D0232074

EYEWITNESS TRAVEL

MILAN
& THE LAKES

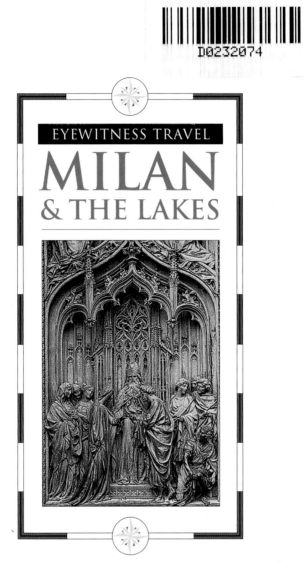

EYEWITNESS TRAVEL

MILAN
& THE LAKES

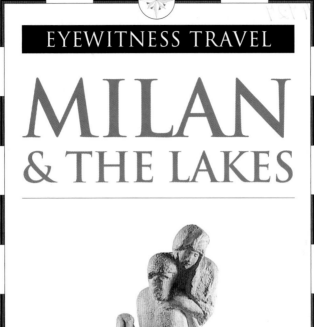

CORK CITY LIBRARIES
8054 724

LONDON, NEW YORK,
MELBOURNE, MUNICH AND DELHI
www.dk.com

Produced by Fabio Ratti
Editoria Libraria e Multimediale, Milan, Italy

PROJECT EDITORS Barbara Cacciani, Giovanni Francesio
EDITORS Emanuela Damiani, Mattia Goffetti,
Alessandra Lombardi, Marco Scapagnini
DESIGNERS Oriana Bianchetti, Silvia Tomasone

Dorling Kindersley Ltd
PROJECT EDITOR Fiona Wild
SENIOR ART EDITOR Marisa Renzullo
DTP DESIGNERS Maite Lantaron, Samantha Borland,
Sarah Meakin
PRODUCTION Marie Ingledew

CONTRIBUTOR
Monica Torri

ILLUSTRATORS
Giorgia Boli, Alberto Ipsilanti,
Daniela Veluti, Nadia Viganò

ENGLISH TRANSLATION
Richard Pierce

Printed and bound in China by L. Rex Printing Co., Ltd

First published in the UK in 2000 by
Dorling Kindersley Ltd,
80 Strand, London WC2R 0RL

13 14 15 16 10 9 8 7 6 5 4 3 2 1

Reprinted with revisions 2003, 2005, 2007, 2009, 2011, 2013

Copyright 2000, 2013 Dorling Kindersley Ltd
A Penguin Company

ALL RIGHTS RESERVED. NO PART OF THIS PUBLICATION MAY BE REPRODUCED,
STORED IN A RETRIEVAL SYSTEM, OR TRANSMITTED IN ANY
FORM OR BY ANY MEANS, ELECTRONIC, MECHANICAL, PHOTOCOPYING,
RECORDING OR OTHERWISE, WITHOUT THE PRIOR WRITTEN PERMISSION
OF THE COPYRIGHT OWNER.

A CIP CATALOGUE RECORD IS AVAILABLE FROM THE BRITISH LIBRARY.

ISBN 978-1-40938-613-1

FLOORS ARE REFERRED TO THROUGHOUT IN ACCORDANCE WITH EUROPEAN
USAGE; IE THE "FIRST FLOOR" IS THE FLOOR ABOVE GROUND LEVEL.

*Front cover main image: The ceiling of
a shopping mall, Galleria Vittorio Emanuele II, Milan*

MIX
Paper from
responsible sources
FSC™ C018179
www.fsc.org

**The information in this
DK Eyewitness Travel Guide is checked regularly.**
Every effort has been made to ensure that this book is as up-to-date
as possible at the time of going to press. Some details, however,
such as telephone numbers, opening hours, prices, gallery hanging
arrangements and travel information are liable to change. The
publishers cannot accept responsibility for any consequences arising
from the use of this book, nor for any material on third party
websites, and cannot guarantee that any website address in this
book will be a suitable source of travel information. We value the
views and suggestions of our readers very highly. Please write to:
Publisher, DK Eyewitness Travel Guides, Dorling Kindersley, 80 Strand,
London WC2R 0RL, UK, or email: travelguides@dk.com

CONTENTS

Statue at the entrance to the
Pinacoteca di Brera *(see pp114–7)*

INTRODUCING
MILAN
AND THE LAKES

Naviglio Grande, in the southern
district of Milan *(see p89)*

Leonardo da Vinci's *Last Supper,* in Santa Maria delle Grazie *(see pp72–3)*

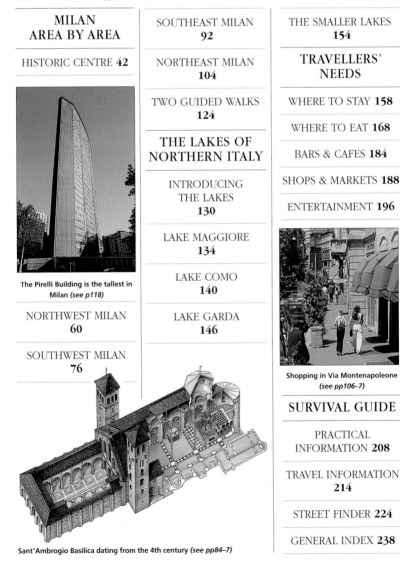
Sant'Ambrogio Basilica dating from the 4th century *(see pp84–7)*

HOW TO USE THIS GUIDE

This guide helps you to get the most out of your visit to Milan and the lakes of Northern Italy by providing detailed descriptions of sights, practical information and expert advice. *Introducing Milan*, the first chapter, sets the city in its geographical and historical context, and *Milan at a Glance* provides a brief overview of the architecture and cultural background. *Milan Area by Area* describes the main sightseeing areas in detail, with maps, illustrations and photographs. A special section is dedicated to the lakes of Northern Italy, which are all within easy travelling distance of Milan's city centre. Information on hotels, restaurants, bars, cafés, shops, sports facilities and entertainment venues is covered in the chapter *Travellers' Needs,* and the *Survival Guide* section contains invaluable practical advice on everything from personal security to using the public transport system. The guide ends with a detailed Street Finder map and a map of the public transport network in Milan.

FINDING YOUR WAY AROUND THE SIGHTSEEING SECTION

The city of Milan is divided into five sightseeing areas, each with its own colour-coded thumb tab. Each area has its own chapter, which opens with a numbered list of the sights described. The lakes of Northern Italy are covered in a separate chapter, also colour coded. The chapter on the lakes opens with a road map of the region. The major sights are numbered for easy reference.

1 Introduction to the Area
On this page the major sights are numbered, listed by category and plotted on an area map, which also shows where public transport stops, taxi ranks and car parks are located.

A locator map shows where you are in relation to the other areas of the city.

Each area has a colour-coded thumb tab.

Locator map

The area shaded pink is shown in greater detail on the Street-by-Street map.

2 Street-by-Street Map
This gives a bird's-eye view of the most interesting parts of each sightseeing area. The numbering of the sights ties in with the area map on the preceding page as well as with the fuller descriptions provided on the pages that follow.

A suggested route for a walk covers the most interesting streets in the area.

MILAN AREA BY AREA

The five coloured areas shown on this map *(see pp14–15)* correspond to the main sightseeing areas of Milan – each of which is covered by a full chapter in the *Milan Area by Area* section *(see pp40–123)*. These areas are also highlighted on other maps, for example in the section *Milan at a Glance (see pp28–35)*. The colours on the margins of each area correspond to those on the colour-coded thumb tabs.

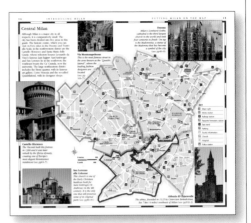

Numbers refer to each sight's position on the area map and its place in the chapter.

Practical information provides everything you need to know to visit the sights, including map references to the *Street Finder (see pp224–37)*.

3 Detailed Information on Each Sight

All the most important monuments and other sights are described individually. They are listed in order, following the numbering on the area map. The key to the symbols used is shown on the back flap for easy reference.

The story boxes discuss particular aspects of the places described.

Stars indicate the features you should not miss.

4 The Top Sights

All the most important sights are described individually in two or more pages. Historic buildings and churches are dissected to reveal their interiors. and museums and galleries have colour-coded floorplans to help you locate the major works on exhibit.

The Visitors' Checklist provides all the practical information needed to plan your visit.

INTRODUCING
MILAN

ALLI LETTORI.

Quanto la nobilissima Città di Milano sia bella, grande, forte, e populata, e d'acque; per le quali anco uengono barche: abondantissima, e d'ogni sorti d'arti piena. e d'il suo territorio fertilissimo. Ciascuno che l' habbia uiste, o praticata; o che leggerà chi di esse ne ha scritto facilmente lo può sapere: e però qui si lassa di narrarlo, ma solo si metterà nell' altro spatio quello di essa più notabile ne appar.

FOUR GREAT DAYS IN MILAN AND THE LAKES

A couple of days in Milan will give you a good idea of the city's riches. Two of the itineraries below focus on attractions such as Leonardo's *Last Supper*, the Duomo, the Brera art gallery and the fashion boutiques. If you need a change of pace,

La Scala's **Museo Teatrale**

head to the lakes. The trips to Lake Como and Lake Maggiore will show why these locations are such sought-after retreats, drawing everyone from Catullus to Hemingway. The price guides given include travel, food and admission costs.

ART AND SHOPPING IN CENTRAL MILAN

- Galleries of Old Masters
- Fashion boutiques
- Atop the Duomo
- Opera at Teatro alla Scala

TWO ADULTS allow at least €99

Morning
Start at 10am with the Old Masters – Leonardo, Raphael, Caravaggio – in the **Pinacoteca Ambrosiana** *(see pp56–9)*. Then work your way east to Via Torino and the **Piazza del Duomo** *(see pp44–5)*. Ascend to the roof of Italy's second-largest cathedral *(see pp46–9)* and wander amid the spires for views of the city. Pause for lunch at **Caffè Zucca** *(see p187)*, then browse around Milan's splendid 19th-century shopping mall, **Galleria Vittorio Emanuele II** *(see p50)*.

Afternoon
Piazza della Scala is flanked by the world-renowned **Teatro alla Scala** opera house *(see pp52–3)* and its **Museo Teatrale**, devoted to luminaries such as Verdi and Toscanini. The season runs year-round; *see p201* for box office details.

Nearby is the Quadrilatero d'Oro, a "Golden Rectangle" (bounded by Via Manzoni, Via Montenapoleone, Via Sant' Andrea and Via della Spiga) of boutiques by the likes of Dolce & Gabbana, Gucci and Ferragamo. If you prefer art to shopping, two excellent museums in the area, **Poldi Pezzoli** *(see p108)* and **Bagatti Valsecchi** *(see p109)*, showcase the private collections of Milan's 19th-century elite.

Finish up at the **Pinacoteca di Brera** *(see pp114–17)*, in the Brera district, which is packed with lively bars.

The fountain in front of the Castello Sforzesco

MEDIEVAL AND RENAISSANCE MILAN

- Leonardo's *Last Supper*
- Ancient churches
- Roman remains
- Trendy Navigli district

TWO ADULTS allow at least €83

Morning
Start at 9am with the collections of sculpture (including Michelangelo's *Rondanini Pietà*) and Renaissance paintings at the **Castello Sforzesco** *(see pp64–7)*. Pop into the **Museo Archeologico** *(see p74)* to ponder Milan's early history while you await your scheduled noon entry time (reserved at least six weeks in advance) to Leonardo's *Last Supper*, in **Santa Maria delle Grazie** *(see pp72–3)*. Double back along Corso Magenta to the corner with Via Carducci to enjoy a light lunch at the Art Nouveau **Bar Magenta** *(see p186)*.

Gothic spires of the Duomo, the second-largest cathedral in Italy

◁ *L'Arena: veduta della porta trionfala dall'esterno*, 1835-1839 by Johann Jakob Falkeisen held in Museo di Milano

Afternoon

Visit the 4th-century church of **Sant'Ambrogio** *(see pp84–7)*, then head for the **Museo della Scienza e della Tecnologia Leonardo da Vinci** *(see p88)*, which holds replicas of some of Leonardo's inventions. Make your way along the Parco delle Basiliche, where you will find another 4th-century church, **San Lorenzo** *(see pp80–81)*, preceded by a row of Roman columns; the **Museo Diocesano** *(see p90)*, a repository for art from church treasuries across Lombardy; and **Sant'Eustorgio** *(see p90)*, a church filled with Renaissance frescoes. Finish in the nearby Navigli area, with its many bars and restaurants.

A view of Lake Maggiore and snow-capped mountains from Stresa

A FAMILY DAY ON LAKE MAGGIORE

- **Island-hop by ferry**
- **Explore glorious gardens**
- **Lunch by the lakeside**
- **Breathtaking panoramas**

FAMILY OF 4 allow at least €116

Morning

The best way to enjoy Lake Maggiore is by flitting between its three tiny **Borromean Islands** *(see p137)*. Start island-hopping at the lakeside town of **Stresa** *(see p137)*. Spend the morning at Isola Bella and Isola Madre, where peacocks wander the exotic gardens and the palace rooms are filled with quirky exhibits, including marionette stages and liveried mannequins. Then head to the village on Isola dei Pescatori for a leisurely lunch by the lake.

Afternoon

Hop off the ferry heading to Stresa at the Mottarone stop, where you can take a cable car (open daily) to the top of Monte Mottarone. You will be rewarded with spectacular views. It is a three-hour trek back down, so you may want to buy a return ticket. Stresa's cafés are a 20-minute stroll back along a lakeside path lined with crumbling villas.

Those with a car might find time to stop outside the town of **Arona** *(see p136)* to climb the 35-m (115-ft) high statue of San Carlo Borromeo. Kids (aged eight plus only) love to clamber up the spiral staircase inside the statue to the head, and peer out of the eyes or nostrils at a lake panorama.

A DAY ON ELEGANT LAKE COMO

- **Lavishly decorated Duomo**
- **Ornate gardens**
- **Lakeside strolls**
- **Palatial villas**

TWO ADULTS allow at least €48

Morning

Begin the day at **Como** *(see p142)*, on the southwest arm of the lake. Wander along the lakeside promenade, browse the silk outlets, and visit the impressive Duomo and the museum of notable scientist Alessandro Volta. Then head up to the lovely resort town of **Bellagio** *(see p145)*. The tip of Bellagio's promontory is occupied by the grounds of Villa Serbelloni, which you can visit only by guided tour (sign up at the tourist office).

Afternoon

Take a ferry to **Varenna** *(see p144)*, on the eastern shore, and stop for lunch. Then tour the formal gardens at Villa Cipressi and Villa Monastero, or hike up to the ruins of medieval Castello di Vezio for stunning lake views. Afterwards cross by ferry to the western shore and the town of **Tremezzo** *(see p143)*, home to the 18th-century Villa Carlotta, with its terraced gardens and works by Canova and Hayez. Return to Bellagio for a leisurely evening stroll through its pretty alleyways.

Villa Monastero, one of many elegant lakeside villas on Lake Como

Putting Milan on the Map

Milan is the capital of Lombardy (Lombardia), the most densely populated and economically developed region in Italy. The population of Milan is over 1,300,000 (second only to Rome). This figure does not include the many people who live in the suburbs – which have spread outwards over the years – who depend on the city both for work (there are large numbers of commuters) and entertainment. The city lies in the middle of the Po river valley (Valle Padana) and has always been a key commercial centre. Today it forms part of an industrial triangle with the cities of Turin and Genoa. Milan's position makes it an ideal starting point for visits to the Alpine lakes. Lake Maggiore and Lake Como are close to Milan, whereas Lake Garda is further east, with the western shore part of Lombardy, the eastern shore part of the Veneto.

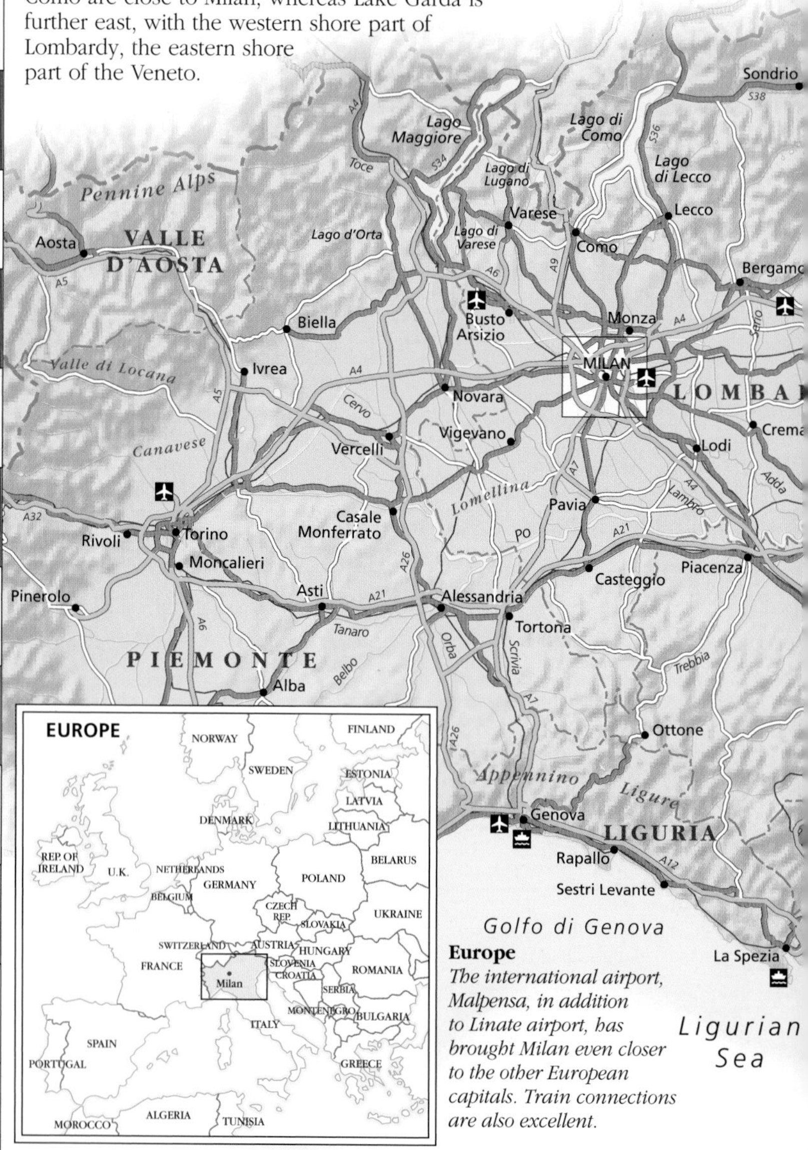

Sondrio

Lago Maggiore
Lago di Como
Lago di Lecco
Pennine Alps
Aosta
VALLE D'AOSTA
Lago d'Orta
Lago di Lugano
Lago di Varese
Varese
Lecco
Como
Bergamo
Biella
Busto Arsizio
Monza
MILAN
Valle di Locana
Ivrea
Novara
LOMBA
Canavese
Vercelli
Vigevano
Crema
Lodi
Lomellina
Pavia
Casale Monferrato
Torino
Rivoli
Moncalieri
PO
Piacenza
Casteggio
Pinerolo
Asti
Alessandria
Tortona
PIEMONTE
Alba
Tanaro
Trebbia
Ottone
Appennino Ligure

EUROPE

NORWAY
SWEDEN
FINLAND
ESTONIA
LATVIA
LITHUANIA
DENMARK
REP. OF IRELAND
U.K.
NETHERLANDS
GERMANY
POLAND
BELARUS
BELGIUM
CZECH REP.
SLOVAKIA
UKRAINE
SWITZERLAND
AUSTRIA
HUNGARY
FRANCE
SLOVENIA
CROATIA
ROMANIA
Milan
ITALY
SERBIA
MONTENEGRO
BULGARIA
SPAIN
GREECE
PORTUGAL
MOROCCO
ALGERIA
TUNISIA

Genova
LIGURIA
Rapallo
Sestri Levante

Golfo di Genova

Europe
The international airport, Malpensa, in addition to Linate airport, has brought Milan even closer to the other European capitals. Train connections are also excellent.

La Spezia

Ligurian Sea

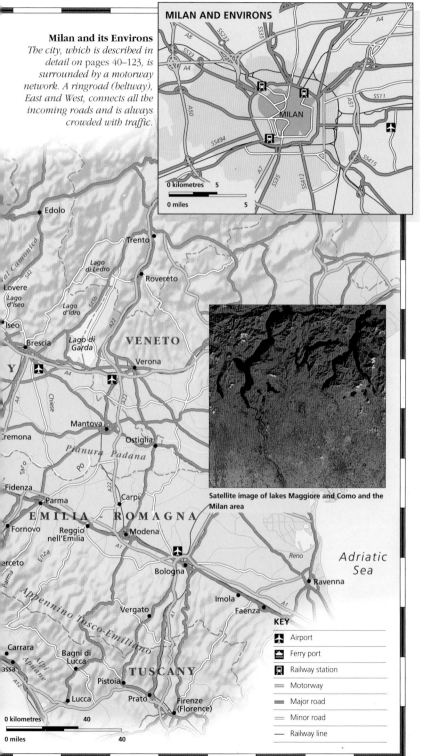

MILAN AND ENVIRONS

Milan and its Environs
The city, which is described in detail on pages 40–123, is surrounded by a motorway network. A ringroad (beltway), East and West, connects all the incoming roads and is always crowded with traffic.

MILAN

0 kilometres 5

0 miles 5

Edolo

Trento

Val Camonica

Lago di Ledro

Roveréto

Lovere
Lago d'Iseo

Lago d'Idro

Iseo

Brescia

Lago di Garda

VENETO

Verona

Y

Chiese

Mantova

Ostiglia

Cremona

Pianura Padana

Po

Taro

Fidenza

Carpi

Parma

EMILIA - ROMAGNA

Fornovo

Reggio nell'Emilia

Modena

Enza

erceto

Reno

Bologna

Adriatic Sea

Parma

Ravenna

Imola

Vergato

Faenza

Satellite image of lakes Maggiore and Como and the Milan area

Appennino Tosco-Emiliano

KEY

Carrara

Bagni di Lucca

Alpi Apuane

assa

TUSCANY

Pistoia

Lucca

Prato

Firenze (Florence)

✈	Airport
⛴	Ferry port
🚉	Railway station
═══	Motorway
▬▬▬	Major road
═══	Minor road
───	Railway line

0 kilometres 40

0 miles 40

Central Milan

Although Milan is a major city in all respects, it is comparatively small. The city has been divided into five areas in this guide. The historic centre, which you can visit on foot, takes in the Duomo and Teatro alla Scala; in the northwestern district are the Castello Sforzesco and Santa Maria delle Grazie, whose refectory houses Leonardo da Vinci's famous *Last Supper*. Sant'Ambrogio and San Lorenzo lie in the southwest; the southeast boasts the Ca' Granda, now the university. The large northeastern district includes the Brera quarter, with its famous art gallery, Corso Venezia and the so-called Quadrilateral, with its designer shops.

Via Montenapoleone
This is the most famous street in the area known as the "Quadrilateral", where the leading fashion designers are located (see pp 106–7).

Castello Sforzesco
The Visconti built this fortress in 1368 and it was later rebuilt by the Sforza dynasty, creating one of Europe's most elegant Renaissance residences (see pp64–7).

0 metres   600

0 yards   600

San Lorenzo alle Colonne
This church is one of the Early Christian basilicas built for Sant'Ambrogio (St Ambrose) in the 4th century. It is the only one that still preserves some of its original parts (see pp80–81).

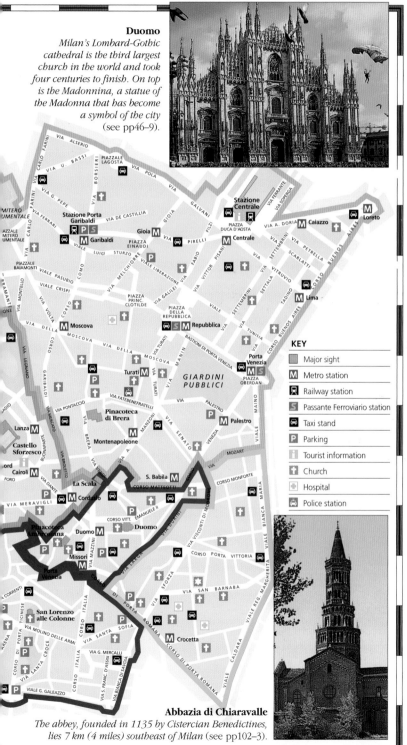

Duomo
Milan's Lombard-Gothic cathedral is the third largest church in the world and took four centuries to finish. On top is the Madonnina, a statue of the Madonna that has become a symbol of the city (see pp46–9).

KEY

▢	Major sight
Ⓜ	Metro station
Ⓢ	Passante Ferroviario station
🚕	Taxi stand
P	Parking
ℹ	Tourist information
✝	Church
✚	Hospital
🚓	Police station

Abbazia di Chiaravalle
The abbey, founded in 1135 by Cistercian Benedictines, lies 7 km (4 miles) southeast of Milan (see pp102–3).

THE HISTORY OF MILAN

A*ccording to the words of a 17th-century ambassador, "Milan never fails to be a great city, and when it declines it soon becomes great again". The sentiments encapsulate one of the characteristics of the city – its ability to rise from the ruins of wars, epidemics, sieges and bombings suffered over the centuries, and to regain dynamism and prosperity once more.*

THE PREHISTORIC AND ROMAN CITY

In the 3rd–2nd millennium BC, the area covered by Milan today was inhabited by the Ligurians. It was later settled by Indo-European populations and then, in the 5th century BC, by the Etruscans. Around the lakes, archaeologists have unearthed fascinating pre-Roman objects that reveal the presence of a Celtic civilization in the 9th–6th centuries BC. Milan itself was founded in the early 4th century BC when the Gallic Insubre tribes settled there.

The origins of the city are somewhat obscure, as is its name, which most scholars say derives from *Midland* (or "middle of the plain"), while others say it derives from *scrofa semilanuta* (half-woolly boar), the city emblem in ancient times. In 222 BC the Romans, led by the consuls Gnaeus Cornelius Scipio Calvus and Claudius Marcellus, defeated the Celts and conquered the Po river valley and its cities. Milan soon became a flourishing commercial centre and in the Imperial era

Slab with a relief of the half-woolly boar, once the city emblem

attained political and administrative independence. In AD 286 it became the capital of the Western Roman Empire (until 402) and was the residence of Emperor Maximian. By the late Imperial era Milan was the most important city in the West after Rome and it became a leading religious centre after Constantine's Edict of Milan in 313, which officially recognized Christianity as a religion. Sant'Ambrogio (Ambrose) exerted great influence at this time. He was the first great figure in Milan's history: a Doctor of the Church, he built four basilicas (San Simpliciano, Sant'Ambrogio, San Lorenzo, San Nazaro) and was a leading opponent of the Arian heresy (which denied the divinity of Christ). Sant'Ambrogio was the first in a long series of bishops who ran the city's affairs in the early Middle Ages. Roman Milan was a substantial size: the Republican walls, enlarged to the northeast during the Imperial Age, defined an area that was roughly the same size as the present-day city centre.

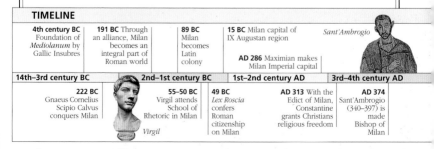

TIMELINE

| 4th century BC Foundation of *Mediolanum* by Gallic Insubres | 191 BC Through an alliance, Milan becomes an integral part of Roman world | 89 BC Milan becomes Latin colony | 15 BC Milan capital of IX Augustan region | *Sant'Ambrogio* |
| AD 286 Maximian makes Milan Imperial capital | | | | |

| 14th–3rd century BC | 2nd–1st century BC | 1st–2nd century AD | 3rd–4th century AD |
| 222 BC Gnaeus Cornelius Scipio Calvus conquers Milan / *Virgil* | 55–50 BC Virgil attends School of Rhetoric in Milan | 49 BC *Lex Roscia* confers Roman citizenship on Milan | AD 313 With the Edict of Milan, Constantine grants Christians religious freedom | AD 374 Sant'Ambrogio (340–397) is made Bishop of Milan |

◁ The *Sforzesca Altarpiece* (1494), now in the Brera art gallery, with portraits of Beatrice d'Este and Lodovico il Moro

THE EARLY MIDDLE AGES AND THE COMMUNE OF MILAN

The 5th and 6th centuries marked a period of decline for Milan. In 402 it lost its status as Imperial capital, was sacked by Attila's Huns in 452, conquered by the Germanic Eruli in 476 and then by Ostrogoths in 489. During the war between the Greek Byzantines and Goths, the city, allies of the former, was attacked by the Goths and utterly destroyed. Reconstruction began in 568, when the city was reconquered by the Byzantine general Narses, who was forced to cede it to the Lombards in the following year. Milan was then ruled by the city of Pavia. The few remaining citizens, led by their bishop Honorius, fled to Liguria: what had been one of the most prosperous cities in the Western Roman Empire was reduced to ruins in the 6th and 7th centuries. The Edict of Rothari of 643 describes in detail Lombard administrative structures of the time.

Emperor Frederick Barbarossa at the Battle of Legnano (1176) in a 1308 miniature

In 774, the Franks defeated the Lombards and conquered Northern Italy. The archbishops regained power and there was a revival of the economy with the rise of an artisan and merchant class, which in the 11th century led to the birth of the commune. After centuries in which Monza and Pavia had been the focal points of Lombardy, Milan was once again the political centre of the region. The aristocrats and mercantile classes struggled for power in the 11th century, but then joined forces

King Rothari proclaims his edict (643), miniature, Codex Legum Longobardorum

to defend the city against the emperor. Once again the city was led by a series of archbishops, some of whom, such as Ariberto d'Intimiano (1018–45), were both bishops and generals. In 1042 the free commune of Milan was founded and a new city wall built. It was demolished in 1162 when, after a siege, the Milanese were forced to open their gates to Frederick Barbarossa: for the second time the city was burned to the ground. Milan and other northern communes together formed the Lombard League, which defeated Barbarossa's troops at Legnano in 1176. Seven years later the Treaty of Constance sanctioned the freedom of these communes.

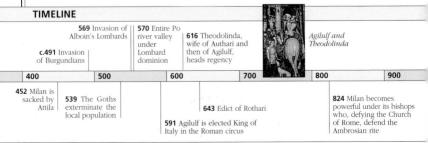

TIMELINE

400	500	600	700	800	900

569 Invasion of Alboin's Lombards

c.491 Invasion of Burgundians

570 Entire Po river valley under Lombard dominion

616 Theodolinda, wife of Authari and then of Agilulf, heads regency

Agilulf and Theodolinda

452 Milan is sacked by Attila

539 The Goths exterminate the local population

643 Edict of Rothari

591 Agilulf is elected King of Italy in the Roman circus

824 Milan becomes powerful under its bishops who, defying the Church of Rome, defend the Ambrosian rite

In the 13th century, Milan created a formidable canal network, the Navigli, which linked the city to Ticino in Switzerland. However, power struggles among the leading families sapped the strength of the entire city and fore-shadowed its decline.

THE GREAT DYNASTIES

In 1277 at Desio, the Visconti, under Archbishop Ottone, overthrew the Torriani family. The Visconti then summoned the leading artists of the time, including Giotto, to Milan to embellish the city and its palazzi, and they commissioned new buildings such as the Castello and the Duomo *(see pp46–9)*. The height of Visconti power was achieved under Gian Galeazzo, who became duke in 1395 and undertook an ambitious policy of expansion. Milan soon ruled most of Northern Italy and even controlled some cities in Tuscany, but the duke's dream of a united Italy under his lead came to

Coat of arms of the
Visconti family

an end with his death in 1402. The Visconti dynasty died out in 1447 and for three years the city enjoyed self-government under the Ambrosian Republic. In 1450 the *condottiere* Francesco Sforza initiated what was perhaps the most felicitous period in the history of Milan: he abandoned the Visconti expansionist policy and secured lasting peace for the city, which flourished and grew to a population of 100,000. The Visconti castle was rebuilt and became the Castello Sforzesco *(see pp64–7)*, while architects such as Guiniforte Solari and Filarete began work on the Ospedale Maggiore, better known as Ca' Granda *(see p97)*. However, Milan's cultural golden age came with Lodovico Sforza, known as "il Moro" (1479–1508). He was an undisciplined politician but a great patron of the arts. His policy of alliances and strategic decisions marked the end of freedom for Milan, which in 1499 fell under French dominion, yet during his rule Milanese arts and culture were second only to Medici Florence. From 1480 on, great men such as Bramante and Leonardo da Vinci were active in Milan. The former restored numerous churches and designed Santa Maria delle Grazie *(see p71)*, in whose refectory Leonardo painted *The Last Supper (see pp72–3)*, one of his many master-pieces. Leonardo also worked on major city projects such as the Navigli network of canals.

Milan in a 15th-century print

1038 Archbishop Ariberto d'Intimiano leads Milanese against Corrado II and uses *Carroccio* cart with city banner as symbol of Milan	1158 Barbarossa lays siege to Milan. In 1162 the city is destroyed by Imperial troops	1277 Rise of the Visconti	1447–50 Ambrosian Republic	1482–99 Leonardo da Vinci in Milan
		1395 Gian Galeazzo Visconti becomes duke		1499 Lodovico cedes duchy to Louis XII

1000	1100	1200	1300	1400	1500

| 1057 The Pataria movement against abuses of the clergy | 1154 Frederick Barbarossa suppresses commune at Roncaglia | 1176 Lombard League defeats Barbarossa at Legnano | 1450 Rise of the Sforza 1494 Lodovico il Moro rules *Frederick Barbarossa* | 1525 Sforza return to power 1535 Charles V takes over duchy |

The Visconti and Sforza

The period of the Signorie, or family lordships, from the late 13th to the early 16th century, was one of the most successful in the history of Milan. The Visconti dynasty succeeded – especially during Gian Galeazzo's rule – in expanding the city's territories, albeit for a brief span of time. The Sforza dukedom is best known for the cultural and artistic splendour commissioned by Lodovico il Moro, who invited the leading artists and architects of the time to his court.

Gian Galeazzo *imprisoned his uncle Bernabò in 1385 and became sole ruler of Milan. He was made a duke by Emperor Wenceslaus ten years later.*

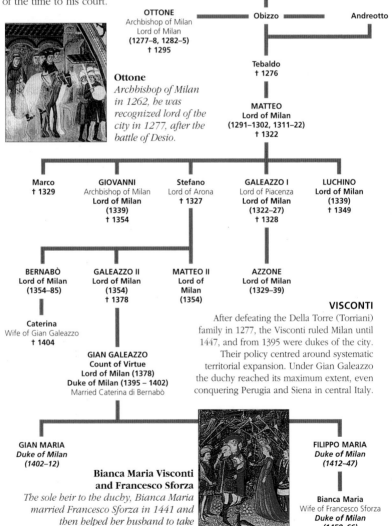

Ottone
Archbishop of Milan in 1262, he was recognized lord of the city in 1277, after the battle of Desio.

Umberto
† before 1248

OTTONE
Archbishop of Milan
Lord of Milan
(1277–8, 1282–5)
† 1295

Obizzo

Andreotto

Tebaldo
† 1276

MATTEO
Lord of Milan
(1291–1302, 1311–22)
† 1322

Marco † 1329	**GIOVANNI** Archbishop of Milan **Lord of Milan** **(1339)** † 1354	**Stefano** Lord of Arona † 1327	**GALEAZZO I** Lord of Piacenza **Lord of Milan** **(1322–27)** † 1328	**LUCHINO** **Lord of Milan** **(1339)** † 1349

BERNABÒ **Lord of Milan** **(1354–85)**	**GALEAZZO II** **Lord of Milan** **(1354)** † 1378	**MATTEO II** Lord of Milan **(1354)**	**AZZONE** **Lord of Milan** **(1329–39)**

Caterina
Wife of Gian Galeazzo
† 1404

GIAN GALEAZZO
Count of Virtue
Lord of Milan (1378)
Duke of Milan (1395 – 1402)
Married Caterina di Bernabò

VISCONTI

After defeating the Della Torre (Torriani) family in 1277, the Visconti ruled Milan until 1447, and from 1395 were dukes of the city. Their policy centred around systematic territorial expansion. Under Gian Galeazzo the duchy reached its maximum extent, even conquering Perugia and Siena in central Italy.

GIAN MARIA
Duke of Milan
(1402–12)

Bianca Maria Visconti and Francesco Sforza
The sole heir to the duchy, Bianca Maria married Francesco Sforza in 1441 and then helped her husband to take over power in Milan.

FILIPPO MARIA
Duke of Milan
(1412–47)

Bianca Maria
Wife of Francesco Sforza
Duke of Milan
(1450–66)

SFORZA

After the three-year Ambrosian Republic, the city had a new duke in 1450, Francesco Sforza, the *condottiere* son of Muzio Attendolo, known as "Sforza". The 50 years of Sforza family rule were the most prosperous and splendid Milan had ever enjoyed. Art and commerce flourished, particularly under Lodovico il Moro. However, his unscrupulous foreign policy led to the fall of the dukedom and the end of freedom in Milan.

Francesco I
This great warrior had fought for Filippo Maria Visconti, and married his daughter Bianca Maria. In 1454 he began expanding the duchy through peaceful means until it included Genoa and Corsica.

Muzio Attendolo
Count of Cotignola
† 1424

FRANCESCO I
Natural son of Lucia Terzani,
married Bianca Maria Visconti
Duke of Milan from 1450
† 1466

GALEAZZO MARIA
Duke of Milan from 1466
† 1476

LODOVICO called IL MORO
Duke of Milan from 1494
† 1508

Ascanio
Became cardinal in 1484
† 1505

GIAN GALEAZZO MARIA
Duke of Milan from 1476
† 1494

Bianca Maria
wife of Emperor Maximilian
of Habsburg
† 1510

Lodovico Il Moro
Born in 1452, he usurped power from his nephew Gian Galeazzo Maria in 1480. After being defeated at Novara (1500) he was exiled to France and died there in 1508.

Bona
wife of Sigismund I
King of Poland
† 1558

ERCOLE MASSIMILIANO
Duke of Milan (1512–15)
† 1530

FRANCESCO II
Duke of Milan
(1521–24; 1525; 1529–35) † 1535

The Castello Sforzesco *is one of the symbols of the Signoria period in Milan.*

WHERE TO SEE VISCONTI AND SFORZA MILAN

The Milan of the Visconti family is basically Gothic. The main monuments either started or completed under Visconti rule are the Duomo *(see pp46–9)*, San Gottardo *(see p54)* and San Marco (which, however, has been radically altered: *see p112*). Under the Sforza family there was a transition from Gothic to Renaissance architecture, as can be seen in San Pietro in Gessate *(see p99)* and especially in Santa Maria delle Grazie, where Leonardo painted *The Last Supper (see pp71–3)*. The Ospedale Maggiore, or Ca' Granda *(see p97)* was designed by Filarete for Francesco Sforza, and the Castello Sforzesco *(see pp64–7)* was built by the Visconti but enlarged and embellished by the Sforza, hence the name.

FRANCE AND SPAIN

The Renaissance petered out in the 16th century and was followed by a long period of decline. Milan was greatly affected by the loss of political and military importance on the part of the Italian states, now battlefields for other European powers, and because of its wealth and strategic position the city was a key target. The presence of foreign troops was so common that it gave rise to a bitterly sarcastic proverb: "Franza o Spagna purché se magna" (France or Spain, it doesn't matter, as long as we have something on our platter). When Francesco Sforza died in 1535, Emperor Charles V appointed a governor for Milan and the city thus officially became an Imperial province. However, the city nonetheless con-

Charles V in a portrait by Titian (1532–3)

tinued to thrive and the population grew to 130,000. Its territory expanded and from 1548 to 1560 new city walls were built (called the Spanish walls) corresponding to today's inner ring road. The walls were the most important public works undertaken during Spanish rule. All that is left now is Porta Romana arch, though not in its original position. Many Baroque buildings, such as Palazzo Durini and those facing Corso di Porta Romana, were also built in this period. Among the leading figures in Spanish Milan was San Carlo Borromeo (1538–84), cardinal and archbishop of Milan, patron of the arts and benefactor, who rebuilt many churches and was one of the leading figures in the Counter Reformation. His nephew Federico (1564–1631) was also later archbishop of Milan and was immortalized in Manzoni's novel *I Promessi Sposi (The Betrothed)*, a wide-ranging portrait of Milan under Spanish rule. Economic and social decline reached its lowest point with the 1630 plague, which brought the city's population down to 60,000.

ENLIGHTENMENT MILAN

Spanish rule ended in 1706, when during the War of Spanish

Title page of a rare 1827 edition of Manzoni's novel

ALESSANDRO MANZONI'S THE BETROTHED

Considered one of the greatest novels in Italian literature and a masterpiece of 19th-century European narrative, *The Betrothed (I Promessi Sposi)* is also a splendid portrait of Milan under Spanish rule in the 1600s. Manzoni rewrote it several times and had three different editions published (1820, with the title *Fermo e Lucia*, 1827 and 1840). The novel is set in 1628–31 and portrays different phases of Milanese life. In chapter 12 the hero Renzo is involved in the bread riots (in Corso Vittorio Emanuele, a plaque marks the site of the bakery), while from chapter 31 onwards there are vivid descriptions of the city devastated by the plague of 1630.

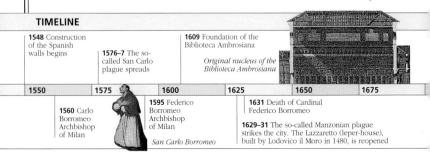

TIMELINE

1548 Construction of the Spanish walls begins

1576–7 The so-called San Carlo plague spreads

1560 Carlo Borromeo Archbishop of Milan

San Carlo Borromeo

1609 Foundation of the Biblioteca Ambrosiana

Original nucleus of the Biblioteca Ambrosiana

1595 Federico Borromeo Archbishop of Milan

1631 Death of Cardinal Federico Borromeo

1629–31 The so-called Manzonian plague strikes the city. The Lazzaretto (leper-house), built by Lodovico il Moro in 1480, is reopened

1550	1575	1600	1625	1650	1675

French troops at the city walls

The leading architect of the time was Giuseppe Piermarini, who designed the Teatro alla Scala *(see pp52–3)*, rebuilt Palazzo Reale in a Neo-Classical style, planned the urban renewal of the historic centre and designed the Corso Venezia gardens. The city's flourishing cultural life did not diminish even when the Austrians had to flee from Napoleon's troops in 1796. As the capital of the short-lived Cisalpine Republic, Milan was the setting for Napoleon's coronation in the Cathedral (1804) and witnessed the construction of various new building projects, including the Foro Bonaparte, the Arena and the Arco della Pace. After Napoleon's defeat, the Congress of Vienna handed Milan back to the Habsburgs, whose government, however, was quite different from the one under Maria Theresa. There were many abortive revolts, and Milan became one of the focal points of Romanticism and the struggle for Italian independence and unity as propounded in the local periodical *Il Conciliatore*. The publication was repressed by censors and its main exponents (Pellico, Confalonieri and Maroncelli) were imprisoned. The independence movement continued to grow, with the help of the operas of Verdi, and reached its peak with the revolt known as the *Cinque Giornate di Milano*, when the Milanese succeeded, albeit briefly, in driving the Austrian troops out of the city.

Maria Theresa of Austria

Succession Austrian troops occupied the city. Milan remained part of the Austro-Hungarian Empire until 1859, except for the Napoleonic period and the Cinque Giornate rebellion *(see pp24–5)*. Economic and, in particular, cultural revival marked the 18th century. Milan was one of the capitals of the Enlightenment, encouraged by Maria Theresa's wise administration (1740–80). From June 1764 to May 1766 a group of Milanese intellectuals, including Cesare Beccaria and the Verri brothers, published the periodical *Il Caffè*, influencing Italian cultural life by propounding the ideas of the French "Encyclopedists".

Abbé Longo, Alessandro Verri, Giovanni Battista Biffi and Cesare Beccaria, the founders of *Il Caffè*

6 Eugene of by drives out last nish governor		**1778** Inauguration of La Scala opera house	**1796** French troops enter Milan		**1848** Cinque Giornate revolt	
	1740 Beginning of Maria Theresa's rule in Milan		**1805** Italic Kingdom proclaimed	**1820** Pellico imprisoned by Austrians	**1848** Radetzky occupies Milan	
1725	**1750**	**1775**	**1800**	**1825**	**1850**	
1714 Treaty of Utrecht: Lombardy ceded to Austria	*Cesare Beccaria*	**1764–66** Pietro Verri publishes *Il Caffè* **1764** Cesare Beccaria publishes *On Crimes and Punishment*	**1818** *Il Conciliatore* published **1797** Cisalpine Republic	**1839** Cattaneo founds *Il Politecnico* **1849** Austria-Piedmont peace treaty	**1859** Milan liberated by French-Piedmontese troops	

The Cinque Giornate Revolt

The Italian flag in 1848

This historic event was preceded by the "smoking strike", held during the first three days of 1848, when the Milanese refused to buy tobacco as a protest against Austrian taxation. The "Five Days" revolt began on 18 March 1848. Clashes broke out after a demonstration and continued in a disorderly fashion for two days, during which the Austrians, led by Field Marshal Radetzky, were initially besieged inside the Castello Sforzesco. After the formation of a War Council and a Provisional Government on 22 March at Porta Tosa, the Imperial troops were defeated and driven out of Milan.

Carlo Cattaneo (1801–69)
Cattaneo was one of the leaders in the Cinque Giornate, and later went into exile in Switzerland.

Carlo Alberto's Proclamation
With this declaration, Carlo Alberto, king of Sardinia, put himself at the head of the revolt. Yet when the opportune occasion arose he failed to attack the Austrians and in August 1848 he was forced to cede Milan to the Austrian Radetzky.

Behind the barricades were people from all social classes, demonstrating the unity of the Milanese in the battle for independence.

The Austrian Army
Field Marshal Radetzky had some 74,000 men (about a third of them Italians) at his disposal, divided into two army corps. The first and larger one was stationed in Milan.

PORTA TOSA
This painting by Carlo Canella, now in the Museo di Milano, represents the *Battle at Porta Tosa*, when the Milanese dealt the final blow to the Austrian troops on 22 March. After this historic event, the city gate, which is situated in the eastern part of the city, was renamed Porta Vittoria (Victory Gate).

Pasquale Sottocorno
Despite being crippled, this 26-year-old shoemaker managed to set fire to the military engineers' building where the enemy troops were barracked, and capture the hospital of San Marco, which was another Austrian stronghold.

ABITANTI DELLA LOMBARDIA!

Alla testa del prode e vittorioso mio esercito sono entrato sul vostro suolo come il liberator vostro da una dominazione rivoluzionaria e tirannica. Molti di voi, sedotti da perfide suggestioni, hanno dimenticato i sacri doveri verso il legittimo loro Sovrano. Tornate devoti sotto lo scettro benigno del nostro Imperatore e Re. Io vi offro la mano a sincera conciliazione.

Abitanti la Lombardia, ascoltate il benevolo mio consiglio. Confidenti accogliete le brave mie Truppe. Esse guarentiranno al cittadino pacifico ogni maggior sicurezza della persona e della proprietà, ma contro chi si ostinasse nel cieco delirio della ribellione procederanno irremissibilmente con tutta la severità della legge marziale.

A voi sta la scelta; a me l'impegno di esattamente adempire la mia parola.
Dal Quartier-Generale di Valleggio 27 Luglio 1848.

RADETZKY

The Austrians, forced into retreat

The Austrians Return
After he had defeated King Carlo Alberto at Custoza (25 July), Radetzky returned to Lombardy, as announced in this proclamation of 27 July. He recaptured Milan on 6 August.

Over 1,600 barricades were set up throughout the city during the insurrection.

The Soldier's Widow
In Italy the struggle for independence was closely linked to Romanticism, as can be seen in works dating from this period, such as this 1851 sculpture by Giovanni Pandiani.

THE CINQUE GIORNATE REVOLT

Radetzky

The revolt spreads throughout the city and barricades are built everywhere

Radetzky proposes an armistice but is rejected

18 March	19 March	20 March	21 March	22 March
Demonstration in the Monforte district for freedom of the press and the establishment of a Civil Guard. Radetzky is besieged in the Castello Sforzesco		Formation of the War Council and Provisional Government	*Guardia Nobile helmet*	The Imperial troops suffer defeat in the last battle at Porta Tosa (renamed Porta Vittoria) and abandon Milan

MILAN AFTER ITALY'S UNIFICATION

In 1861 the population of Milan was 240,000, which shows how much the city had grown under Austrian rule. However, the real demographic explosion was yet to come. Although Milan did not become the political capital after the unification of Italy, it became the economic and cultural capital of the country. Infrastructures created by the Austrians were exploited to the full and by 1920 the city had developed into a thriving industrial metropolis. Business was booming, *Corriere della Sera*, the leading Italian daily newspaper, was founded, the city increased in size and the population exploded (there were 850,000 inhabitants in 1923). This over-rapid growth inevitably brought major social consequences: the first trade

A Corriere della Sera poster

union centre was founded, and socialist groups grew in strength. Demonstrations and strikes became more and more frequent, and social tensions exploded in 1898, when a protest against the high cost of living was violently repressed by cannon fire, on the orders of General Bava Beccaris. The early 20th century witnessed the rise of an important avant-garde movement in Milan (the

The 1898 demonstration quelled by Bava Beccaris

second in the city after the Scapigliatura movement of the second half of the 19th century): Futurism, which was founded by Filippo Tommaso Marinetti (a plaque in Corso Venezia commemorates the event). The Futurists were not only important from an artistic standpoint, but also because their ideas and actions fitted in perfectly with the cultural temper of the times, characterized by the pro-intervention attitude regarding World War I and then the rise of Fascism. In fact, Fascism and Mussolini had a very close relationship with Milan. The original nucleus of the movement was founded in Milan in 1919. In 1943, after the fall of the regime and the foundation of the Repubblica Sociale puppet government, Milan – severely damaged by bombing raids – was the last large Italian city to remain under the control of the remaining Fascists and the Germans. On 26 April 1945, the story of Mussolini and Italian Fascism played out its final moments in Milan: the corpses of il Duce, his mistress Claretta Petacci and some party officials were put on display in Piazzale

Milan after the 1943 bombings

TIMELINE

1866–7 Mengoni builds the Galleria Vittorio Emanuele II

1876 Foundation of *Corriere della Sera*

1900 Umberto I assassinated by Gaetano Bresci

1919 Fascists meet in Piazza San Sepolcro

1943 The city is heavily bombed

1860 — 1870 — 1880 — 1890 — 1900 — 1910 — 1920 — 1930 — 194

1872 Pirelli company founded

1873 Alessandro Manzoni dies

1898 Insurrection thwarted by Bava Beccaris

1901 Verdi dies at the Grand Hotel et de Milan

1906 Falck firm founded

Fiera poster

1920 Fiera di Milano founded

1946 Toscani conducts th opening concert the restore La Sca

Loreto, exactly the same place where some partisans had been executed a few weeks earlier.

THE POSTWAR PERIOD

On 11 May 1946, Arturo Toscanini conducted a concert celebrating the re-opening of the Teatro alla Scala, which had been destroyed by bombs during the war.

Logo of Teatro alla Scala

This historic event demonstrated the desire for recovery and reconstruction that characterized postwar Milan. The linchpin of an industrial triangle with Turin and Genoa, Milan now had 1,800,000 inhabitants. This period of secure growth, disturbed only by student protests in 1968, ended on 12 December 1969, when the explosion of a terrorist bomb in a bank in Piazza Fontana, causing a massacre, began the long, grim period of terrorist activity. The 1980s saw the development of the fashion industry that has made Milan one of the world leaders in this field. The most significant event in the city's recent history was the 1992 anti-corruption investigations which forced many members of the ruling parties to step down from power.

PRESENT-DAY MILAN

Thanks to the dynamism, productivity and inventiveness of its people, today's Milan is a leading European city, but it still has a number of problems: the decline in population, now 1.33 million, is proof of a growing dissatisfaction with a city that is considered, for example, unsuitable for children. The rapid increase in commuter traffic has not been matched by adequate long-distance public transport, which is why the city is frequently blocked by heavy traffic. Last, although Milan is probably the most multicultural city in Italy, clandestine immigration causes its own social problems. Despite this, Milan is an avant-garde city by all standards, a financial, professional and cultural leader in Italian life.

THE GROWTH OF MILAN

This map shows the growth of Milan from the original Roman city to the present-day metropolis.

KEY

- The Roman city
- The Medieval city
- Up to the 18th century
- The 19th century
- The early 20th century
- Present-day Milan

1950 Creation of Metanopoli, satellite city of San Donato Milanese		*The Pirelli Building*	1973 Telemilano (later Canale 5) first private TV station in Italy	1992 Outbreak of political corruption scandal		2004 Teatro alla Scala re-opens after extensive restoration	

1950	1960	1970	1980	1990	2000	2010	2020
	1955–60 The Pirelli Building is constructed	1973 Bomb in Via Fatebenefratelli	1997 Dario Fo, actor and playwright, wins Nobel Prize for Literature		2000 "Needle, Thread and Knot" sculpture erected in Piazza Cadorna		2015 EXPO 2015 World Fair to be held in Milan
	1969 Bomb at Piazza Fontana						

MILAN AT A GLANCE

One of the many clichés about Milan is that it is a practical, industrious, even drab city, wholly dedicated to work and the world of commercial gain. In fact, besides being a leading metropolis in Europe from a financial standpoint and in terms of productivity, it is also rich in history and culture, architecture and art. The historic centre has no single dominating architectural style, and the buildings are perhaps more varied than any other city centre in Italy. The museums and galleries are among the finest in Northern Italy, and many of the leading figures in the fields of Italian art, design, culture and politics were either born in Milan or achieved success here. The following eight pages will provide brief descriptions of some of the major aspects of the city, while below is a selection of top attractions that no visitor to Milan should miss.

MILAN'S TOP TEN ATTRACTIONS

Sant'Ambrogio
See pp84–7

Teatro alla Scala
See pp52–3

Pinacoteca Ambrosiana
See pp56–9

Ca' Granda
See p97

San Lorenzo alle Colonne
See pp80–81

Abbazia di Chiaravalle
See pp102–3

Duomo
See pp46–9

Castello Sforzesco
See pp64–7

Pinacoteca di Brera
See pp114–17

The Last Supper
See pp72–3

◁ Statues decorating the exterior of the Duomo

Famous Residents and Visitors

Many leading figures in Italian cultural life are connected in some way with Milan, from intellectuals, journalists and politicians to composers, writers and poets. The Italian novelist Alessandro Manzoni was born in Milan, and many other artists have been drawn here, hoping to make their fortune (an illustrious example is Giuseppe Verdi) or, more simply, to find work. One of the most widespread, and perhaps most accurate, sayings about Milan is that it is an open, receptive city ready to give strangers and foreigners a sincere, if brusque, welcome.

Carlo Emilio Gadda (1893–1973)
Milanese by birth, Gadda was one of the great 20th-century authors. One of his major works, L'Adalgisa celebrates the lives of middle-class Milanese and ends with the hero cleaning the tombs in the Monumental Cemetery.

Giorgio Strehler (1921–97)
In 1947 the great Trieste-born director founded the Piccolo Teatro della Città di Milano with Paolo Grassi. It was the first permanent theatre in Italy.

NORTHWEST
(see pp60–75)

Leonardo da Vinci (1452–1519)
In 1482 Lodovico il Moro invited Leonardo da Vinci to his court in Milan, where he remained for almost 20 years. He left a number of works, including the Codex Atlanticus, now in the Biblioteca Ambrosiana and The Last Supper, in Santa Maria delle Grazie (see pp72–3).

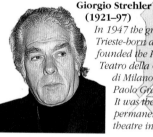

SOUTHWEST
(see pp76–91)

0 metres	700
0 yards	700

Benito Mussolini (1883–1945)
In 1919, in Milan's Piazza San Sepolcro, Mussolini founded the Fasci Nazionali di Combattimento, the first nucleus of the future Fascist movement. On 16 December 1944 Mussolini gave his last speech at the Teatro Lirico in Milan. A few months later, on 26 April 1945, his corpse was hung upside down in Piazzale Loreto.

Giuseppe Verdi (1813–1901)

Born in Busseto, in the province of Parma, Verdi moved to Milan at a very early age. His third opera, Nabucco *(1842), brought him fame. He died at the Grand Hotel et de Milan, which he had made his home.*

Alessandro Manzoni (1785–1873)

Manzoni wrote what is considered the greatest Italian novel, The Betrothed, *as well as plays and poetry. His house in Piazza Belgioioso (see p51) is open to the public.*

Cesare Beccaria (1738–94)

A leading exponent of the Enlightenment movement in Milan, Beccaria wrote its most representative work, On Crimes and Punishment. *In the square named after him is a monument in his honour.*

NORTHEAST
(see pp104–23)

STORIC
NTRE
pp42–59

SOUTHEAST
(see pp92–103)

The Verri Brothers

Pietro (1728–97) and Alessandro (1741–1816) Verri met other noted Enlightenment figures at the Caffè Greco, opposite the Duomo, where they conceived the influential periodical Il Caffè.

Carlo Porta (1775–1821)

A poet who wrote in Milanese dialect, Porta offered a vivacious description of the society of his time in his satirical poems. There is a monument in his honour in Piazza Santo Stefano, which was the setting for one of his best-known works, Ninetta del Verzee.

Milan's Best: Churches and Basilicas

The churches of Milan are built in two basic architectural styles: Lombard Romanesque, which can be seen elsewhere in the region, and the Counter-Reformation Mannerism of Milan under the Borromeos. The only exception is the Duomo, a splendid example of Lombard Gothic. There are very few examples of older styles. This is partly the result of destructive invasions and time, but is mostly due to the fact that the city is built just above the water table, and older buildings had to be demolished to make way for new ones.

Santa Maria delle Grazie
Besides being home to Leonardo's Last Supper, *this church, designed by Solari and Bramante, is a marvellous example of Renaissance architecture (see pp71–3).*

NORTHWEST
(see pp60–75)

Basilica of Sant'Ambrogio
The famous church founded by Sant'Ambrogio has a long architectural history, culminating in the restoration carried out to repair damage caused by the bombs of World War II (see pp84–7).

SOUTHWE
(see pp76–9

Basilica of San Lorenzo
This late 4th-century basilica still has some original architectural elements, such as the columns that surround the courtyard (see pp80–81).

Basilica of Sant'Eustorgio
Inside this 9th-century basilica are several aristocratic chapels, including the Cappella Portinari, one of the great examples of Renaissance architecture in Milan (see p90).

San Marco
The basic structure is 13th-century Romanesque, while the Neo-Gothic façade was restored in 1871. The three statues depicting San Marco between Sant'Ambrogio and Sant'Agostino (above) are works of the Campionese school (see p112).

San Fedele
This typical example of Counter-Reformation architecture was begun in 1569. Pellegrini's original design was completed by Bassi, who built the façade, and by Richini (see p50).

NORTHEAST
(see pp104–23)

**STORIC
NTRE**
e pp42–55)

SOUTHEAST
(see pp92–103)

Duomo
Milan's cathedral is the third largest church in the world (see pp46–9). It was begun by the Visconti family in 1386 and finished by Napoleon in 1805 – more than four centuries later.

0 metres	700
0 yards	700

Basilica of San Nazaro Maggiore
Founded by Sant'Ambrogio towards the end of the 4th century, the basilica has been altered many times, but restoration work has revived its original austere beauty. Do not miss the Trivulzio Chapel (see p96).

Milan's Best: Museums and Galleries

**17th-century clock,
Museo della Scienza
e della Tecnologia
Leonardo da Vinci**

Besides housing priceless works of art, the museums and art galleries of Milan also reflect the history of the city. The Pinacoteca di Brera was founded at the height of the Enlightenment period and the Ambrosiana is the result of the patronage of religious art by the Borromeo family. The Castello Sforzesco collections date from the period of the *Signorie*, while the Galleria d'Arte Moderna and the Museo dell'Ottocento are a sign of civic commitment to fine arts. The Museo Bagatti Valsecchi and Poldi Pezzoli, private collections, are typical manifestations of the Milanese love of art.

Pinacoteca di Brera
One of Northern Italy's largest art galleries has works from the 14th to the 19th century. Above, Pietà *by Giovanni Bellini (see pp114–17).*

Musei del Castello
The Castello Sforzesco museums are rich in sculpture, furniture and applied arts and also include a gallery with works by great artists, such as this Madonna and Child with the Infant St John the Baptist by Correggio (see pp64–7).

NORTHWEST
(see pp60–75)

**Museo Nazionale della
Scienza e della Tecnologia
Leonardo da Vinci**
The Science and Technology Museum has wooden models of Leonardo's inventions and a section given over to clocks, computers and means of communication and transport (see p88).

SOUTHWEST
(see pp76–91)

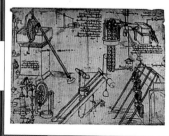

Pinacoteca Ambrosiana
This art gallery was founded by Cardinal Federico Borromeo in the 17th century to provide models for the students at the Fine Arts Academy. The collections include works by artists such as Caravaggio and Raphael (see pp56–9), while the Biblioteca Ambrosiana (library) contains the precious Codex Atlanticus by Leonardo da Vinci.

Museo Poldi Pezzoli
Together with the many works by Italian artists in this splendid residence-cum-museum (see p108) is Lucas Cranach's Portrait of Martin Luther.

Galleria d'Arte Moderna
Villa Belgiojoso – Galleria d'Arte Moderna (see p121) houses important 19th-century Italian art collections, the Vismara Collection and the Grassi Collection. Right, Matilda Juva Branca *(1851) by Francesco Hayez.*

NORTHEAST
(see pp104–123)

Museo Bagatti Valsecchi
This marvellous example of a 19th-century private residence contains 16th-century handicrafts, furniture, arms, ivory pieces, paintings and ceramics (see p109).

Museo Teatrale alla Scala
The Museo Teatrale was founded in 1913 and tells the story of the opera house. It holds a vast collection of musical instruments, portraits and documents dedicated to the greatest musicians, from Giuseppe Verdi to Arturo Toscanini (see p52).

HISTORIC CENTRE
(see pp42–59)

SOUTHEAST
(see pp92–103)

Palazzo Reale
The former royal palace has a long and distinguished history that can be divided into four historic phases: Neo-Classical, Napoleonic, Restoration and the Unification of Italy. The sumptuous interiors create a grand backdrop for the art exhibitions that take place here (see p54).

| 0 metres | 700 |
| 0 yards | 700 |

MILAN THROUGH THE YEAR

Milan offers a range of different events and attractions at different seasons of the year, from traditional to commercial. The city's citizens are still attached to traditional religious celebrations such as the Carnevale Ambrosiano (Milanese Carnival) and the festivities that take place around 7 December, the Festival of Sant'Ambrogio, the city's patron saint. This is also the date of opening night at La Scala, the world-famous opera house. Such traditional and characteristic festivities alternate with other events that are perhaps more in keeping with the image of a modern, industrial city. Among these are Fashion Week, one of the world's top fashion shows, held twice a year, and SMAU, an important international multimedia and communications technology trade show.

Private courtyards in Milan, open to the public in the spring

SPRING

After the long Milanese winter, local inhabitants welcome the arrival of spring with a sigh of relief. The pleasant spring breezes clear the air of the notorious Milanese smog and the city seems to take on different colours. On very clear days, if you look northwards you will see the peaks of the Alps, which are still covered with snow – one of the finest views the city affords at this time of year.

Towards the end of spring, the clear weather may very well give way to showers and even violent storms, which may blow up in the space of just a few hours, causing problems with city traffic.

This is the season when tourist activity resumes at the lakes. Boat services start up again and the water becomes a major weekend attraction for the Milanese once more.

MARCH

Cartoomics *(three days mid-Mar)*. Fieramilanocity, an event for fans of comics and animation, also features areas dedicated to science fiction and the Star Wars films. It has plenty of activities for kids.

Milano–San Remo *(third Sat)*. Part of the city centre hosts the start of this prestigious international bicycle race.

Oggi Aperto *(third weekend)*. Monuments and historic buildings that are usually closed to the public are opened up for the weekend.

Stramilano *(end Mar)*. This celebrated marathon is for professionals and amateurs alike and attracts an average of 50,000 competitors every year.

APRIL

Fiera dei Fiori
(Mon after Easter). In and around Via Moscova, near the Sant'Angelo Franciscan convent, is this fair devoted mainly to flower growing.

Barclays Milano City Marathon *(mid-Apr)*. This relay marathon for teams of four runners starts at Fiera di Rho, takes in many of the city's famous sights, and ends at Piazza Castello.

MAY

Milano Cortili Aperti.
The courtyards of the city's private residences are open to the public.

Pittori sul Naviglio.
Outdoor art display along the Alzaia Naviglio Grande canal *(see p89)*.

Estate all'Idroscalo.
Near Linate airport, the Milan seaplane airport inaugurates its summer season with sports events, water entertainment and concerts.

Sagra del Carroccio.
At Legnano, 30 km (19 miles) from Milan, there is a commemoration of the battle of 1176, when the Lombard League defeated Emperor Frederick Barbarossa. There are many costume parades, folk festivities and events.

The March Milan–San Remo race, opening the Italian cycling season

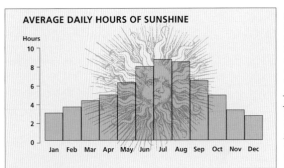

AVERAGE DAILY HOURS OF SUNSHINE

Hours

Sunshine Hours
The hours of sunshine in Milan are in line with the Mediterranean average. However, in autumn and winter the weather can be very foggy, which is a typical feature of the climate in the Po river valley, exacerbated by city pollution. The lakes, surrounded by the Alps, are more shaded in the morning and evening.

Parco Sempione, a major venue for summer entertainment

SUMMER

June is one of the most pleasant months to visit Milan because the climate is mild and the programme of cultural and sports events is truly packed. In July the torrid, muggy summer heat (the temperature may be as high as 40° C/104° F), together with the heavy traffic, can make sightseeing quite uncomfortable.

In August, most of the factories and offices close for the summer holidays and the empty city is an unusual and, in some respects, quite pleasant sight. The same streets that were crowded a week earlier are now quiet, even restful.

Despite the exodus, many events, both cultural and recreational, are held in Milan during the summer.

This is the busiest season for visiting the lakes of Northern Italy, but also the sunniest. Even at the peak of the summer heat, the water can have a cooling effect.

JUNE

Festa del Naviglio *(first Sun).* You can find everything under the sun at this festival, held in the atmospheric setting of the illuminated Navigli canals: street artists and performers, concerts, sports, an antiques market, handicrafts, regional cooking.

Milano d'Estate *(Jun-Aug).* This marks the beginning of summer entertainment in the city (concerts, exhibits, various cultural events), which takes place in the Parco Sempione.

Sagra di San Cristoforo *(third Sun).* The patron saint of travellers, St Christopher, is celebrated along the Naviglio, in the square facing the church. In the evening decorated barges glide along the canals.

Estate all'Umanitaria. The Humanitarian Association organizes a festival of cinema, dance, music, theatre and cartoons and shows for children.

Fotoshow *(odd years).* An interesting video, photography and optics show in the Fiera (Exhibition Centre) pavilions.

Orticola. Flower growing and garden furnishings show and market in the Porta Venezia public gardens *(see p120).*

Sagra di San Giovanni. At Monza, a few miles north of Milan, the patron saint's feast day is celebrated with sports and cultural events, some of which are held at a splendid venue – the park at the Villa Reale.

JULY AND AUGUST

Festival Latino-Americano. The Forum di Assago hosts this lively festival of Latin-American music, handicrafts and cuisine.

Arianteo. At the Giardini Pubblici *(see p120),* the Anteo motion-picture theatre organizes a series of outdoor showings, which includes all the most important films featured in Milan's cinemas and theatres during the year.

The Festa del Naviglio, marking the beginning of summer events

AVERAGE MONTHLY RAINFALL

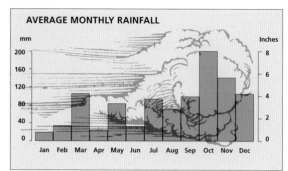

mm / Inches

200, 160, 120, 80, 40, 0

Jan Feb Mar Apr May Jun Jul Aug Sep Oct Nov Dec

Rainfall
The average monthly rainfall in the Milan area can vary quite considerably during the year. The wettest season is certainly autumn, when it may rain for several days without a break. In late spring and summer the average rainfall level may increase because of unexpected storms.

AUTUMN

September in Milan really gives you the impression of life beginning anew. In general, by the last week of August the Milanese have returned from holiday, but it is only in September that things get back into full swing.

A Ferrari in action at Monza

As far as the weather is concerned, fog and rain alternate with lovely clear days with that typical "Lombard sky" which Alessandro Manzoni, in *The Betrothed*, described as being "so beautiful when it is beautiful, so blue, so serene".

SEPTEMBER

Premier League Football (soccer). By September the Italian football season is under way (the opening match takes place on the last Sunday in August). The football season is of great importance to the city, which is home to two of Italy's top teams, Inter and Milan.
Panoramica di Venezia (*early Sep*). Milan cinemas show films from the Venice Film Festival while they are being screened there. **Gran Premio di Monza.** Held at one of the top motor racing circuits, the Grand Prix of Italy is often crucial to the outcome of the Formula One competition.
Mi Milano Prêt-à-Porter (*last weekend*). A major fashion show for leading Italian and international fashion designers.

OCTOBER

Fiera Di Chiaravalle (*first Mon*). This famous fair is held in the shade of the *ciribiciaccola* (as the Milanese call the bell tower of the Chiaravalle Cistercian abbey, *see pp102–3*). The fair features music, dancing and an art exhibition.

The Fiera, host to both SMAU and fashion shows

SMAU (*first week*). International multimedia show held in the Fiera Exhibition Centre: IT, from computers for offices to CD-Roms and Virtual Reality.
Bagutta-Pittori all'Aria Aperta (*mid-Oct*). The famous Via Bagutta plays host to a fascinating outdoor exhibition for artists' work.

NOVEMBER

Premio Bagutta Milan's most important literary prize is awarded.

San Siro stadium, packed with fans at the beginning of the season

PUBLIC HOLIDAYS

New Year's Day (1 Jan)
Epiphany (6 Jan)
Easter Sunday & Monday
Liberation Day (25 Apr)
Labour Day (1 May)
Festa della Repubblica (2 June)
Ferragosto (15 Aug)
All Saints' Day (1 Nov)
Sant'Ambrogio (7 Dec)
Immaculate Conception (8 Dec)
Christmas (25 Dec)
Santo Stefano (26 Dec)

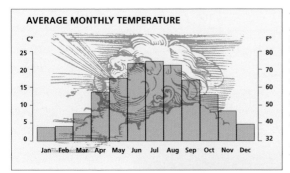

AVERAGE MONTHLY TEMPERATURE

Temperature
Milan is inland and there are big differences in temperature between winter and summer. The winters can be very cold indeed, particularly in December and January, typical of continental Europe, while there may be torrid heat in summer. The climate is always very humid.

WINTER

Characterized by severe cold (heavy snowfall is not rare), the Milanese winter is "warmed up" by a rich and fascinating programme of cultural events, major holidays and special occasions. The city becomes especially lively around the feast day of Sant'Ambrogio (St Ambrose), the local patron saint, and then for Christmas, which is preceded by the usual shopping sprees in the city-centre shops. On the cultural side, the theatres of Milan present a high-quality theatre season, headed by the world-famous Piccolo Teatro.

Typical antiques stalls at the Oh bej Oh bej fair

antiques as well as other articles. It is held in the streets around the basilica of Sant'Ambrogio *(see pp84–7)*.
La Scala. The season at the world-famous opera house *(see pp52–3)* starts on 7 December. The opening night is a major cultural event, and an important occasion in the Milanese social calendar.

JANUARY

Corteo dei Re Magi *(6 Jan)*. A traditional procession with a *tableau vivant* of the Nativity goes from the Duomo to Sant'Eustorgio.
Fiera di Senigallia *(every Sat all year long)*. Along the Darsena is a colourful market offering ethnic handicrafts, records and bicycles.
Mercato dell'Antiquariato di Brera *(third Sat of month, all year)*. Stalls with antiques, books, postcards, jewellery.

FEBRUARY

Carnevale Ambrosiano. The longest carnival in the world ends on the first Saturday of Lent. Floats and

Milanese characters, such as Meneghin, take part in a parade to Piazza del Duomo.
BIT *(mid-Feb)*. The Fiera (Milan's Exhibition Centre) hosts an international tourist trade show.
Mi Milano Prêt-à-Porter *(late Feb)*. The autumn-winter collections of the leading international and Italian fashion designers go on show.

Christmas decorations in the Galleria Vittorio Emanuele II

DECEMBER

Festa di Sant'Ambrogio *(7 Dec)*. This is the feast day of the patron saint of Milan, just before Immaculate Conception *(8 Dec)*. Sant'Ambrogio is celebrated with many events: the jam-packed **Fiera degli Oh bej Oh bej**, a vast street fair featuring

Taking part in the Carnevale Ambrosiano in Piazza del Duomo

Piazza Duomo and entrance to Galleria Vittorio Emanuele ▷

MILAN AREA
BY AREA

HISTORIC CENTRE

Leonardo da Vinci,
in Piazza della Scala

The area around the Duomo was the religious centre of Milan in the 4th century. Up to the 14th century it was the site of the basilicas of Santa Tecla and Santa Maria Maggiore and the Early Christian baptisteries, San Giovanni alle Fonti and Santo Stefano. These were all demolished to make room for the new cathedral. The political and administrative centre of the city was the nearby Palazzo della Ragione. At that time Milan was only slightly larger than the present-day historic centre; in fact, what is today Piazza della Scala was on the edge of town. Piazza del Duomo was the focus of small businesses until the 18th century, and a stage for the city's major religious and civic ceremonies. In the 19th century it became the nucleus from which avenues radiated. In the 1860s the decaying dwellings and the shops around the Duomo were demolished to make way for the construction of the then futuristic Galleria, the symbol of Milan after the unification of Italy. The damage caused by bombs in World War II created large empty areas later occupied by many modern buildings. The Historic Centre is always thronging with visitors, drawn by the world-famous churches, museums and galleries and also by the excellent shops.

SIGHTS AT A GLANCE

Streets, Squares and Historic Buildings
Casa degli Omenoni **6**
Casa Manzoni and
  Piazza Belgioioso **7**
Galleria Vittorio Emanuele II **2**
Palazzo Borromeo **15**
Palazzo Marino **4**
Palazzo Reale **10**
Piazza del Liberty and Corso
  Vittorio Emanuele II **8**
Piazza Mercanti **12**

Churches
Duomo see pp46–9 **1**
San Fedele **5**
San Giorgio al Palazzo **16**
San Gottardo in Corte **9**
San Sepolcro **14**
Santa Maria presso San Satiro **17**

Galleries
Museo del Novecento **11**
Pinacoteca Ambrosiana
  see pp56–9 **13**

Theatres
Teatro alla Scala see pp52–3 **3**

KEY

▦ Street-by-Street map
   See pp44–5

Ⓜ Metro

🚕 Taxi

GETTING THERE
Underground metro lines 1 (red) and 3 (yellow) have stops in Piazza del Duomo; line 3 also stops in Piazza Missori. Tram 1 stops in front of La Scala and trams 3, 12, 14, 16, 19 and 27 stop in Via Orefici. Bus No. 60, the terminus of which is in Piazza San Babila, goes to the Stazione Centrale (main railway station).

0 metres 400
0 yards 400

◁ The Galleria Vittorio Emanuele II, Milan's elegant "drawing room" since 1867

Street-by-Street: Piazza del Duomo

Piazza del Duomo, designed by Giuseppe Mengoni and opened in 1865 after protracted difficulties, is the ideal starting point for a visit to Milan's historic centre. The area is packed with visitors fascinated by the "great machine of the Duomo", as Alessandro Manzoni describes the cathedral in *The Betrothed*. There are numerous spots where the Milanese like to meet for an aperitif on Sunday morning. Young people prefer to go to Corso Vittorio Emanuele II, which has most of the cinemas as well as many shops and department stores.

Sculpture, Casa degli Omenoni

San Fedele
This church, a typical example of Counter-Reformation architecture, is popular with the old Milanese aristocracy ❺

Casa degli Omenoni

★ Teatro alla Scala
This was the first monument in Milan to be rebuilt after the 1943 bombings ❸

Palazzo Marino

Zucca in Galleria is a popular café, decorated with mosaics and decor dating from 1921.

Piazza Mercanti

★ Galleria Vittorio Emanuele II
The Galleria was one of the first iron and glass constructions in Italy ❷

| 0 metres | | 100 |
| 0 yards | | 100 |

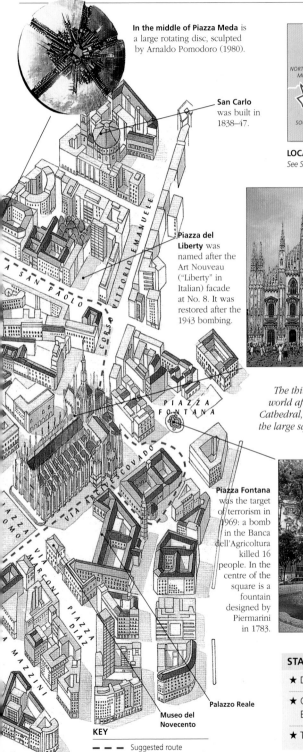

In the middle of Piazza Meda is a large rotating disc, sculpted by Arnaldo Pomodoro (1980).

San Carlo was built in 1838–47.

LOCATOR MAP
See Street Finder, maps 3, 4, 7, 8

Piazza del Liberty was named after the Art Nouveau ("Liberty" in Italian) facade at No. 8. It was restored after the 1943 bombing.

★ **Duomo**
The third largest church in the world after St Peter's and Seville Cathedral, the Duomo towers over the large square named after it ❶

Piazza Fontana was the target of terrorism in 1969: a bomb in the Banca dell'Agricoltura killed 16 people. In the centre of the square is a fountain designed by Piermarini in 1783.

Palazzo Reale

Museo del Novecento

KEY

– – – Suggested route

STAR SIGHTS

★ Duomo

★ Galleria Vittorio Emanuele II

★ Teatro alla Scala

Duomo ❶

The construction of the Duomo began in 1386, with the city's bishop, Antonio da Saluzzo, as its patron. Duke Gian Galeazzo Visconti invited Lombard, German and French architects to supervise the works and insisted they use Candoglia marble, which was transported along the Navigli canals. The official seal AUF (*ad usum fabricae*), stamped on the slabs, exempted them from customs duty. The cathedral was consecrated in 1418, yet remained unfinished until the 19th century, when Napoleon, who was crowned King of Italy here, had the façade completed.

Statue in the interior

La Madonnina
The 4.16-m (14-ft) gilded statue of the Madonna was sculpted by Giuseppe Bini in 1774.

Flying buttresses

★ **Stained-glass Windows**
Most of the windows depict scenes from the Bible, and date from the 19th century. The oldest one – the fifth in the right-hand aisle – dates back to 1470–75 and depicts the life of Christ, while the newest (the seventh) dates from 1988.

★ **Trivulzio Candelabrum**
This masterpiece of medieval goldsmithery was donated in 1562 by Gian Battista Trivulzio. On the pedestal there are fantastic monsters and figures representing arts, crafts and the virtues.

Crypt

THE BUILDING OF MILAN CATHEDRAL

1386 The first stone of the Duomo is laid	**1567** Pellegrino Tibaldi ("il Pellegrini") redesigns the presbytery	**1656** Carlo Buzzi continues façade in Gothic style	**1774** The Madonnina is placed on the tallest spire		**1838–65** The Bertinis make the apse windows

1300	1400	1500	1600	1700	1800	1900

1418 Pope Martin V consecrates the high altar	**1500** Central spire inaugurated	**1617** Francesco Maria Richini begins work on the façade	**1813** façade completed with Gothic spires	**1981–4** Presbytery piers restored

Martin V

★ Roof Terraces

The view of the city from the roof terraces is simply unforgettable. You can also have a close-up look at the central spire. The roof bristles with spires, the oldest of which dates from 1404.

VISITORS' CHECKLIST

Piazza Duomo. **Map** 7 C1.
Tel 02-72 02 33 75. **M** 1, 3
Duomo. 🚋 1, 2, 3, 12, 14, 15,
16, 19, 24, 27. ◯ 7:30am–
7:30pm daily. ◻ ◻
Baptistery/Digs ◯ 9am–
5:30pm. ◻ 🖻 **Treasury**
◯ 9:30am–5:30pm Mon–Sat
(5pm Sat); 1:30–3:30pm Sun.
◻ 🖻 **Roof Terraces** ◯ 9am–
6:30pm (9pm summer). 🖻 ♿

About 3,500 statues lend movement to the massive Duomo. They are typically medieval, representing saints, animals and monsters.

A plaque confirms that the Duomo is dedicated to Maria Nascente.

The Interior

The 5 aisles in the nave are separated by 52 piers, whose capitals are decorated with statues.

Main entrance

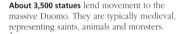

STAR FEATURES

★ Stained-glass Windows

★ Trivulzio Candelabrum

★ Roof Terraces

The Doors

The five doors were made from 1840 to 1965. Right, The Flagellation *by Ludovico Pogliaghi, a bronze relief in the central door.*

Exploring the Duomo

Statue of Sant'Ambrogio

So that the Duomo could be built, a great Jubilee was proclaimed in 1390 in order to urge the Milanese to contribute money and manual labour to carry out the work. The initial plan was to build it in fired bricks, as the excavations in the northern sacristy have revealed, but in 1387 Duke Gian Galeazzo Visconti, who wanted the cathedral to be seen as a great symbol of his power, demanded that marble should be used instead and that the architectural style should be International Gothic. Building continued over five centuries, resulting in the obvious mixture of styles that characterizes the cathedral.

The presbytery, with the small ciborium dome in the foreground

THE FAÇADE

Up to the first level of windows the façade is Baroque. It was completed in the 19th century with Neo-Gothic ogival windows and spires, revealing the difficulties entailed in building the Duomo.

THE INTERIOR

Tall cross vaults cover the interior and the 5 aisles in the nave are separated by 52 piers (for the 52 weeks of the year). The capitals on the piers are decorated with statues of saints. Behind the façade, embedded in the floor, is a meridian ①, installed in 1786 by the Brera astronomers. It marked astronomical noon, thanks to a ray

of sunlight that enters from the first bay of the south aisle on the right-hand side.

This is a good starting point for a visit to the Duomo. To the right is the sarcophagus of Archbishop Ariberto d'Intimiano ②, bearing a copy of the crucifix that he donated to the San Dionigi monastery (the original is in the Museo del Duomo). Next to this, on the left, is a plaque with the date of the foundation of the cathedral. The corresponding stained-glass window, executed in the old mosaic technique, relates the *Life of St John the Evangelist* (1473–7). The stained-glass windows in the next three bays, showing episodes from the Old Testament, date from the

Stained-glass window, detail

16th century. In the fifth bay there is a stained-glass window executed between 1470 and 1475 that illustrates the *Life of Christ* ③. Compare this with the other window in the seventh bay – it was made in 1988 and is dedicated to Cardinals Schuster and Ferrari ④. The presbytery ⑤ is constructed in the style imposed in 1567 by Pellegrini who, at the request of San Carlo Borromeo, made this part of the Duomo the Lombard model of a typical Counter-Reformation church.

In the middle, under the ciborium behind the altar, is the Tabernacle ⑥, donated by Pius IV to his nephew San Carlo (St Charles). In front of them are two 16th-century gilded copper pulpits ⑦ with

FLOOR PLAN

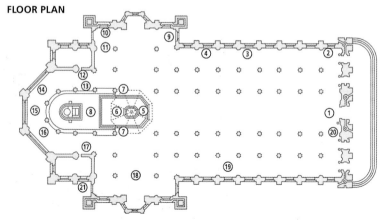

THE HOLY NAIL OF THE CROSS

Tabernacle of the Nail of the Cross

In the vault above the choir, a red light marks the location of the niche where a nail from Christ's Cross has been kept since 1461. The nail, which was once kept in the early medieval Santa Maria Maggiore, is in the shape of a horseshoe and was found by St Helena and later given to her son, Emperor Constantine. It was later donated to Sant'-Ambrogio and carried by San Carlo in procession during the 1576 plague. It is shown to the public every 14 September, when the Bishop of Milan is raised up to the level of the niche which holds the nail in a kind of decorated balcony, drawn by invisible pulleys.

episodes from the Old and New Testaments, surmounted by the organs painted by Giovanni Ambrogio Figino, Camillo Procaccini and Giuseppe Meda.

Behind the altar is an extra-ordinary wooden choir with the *Life of Sant'Ambrogio* ⑧, carved in 1572–1620. In the right-hand transept is the funerary monument of Gian Giacomo Medici ⑨, the brother of Pope Pius IV, which was once attributed to Michelangelo but is in fact the work of Leone Leoni (1560–63). Past the chapel dedicated to St John the Good, Bishop of Milan in the 7th century, above the side entrance is the splendid stained-glass window of St Catherine of Alexandria ⑩, designed by the Arcimboldi brothers in 1556. A little further on is the strange statue of the flayed St Bartholomew ⑪, signed and dated 1562 by Marco d'Agrate.

At the beginning of the ambulatory there is a *Deposition* on the southern door of the sacristy ⑫ (1393), dedicated to the "Mysteries of the Virgin Mary". Steps ⑬ lead to the crypt (1606), where San Carlo Borromeo is buried, the Duomo Treasury, with its exceptional collection of church vestments and objects, and the Coro Jemale, a small 16th-century room decorated with fine stucco-work (check out the relief sculpture cycle of the *Life of the Virgin Mary*, a 17th-century masterpiece). The apse is illuminated by the

three huge 19th-century stained-glass windows by the Bertini brothers with episodes from the Old ⑯ and New ⑭ Testaments and the Apoca-lypse ⑮. The ambulatory ends at the northern portal of the sacristy ⑰, with *Christ the Lord and Judge* (1389). The left-hand transept is dominated by the 5-m (16-ft) bronze Trivulzio Candelabrum ⑱, a 12th-century masterpiece by the goldsmith Nicola da Verdun. The candelabrum carries scenes from the Old Testament and the Three Wise Men riding towards the enthroned Virgin. Going down the north aisle, you will see the Chapel of the Crucifix ⑲ carried by San Carlo in pro-cession during the 1576 plague. Behind this is a window with a depiction of the *Discovery of the True Cross by St Helena* (1570–77). To the left of the entrance, steps lead down to the

Chalice in the Duomo Treasury

remains of an Early Christian apse of Santa Tecla and an octagonal baptistery ⑳ where, according to tradition, Sant'Ambrogio (St Ambrose) baptized St Augustine in AD 387. From San Carlo's feast day to Epiphany, the *Quadroni di San Carlo* go on display in the nave. These paintings, the work of leading 17th-century Lombard artists, depict the story of the life and miracles of San Carlo.

ROOF TERRACES

On the way to the lift ㉑ which goes up to the roof, you should go to the apse to admire the central stained-glass window, designed by Filippino degli Organi in 1402. From the roof there is a magnificent view of the city and the mountains to the north, as well as the Duomo spires and statues and even the buttresses below.

MUSEO DEL DUOMO

The Cathedral museum, founded in 1953, is at No. 15 Via Arcivescovado. It houses paintings, sculptures, religious objects and stained-glass windows from the Duomo. Among the best works are *St Paul the Hermit*, Tintoretto's *Christ among the Doctors* (1530) and a wooden model of the Duomo, begun in 1519. It focuses on both the hist-orical and artistic elements of the Duomo, and also docu-ments the restoration of the four central piers (1981–4).

The right side of the presbytery of the Milan Duomo

Palazzo Marino, the Town Hall since 1860, and the 1872 statue of Leonardo da Vinci on the right

Galleria Vittorio Emanuele II ❷

Piazza della Scala, Piazza del Duomo. **Map** 7 C1. M *1, 3 Duomo.*

The Galleria is an elegant arcade lined with cafés, shops and a famous restaurant, Savini *(see p173).* Work began in 1865, overseen by the architect Giuseppe Mengoni, and it was opened two years later by the king, Vittorio Emanuele II, after whom it was named. The gallery was designed to connect Piazza del Duomo and Piazza della Scala, and formed part of an ambitious urban renewal project. On the floor in the central octagonal area, directly under the 47-m (154-ft) high glass dome, is the heraldic symbol of the Savoy family, a white cross on a red ground. Around it are the arms of four major Italian cities: the bull of Turin, the wolf of Rome, the lily of Florence and the red cross on a white ground (Milan). On the vault are mosaics of Asia, Africa, Europe and America.

Teatro alla Scala ❸

See pp52–3.

Palazzo Marino ❹

Piazza della Scala. **Map** 3 C5. M *1, 3 Duomo.* ⊘ *to the public.*

This palazzo was designed in 1558 by Galeazzo Alessi for the banker Tommaso Marino, but remained unfinished until 1892, when Luca Beltrami completed the façade. From Via Marino on the right you can see the richly decorated, porticoed courtyard of honour.

According to tradition the palazzo, home of Milan Town Hall since 1860, was the birthplace of Marianna de Leyva, the famous nun of Monza described by Alessandro Manzoni in *The Betrothed* as the "Signora".

San Fedele ❺

Piazza San Fedele. **Map** 3 C5.
Tel *02-86 35 22 15.* M *1, 3 Duomo.*
🚋 *1, 2.* 🚌 *61.* ⏰ *7:30am–1:15pm, 4:30–6pm Mon–Fri.* ✝ *7:50am, 12:45pm Mon–Fri; 6:30pm Sat; 11am, 7pm Sun.*

This church is the Milanese seat of the Jesuit Order, commissioned by San Carlo Borromeo from Pellegrino Tibaldi in 1569. The work was continued by Martino Bassi and the dome, crypt and choir were designed by Francesco Maria Richini (1633–52). With its austere architecture and nave without aisles, this is a typical Counter-Reformation church. The façade is being restored, but the interior has three interesting paintings. By the first altar on the right is *St Ignatius's Vision* by Giovan Battista Crespi, known as "il Cerano" (c.1622). A *Transfiguration* by Bernardino Campi (1565) is in the atrium after the second altar on the left; Campi also painted the *Blessed Virgin and Child,* by the second altar (left). These last two works came from Santa Maria della Scala, which was demolished to make room for La Scala opera house *(see pp52–3).*

The wooden furniture is also worth a closer look: the confessionals (1596) have scenes from the life of Christ carved by Giovanni Taurini, and the cupboards in Richini's sacristy (1624–28) are by Daniele Ferrari (1639). A statue of writer Alessandro Manzoni, whose death certificate is kept in San Fedele, stands in the square.

Galleria Vittorio Emanuele II, inaugurated in 1867

Casa degli Omenoni ❻

Via Omenoni 3. **Map** 3 C5.
Ⓜ 1, 3 Duomo. 🔾 to the public.

Eight telamones, which the Milanese call *omenoni* ("large men"), are the most striking feature of this house-cum-studio, built by the sculptor Leone Leoni in 1565. The artist collected many works of art, including paintings by Titian and Correggio and Leonardo da Vinci's famous *Codex Atlanticus (see p59)*.

A reference to Leoni can be seen in the relief under the cornice, in which Calumny is torn up by lions *(leoni)*.

The entrance to the Casa degli Omenoni

Casa Manzoni and Piazza Belgioioso ❼

Via Morone 1. **Map** 4 D5. **Tel** 02-86 46 04 03. Ⓜ 3 Montenapoleone.
🚋 1. 🚌 61. 🔾 9am–noon, 2–4pm Tue–Fri. 🏛 public hols. ♿

This is the house where Italian author Alessandro Manzoni lived from 1814 until his death in 1873 after a fall

Part of the façade of Palazzo Liberty, at No. 8 Piazza del Liberty

on the steps of San Fedele. The perfectly preserved interior includes Manzoni's studio on the ground floor, where he received Garibaldi in 1862 and Verdi in 1868. Next to this is the room where poet and author Tommaso Grossi had his notary office, while on the first floor is Manzoni's bedroom. The house is now the seat of the National Centre for Manzoni Studies, which was founded in 1937. It includes a library with works by Manzoni and critical studies of his oeuvre, as well as the Lombard Historical Society Library with over 40,000 volumes. The brick façade overlooks Piazza Belgioioso, named after the palazzo at No. 2 (closed to the public). This monumental palazzo was designed by Piermarini in 1777–81 for Prince Alberico XII di Belgioioso d'Este. The façade bears heraldic emblems. In the interior a fresco by Martin Knoller represents the apotheosis of Prince Alberico.

Piazza del Liberty and Corso Vittorio Emanuele II ❽

Map 8 D1. Ⓜ 1, 3 Duomo, 1 San Babila. 🚋 15, 23. 🚌 60, 61, 73.

Once past the arch at the end of Piazza Belgioioso, go through Piazza Meda (1926) and past Corso Matteotti, which was built in 1934 to link Piazza della Scala with Piazza San Babila, and then go down Via San Paolo, which will take you to Piazza del Liberty. This small square owes its name to the Art Nouveau (Liberty) façade on No. 8, restored by Giovanni and Lorenzo Muzio in 1963 with architectural elements from the Trianon café-concert, a building dating from 1905 which was moved from Corso Vittorio Emanuele II.

Go along Via San Paolo to reach Corso Vittorio Emanuele II. This is Milan's main commercial street, and was once called "Corsia dei Servi" (Servants' Lane). It follows the course of an ancient Roman street and in 1628 was the scene of bread riots, described by Manzoni in *The Betrothed*. Near San Carlo al Corso, at No. 13 is the *Omm de preja* (local dialect for *uomo di pietra* or "man of stone") statue, a copy of an ancient Roman work. It is also called "Sciur Carera", a misspelling of the first word of a Latin inscription under the statue *(carere debet omni vitio qui in alterum dicere paratus est)*.

The *Omm de preja* statue

Casa Manzoni, now home to the National Centre for Manzoni Studies

Teatro alla Scala ❸

Poster for
Turandot

Built by Giuseppe Piermarini in 1776-8, this opera house owes its name to the fact that it stands on the site of Santa Maria della Scala, a church built in 1381 for Regina della Scala, Bernabò Visconti's wife. The theatre opened in 1778; it was bombed in 1943 and rebuilt three years later. After an extensive restoration programme that saw the addition of a new stage tower designed by Mario Botta, La Scala reopened in 2004. The opening night of the opera season is 7 December, the feast day of Sant'Ambrogio, Milan's patron saint.

Teatro alla Scala in 1852, by Angelo Inganni

The chandelier, made of Bohemian crystal (1923), holds 383 lightbulbs.

★ Foyer
This large, mirror-lined salon was renovated in 1936. There is a bust of the legendary conductor Arturo Toscanini.

The boxes were like small living rooms where romantic trysts and parlour games were arranged.

The façade was designed by Piermarini so that passers-by in Via Manzoni could catch a glimpse of it.

Entrance

★ Museo Teatrale
The theatre museum was founded in 1913 and boasts a fine collection of sculpture, original scores, paintings and ceramics related to the history of La Scala as well as of theatre in general.

STAR FEATURES

★ Auditorium

★ Foyer

★ Museo Teatrale

THE BALLET SCHOOL

La Scala's Ballet School was founded in 1813. Originally there were 48 students who studied dance, mime or specialist disciplines. At the end of an eight-year course, the best students were awarded merits of distinction and became part of the theatre's *corps de ballet* with an annual stipend of €1.5. This rigorously disciplined school has produced such artists as Carla Fracci and Luciana Savignano.

Students at the Ballet School

VISITORS' CHECKLIST

Piazza della Scala. **Map** 3 C5.
M *1, 3 Duomo.* 🚊 *1, 61.*
Tel 02-88 791. **Museo
Teatrale alla Scala:** Largo
Ghiringhelli 1 (Piazza Scala).
Tel 02-88 79 74 73. ◯ *9am–
noon, 1:30–5pm daily.* 🎫
*(includes a look at the theatre
from a balcony, provided there
are no rehearsals or shows).* ♿
📷 www.teatroallascala.org

A tank filled with water, placed over the wooden vault, was ready for use in case of fire.

Dressing rooms

The orchestra pit was introduced in 1907. Before then the orchestra played behind a balustrade on the same level as the stalls.

Stage
This is one of the largest stages in Italy, measuring 1,200 sq m (13,000 sq ft).

★ Auditorium
Made of wood covered with red velvet and decorated with gilded stuccowork, the interior boasts marvellous acoustics and has a seating capacity of 2,015.

The entrance to the church of San Gottardo in Corte

San Gottardo in Corte ❾

Via Pecorari 2. **Map** 8 D1. **Tel** 02-86 46 45 00. Ⓜ 1, 3 Duomo. 🚊 2, 3, 12, 15, 23, 27. 🚌 54, 60. ⭕ 8am–noon, 2–6pm Mon–Fri (to 5:30pm Fri), 2–4pm Sat, 8am–noon Sun.

Azzone Visconti, lord of Milan, ordered the construction of this church in 1336 as the ducal chapel in the Broletto Vecchio (Courthouse) courtyard. The interior was rebuilt in Neo-Classical style by Piermarini. On the left-hand wall is a *Crucifixion* by the school of Giotto.

Azzone Visconti's funerary monument, by Giovanni di Balduccio, is in the apse: the reclining statue of Visconti is flanked by the figures of two women. The octagonal brick bell tower with small stone arches and columns is by Francesco Pecorari (c.1335).

Palazzo Reale ❿

Piazza del Duomo. **Map** 7 C1. **Tel** 02-88 46 52 30. Ⓜ 1, 3 Duomo. 🚊 12, 15, 23, 24, 27. 🚌 54, 60. ⭕ 9:30am–5:30pm Tue–Sun.

The seat of the commune administration in the 11th century, this building was drastically rebuilt by Azzone Visconti in 1330–36. At the height of its importance, it was the headquarters of the lords of Milan. Galeazzo Maria Sforza's decision to move the palace began the decline of the Palazzo Reale. In 1598 it housed the first permanent theatre in Milan. Made of wood, it was rebuilt in 1737 and Mozart played here as a child. In 1776 it was destroyed by a fire.

The present Neo-Classical appearance dates from 1778, when Giuseppe Piermarini made it into a residence for Archduke Ferdinand of Austria. In 1920 Vittorio Emanuele III granted the place temporarily to the city of Milan, and in 1965 the city purchased it to use as offices and museums and for important temporary exhibitions by sculptors and painters such as Claude Monet and Pablo Picasso.

Unique Forms of Continuity in Space (1913) by Umberto Boccioni

Museo del Novecento ⓫

Palazzo dell'Arengario, Piazza del Duomo. **Map** 7 C1. **Tel** 02-88 44 40 72. Ⓜ 1, 3 Duomo. 🚊 12, 14, 15, 23, 24, 27. 🚌 54, 60. ⭕ call for details. ♿

Construction of the Arengario, designed by architect Piero Portaluppi and others, began in the late 1930s as part of a modernisation plan for the city. The name *arengario* refers to the place where medieval town councils were held.

The building now houses the Museo del Novecento (Museum of 20th-Century Art). Architect Italo Rota's design includes an exterior steel and glass bridge to connect the building to the Palazzo Reale, creating an important museum complex. The museum traces the history of 20th-century Italian art, with sections devoted to movements like Futurism, Metaphysical Art, Arte Povera and Abstractionism. Works by 20th-century Milanese artists are also featured.

Piazza Mercanti ⓬

Map 7 C1. Ⓜ 1 Cairoli–Cordusio.

This corner of medieval Milan was the seat of public and civic activities and also housed the prison. Palazzo della Ragione was built in 1233 by the chief magistrate (and virtual ruler) Oldrado da Tresseno, who is portrayed in a relief by Antelami on the side facing the square. This courthouse is also known as "Broletto Nuovo" to distinguish it from the older Broletto Vecchio near Palazzo Reale. Markets were held under the porticoes, while the Salone dei Giudici on the first floor was used as the law court. In 1773 another storey was added to house the notarial archive. On one side

Palazzo Reale, now used as a venue for temporary exhibitions

The well in Piazza Mercanti and, on the left, Palazzo delle Scuole Palatine

of the square is the Loggia degli Osii, built by Matteo Visconti in 1316. The façade is decorated with the arms of the districts of Milan and statues of the Virgin Mary and saints (1330). Next is the Palazzo delle Scuole Palatine (1645), the façade of which bears statues of St Augustine and the Latin poet Ausonius. The Palazzo dei Panigarola (to the right), which was rebuilt in the 15th century, was used to register public documents.

In the centre of the square is a 16th-century well. In Via Mercanti is the Palazzo dei Giureconsulti, dominated by the Torre del Comune, built by Napo Torriani in 1272. At the foot of this tower is a statue of Sant'Ambrogio.

Pinacoteca Ambrosiana ⓭

See pp56–9.

San Sepolcro ⓮

Piazza San Sepolcro. **Map** 7 B1.
Ⓜ *1, 3 Duomo.* 🚌 *1, 2, 3, 14, 16, 19, 27.* 🕐 *noon–2pm Mon–Fri.*
✝ *5pm pre-hols; noon (winter), 5pm hols.* 📷

San Sepolcro was founded in 1030 in the area of the ancient Roman Forum and rebuilt in 1100 at the time of

the second Crusade. The Neo-Romanesque façade was built in 1897, while the interior is basically Baroque. There are two terracotta groups by Agostino De Fondutis (16th century) depicting *Christ Washing His Disciples' Feet* and *The Flagellation of Christ with Caiaphas and St Peter.* The only remaining part of the 1030 church is the Romanesque crypt, with a sculpture group of the *Deposition* by the De Fondutis school in the apse.

Palazzo Borromeo ⓯

Piazza Borromeo 7. **Map** 4 D4.
Ⓜ *1 Cordusio.* 🚌 *2, 3, 14, 16, 27.* 🕐 *courtyard only.*

This prestigious early 15th-century residence was badly damaged by the 1943 bombings and the only remaining original architectural element is the ogival portal, with leaf decoration and the coat of arms of the Borromeo family. The partly rebuilt second courtyard has porticoes on three sides and on the fourth, between the brick windows, is the original decoration with the family motto *Humilitas*. This courtyard leads to the 15th-century Sala dei Giochi, which is decorated with frescoes of the games played by the aristocracy of the time, including the *Game of Tarot* by a painter known as the Master of the Borromeo Games. The red background developed as the result of a chemical reaction which changed the original blue of the sky.

The Borromeo family coat of arms with the motto *Humilitas*

San Giorgio al Palazzo ⓰

Piazza San Giorgio 2. **Map** 7 B1.
Tel *02-805 71 48.* 🚌 *2, 3, 14.*
🕐 *7:30am–noon, 3:30–6pm daily.*
✝ *8am Mon–Fri; 6pm pre-hols; 11am hols.*

Founded in 750, this church was named after an ancient Roman *palatium* which stood here. It was radically changed in 1623 and 1800–21 by the architects Richini and Cagnola respectively, and little remains of the original or Romanesque (1129) structures. The third chapel in the right-hand aisle contains paintings by Bernardino Luini (1516) with scenes from the Passion. On the vault there is a fresco of the Crucifixion.

Santa Maria presso San Satiro ⓱

Via Speronari 3. **Map** 7 B1.
Tel *02-87 46 83.* Ⓜ *1, 3 Duomo.*
🚌 *1, 2, 3, 14, 15, 16, 24, 27.*
🕐 *7:30–11:30am, 3:30–6:30pm Mon–Fri; 3:30–7pm Sat; 10am–noon, 3:30–7pm Sun.* ✝ *7:45am, 6pm Mon–Sat; 11am, 6pm Sun.*

The original nucleus of this church, founded by archbishop Ansperto da Biassono, dates from 876. The only remnant is the Sacello della Pietà (chapel of pity), which was altered by Bramante in the 15th century, and the Lombard Romanesque bell tower. In 1478 Bramante was asked to rebuild the church to salvage a 13th-century fresco on the façade, which was said to have miraculous powers. Bramante set it on the high altar, solving the problem of lack of space by creating a sort of *trompe l'oeil* apse of only 97 cm (38 in) with stuccowork and frescoes. The transept leads to the Chapel of San Satiro with a terracotta *Pietà* (c.1482). In the right-hand aisle is the octagonal baptismal font decorated by De Fondutis.

Pinacoteca Ambrosiana ⓭

The Ambrosiana art gallery was founded in 1618 by
Cardinal Federico Borromeo, the cousin of San Carlo
and his successor in charge of the archdiocese of
Milan. A true art connoisseur, Borromeo planned
the gallery as part of a vast cultural project which
included the Ambrosiana Library, opened in 1609,
and the Accademia del Disegno (1620) for the training
of young Counter-Reformation artists. The gallery,
founded to provide inspiration for emerging artists,
held 172 paintings – some of which already belonged
to Borromeo, while others were purchased later after
painstaking research by the cardinal. The collection
was then enlarged thanks to private donations.

★ Portrait of a Musician
*This is the only Milanese
wood panel painting by
Leonardo da Vinci. The
subject is Franchino
Gaffurio, the Sforza
court composer.*

Adoration of the Magi
*Cardinal Borromeo considered this painting by Titian
(purchased in 1558) a treasure trove for painters "for
the multitude of things therein".*

STAR EXHIBITS

★ Portrait of a Musician

★ Cartoon for the
   School of Athens

★ Basket of Fruit

★ Madonna del
   Padiglione

The Library is on
the ground floor.

**★ Madonna
del Padiglione**
*The restoration
of this work by
Botticelli has
revealed its
masterful and
elegant brushwork.*

GALLERY GUIDE

The most famous works are held in the Borromeo Collection, which was subsequently enriched with important 15th–16th-century paintings and sculptures. The Galbiati Wing contains 16th–20th-century paintings, a collection of objects, the Sinigaglia Collection of miniature portraits and scientific instruments.

Nicolò da Bologna Room

San Sepolcro was annexed to the gallery in 1932.

VISITORS' CHECKLIST

Piazza Pio XI 2.
Map 7 B1 **Tel** 02-80 69 21.
Ⓜ 1, 3 Duomo, 1 Cordusio.
🚋 2, 3, 14, 19, 24, 27.
◯ 10am–6pm Tue–Sun
(last adm: 5:30pm). 🏷
♿ partial. 📷 📹 🎦
www.ambrosiana.eu

Centrepiece with Fishing Scene
This is part of the prestigious collection of Neo-Classical gilded bronze objects donated to the Ambrosiana by Edoardo De Pecis in 1827.

KEY

▢ Borromeo Collection and 15th–16th-century paintings

▢ Galbiati Wing

▢ De Pecis Collection & 19th century

▨ Sculpture

★ **Basket of Fruit**
Caravaggio painted this extraordinarily realistic work around 1594. The fruit alludes to the symbolism of the Passion of Christ.

★ **Cartoon for the School of Athens**
This was a preparation for the painting now in the Vatican. Raphael used the faces of contemporary artists – Leonardo, for instance, appears in the guise of Aristotle.

Exploring the Pinacoteca Ambrosiana

After seven years of painstaking restoration work, the Pinacoteca was reopened in October 1997. It is housed in a palazzo originally designed by Fabio Mangone in 1611. It was enlarged in the 19th century and again in 1932, when San Sepolcro was added. The new rooms were inaugurated on the third centenary of the death of Federico Borromeo, when about 700 paintings were exhibited, arranged in rows or set on easels. Today the Pinacoteca, whose collections are even larger thanks to donations, has 24 rooms and is one of Milan's finest museums.

17th-century silver stoup

Portrait of a Young Man, attributed to Giorgione

THE BORROMEO COLLECTION, 15TH–16TH-CENTURY PAINTINGS

The visit begins in the atrium, which has plaster casts of Trajan's Column, narrating the emperor's victories against the Dacians; on the staircase there are other casts of the *Laocoön* and Michelangelo's *Pietà*. Rooms 1, 4, 5, 6 and 7 house the Borromeo Collection, which boasts many of the best-known works in the gallery. Room 1, which features Venetian and Leonardo-esque painting, opens with the *Holy Family with St Anne and the Young St John the Baptist* by Bernardino Luini (c.1520). Next to this is Titian's *Adoration of the Magi* (1559–60), which is still in its original frame

bearing the carved initials of Henry II of France and his wife, who commissioned the work. The main scene is at the far left, while animals and minor figures fill the right-hand half of this original composition. On the opposite wall is a series of portraits, including *Profile of a Lady* by Ambrogio De Predis, and those of *The Young Jesus with Lamb* and *Benedictory Christ* by Luini, ending with Titian's *Man in Armour*. Rooms 2 and 3 have works acquired after 1618. One is Leonardo da Vinci's *Portrait of a Musician* with its innovative three-quarter profile position and intense expression; it was probably painted in early 1485. Next to it is Botticelli's *Madonna del Padiglione*, with its many symbols of the Virgin Mary, and *Sacred Conversation* by Bergognone (c.1485). Another unmissable work is *Adoration of the Child*, by the workshop of Domenico Ghirlandaio. Room 3 features 15th–16th-century Leonardo-esque and Lombard

Holy Family with St Anne and the Young St John the Baptist by Bernardino Luini

Adoration of the Child, Domenico Ghirlandaio's workshop

paintings, among which is Salaino's *St John the Baptist*, whose finger pointing upwards alludes to the coming of Christ. Next to this are three works by Bartolomeo Suardi, known as "il Bramantino". In his *Madonna of the Towers* (which may have had an anti-heretic function), next to the Virgin are St Ambrose and St Michael Archangel kneeling and offering a soul to the Christ Child. Room 4 has copies from Titian and Giorgione and the *Rest on the Flight into Egypt*, traditionally attributed to Jacopo Bassano (c.1547). In room 5 is a Raphael study for *The School of Athens*, the only great Renaissance cartoon that has come down to us. It was purchased by Cardinal Borromeo in 1626. Raphael executed the cartoon in 1510 as a study for his marvellous fresco in the Vatican. The fresco's architectonic setting and figure of Heraclitus (portrayed with Michelangelo's face) are not seen in the cartoon because Raphael only added them when, halfway through painting, he got a glimpse of the Sistine Chapel and was deeply impressed.

One of the most famous works in the museum, *Basket of Fruit,* is in room 6. Caravaggio painted it in the

For hotels and restaurants in this area see p160 and pp172–3

late 1500s on a used canvas. The withered leaves represent the vanity of beauty.

The large body of Flemish paintings in the Borromeo Collection is on display in room 7, where you can compare the works of Paul Bril and Jan Brueghel. *Landscape with St Paul* is the most dramatic of the several Bril works on display. Bril worked with the early 17th-century's most popular sacred scenes, but set them in his beloved, intricately executed landscape form. Interesting works by Brueghel include *The Mouse with Roses* and *Allegories of Water and Fire*, which Napoleon removed and took back to France. They were later returned.

THE GALBIATI WING

The Sala Della Medusa and the Sala delle Colonne feature Renaissance paintings and a collection of objects, the most curious of which are Lucrezia Borgia's blonde hair and Napoleon's gloves.

A short passageway leads to the Spiriti Magni courtyard, decorated with statues of illustrious artists. The three rooms that follow feature 16th-century Italian and Venetian paintings, including an *Annunciation* by Bedoli (room 11), the *Portrait of Michel de l'Hospital* by Giovan Battista Moroni (1554) and Moretto's altarpiece, *Martyrdom of St Peter of Verona* (c.1535, room 12). This latter room, known as the "exedra room", is decorated with a mosaic reproducing a miniature by Simone Martini from the volume of Virgil annotated by Petrarch in the Biblioteca Ambrosiana.

Italian and Flemish painting of the 16th and 17th centuries is on display in the Sala Nicolò da Bologna, on the upper floor, along with an unfinished *Penitent Magdalen* (1640–42) by Guido Reni. Seventeenth-century Lombard paintings are on display in rooms 14, 15 and 16. Among the interesting works are *Still Life with Musical Instruments*

by Evaristo Baschenis (room 14) and Morazzone's *Adoration of the Magi* (room 15), while the following room has works by Francesco Cairo and Daniele Crespi, as well as *Magdalen* by Giulio Cesare Procaccini. Paintings by Magnasco, Magatti, Fra Galgario and Londonio represent 18th-century Italian art in room 17, but the jewels are two works by Tiepolo on the wall near the entrance.

Funerary monument by il Bambaia

Lucrezia Borgia's hair

DE PECIS COLLECTION AND 19TH CENTURY

Rooms 18 and 19 form the largest section of the Pinacoteca Ambrosiana, donated by Giovanni Edoardo De Pecis in 1827. This collection consists mostly of Italian and Flemish paintings and includes a series of small

Neo-Classical bronze pieces and a *Self Portrait* by sculptor Antonio Canova, inspired by Roman portraiture. The exhibition in this wing ends with a selection of 19th- and early 20th-century canvases, including works by Andrea Appiani *(Portrait of Napoleon)*, Mosé Bianchi and Francesco Hayez. Emilio Longoni is represented with his masterpiece *Locked out of School* (1888). Room 21 has 15th–17th-century German and Flemish art as well as the *Dantesque Stained Glass* by Giuseppe Bertini, the Duomo master glassblower. It was executed in 1865 and depicts the author of the *Divine Comedy* surrounded by his characters and with the Virgin Mary above him.

SCULPTURE

Room 22 is given over to sculpture. There are ancient Roman, Romanesque and Renaissance pieces as well as the highly elegant bas-reliefs by Agostino Busti – known as "il Bambaia" – sculpted for the tomb of Gaston de Foix around 1516.

BIBLIOTECA AMBROSIANA

Virgil illuminated by Simone Martini

This was one of the first libraries open to the public. It boasts over 750,000 printed volumes, 2,500 of which are incunabula, and 36,000 manuscripts. Among them is the 5th-century *Ilias Picta*, a copy of Virgil's book annotated by Petrarch and illuminated by Simone Martini; a volume of Aristotle with annotations by Boccaccio; as well as Arab, Syrian, Greek and Latin texts. The Ambrosian Library also has over 1,000 pages of Leonardo da Vinci's *Codex Atlanticus*, purchased in 1637, removed by Napoleon in 1796 and only partly returned in 1815. The Library opened in 1609, already equipped with shelves and wooden footstools to protect readers from the cold floors.

NORTHWEST MILAN

In the 14th century, when the construction of the Castello Sforzesco began, this district stood outside the city walls and was covered in woods. After the demolition of the Spanish walls around the Castello in the early 19th century, a new plan for the area was drawn up (but only partly realized). The aim was to transform the zone into a monumental quarter by building the Arco della Pace and a number of elegant buildings, which were to be used as offices, luxury residences, markets and theatres. By the end of the century, Via Dante, which leads to the Castello and is lined with fine buildings, was complete, as was the Corso Magenta residential district around Santa Maria delle Grazie. Northwest Milan also hosts two historic theatres: Dal Verme (1872) and the Piccolo Teatro (now called Teatro Grassi), founded in 1947.

The personification of a river, part of the Arco della Pace (Arch of Peace)

GETTING THERE

Fieramilanocity (Amendola, Lotto) and Castello (Cairoli) are served by metro lines 1 and 2. A number of tramlines pass Piazza Cordusio (No. 16 goes to Santa Maria delle Grazie or San Siro stadium).

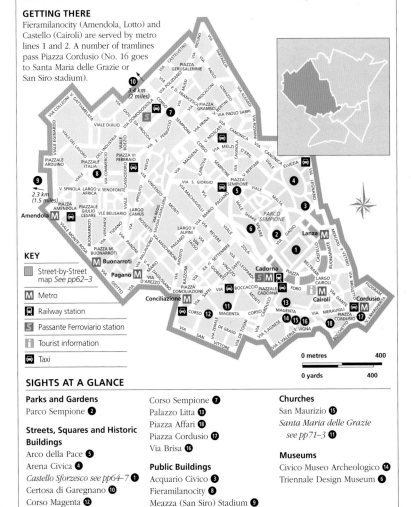

KEY

- Street-by-Street map See pp62–3
- M Metro
- Railway station
- S Passante Ferroviario station
- Tourist information
- Taxi

0 metres 400
0 yards 400

SIGHTS AT A GLANCE

Parks and Gardens
Parco Sempione 2

Streets, Squares and Historic Buildings
Arco della Pace 5
Arena Civica 4
Castello Sforzesco see pp64–7 1
Certosa di Garegnano 10
Corso Magenta 12
Corso Sempione 7
Palazzo Litta 13
Piazza Affari 18
Piazza Cordusio 17
Via Brisa 16

Public Buildings
Acquario Civico 3
Fieramilanocity 8
Meazza (San Siro) Stadium 9

Churches
San Maurizio 15
Santa Maria delle Grazie see pp71–3 11

Museums
Civico Museo Archeologico 14
Triennale Design Museum 6

◁ The Salone degli Specchi in Palazzo Litta, a fine example of the 18th-century Lombard style

Street-by-Street: Around the Castello Sforzesco

Visconti coat of arms

The Castello Sforzesco and Sempione park today are the result of late 19th-century landscaping and restoration. Architect Luca Beltrami managed to thwart attempts to demolish the castle by converting it into a museum centre. He restored many of its original elements. In the early 1800s, the Arco della Pace and the Arena were built in the Parco Sem-pione, which was landscaped as an "English" garden by Emilio Alemagna. To mark the 1906 opening of the Galleria del Sempione, an International Exposition was held, featuring new products that later became household names in Italy.

Arena Civica
This amphitheatre, built in 1806, was used for boating displays, when it was filled with water from the Naviglio canals ❹

★ Parco Sempione
The 47-hectare (116-acre) English-style garden was designed by Emilio Alemagna in 1893. It contains a number of historic buildings and monuments ❷

Corso Sempione
Napoleon built this avenue leading to the Castello, modelling it on the Champs-Elysées in Paris ❼

PIAZZALE SEMPIONE

VIALE BYRON

VIALE BAR

V. LA M. L. L. A

★ Arco della Pace
Modelled on the triumphal arch of Septimius Severus, the Arch of Peace was built to celebrate Napoleon's victories. However, it was inaugurated by Francis II in memory of the peace declared in 1815 ❺

STAR SIGHTS

★ Castello Sforzesco

★ Parco Sempione

★ Arco della Pace

Acquario Civico
The Civic Aquarium was built in 1906 as an exhibition and educational centre. The building still has its original decoration of tiles and reliefs ❸

The Foro Buonaparte is a semicircular boulevard lined with imposing late 19th-century buildings.

LOCATOR MAP
See Street Finder, maps 2, 3

KEY

– – – Suggested route

Via Dante, one of the city's most elegant streets, is a pedestrian precinct, and one of the few in Milan where you can sit and have a drink outdoors.

★ Castello Sforzesco
The castle, a symbol of Milan, was initially the palace of the Visconti, who built it in 1368 and named it Castello di Porta Giovia, and then of the Sforza, who embellished it, turning it into a magnificent Renaissance residence ❶

Triennale Design Museum
The Palazzo dell'Arte is home to the Triennale Design Museum, which features decorative art, fashion and handicrafts ❻

| 0 metres | 400 |
| 0 yards | 400 |

Castello Sforzesco ●

Umberto I, the Filarete Tower

Built in 1368 by Galeazzo II Visconti as a fortress, the Sforza castle was enlarged in the 14th century by Gian Galeazzo and then by Filippo Maria, who transformed it into a splendid ducal palace. It was partly demolished in 1447 during the Ambrosian Republic. Francesco Sforza, who became lord of Milan in 1450, and his son Lodovico il Moro made the castle the home of one of the most magnificent courts in Renaissance Italy, graced by Bramante and Leonardo da Vinci. Under Spanish and Austrian domination, the Castello went into gradual decline, as it resumed its original military function. It was saved from demolition by the architect Luca Beltrami, who from 1893 to 1904 restored it and converted it into an important museum centre.

★ Trivulzio Tapestries
The 12 tapestries designed by Bramantino, depicting the months and signs of the zodiac, are masterpieces of Italian textile art.

The Torre Castellana was where Lodovico il Moro kept his treasury. It was "guarded" by a figure of Argus, in a fresco by Bramantino at the Sala del Tesoro entrance.

The Cortile della Rocchetta was the last refuge in the event of a siege. Its three porticoes, formerly frescoed, were designed by Ferrini and Bramante. The oldest wing (1456–66), opposite the entrance to the Corte Ducale, was the apartment of Lodovico and his wife before he became duke.

The holes in the castle walls, now used by pigeons, were made to anchor the scaffolding used for maintenance work.

Porta Vercellina
Only ruins remain of the great fortified structure that once protected the gate of Santo Spirito.

Cappella Ducale
The Ducal chapel still has the original frescoes painted in 1472 by Stefano de Fedeli and Bonifacio Bembo for Galeazzo Maria Sforza. On the vault is a Resurrection and on the wall to the left of the entrance is an Annunciation *with saints looking on.*

VISITORS' CHECKLIST

Piazza Castello. **Map** 3 B5.
Tel 02-88 46 37 00. M 1 Cairoli–Cadorna, 2 Lanza–Cadorna. 1, 4, 12, 14. 18, 50, 57, 58, 61, 94. **Castello** 7am–6pm daily (to 7pm in summer).
Musei Civici 9am–5:30pm Tue–Sun (last adm: 5pm).
1 Jan, Easter, Easter Mon, 1 May, 25 Dec.
www.milanocastello.it

Ducal court

★ **Sala delle Asse**
This pergola, painted to look like an open air space, was the work of Leonardo (1498). The room owes its name to the planks (asse) once thought to cover the walls.

★ **Rondanini Pietà**
Michelangelo's final work, held in the Civiche Raccolte, was altered several times and never completed. Christ's arm on the left and a different angle for Mary's face, visible from the right, are part of the first version.

STAR FEATURES

★ Rondanini Pietà

★ Sala delle Asse

★ Trivulzio Tapestries

The Filarete Tower collapsed in 1521 when the gunpowder kept there exploded. It was rebuilt in 1905 by Luca Beltrami, who worked from drawings from the period.

Exploring the Civic Museums in the Castello Sforzesco

Since 1896, the Castello Sforzesco has housed the Civic Museums with one of the largest collections of art in Milan. The Corte Ducale is home to the Raccolte di Arte Antica and the art and sculpture gallery, as well as the furniture collection, while the Rocchetta holds decorative arts (ceramics, musical instruments and gold) and the Trivulzio Tapestries. In addition, the photography archive and the Achille Bertarelli Collection, featuring about 700,000 prints, books and photographs from the 19th century, are here. Major institutions, such as the Art Library and the Trivulziana Library can also be found within the same building.

Relief of the Three Magi, School of Antelami (12th century)

CIVICHE RACCOLTE d'ARTE ANTICA

The displays making up the collections of Ancient Art are arranged in chronological order (except for Room 6) in rooms facing the Corte Ducale, where the 14th-century Pusterla dei Fabbri postern, rebuilt after being demolished in 1900, has 4th-6th-century sculpture. In room 1 ① is the Sarcophagus of Lambrate (late 4th century) and a bust of the Empress Theodora

(6th century). Room 2 ② features Romanesque and Campionese sculpture, with a fine early 12th-century telamon. The relief of the Three Magi is by the school of Benedetto Antelami, the great 12th-century sculptor and architect. The main attraction, however, is the *Mausoleum of Bernabò Visconti*, sculpted by Bonino da Campione in 1363 for the lord of Milan. He is portrayed on horse-back between Wisdom and Fortitude, while on the sarcophagus are *Scenes from the Passion*. Room 3 ③ has a window with a 14th-century Tuscan *Benedictory Christ*. Room 4 ④ is given over to Giovanni di

Balduccio, with fragments from the façade of Santa Maria di Brera (14th century). A passage leads to the Cappelletta ⑤, dominated by a 14th-century wooden Crucifix.

Room 6 ⑥ features reliefs from the Porta Romana (1171) narrating the *Return of the Milanese after Being Driven out of Town by Barbarossa* and *St Ambrose Expelling the Arians*. In room 7 ⑦ is the *Gonfalone* (Standard) of Milan designed by Giuseppe Meda in 1566, with scenes from Sant'Ambrogio's life. On the walls are 17th-century Flemish tapestries. The Sala delle Asse ⑧ is known for its fine fresco decoration on the vault, designed by Leonardo in 1498, which, despite its poor condition, is a good example of Sforza decoration. From here you go to the bridge over the moat ⑨ ⑩, with important small sculptures by Agostino Busti (Il Bambaia). Next is the Sala dei Ducali ⑪, named after the arms of Galeazzo Maria Sforza, with Lodovico's set above. Here the early 15th-century sculpture is dominated by Agostino di Duccio's relief of *St Sigismund on a Journey* from the Malatesta Temple in

The Mausoleum of Bernabò Visconti

PLAN OF THE CASTELLO SFORZESCO

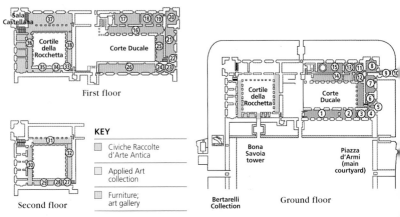

First floor

Second floor

KEY

- ▢ Civiche Raccolte d'Arte Antica
- ▢ Applied Art collection
- ▢ Furniture; art gallery

Bona Savoia tower

Bertarelli Collection

Ground floor

Piazza d'Armi (main courtyard)

For hotels and restaurants in this area see pp160–61 and p173

The armour collection in the Sala Verde

Rimini. Left, is the door to the Cappella Ducale ⑫, with a braided Virgin, *Madonna del Coazzone*, a 15th-century work attributed to Pietro Antonio Solari. On the vault is a *Resurrection* painted around 1472 by Bonifacio Bembo and Stefano de' Fedeli. Late 15th-century sculpture is featured in the Sala delle Colombine ⑬, with the Visconti coat of arms and motto, *A Bon Droit*. One of the finest works here is Antonio Mantegazza's *Kneeling Apostles*. The 1463 Portale del Banco Medicea (portal) in the Sala Verde ⑭ is attributed to Filarete. This room also has some fine armour.

The last room, the Sala degli Scarlioni ⑮, boasts two world-famous sculptures: Gaston de Foix's funerary monument with marvellous reliefs, and Michelangelo's *Rondanini Pietà*. The former is by Agostino Busti, known as "Il Bambaia", and commemorates the death on the battlefield of the young captain of the French troops in 1512. Behind a partition is Michelangelo's unfinished masterpiece, which he was working on until a few days before his death in 1564 (he had begun it in 1552–3): the standing Mother of Christ supporting the heavy body of her Son. The exit route goes through the Cortile della Fontana, where the only original window left in the castle can be seen. It was used by Beltrami as a model in his restoration of the Castello.

FURNITURE COLLECTION AND PINACOTECA

Showcasing the traditions from which Milanese furniture design has grown, "From the Sforza to Design" is the name given to the furniture collection ⑯, ⑰, ⑱, ⑲, housing pieces from the 15th to the 20th centuries. Beginning with Court and Church furniture from the 15th to the 16th centuries and Baroque inlaid furniture, as well as collections from aristocratic Milanese families, the collection ends with 20th-century pieces by important Milanese designers such as Giò Ponti and Ettore Sottsass.

The art gallery houses works in chronological order from the mid-15th to the 18th centuries. It begins in

Madonna in Glory and Saints, by Andrea Mantegna

room 20, the former Falconry Tower ⑳, with 14th–15th-century Italian paintings, while rooms 21 ㉑ and 22 ㉒ contain works by Milanese artists such as Vincenzo Foppa. Room 23 ㉓ contains major works such as Mantegna's *Madonna in Glory and Saint John* (1497), Antonello da Messina's *Saint Benedict* (c. 1470–73), Lorenzo Veneziano's *Resurrection* (1371), Giovanni Bellini's *Madonna and Child* (c. 1460–65) and *Madonna of Humility* by Filippo Lippi (1430). Room 24 ㉔ features Correggio's *Portrait of a Man Reading* along with examples of Cremonese Mannerism, an Italian art movement founded during the Renaissance period. In room 25 ㉕ Venetian paintings are displayed, boasting examples by Titian and Tintoretto, which contrast with pieces from the 16th-century schools of Brescia and Bergamo. Room 26 ㉖, the former Salone della Cancellaria, houses works by "plague painters" such as Morazzone and Il Cerano (Crespi), finishing with two views of Venice by Canaletto.

APPLIED ART COLLECTION

Return to the entrance for access to the first floor to see the collection of old musical instruments ㊱ ㊳, which includes a Flemish double virginal with ottavino. Between these two rooms is the large Sala della Balla (ballroom) ㊲, with Bramantino's splendid Trivulzio Tapestries representing the 12 months (1503–09). On the second floor (rooms 28–32) is a large collection of fine Italian and European glass, ceramics, majolica and porcelain, ivory works, gold medieval jewellery and scientific instruments.

Lastly, in the basement of the Corte Ducale, are a Prehistoric and an Egyptian section with funerary cult objects, including a tomb from c.640 BC.

Parco Sempione ❷

Piazza Castello–Piazza Sempione
(Eight entrances around perimeter).
Map 2 F3–4, 3 A3–4. Ⓜ *1 Cadorna,
Cairoli, 2 Lanza, Cadorna.* Ⓕ *Ferrovie
Nord, Cadorna.* 🚋 *1, 4, 12, 14, 19,
27.* 🚌 *18, 43, 57, 58, 61, 94.*
🔘 *Mar–Apr: 6:30am–9pm; May:
6:30am–10pm; Jun–Sep: 6:30am–
11:30pm; Oct: 6:30am–9pm; Nov–
Feb: 6:30am–8pm.*

Although it covers an area of
about 47 ha (116 acres), this
park occupies only a part of
the old Visconti ducal garden,
enlarged by the Sforza in the
15th century to make a 300-ha
(740-acre) hunting reserve. The
area was partly abandoned
during Spanish rule, and in the
early 1800s part of it was used
to create a parade ground
extending as far as the Arco
della Pace. The present-day
layout was the work of Emilio
Alemagna, who in 1890–93
designed it along the lines of
an English garden. In World
War II the park was used
to cultivate wheat, but after
the reconstruction period it
returned to its former
splendour as a locals' haunt,
especially in spring and
summer, when it plays host to
many entertainment events.
Walking through the park
after dark is not advisable.
   Standing among the trees are
the monuments to Napoleon
III (designed by Francesco
Barzaghi), De Chirico's

Metaphysical construction
Mysterious Baths, the sulphur
water fountain near the Arena
and the Torre del Parco, a
108-m (354-ft) tower made
of steel tubes in 1932 after
a design by Gio Ponti.

Acquario Civico ❸

Via Gadio 2. **Map** 3 B4.
Tel 02-88 46 57 50.
Ⓜ *2 Lanza.* 🚋 *4, 12, 14.*
🚌 *43, 57.* 🔘 *9am–1pm, 2–5:30pm
Tue–Sun.*

The Civic Aquarium was built
by Sebastiano Locati for the
1906 National Exposition, and
it is the only remaining
building. Its 36 tanks
house about 100
species (fish,
crustaceans,
molluscs and
echinoderms)
typical of the
Mediterranean
sea and Italian
freshwater
fauna. There are
also rare kinds
of tropical fish
on display.
   The aquarium
museum is also home
to the Hydrobiological
Station, which has a library
specializing in the subject.
The aquarium building itself
(1906) is a fine example of
Art Nouveau architecture
and is decorated with

**Sea creature decorating the
facade of the Aquarium**

Richard-Ginori ceramic tiles
and statues of aquatic
animals, dominated by Oreste
Labò's statue of Neptune.

Arena Civica ❹

Via Legnano, Viale Elvezia.
Map 3 A-B3. Ⓜ *2 Lanza.*
🚋 *2, 4, 12, 14.* 🚌 *43, 57.*
🔘 *for exhibitions and events only.*

This impressive Neo-Classical
amphitheatre, designed in
1806 by Luigi Canonica, was –
together with the Arco della
Pace, Caselli Daziari and
Foro Buonaparte – part of
the project to transform the
Castello Sforzesco area into
a monumental civic
centre. Napoleon
was present at the
Arena inaugura-
tion, and it was
the venue for
various cultural
and sports
events, from
horse and mock
Roman chariot races
to hot-air balloon
launchings, mock
naval battles and
festivities. With
a seating capacity of 30,000,
it has also been a football
stadium, but San Siro *(see
p70)* is now the more
important ground. The Arena
is mainly a venue for athletics
(it has a 500-m, 1,640-ft track),
concerts and civil weddings.

View of the Parco Sempione: in the foreground, the artificial lake and in the background, the Castello Sforzesco

Arco della Pace ❺

Piazza Sempione. **Map** 2 F3. 🚋 *1, 7, 19.* 🚌 *43, 57, 61.*

Work on Milan's major Neo-Classical monument was begun by Luigi Cagnola in 1807 to celebrate Napoleon's victories. It was originally called the Arch of Victories, but building was interrupted and not resumed until 1826 by Francis I of Austria, who had the subjects of the bas-reliefs changed to commemorate the peace of 1815 instead. The Arch of Peace was inaugurated on 10 September 1838 on the occasion of Ferdinand I's coronation as ruler of the Lombardy–Veneto kingdom. The arch is dressed in Crevola marble and decorated with bas-reliefs depicting episodes of the restoration after Napoleon's fall. On the upper level are personifications of the rivers in the Lombardy–Veneto kingdom: the Po, Ticino, Adda and Tagliamento.

At the top of the monument stands the huge bronze Chariot of Peace, by Abbondio Sangiorgio, surrounded by four Victories on horseback. The chariot originally faced France. However, when Milan was ceded to Austria in 1815, it was turned to face the centre of the city, and was the site of the triumphal entrance into Milan of Victor Emmanuel II, first king of Italy upon unification in 1861.

Tree-lined Corso Sempione

Triennale Design Museum ❻

Viale Alemagna 6. **Map** 3 A4. **Tel** *02-72 43 42 08.* Ⓜ *1–2 Cadorna.* 🚋 *61.* ⭘ *10:30am–8:30pm Tue–Sun (to 11pm Thu & Fri; last adm: 7:25pm).* 📷 ♿ 🖥 ⌨ **www**.triennale.it

The Palazzo dell'Arte, south-west of Parco Sempione, was built by Giovanni Muzio in 1932–3 as a permanent site for the International Exhibition of Decorative Arts. The Triennale show was founded in 1923 to foster the development of Italian arts and always played a primary role in promoting architectural development. The building now houses the Triennale Design Museum, offering both a permanent collection and temporary exhibitions showcasing Milan as a centre for cutting-edge design. The museum includes an excellent decorative arts bookstore as well as a research library with

Obelisk in front of the Palzzo dell'Arte

specialized and often rare research resources in the fields of architecture, art and fashion. The DesignCafé is worth a visit to take in the surroundings and Michelin-starred cuisine. Next to the museum is the Teatro dell'Arte, redesigned in 1960.

Corso Sempione ❼

Map 2 D1, E2, F3. 🚋 *1, 19, 33.* 🚌 *37, 43, 57.*

Modelled on the grand boulevards of Paris, Corso Sempione was the first stage of a road built by Napoleon to link the city with Lake Maggiore, Switzerland and France via the Simplon Pass. The first section, starting at the Arco della Pace, is pedestrianized. The Corso is lined with late 19th-century and early 20th-century houses and is now the main thoroughfare in a vast quarter. The initial stretch (to-wards the park) is considered an elegant area, with good shops, bars and restaurants, the headquarters of Milanese banks and Italian State Radio and TV, RAI (at No. 27). Opposite, at No. 36, is a residence designed by Giuseppe Terragni and Pietro Lingeri in 1935, one of the first examples of Rationalist architecture in Milan.

The semicircular Via Canova and Via Melzi d'Eril cross the Corso, every angle of which offers a different view of the Arco della Pace.

The horses on the Arco della Pace, each cast in one piece

Fieramilanocity **8**

Largo Domodossola 1. **Map** 1 C3.
Tel 02-499 71. **Fax** 02-49 97 76 05.
M 1 Amendola Fieramilanocity, Lotto,
Domodossola. 🚋 27. 🚌 37, 48, 68,
78. Shuttle from Linate airport. ATM
circle line buses (free). ⬜ for
exhibitions only. 🖼️ ♿ 🍴 🖥️
www.fieramilano.it

San Siro Stadium, now named after footballer Giuseppe Meazza

The Fiera Campionaria, or Trade Fair, was founded in 1920 to stimulate the domestic market in postwar Italy. It was originally located near Porta Venezia and in 1923 was moved to the ground behind the Castello Sforzesco. It was fitted out with permanent pavilions and buildings, many of which were damaged or destroyed in World War II. Some original Art Nouveau buildings have survived at the entrance in Via Domodossola and the Palazzo dello Sport (sports arena). The old main entrance to the Fiera is in Piazza Giulio Cesare, which is dominated by a Four Seasons fountain, placed there in 1927.

Fiera di Milano logo

One of the leading exhibition centres in Europe, the Fiera di Milano has become a symbol of Milanese industriousness. It hosts 78 specialist international shows attracting 2.5 million visitors every year.

Specialist trade fairs are held at an innovative centre known as Fieramilano, located just outside Milan, in Rho. Plans are afoot to enhance the centre, which will house Expo 2015.

Meazza (San Siro) Stadium **9**

Piazzale A. Moratti. **Tel** 02-48 79 82 02. **M** 1 Lotto (**Map** 1 A2); shuttle bus for Inter & Milan games. 🚋 16.
San Siro Museum Entrance gate 14. ⬜ 10am–5pm Mon–Sat.
🖼️ 📷 **www**.sansiro.net

Named after Giuseppe Meazza, the famous footballer who played for the local teams, Inter and Milan, Italy's top stadium is commonly known as San Siro, after the surrounding district. It was built in 1926, rebuilt in the 1950s with a capacity of 85,000, and then renovated in 1990, when another ring of tiers and a roof were added (see Entertainment pp202–3). The stadium and changing rooms can be visited on the museum tour.

Certosa di Garegnano **10**

Via Garegnano 28. **Tel** 02-38 00 63 01. 🚋 14. 🚌 40. ⬜ 8am–noon, 3:30–5:30pm daily. 🕇 6pm prehols; 8:30, 10 & 11:30am & 6pm.

The church that forms the heart of this important Carthusian monastery, dedicated to Our Lady of the Assumption, was founded in 1349 by Archbishop Giovanni Visconti. Sadly, the Certosa is well-known because the main cloister was ruined by the con-struction of the A4 motorway. The courtyard is of impressive size, with the monks' houses, each with a kitchen garden, around the sides. The rules imposed by the semi-closed order required each monk to live independently. The complex was rebuilt in late Renaissance style in 1562; the façade, completed in 1608, was decorated with obelisks and statues, crowned by a statue of Our Lady. A porticoed atrium with an exedra-shaped vestibule provides a harmonious introduction to the complex.

Vincenzo Seregni designed the interior in the 1500s. The aisleless nave is crowned by a barrel vault flanked by blind arcades. The church is famous for the frescoes by Daniele Crespi, a leading 17th-century Lombard artist. He reputedly painted the ⬦ ⬦ ⬦ (The Legend of ⬦ ⬦ ⬦ion f the Order) ⬦ thank the Carthusian monks for offering refuge after he had been charged with murder. The cycle begins by the first arch on the right, continues on the wall behind the façade, designed by Simone Peterzano, and is resumed on the vault, where there are four medallions. In the first bay on the left Crespi included a self-portrait of himself as a servant blowing a horn and added the date (1629) and his signature in a scroll.

Simone Peterzano painted the frescoes in the presbytery and apse (1578), with scenes from the life of Mary. The chapel on the right has two macabre 17th-century paintings informing novices of the various forms of torture they might encounter while spreading Christianity. On leaving, look at the 14th-century cloister on the right, the only surviving part of the original monastery.

Façade of the Certosa di Garegnano (1608)

Santa Maria delle Grazie ⓫

Piazza Santa Maria delle Grazie.
Map 2 F5. *Tel* 02-46 76 111. Ⓜ 1,
2 Cadorna, 1 Conciliazione. ⓉⓉ 16.
Ⓞ 7am–noon, 3–7pm Mon–Sat,
7:30am–12:15pm, 3:30–8:15pm
Sun. Ⓣ 7:30, 8 (except Jul–mid-Sep),
8:30 & 9:30am, 6:30pm Mon–Sat;
6:30pm pre-hols; 7, 9:30, 10:30 &
11:30am, 6:30 & 8pm (except Jul &
Aug) hols.

Construction of this church designed by Guiniforte Solari, began in 1463 and was completed in 1490. Two years later Lodovico il Moro asked Bramante to change the church into the family mausoleum: Solari's apse section was demolished and replaced by a Renaissance apse. After il Moro lost power in 1500, the Dominicans continued to decorate the church, later assisted by the court of Inquisition, which had moved here in 1558. Restoration was undertaken only in the late 19th century. In 1943 a bomb destroyed the main cloister, but the apse and the room containing Leonardo's *Last Supper* were miraculously left intact; restoration work has continued since then. On the exterior, Solari's wide brick façade is worthy of note. The doorway was designed by Bramante; it is preceded by a porch supported by Corinthian columns and the lunette has a painting by Leonardo da Vinci

Frescoed cross vaulting in Santa Maria delle Grazie

with the Madonna between Lodovico and his wife, Beatrice d'Este. The sides and polygonal apse are also of interest. As you enter the church you notice the difference between Solari's nave, which echoes Lombard Gothic architecture – entirely covered with frescoes and with ogival arches – and Bramante's design for the apse, which is larger, better lit and is almost bare of decoration. The two parts of the church reflect Bramante's impact on Milanese culture; he introduced the Renaissance style that dominated Tuscany and Umbria in the early 15th century. The all-pervasive painting decoration of the aisle walls is by Bernardino Butinone and Donato Montorfano (1482–6). The Della Torre chapel is the first one in the right-hand aisle: the altar has a 15th-century fresco and to the left is the tomb of Giacomo Della Torre, with bas-relief sculpture by the Cazzaniga brothers (1483). The fourth chapel, dedicated to Santa Corona, has frescoes by Gaudenzio Ferrari. The next chapel is a *Cru* Giovanni Demìo (1542).

The nave of Santa Maria delle Grazie

The apse, decorated only with graffiti to maintain the purity of the architectural volumes, is a perfect cube crowned by a hemisphere. It was built to house the tomb of Lodovico il Moro and Beatrice d'Este, but the work never reached Santa Maria delle Grazie (it is now in the Charterhouse of Pavia). The decoration of the dome is rich in Marian symbols, while the Doctors of the Church appear in the roundels in the pendentives. The carved and inlaid wooden stalls of the choir are lovely.

A door on the right leads to the small cloister known as Chiostrino delle Rane because of the frogs *(rane)* in the central basin. The cloister leads to the old sacristy, with its painted wardrobes, one of which conceals a secret underground passageway, used by Lodovico to come from the Castello on horseback. Back in the church, the chapels in the north aisle begin with the Madonna delle Grazie chapel, with Cerano's *Madonna Freeing Milan of the Plague* (1631) on the entrance archway. The altarpiece, *Madonna delle Grazie*, dates from the 15th century. The sixth chapel has a *Holy Family with St Catherine* by Paris Bordone, and the first chapel contains the cloak of St Catherine of Siena.

The façade of Santa Maria delle Grazie, designed by Guiniforte Solari

Leonardo da Vinci's *Last Supper*

Lodovico il Moro

This masterpiece was painted for Lodovico il Moro in the refectory of Santa Maria delle Grazie in 1495–7. Leonardo depicts the moment just after Christ has uttered the words, "One of you will betray me". The artist captures their amazement in facial expressions and body language in a remarkably realistic and vivid *Last Supper*. It is not a true fresco, but was painted in tempera, allowing Leonardo more time to achieve the subtle nuances typical of his work. The room was used as a stable in the Napoleonic era and was badly damaged by bombs in 1943. Fortunately, the work was saved because it was protected by sandbags.

Jesus Christ
The isolated, serene figure of Christ contrasts with the agitated Apostles. Half-closed lips show he has just spoken.

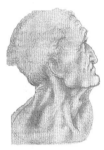

Judas
Unable to find a truly evil face for Judas, Leonardo drew inspiration from that of the prior in the convent, who kept on asking when the work would be finished.

The Last Supper is famous for the gesturing hands of the Apostles, which are so harmonious and expressive that critics have said they "speak".

The Apostle Andrew, with his arms upraised, expresses his horror at Christ's words.

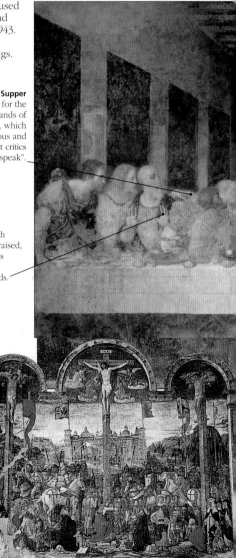

The Crucifixion by Montorfano
The Dominicans asked Donato Montorfano to paint a fresco of the Crucifixion on the opposite wall to depict Christ's sacrifice. In this dense composition the despairing Magdalen hugs the cross while the soldiers on the right throw dice for Christ's robe. On either side of the work, under the cross, Leonardo added the portraits – now almost invisible – of Lodovico il Moro, his wife Beatrice and their children, signed and dated (1495).

THE RESTORATION

It was not the humidity but the method used by Leonardo, *tempera forte*, that caused the immediate deterioration of the *Last Supper*. As early as 1550 the art historian Vasari

called it "a dazzling blotch" and regarded it as a lost work. There have been many attempts to restore the *Last Supper*, beginning in 1726, but in retouching the picture further damage was done. The seventh restoration ended in spring 1999: although it lacks the splendour of the original, it is at least authentic.

Material used for restoration

VISITORS' CHECKLIST

Piazza Santa Maria delle Grazie 2. **Map** 2 F5. *Tel* Compulsory advance booking: 02-92 80 03 60. M 1, 2 Cadorna. 16. 18. 8:15am–6:45pm Tue–Sun. pub hols, 1 May, 15 Aug. www.cenacolovinciano.org

The tablecloth, plates and bowls were probably copied from those in the convent to give the impression that Christ was at table with monks.

Sketches of the Apostles
Leonardo used to wander around Milan in search of faces to use for the Apostles. Of his many sketches, this one for St James is now in the Royal Library in Windsor.

CHRIST AND THE APOSTLES

13 12 11 10 9 8 1 2 3 4 5 6 7

1 Christ
2 Thomas
3 James the Greater
4 Philip
5 Matthew
6 Thaddaeus
7 Simon
8 John
9 Peter
10 Judas
11 Andrew
12 James the Lesser
13 Bartholomew

Corso Magenta ⓬

Map 3 A5. Ⓜ *1 Conciliazione, 1, 2
Cadorna.* 🚊 *16, 19.* 🚌 *18.*

This street is fascinating, with
its elegant shops and historic
buildings making it one of
the loveliest and most elegant
quarters in Milan. At No. 65,
just past Santa Maria delle
Grazie, is a building incor-
porating the remains of the
Atellani residence, decorated
by Luini,
where
Leonardo da
Vinci stayed
while working
on the *Last
Supper.* Piero
Portaluppi
carried out
the work on
No. 65 in
1919. In the
garden at the
back there are
some vines,
said to be the
remains of the
vineyard that Lodovico il Moro
gave to the great artist. The
next building (No. 61), Palazzo
delle Stelline, originally a girls'
orphanage, is now a conven-
tion centre and houses the
Fondazione Stelline, which
holds art exhibitions. The
Fondazione also has a garden,
created from the land given
to Leonardo. At the corner of
Via Carducci, which was built
over the original course of the
Naviglio canal, is Bar Magenta
(see p186). The medieval city
gate, the Porta Vercellina,
once stood at this junction.

Pastry shop
sign in Corso
Magenta

Palazzo Litta ⓭

Corso Magenta 24. **Map** 3 A5. Ⓜ *1,
2 Cadorna.* 🚊 *16, 27.* 🚌 *18, 50, 58,
94.* 🔲 *during cultural events only.*

Considered one of the most
beautiful examples of 18th-
century Lombard architecture,
this palazzo was first built in
1648 for Count Bartolomeo
Arese by Francesco Maria
Richini. At the end of the
century the interior was
embellished and in 1763 the
pink façade was built at the
request of the heirs, the Litta
Visconti Arese. The façade,

The Sala Rossa in Palazzo Litta, with mementos of Napoleon's visit here

by Bartolomeo Bolli, is late
Baroque, the door flanked by
large telamones. Since 1905
the building has housed the
State Railway offices.
   Inside is a number of
sumptuous rooms looking
onto a 17th-century courtyard.
The broad staircase, designed
by Carlo Giuseppe Merlo in
1740 and decorated with
precious marble and the
family coat of arms (a black
and white check), has a
double central flight. It leads
up to the *piano nobile*, where
one of the rooms is named
the Sala Rossa (Red Room)
after the colour of its wallpaper (a copy of the original).
Set in the floor is a pearl,
there to commemorate a
tear said to have been shed
during a meeting between the
Duchess Litta and Napoleon.
   The next room is the Salone
degli Specchi, which seems to
be enlarged to infinity by the
large mirrors *(specchi)* on the
walls. The vault decoration is
by Martin Knoller. The Salotto
della Duchessa is
the only room in
the palazzo which
still has its original
18th-century wall-
paper. The Teatro
Litta stands to
the left of the
palazzo, the
oldest theatre
in the city.

Civico Museo Archeologico ⓮

Corso Magenta 15. **Map** 3 A5.
Tel *02-88 44 52 08.* Ⓜ *1, 2
Cadorna.* 🚊 *16, 27.* 🚌 *18, 50, 58,
94.* 🔲 *9am–5:30pm Tue–Sun.* 🈲
🔲 *(phone ahead).* 🚫

The Archaeological Museum
is well worth a visit for the
finds and to see the only
remaining part of the city's
Roman walls. At the entrance,
graphic reconstructions
illustrate urban planning and
architecture in Milan from the
1st to the 4th century AD. The
visit begins in a hall on the
right, with clay objects,
including a collection of oil
lamps. This is followed by
Roman sculpture. One of the
most interesting pieces
in the series of portraits
dating from Caesar's era to
late antiquity (1st–4th century
AD), is the *Portrait of Maximin* (mid-3rd century AD).
At the end of this room is a

Roman sarcophagus of a lawyer, on display in the
Civico Museo Archeologico

huge fragment of a torso of Hercules from the Milanese thermae, dating from the first half of the 2nd century AD. Behind this are some 3rd-century AD floor mosaics found in Milanese houses.

By the window are two of the most important works in the museum: the Parabiago Patera and the Diatreta Cup. The Patera is a gilded silver plate with a relief of the triumph of the goddess Cybele, mother of the gods, on a chariot pulled by lions and surrounded by the Sun and Moon and sea and Zodiac divinities (mid-4th century AD). The marvellous Diatreta Cup, also dating from the 4th century AD, comes from Novara and consists of a single piece of coloured glass, with finely wrought, intricate decoration. Winding around the cup is the inscription *Bibe vivas multis annis* ("Drink and you will live many years"). The entrance hall leads to a courtyard, where you will see the Torre di Ansperto, a Roman tower from the ancient Maximinian walls. Off of the courtyard is a three-storey exhibition space displaying early medieval, Etruscan and Greek Collections. The basement houses art from Gandhar and Caesaera (Israel), as well as Roman and Mediolanum flooring.

Stela with portraits, Museo Archeologico

San Maurizio ⓯

Corso Magenta 13.
Map 3 A5. **Tel** 02-86 66 60
(Santa Maria alla Porta).
Ⓜ *1, 2 Cadorna.* 🚊 *16, 27.*
🚌 *50, 58, 94.* ◯ *9:30am–5:30pm Tue–Sat.* 🕕 *6pm Mon–Fri, 10:15am (Greek–Albanian) Sun.*

In 1503 Gian Giacomo Dolcebuono began construction of this church, which was intended for the most powerful closed order of Benedictine nuns in Milan, with one hall for the public and another for the nuns. In the first hall, to the right of the altar, is the opening through which the nuns receive the Body of Christ. Most of the decoration was done by Bernardino Luini. He painted the frescoes in the first hall, including the *Life of St Catherine* (third chapel to the right) and those on the middle wall. The second chapel on the right was decorated by Callisto Piazza, the chapels to the left by pupils of Luini. On the altar is an *Adoration of the Magi* by Antonio Campi. The middle wall of the second hall, occupied by the choir, has frescoes by Foppa, Piazza, an *Annunciation* attributed to Bramantino and *Episodes of the Passion*. Concerts are held here in the winter.

The Roman ruins in Via Brisa

Via Brisa ⓰

Map 7 B1. Ⓜ *1, 2 Cadorna.*
🚊 *16, 27.* 🚌 *50, 58.*

Excavations carried out after the 1943 bombing of this street revealed Roman ruins which were probably part of Maximin's imperial palace: the foundation of a round hall surrounded by apsidal halls and preceded by a narthex. Note the columns that raised the pavement to allow warm air to pass into the palace.

Piazza Cordusio ⓱

Map 7 C1. Ⓜ *1 Cordusio.*
🚊 *1, 2, 3, 12, 14, 16, 27.*

This oval-shaped piazza was named after the *Curtis Ducis*, the main seat of the Lombard duchy. The area, Milan's financial district, was laid out from 1889 to 1901. Buildings include Luca Beltrami's Assicurazioni Generali building, Casa Dario, and the main offices of Credito Italiano, designed by Luigi Broggi.

Piazza Affari ⓲

Map 7 B1 (9 B3). Ⓜ *1 Cordusio.*
🚊 *3, 16, 27.*

The heart of the financial district, this square was laid out in 1928–40 to house the city's markets (especially farm produce). The Borsa Valori, Italy's most important Stock Exchange, stands here. Founded in 1808, it is housed in a building designed by Paolo Mezzanotte in 1931. Ruins of a 1st-century BC Roman theatre were found in the basement area.

The Milan Stock Exchange in Piazza Affari, built in 1931

SOUTHWEST MILAN

Vault mosaic, Sant'Ambrogio

Religious complexes once covered this district, preventing further building until the early 19th century. The suppression of the monasteries in the late 18th century paved the way for the urbanization of the area between the medieval and Spanish walls, crossed by two large avenues, Corso Italia and Corso di Porta Ticinese. Beyond Porta Ticinese, which leads to the southern part of Milan, is Corso San Gottardo. The area is bordered by the inner ring road, which follows the course of the medieval walls, and the outer ring road, which replaced the Spanish walls. Further on is the Naviglio canals quarter, with the Naviglio Grande and the Pavese, the last vestiges of what was once a major network for communications and commerce. Barges used the Naviglio Grande to transport the Candoglia marble used to build the Duomo and, in the 1950s, the material for postwar reconstruction.

SIGHTS AT A GLANCE

Streets, Squares and Historic Buildings

Largo Carrobbio and Via Torino ❸
Piazza della Vetra and medieval Porta Ticinese ❷
Via Circo ❹

Churches

San Bernardino alle Monache ❺
San Lorenzo alle Colonne see pp80–81 ❶
San Paolo Converso ⓬
San Vittore al Corpo ❽

Sant'Alessandro ⓭
Sant'Ambrogio see pp84–7 ❻
Sant'Eustorgio ❿
Santa Maria dei Miracoli presso San Celso ⓫

Museums and Galleries

Museo Diocesano ❾
Museo Nazionale della Scienza e della Tecnologia Leonardo da Vinci ❼

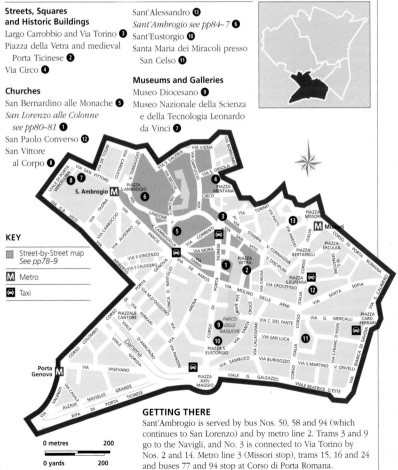

KEY

▦ Street-by-Street map *See pp78–9*

Ⓜ Metro

🚕 Taxi

0 metres 200
0 yards 200

GETTING THERE

Sant'Ambrogio is served by bus Nos. 50, 58 and 94 (which continues to San Lorenzo) and by metro line 2. Trams 3 and 9 go to the Navigli, and No. 3 is connected to Via Torino by Nos. 2 and 14. Metro line 3 (Missori stop), trams 15, 16 and 24 and buses 77 and 94 stop at Corso di Porta Romana.

◁ The Canons' bell tower rises above the atrium of the 4th-century church of Sant'Ambrogio

Street-by-Street: From Sant'Ambrogio to San Lorenzo

Situated just outside the Roman walls, this area was occupied by Early Christian cemeteries and Imperial Age buildings such as the Arena and Circus. Though little remains of this ancient heritage, it is significant, particularly the columns of the triumphal entrance to the basilica of San Lorenzo. Nine kings of Italy were crowned in Sant'Ambrogio in the 9th–15th centuries with four buried here. Napoleon came here in 1805, and Ferdinand of Austria in 1838, after their respective coronations in the Duomo. On the feast day of Sant' Ambrogio, 7 December, the *Oh bej Oh bej* ("how beautiful" in Milanese dialect) fair is held in the streets.

Statue, Università Cattolica

Via Circo
The remains of an ancient Roman circus, used for public spectacles, were found in this street ❻

Cloister of Santa Maria Maddalena al Cerchio

The Università Cattolica (1921) is located in the monastery and cloisters of old Sant'Ambrogio, built by Bramante in 1497.

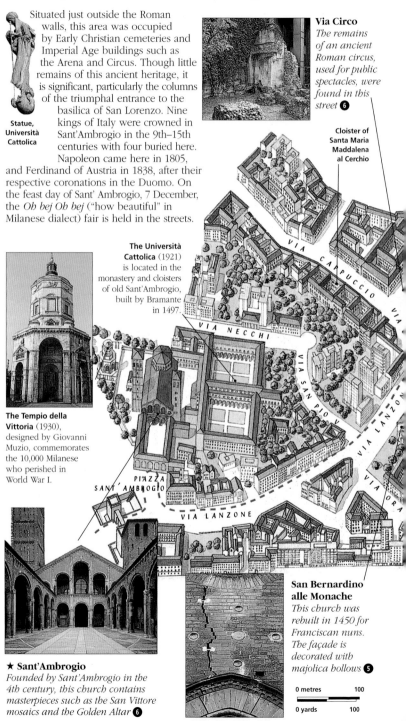

The Tempio della Vittoria (1930), designed by Giovanni Muzio, commemorates the 10,000 Milanese who perished in World War I.

VIA NECCHI

VIA CAPPUCCIO

VIA SAN PIO V

VIA LANZ

VIA ORA

PIAZZA SANT'AMBROGIO

VIA LANZONE

San Bernardino alle Monache
This church was rebuilt in 1450 for Franciscan nuns. The façade is decorated with majolica hollows ❺

★ **Sant'Ambrogio**
Founded by Sant'Ambrogio in the 4th century, this church contains masterpieces such as the San Vittore mosaics and the Golden Altar ❻

| 0 metres | 100 |
| 0 yards | 100 |

Largo Carrobbio
The name of the crossroads at the end of Via Torino may derive from Quadrivium, meaning a place where four streets converge **3**

LOCATOR MAP
See Street Finder, map 7, 8

A tower from the Roman Porta Ticinese is hidden in the courtyard of a building between Via del Torchio and Via Medici.

In Largo Carrobbio the small deconsecrated church of San Sisto houses the Museo Messina.

Piazza della Vetra
From this square there are spectacular views of the apses of San Lorenzo and Sant'Eustorgio. Until 1840 the piazza was the scene of executions **2**

VIA TORINO

LARGO CARROBBIO

VIA SAN VITO

VIA PIO IV

VIA CESARE CORRENTI

PORTA TICINESE

VIA MORA

VIA MOLINO DELLE ARMI

VIA DE AMICIS

KEY

- - - Suggested route

The 16 Corinthian columns may have come from a 2nd–3rd-century AD pagan temple.

Medieval Porta Ticinese

STAR SIGHTS

★ San Lorenzo alle Colonne

★ Sant'Ambrogio

★ **San Lorenzo alle Colonne**
This superb 4th-century basilica consists of a main domed section linked to a series of minor buildings, dating from different periods **1**

San Lorenzo alle Colonne ❶

Dating from the 4th century, San Lorenzo is
one of the oldest round churches in Western
Christendom and may have been the ancient
Imperial palatine chapel. The church was built
utilizing materials from a nearby Roman
amphitheatre. The plan, with exedrae and women's
galleries, is unlike Lombard architecture and reveals
the hand of Roman architects and masons. Some
art historians also see the influence of Byzantine art
in the unusual plan. After several fires the church
was reconstructed in the 11th and 12th centuries
and was again rebuilt after the dome collapsed
in 1573, but the original quatrefoil plan has been
preserved. The chapel of Sant'Aquilino contains
some of the best mosaics in Northern Italy.

Cappella di San Sisto
*This chapel was frescoed by
Gian Cristoforo Storer in the
17th century.*

A bas-relief above the entrance depicts San
Lorenzo, who was burnt over live coals in the
3rd century (a recurring symbol in the church).

Main entrance

★ **Roman Columns**
*The 16 Corinthian columns, from
the 2nd–3rd century, were part
of an unidentified temple and
were placed in their present
location in the 4th century.*

**Statue of
Constantine**
*This bronze work is
a copy of a Roman
statue of the emperor
who issued the Edict of
Milan in AD 313,
bringing persecution of
Christians to an end.*

The dome, the largest in Milan, is supported by an octagonal tambour lit by eight large windows. It was rebuilt by Martino Bassi after it collapsed in 1573.

An upside-down column symbolizes Christianity rising from the ruins of paganism.

VISITORS' CHECKLIST

Corso di Porta Ticinese 39.
Map 7 B2. **Tel** 02-89 40 41 29.
M 3 Missori. 🚋 3. 🚌 94.
🕐 7:30am–6:30pm Mon–Sat
(closed 12:30–2:30pm Tue–Thu),
9am–7pm Sun. ✝ 6:15pm Mon–
Fri; 6pm pre-hols; 9:30, 11:30am,
4pm (in Philippine lang), 6pm hols.
Cappella di Sant'Aquilino 🕐
9am–6:30pm daily. 🖼 🖴 🚫 📷

★ **Cappella di Sant'Aquilino**
This 5th-century chapel has mosaics from the same period: Elijah on the Chariot of Fire *and* Christ with the Apostles. *The entire chapel was once decorated with mosaics.*

Byzantine sarcophagus

Behind the altar, steps lead to the foundations, which have stones taken from the amphitheatre and used for compacting the earth.

The 17th-century presbyteries, designed by Trezzi and Richini, were originally designed to join up with the columns so as to revive the pattern of the ancient quadriporticus.

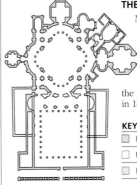

THE STRUCTURE

Most of the walls, towers and three chapels date from the late 4th century. The upper parts of the towers are Romanesque. The dome was built in the late 1500s and the façade in 1894 by Cesare Nava.

KEY

▨	Early Christian
☐	Medieval and modern
▨	Romanesque

STAR FEATURES

★ Roman Columns

★ Cappella di Sant'Aquilino

Piazza della Vetra, linking San Lorenzo to Sant'Eustorgio

Piazza della Vetra and medieval Porta Ticinese ❷

Map 7 B2. 🚋 *2, 3, 14, 15.* 🚌 *94.*

The vast area of greenery dominated by a column bearing the statue of San Lazzaro (1728) is also called Parco delle Basiliche, because it lies between the basilicas of San Lorenzo and Sant'Eustorgio. The name "Vetra" seems to derive from the Latin *castra vetera*, which probably alluded to the Roman military camps positioned here to defend the nearby imperial palace. The name was also given to a canal that was once on the northern side of the square and was lined with tanners' work-shops (the tanners were called *vetraschi*). Until 1840 the square was used for the public hangings of condemned commoners, while nobles were decapitated in front of the law court, the Broletto *(see p54)*.

During the Roman era there was a small port here, at the point where the Seveso and Nirone rivers converged in the navigable Vettabbia canal.

This square is worth visiting just for the magnificent view of the apses of the basilicas. In the 12th century, when the city walls were enlarged to include San Lorenzo, the Roman gate at present-day Largo Carrobbio was replaced by the "new" medieval Porta Ticinese. A moat ran around the new walls and along present-day Via Molino delle Armi, which was named after the water mills *(molini)* used mostly to forge weapons.

Porta Ticinese was remodelled after 1329 by Azzone Visconti and decorated with a tabernacle of the *Madonna and Child with St Ambrose Proffering the Model of the City* by the workshop of Giovanni di Balduccio (14th century). This city gate – the only one, along with Porta Nuova on Via Manzoni – was fortified with two towers in 1865.

Detail of the tabernacle of Porta Ticinese: *Madonna and Child with St Ambrose* by Giovanni di Balduccio's workshop

Largo Carrobbio and Via Torino ❸

Map 7 B2. 🚋 *2, 3, 14.* **Museo Messina** *Via San Sisto 4.* **Tel** *02-86 45 30 05.* 🕐 *2–6pm Tue–Sat.* 🔴 *1 Jan, Easter, 1 May, 15 Aug, 25 Dec.* 🚫 ♿

The vast Carrobbio square, which connects Via Torino and Corso di Porta Ticinese, was either named after the *quadrivium*, a crossroads of four streets, or after *carrubium*, a road reserved for carts. One of the towers flanking the Roman Porta Ticinese still stands at the corner of Via Medici and Via del Torchio. The name of the gate derived from the fact that it opened onto the road for Pavia, which in ancient times was called *Ticinum*. At the junction with Via San Sisto is the deconsecrated 17th-century church of San Sisto. In 1976 it became the museum-studio of sculptor Francesco Messina (who died in 1990) and now houses a collection of his bronze and

Female nude by Francesco Messina (1967)

For hotels and restaurants in this area see p161 and pp173–5

coloured plaster sculpture pieces and graphic art.

Largo Carrobbio is at one end of Via Torino, a major commercial street that developed after the merger of the old city districts, which were filled with the work-shops of oil merchants, silk weavers, hatters and famous armourers – as can be seen by the names of some streets.

The 16th-century Palazzo Stampa, built by Massimiliano Stampa, stands in Via Soncino. When the Sforza dynasty died out in 1535, Stampa intro-duced Spanish dominion to the city by hoisting the flag of Charles V on the Castello Sforzesco in exchange for land and privileges. The imperial eagle still stands on the palazzo tower, over the bronze globe representing the dominions of Charles V.

The cloister at Santa Maria Maddalena al Cerchio

Via Circo ❹

Map 7 B1. 🚋 2, 3, 14. 🚌 50, 58.

The area extending from Largo Carrobbio to Corso Magenta is very rich in 3rd- and 4th-century ruins, particularly mosaics and masonry, much of it now part of private homes. This was the period when the Roman emperor Maximian lived in Milan: his splendid palace was near Via Brisa. In order to create a proper imperial capital, he built many civic edifices to gain the favour of the Milanese: the Arena, the thermae and the huge Circus used for two-horse chariot races. The Circus,

505 m (1,656 ft) long, was one of the largest constructions in the Roman Empire. The only remaining parts are the end curve, visible at the junction of Via Cappuccio and Via Circo, and one of the entrance towers, which became the bell tower of San Maurizio in Corso Magenta.

The Circus, active long after the fall of the Roman Empire, was the venue of the corona-tion of the Lombard king Adaloaldo in 615, while in the Carolingian period it became a vineyard, as the place name of nearby Via Vigna indicates. At No. 7 Via Cappuccio, the 18th-century Palazzo Litta Biumi has incorporated, to the left of the central courtyard, the delightful 15th-century nuns' convent Santa Maria Maddalena al Cerchio, which has been partly rebuilt. Its name, a corruption of the Latin *ad circulum*, refers to the Circus over which it was built. The hood of the nuns' habit *(cappuccio)* is probably the origin of the name of the street where the convent is located. Further along, at No. 13, is Palazzo Radice Fossati (a private house), of medieval origin, with a 13th-century portal and 18th-century frescoes inside.

On Via Sant'Orsola you come to Via Morigi, named after a famous Milanese family who once lived here; all that remains of their residence is a 14th-century tower with a small loggia. The nearby square is domi-nated by the 14th-century Torre dei Gorani, another tower crowned by a loggia with small stone columns.

Fifteenth-century frescoes by the school of Vincenzo Foppa

San Bernardino alle Monache ❺

Via Lanzone 13. **Map** 7 A1.
Tel 02-86 45 08 95. 🚋 2, 3, 14.
🚌 94. ⬜ 4–6pm Fri, 10am–noon Sun.

The church is the only remaining building in a Franciscan nuns' convent dating from the mid-15th century and attributed to the Lombard architect Pietro Antonio Solari. The church was named after the preacher Bernardino da Siena, whose relics are kept here. It was partly rebuilt in 1922. The narrow, elegant brick façade is decorated with majolica bowls and a fine elaborate cornice with small arches.

The interior houses fine 15th-century frescoes painted by the school of Vincenzo Foppa, and others dating from the early 16th century. Of note is *Madonna and Child with Saint Agnes*.

Part of the curve of the Circus built by the Roman emperor Maximian in the late 3rd century AD

Sant'Ambrogio ❻

Detail of the apse mosaic

The basilica was built by Bishop Ambrogio (Ambrose) in AD 379–86 on an Early Christian burial ground as part of a programme to reorganize the Christian face of Milan. The church was dedicated to Ambrogio, a defender of Christianity against Arianism, after his burial here. The Benedictines began to enlarge it in the 8th century, then in the following century Archbishop Anspert built the atrium, which was rebuilt in the 12th century. In the 11th century, reconstruction of the entire church began. The dome collapsed in 1196, and the vaults and pulpit were rebuilt. In 1492 the Sforza family asked Bramante to restructure the rectory and the Benedictine monastery. Sadly, the basilica was badly damaged by bombs in 1943.

The Canons' bell tower was erected in 1124 to surpass in height and beauty the campanile of the nearby Benedictines.

The Capitals
The columns are enlivened by Bible stories and fantastic animals symbolizing the struggle between Good and Evil. Some date from the 11th century.

Anspert's Atrium (11th century) was used by local people as a refuge from danger before the city walls were built.

The Interior
The solemn proportions typical of Lombard Romanesque characterize the interior. The nave is covered by ribbed cross vaulting supported by massive piers.

Apse Mosaic

The mosaic dates from the 4th–8th centuries and was partially restored after the 1943 bombings. It depicts the enthroned Christ and scenes from Sant'Ambrogio's life.

Apse

VISITORS' CHECKLIST

Piazza Sant'Ambrogio 15. **Map** 7 A1. **Tel** 02-86 45 08 95. Ⓜ 2 Sant'Ambrogio. 🚌 50, 58, 94. ⏰ 7am–noon, 3–7pm daily (not during services). ✝ 6:30pm pre-hols; 8, 10 & 11am (in Latin), 12:15, 6 & 7pm hols; 8 & 9am, 6:30pm Mon–Fri. 📷 🚻 **Museo della Basilica** *Tel* 02-86 45 08 95. Enter via presbytery. ⏰ 9am–12:30pm, 2:30–6pm Mon–Sat; 10am–1pm, 3–5pm Sun. ⚫ am pre-hols and hols. 🎫 🚻 **Chapel of San Vittore in Ciel d'Oro** 🎫

★ Chapel of San Vittore in Ciel d'Oro

The chapel was named after the gold (oro) mosaics on the vault. Sant'Ambrogio is depicted in one of the 5th-century panels.

Museum entrance

★ Golden Altar

This golden altar was made by Volvinius (9th century) for the remains of Sant'Ambrogio. The reliefs depict the lives of Christ (front) and Ambrogio (to the rear).

The ciborium is the small 10th-century baldachin that protects the Golden Altar. It is supported by four Roman porphyry columns and decorated with stuccowork.

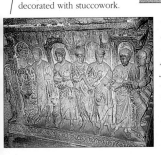

★ Sarcophagus of Stilicho

Situated under the pulpit, this 4th-century master-piece has a wealth of relief figures with religious significance. It is tradition-ally referred to as the tomb of the Roman general Stilicho, but probably contained the remains of the emperor Gratian.

STAR FEATURES

★ Golden Altar

★ Chapel of San Vittore in Cie l d'Oro

★ Sarcophagus of Stilicho

Exploring Sant'Ambrogio

The fact that the church of Sant'Ambrogio houses the remains of the city's patron saint, the church's founder, makes it a special place for the Milanese. Most of its present-day appearance is the result of rebuilding in the 10th and 12th centuries by the Benedictines from the nearby monastery, who made it a model of Lombard Romanesque religious architecture. All that remains of the 4th-century basilica are the triumphal arch and its columns, which became part of the apse. In 1937–40 and in the postwar period the Romanesque structure and delicate colours were restored. From the Pusterla (gate) there is a marvellous view of the church, with its two bell towers and atrium, flanked by the rectory and museum.

Papal statue

PUSTERLA DI SANT'AMBROGIO

The Pusterla di Sant' Ambrogio, one of the minor gates on the medieval walls, is a good starting point for a visit to the church. Rebuilt in 1939, it houses a museum with old weapons and instruments of torture.

A decorated capital in the atrium

ANSPERT'S ATRIUM

Just before the atrium, to the left, is the isolated Roman Colonna del Diavolo (Devil's Column), with two holes halfway up which, according to tradition, were made by the Devil's horns while he was tempting Sant'Ambrogio. The present-day atrium, with its blind arches, dates from the 12th century and replaced one built by Archbishop Anspert in the 9th century.

This large courtyard acts as an entrance foyer for the church proper and sets off the façade. A row of piers

(some Roman) with sculpted capitals continues into the basilica.

The rhythmic pattern of the arches, half-columns and small suspended arches, as well as the proportions, match those in the church, creating a harmonious continuity between exterior and interior. The atrium houses finds and tombstones from this area, which was once an Early Christian cemetery.

The fourth side of the atrium, or narthex, has five bays and is part of the façade, which has an upper loggia with five arches. In the narthex is the main portal (8th–10th centuries), with small columns with figures of animals and the Mystic Lamb, while its wooden wings (1750) have reliefs of the *Life of David*.

The atrium, with finds and tombstones from the surrounding area

THE INTERIOR

The nave provides the best view of the interior, revealing the basilica in all its splendour. The nave has two side aisles divided by arcades supporting the women's galleries with piers with carved capitals. At the beginning of the nave is the Serpent's Column, said to have been erected by Moses in the desert. Beside it, to the left, excavations show the level of the original 4th-century floor.

The pulpit (or ambo) is made of pieces saved when the dome collapsed in 1196. This magnificent monument is decorated with an eagle and a seated man, symbols of the evangelists John and Matthew. Underneath is the sarcophagus of Stilicho (4th century) with reliefs representing (going clockwise) *Christ Giving the Law to St Peter*, four scenes from the Old Testament, *Christ among the Apostles* and the *Sacrifice of Isaac*. Under the octagonal cupola is the ciborium (10th century), the heart of the basilica, supported by columns taken from the 4th-century ciborium. Its painted stucco sides depict various episodes: on the front is *Christ Giving the Keys to St Peter and the Law to St Paul*. The ciborium acts as a baldachin for the Golden Altar, an embossed work that Archbishop Angilberto commissioned from Volvinius in the 9th century. On the back, a silver relief narrates the *Life of Sant'Ambrogio* and has the artist's signature. On the same side, two small doors allowed the faithful to worship the body of St Ambrose, once kept under the altar. The front is made of gold and jewels, and narrates the *Life of Christ*. Behind the ciborium is the wooden choir with the *Life of Sant' Ambrogio* (15th century) and, in the middle, the bishop's throne (4th and 9th centuries), also used by

The Serpent's Column, at the beginning of the nave

the kings of Italy crowned here. Part of the large mosaic in the apse dates from the 6th and 8th centuries. The scene on the left, a *Benedictory Christ*, is of the same period, while the one on the right is the result of 18th-century and postwar reconstruction. Next to the presbytery is the stairway to the crypt, decorated with stucco (c.1740). Under the Golden Altar, an urn (1897) has the remains of Saints Ambrogio, Gervasio and Protasio. Back upstairs, at the end of the south aisle is the stunning San Vittore in Ciel d'Oro Sacellum, the 4th-century funerary chapel of the martyr, which was later incorporated into the basilica. The 5th-century mosaics on the walls show various saints, including Saints Ambrogio, Gervasio and Protasio.

The Risen Christ by
Bergognone (c.1491)

John the Baptist by Bernardo Lanino, who frescoed the *Legend of St George* on the sides (1546). The Baroque chapel of the Holy Sacrament, the fifth, contains the frescoes *The Death of St Benedict* by Carlo Preda and *St Bernard* by Filippo Abbiati (17th and 18th century respectively). In St Bartholomew's chapel (the second) are the *Legends of Saints Vittore and Satiro* (1737) by Tiepolo, detached from the San Vittore Sacellum; they demonstrate the cultural openness of the Cistercians, who commissioned the work. The altarpiece in the second chapel, *The Virgin Mary with St Bartholomew and St John the Baptist*, is attributed to Gaudenzio Ferrari, as is the 1545 *Deposition* in the next chapel, which also has frescoes by Luini on the pillars.

THE SOUTH AISLE

Returning to the entrance in the south aisle, you will see the monks' chapels, built in different eras. St George's chapel – sixth from the entrance – houses an altarpiece of the *Madonna and Child with the Infant St*

THE NORTH AISLE

Go up this aisle from the baptistery (first chapel), which has a porphyry font by Franco Lombardi with the *Conversion of St Augustine* (1940), the saint baptized by Sant'Ambrogio in Milan. It is dominated symbolically

by Bergognone's *The Risen Christ* (c.1491).

In the third chapel is an interesting painting by Luini, a *Madonna with Saints Jerome and Rocco.*

MUSEO DELLA BASILICA

At the end of the north aisle you come out into the Portico della Canonica, the presbytery portico, which was left unfinished by Bramante (1492–4) and rebuilt after World War II. The columns of the central arch, sculpted to resemble tree trunks, are unusual. The entrance to the Basilica Museum, with six rooms featuring objects and works of art from the church, is here. Among the most interesting pieces are a 12th-century multicoloured tondo of St Ambrose; a cast of Stilicho's sarcophagus; St Ambrose's bed; fragments of the apse mosaics and four wooden panels from the 4th-century portal. The museum also has a *Triptych* by Bernardo Zenale (15th century) and *Christ among the Doctors* by Bergognone. In the garden opposite is St Sigismund's oratory, already famous by 1096, with 15th-century frescoes and Roman columns.

Plaque of the Università Cattolica del Sacro Cuore

UNIVERSITÀ CATTOLICA DEL SACRO CUORE

On the right-hand side of the church (entrance at No. 1 Largo Gemelli), in the former Benedictine monastery, is the university founded by padre Agostino Gemelli in 1921. Its two cloisters, with Ionic and Doric columns, were two of the four Bramante had designed in 1497. In the refectory is *The Marriage at Cana* by Callisto Piazza (1545).

Old motion picture camera, the Science and Technology Museum

Museo Nazionale della Scienza e della Tecnologia Leonardo da Vinci **❼**

Via San Vittore 21. **Map** 6 F1. **Tel** 02-48 55 51. **M** 2 Sant'Ambrogio. 🚌 50, 58, 94. 🕐 9:30am–4:30pm Tue–Fri; 9.30am–6pm Sat, hols. 🏛 🕭 🛅 🍴 ♿ (book at Ufficio Didattico). Library, lecture rooms. **www**.museoscienza.org

The Science and Technology Museum is housed in the former Olivetan monastery of San Vittore (16th century) – partly designed by Vincenzo Seregni – which became a military hospital and then a barracks after monasteries were suppressed in 1804. In 1947 it became the home of the museum. In the two court-yards surrounded by the old section of the museum, you can see part of the foundation of the San Vittore fortress and that of the octagonal mauso-leum of Emperor Valentinian II, both ancient Roman.

The museum boasts one of the world's leading science and technology collections. The vast exhibition space is housed in different buildings. The former monastery contains the technological sections on metallurgy, casting and transport, as well as science sections featuring physics, optics, acoustics and astro-nomy. Another section shows the development of calcula-tion, from the first mechanical calculating machine, invented

by Pascal in 1642, to IBM computers. There is also a section on time measurement, with a reconstruction of a 1750 watchmaker's workshop. The printing section shows the 1810 automatic inking method by which 800 sheets an hour could be printed, and also has the father of the modern typewriter (1855).

The cinema photography section shows how the claw device, used to make motion-picture film move, grew out of a sewing machine needle conceived by Singer in 1851. In the rooms given over to telephones and television, there is a reconstruction of the 1856 pantelegraph, the ancestor of the fax machine.

The history of trains begins with the first locomotive in Italy, used for the Naples-Portici line in 1839, and ends with 1970s models. A pavilion in Via Olona houses the air and sea transport section, featuring two historic pieces: the bridge of the transatlantic liner *Conte Biancamano* and a naval training ship.

The Leonardo da Vinci Gallery has fascinating wooden models of the machines and apparatus invented by the genius, shown together with his drawings. Some, like the rotating crane and the helical airscrew, which demonstrate principles of physics and applied mechanics, can be operated by the public.

Façade detail, San Vittore al Corpo

San Vittore al Corpo **❽**

Via San Vittore 25. **Map** 6 F1. **Tel** 02-48 00 53 51. **M** 2 Sant'Ambrogio. 🚌 50, 58, 94. 🕐 7:30am–noon, 3:30–6pm daily. 🕇 8am, 6pm Mon–Fri; 8:30am, 10:30am, noon, 9pm Sun; 10am & 6pm hols. 📷 🎥 available for groups (book in advance).

The original basilica on this site was founded in the 4th century, next to the mausoleum of Emperor Valentinian II, who died in 392. The church was rebuilt in the 11th and 12th centuries by Benedictine monks, and again altered in 1560 by the Olivetans, who replaced the monks. The architect (either Alessi or Seregni) reversed the orientation and made it one of Milan's most sumptuous churches, with splendid late 16th-century paintings. The Baroque Arese Chapel (1668), designed by Gerolamo Quadrio, and the right-hand apse, with scenes from the life of St Gregory by Camillo Procac-cini (1602), are of particular interest. Moncalvo frescoed the angel musicians on the cupola in 1619. The wooden choir stalls, with carvings of episodes from St Benedict's life, date from 1583; above them are three canvases on the same subject by Gio-vanni Ambrogio Figino. Last, the chapel of Sant'Antonio Abate was entirely frescoed in 1619 by Daniele Crespi.

The façade of San Vittore al Corpo

For hotels and restaurants in this area see p161 and pp173–5

Along the Naviglio Grande

One of the 12 locks

Now one of the liveliest quarters in Milan, the Navigli area formed the city's port district until the 19th century. Work on the Naviglio Grande canal first began in 1177, followed by the Pavia, Bereguardo, Martesana and Paderno canals. A system of locks allowed boats to travel along the canals on different levels (Candoglia marble was taken to the Duomo of Milan in the 14th century in this way).

Lodovico il Moro improved this network of canals with the help of Leonardo da Vinci in the 15th century. Barges arrived laden with coal and salt and departed with handmade goods and textiles. Some sections of the canals, which once extended for 150 km (93 miles), were filled in during the 1930s and navigation ceased altogether in 1979. Thanks to the Navigli canals, in 1953 Milan was ranked the 13th port in Italy despite being landlocked.

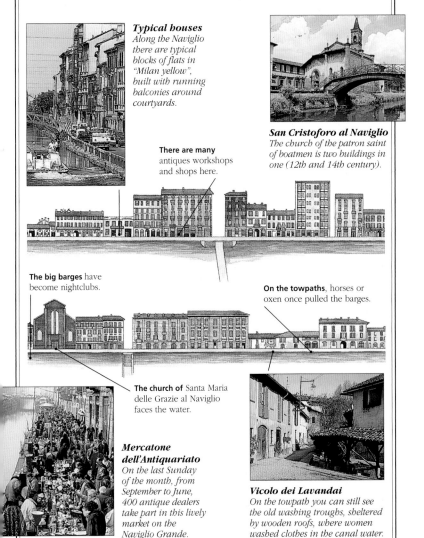

Typical houses
Along the Naviglio there are typical blocks of flats in "Milan yellow", built with running balconies around courtyards.

San Cristoforo al Naviglio
The church of the patron saint of boatmen is two buildings in one (12th and 14th century).

There are many antiques workshops and shops here.

The big barges have become nightclubs.

On the towpaths, horses or oxen once pulled the barges.

The church of Santa Maria delle Grazie al Naviglio faces the water.

Mercatone dell'Antiquariato
On the last Sunday of the month, from September to June, 400 antique dealers take part in this lively market on the Naviglio Grande.

Vicolo dei Lavandai
On the towpath you can still see the old washing troughs, sheltered by wooden roofs, where women washed clothes in the canal water.

Museo Diocesano ❾

Corso di Porta Ticinese 95. **Map** 7
B3. **Tel** 02-89 42 00 19. ⊞ 3, 9.
🚋 94. ☐ 10am–6pm Tue–Sun. 🏛
🎫 Jul–Sep: 7pm–midnight Tue–Sat
(to book, call 02-89 42 00 19). ♿

**A stucco of Sant'Ambrogio kept at
the Museo Diocesano**

The mission of the Museo
Diocesano is to recover and
highlight the artistic heritage
of the Milan diocese, which
extends as far north as the
towns of Varese and Lecco.

This museum of religious
art is housed in the cloisters
of Sant'Eustorgio, next to the
basilica. It features about 320
works of art dating from the
6th to the 19th centuries, from
paintings from the private
collections of past Milanese
archbishops to items rescued
from tiny village churches.
Two of the highlights are the
frescoes of the Stations of
the Cross by late 19th-century
artist Gaetano Previati and the
section devoted to Milan's
patron saint, Sant'Ambrogio.

THE RELICS OF THE MAGI

Emperor Constantine donated the relics in around 315 and
they were taken to Milan by Bishop Eustorgius. Legend has
it that the sarcophagus was so heavy
the cart had to stop at the city gates,
where the original Sant'Eustorgio
basilica was founded and the Apostle
Barnabas baptised the first Milanese
Christians. Barbarossa transferred the
relics to Cologne in 1164. Some were
returned in 1903, an event still celebrated at Epiphany with a procession.

**Tabernacle with
the relics of the Magi**

Sant'Eustorgio ❿

Piazza Sant'Eustorgio 1. **Map** 7 B3.
Tel 02-58 10 15 83. ⊞ 3, 9, 15,
29, 30. 🚋 94. ☐ 7:30am–noon,
3:30–6:30pm. ✝ 7:45am & 5pm
pre-hols; 9:30am, 11am, 12:30pm
(in Portinari Chapel), 5pm hols.
Portinari Chapel Tel 02-89 40 26
71. ☐ 10am–6pm daily.

In the 11th century work began
on building a basilica over one
founded by St Eustorgius in the
4th century, to house the relics
of the Magi. The main body of
the present-day church was
built in the 1300s.
On the right-hand
side of the
façade, which
was rebuilt in
1865, there are
several chapels
dating from
the 13th–15th
centuries. The
Brivio chapel
houses Tommaso Cazzaniga's
tomb of Giovanni Stefano
Brivio (1486). The middle bas-
relief depicts the *Adoration of*

**Sculpture on the façade
of Sant'Eustorgio**

the Magi, and the altarpiece is
a triptych by Bergognone. In
the Baroque Crotta-Caimi
chapel is a fine sarcophagus
by 15th-century sculptor
Protaso Caimi, and a *St
Ambrose on Horseback*. The
Visconti chapel has beautiful
14th-century frescoes: on the
vault are the Evangelists;
below left, a *St George and
the Dragon*; and right, the
Triumph of St Thomas. The
Torriani chapel is frescoed
with symbols of the Evan-
gelists. In the south transept
is the large late-Roman
sarcophagus that
once housed the
relics of the Magi,
and on the altar
is a Campionese
school marble
triptych of the
journey of the
Magi (1347).
The Magi are
also the subject
of the fresco on the left, attributed to Luini. The high altar
houses the remains of St
Eustorgius and bears a marble
altar-front depicting an
unfinished Passion of Christ.

Behind the altar, a passageway leads to the Portinari
chapel, commissioned by
banker Pigello Portinari as his
tomb, and to house the body
of St Peter Martyr. The first
example of a 15th-century
central-plan church in Milan,
it exemplifies the clarity of
Bramante's vision and features
typical Lombard decoration
attributed to Vincenzo Foppa.
Under the dome is the tomb of
St Peter Martyr (1339) by Giovanni di Balduccio, held up by
the eight Virtues and showing
scenes of his ministry. The
small chapel on the left has an
urn containing the saint's skull.

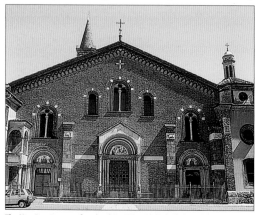

The Neo-Romanesque façade of Sant'Eustorgio, built in 1865

The Sanctuary of Santa Maria dei Miracoli and San Celso

Santa Maria dei Miracoli presso San Celso ⓫

Corso Italia 37. **Map** 7 C3. **Tel** 02-58 31 31 87. 🚋 15. 🚌 94. ◑ 7am–noon, 4–6:30pm daily. 🕇 7:30am, 9am, 6pm daily (except Jul & Aug); 6pm pre-hols; 9 & 11am, noon (except Jul & Aug), 7pm hols. **San Celso** ask sacristan.

San Celso was founded in the 11th century over a church built by St Ambrose in the 4th century to mark the spot where he had found the remains of the martyrs Celso and Nazaro. In 1493 construction began on a sanctuary dedicated to Santa Maria dei Miracoli, designed by Gian Giacomo Dolcebuono and subsequently by Vincenzo Seregni and Alessi. The late 16th-century façade is enlivened by sculptures by Stoldo Lorenzi and Annibale Fontana. The late Renaissance interior has a pavement by Martino Bassi and was frescoed by Cerano and Procaccini. There are major works of art in the various chapels: a painting (1606) by Procaccini; the *Holy Family with St Jerome* altarpiece (1548) by Paris Bordone; Antonio Campi's *Resurrection* (1560); *Baptism of Jesus* by Gaudenzio Ferrari; Moretto da Brescia's *Conversion of St Paul* (1539–40); *Martyrdom of St Catherine* by Cerano (1603); an altarpiece by Bergognone.
    Under the cupola with terracotta Evangelists by De Fondutis and paintings by Appiani (1795) is the high altar (16th century) in semi precious

stones. The wooden choir is from 1570. Statues by Fontana and Lorenzi adorn the pillars. On the Altar of the Madonna is Fontana's *Our Lady of the Assumption*. Below, a 4th-century fresco lies under two embossed silver doors. By the right-hand transept is the entrance to **San Celso**, with 11th–15th-century frescoes and columns with carved capitals.

San Paolo Converso ⓬

Piazza Sant'Eufemia. **Map** 7 C2. 🚋 15. 🚌 94. ◑ for exhibitions only. **Fondazione Metropolitan Tel** 02-86 30 50.

This church was founded in 1549 for the Angeliche di San Paolo convent and is attributed to Domenico Giunti, while the façade was designed by Cerano in 1611. Now deconsecrated, the church has a front section for the public and one to the rear for the nuns. The interior was frescoed in the late 1500s by Giulio and Antonio Campi: in the presbytery are episodes from the life of St Paul, the Ascension of Christ and the Assumption of Mary.
    At the end of Corso di Porta Romana is Piazza Missori, with the remains of San Giovanni in Conca (11th century), once

a Visconti mausoleum. The façade was remade for the Waldensian church in Via Francesco Sforza.

Sant'Alessandro ⓭

Piazza Sant'Alessandro. **Map** 7 C2. **Tel** 02-86 45 30 65. Ⓜ 3 Missori. 🚋 2, 3, 12, 15, 24, 27. ◑ 7:30am–noon, 4–7pm daily. 🕇 11:30am, 6pm Mon–Sat; 6:30pm pre-hols; 7:30am (winter), 10:30am, noon, 6:30pm Sun.

Lorenzo Binago built this church in 1601 for the Barnabiti family. The interior has lavish Baroque furnishings and decoration; the frescoes were painted by Moncalvo and Daniele Crespi. In the presbytery is the *Life of St Alexander* by Filippo Abbiati and Federico Bianchi. The high altar (1741) is decorated with semi-precious stones.
    Next to the church are the Scuole Arcimbolde, schools for the poor founded in 1609 by the Barnabiti family. Opposite is Palazzo Trivulzio, rebuilt by Ruggeri in 1713, with the family coat of arms on the middle window. This family founded the Biblioteca Trivulziana, the library now in the Castello Sforzesco. Nearby Via Palla leads to the Tempio Civico di San Sebastiano, begun by Pellegrino Tibaldi in 1577 and completed in the 1700s. Its interior has works by Legnanino, Montalto and Federico Bianchi.

The cupola and bell tower of Sant'Alessandro, seen from Corso di Porta Romana

SOUTHEAST MILAN

The area between Corso Monforte and Corso di Porta Romana was a typical suburb up to the early 19th century, characterized by aristocratic residences, monasteries and more modest houses typical of the artisans' and commercial districts of Milan. Development of the area began in the 17th century with the construction of Palazzo Durini, one of the most important civic buildings of its time. At the end of the 18th century Corso di Porta Romana and the adjacent streets were changed in keeping with the vast street

A statue in the Guastalla gardens

network renewal plans encouraged by Maria Theresa of Austria. When the empress ordered the suppression of many monasteries, the land where they had stood was purchased by rich nobles. Other areas became available when the Spanish ramparts were demolished. The old atmosphere of Southeast Milan survives above all around the Ca' Granda (now the University), which for almost 500 years was the city hospital, and in the first stretch of Corso di Porta Romana. However, the only vestige of the Verziere, the old vegetable market in Largo Augusto, is the place-name.

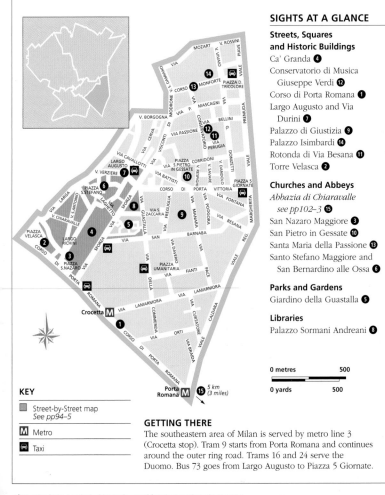

SIGHTS AT A GLANCE

Streets, Squares and Historic Buildings

Ca' Granda ❹
Conservatorio di Musica Giuseppe Verdi ⓬
Corso di Porta Romana ❶
Largo Augusto and Via Durini ❼
Palazzo di Giustizia ❾
Palazzo Isimbardi ⓮
Rotonda di Via Besana ⓫
Torre Velasca ❷

Churches and Abbeys

Abbazia di Chiaravalle see pp102–3 ⓯
San Nazaro Maggiore ❸
San Pietro in Gessate ❿
Santa Maria della Passione ⓭
Santo Stefano Maggiore and San Bernardino alle Ossa ❻

Parks and Gardens

Giardino della Guastalla ❺

Libraries

Palazzo Sormani Andreani ❽

KEY

⬜ Street-by-Street map
   See pp94–5

Ⓜ Metro

🚖 Taxi

GETTING THERE

The southeastern area of Milan is served by metro line 3 (Crocetta stop). Tram 9 starts from Porta Romana and continues around the outer ring road. Trams 16 and 24 serve the Duomo. Bus 73 goes from Largo Augusto to Piazza 5 Giornate.

◁ Detail of *The Legend of St Anthony Abbot*, in San Pietro in Gessate

Street-by-Street: San Nazaro to Largo Augusto

There are many interesting old buildings in this area, which includes the university quarter, with cafés and specialist bookshops, as well as crafts shops on Via Festa del Perdono. Architectural styles range from the 4th-century San Nazaro, founded by St Ambrose, to the Ca' Granda, the old hospital, a marvellous sight when viewed from Largo Richini because of its sheer size and the beauty of its 15th-century arcade. More changes of style come with the palazzi in Corso di Porta Romana and Via Sant'Antonio, and the modern Torre Velasca. The quarter's hospital tradition can be seen in the votive columns at the crossroads, where mass for the sick was celebrated, and the San Bernardino alle Ossa chapel, decorated with the bones of those who died in the hospital.

Sant'Antonio Abat was rebuilt in 1582. It houses paintings by Bernardino Campi, Moncalvo and Ludovico Carracci and is a kind of gallery of early 17th-century painting in Milan.

Torre Velasca
The symbol of modern Milan was built in 1956–8. The tower, 106 m (348 ft) high, houses both offices and flats and is often compared to medieval towers because of the shape of the upper section ❷

Duomo

Corso di Porta Romana
Palazzi with magnificent gardens line this avenue. It follows the route of the ancient Roman road which led from Porta Romana all the way to Rome ❶

KEY

– – – Suggested route

★ **San Nazaro Maggiore**
One of four basilicas founded by Sant'Ambrogio, this church still has some of the original 4th-century masonry. It is preceded by the Trivulzio Chapel, the only Milanese architectural work by Bramantino (1512–50). The view of the back of the church is very striking ❸

STAR SIGHTS

★ San Nazaro Maggiore

★ Ca' Granda

For hotels and restaurants in this area see p162 and p175

Santo Stefano Maggiore and San Bernardino alle Ossa

The San Bernardino ossuary chapel, rebuilt in the 17th century, is entirely covered with human bones and skulls from the cemeteries that were abolished in the 1600s ❻

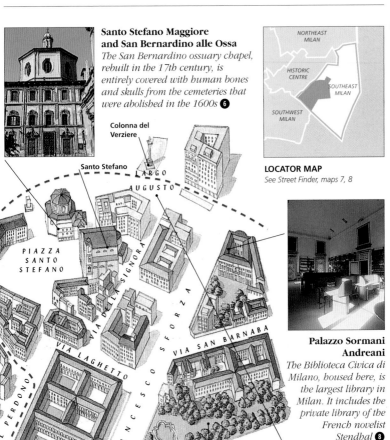

Colonna del Verziere

Santo Stefano

LARGO AUGUSTO

PIAZZA SANTO STEFANO

VIA DELLA SIGNORA

SFORZA

VIA SAN BARNABA

VIA FRANCESCO

VIA LAGHETTO

DEL PERDONO

SAN R O

LOCATOR MAP
See Street Finder, maps 7, 8

NORTHEAST MILAN

HISTORIC CENTRE

SOUTHEAST MILAN

SOUTHWEST MILAN

Palazzo Sormani Andreani

The Biblioteca Civica di Milano, housed here, is the largest library in Milan. It includes the private library of the French novelist Stendhal ❽

Largo Augusto

The Colonna del Verziere here commemorates the end of the 1576 plague ❼

Giardino della Guastalla

Milan's oldest public garden was laid out in 1555. There are several monuments, including a small Neo-Classical temple designed by Luigi Cagnola ❺

★ Ca' Granda

This was the old city hospital, also known as Ospedale Maggiore. It was built in 1456 to bring all the small hospitals of the city together on a single site. It was in use until 1939. Today it is home to Milan's state university ❹

0 metres 300
0 yards 300

Entrance to the Teatro Carcano, in Corso di Porta Romana

Corso di Porta Romana ①

Map 7 C2. M *3 Missori.*
🚎 *12, 15, 16, 24, 27.* 🚋 *77, 94.*

This avenue was laid out over a porticoed stretch of the ancient Roman road outside the city walls (2nd–3rd century AD) that led to Rome.It ran from Porta Romana – then just beyond present-day Piazza Missori – to a triumphal arch (near the widening in the road known as Crocetta), transformed by Barbarossa into a fortified gate in the walls in 1162. The new gate (1171), further back, was demolished in 1793.

The Corso is lined with many noble palazzi. The 17th-century Palazzo Acerbi at No.3; Palazzo Annoni at No. 6, designed by Francesco Maria Richini (1631), famous for its art collection which includes works by Rubens and Van Dyck; Palazzo Mellerio at No.13 and Casa Bettoni (1865) at No.20, with statues of Bersaglieri flanking the door. Via Santa Sofia crosses the Corso, and over the Naviglio canal close to the Crocetta, whose name derives from a votive cross set there during the 1576 plague.

Opposite is the Teatro Carcano (1803), where the great Italian actress Eleonora Duse performed. The Corso ends at the Porta Romana (in Piazzale Medaglie d'Oro), built in 1598. To the right you can see a fragment of the Spanish walls built by Ferrante Gonzaga (1545); they ran for 11,216 m (37,000 ft) and were demolished in 1889.

Torre Velasca ②

Piazza Velasca 5. **Map** 7 C2.
M *3 Missori.* 🚎 *12, 15, 16, 24, 27.* 🚋 *94.*

This tower, built in the late 1950s by architects Belgioioso, Nathan Rogers and Peressutti, is one of the best-known monuments in modern-day Milan. The over-hang of the upper part of the building and its red colour are reminiscent of Italian medieval towers, but the shape actually grew out of the need to create more office space in a limited area.

Cappella Trivulzio, in San Nazaro Maggiore (16th century)

San Nazaro Maggiore ③

Piazza San Nazaro. **Map** 8 D2.
Tel 02-58 30 77 19. M *3 Missori.*
🚎 *16, 24.* 🚋 *77, 94.* 🕐 *7:30am–noon, 3:30–6:30pm.* ✝ *6pm prehols; 8:30, 10, 11:30am, 6pm hols.*
📷 ♿

The original basilica was built by Sant'Ambrogio in AD 382–6 to house the remains of the Apostles Andrew, John and Thomas, which is why it was known as the *Basilica Apostolorum.* It was dedicated to San Nazaro when his remains – found by Sant'Ambrogio near the basilica – were buried here in 396. The church was built outside the walls in an Early Christian burial ground – as can be seen by the sarcophagi outside and the epitaph in the right-hand transept – and looked onto an ancient Roman porticoed street. It was rebuilt after a fire in 1075 reusing much original material.

The church is preceded by the octagonal Trivulzio Chapel, begun in Renaissance style in 1512 by Bramantino and continued by Cristoforo Lombardo. It houses the tomb of Gian Giacomo Trivulzio and his family.

The nave of the church has a cross vault. Either side of the entrance you will see the remains of the Romanesque doorway covered by the Trivulzio Chapel. On the walls, among fresco fragments, are parts of the original masonry. In the crossing, the dome is supported by the 4th-century piers; two altars in the choir contain the remains of the Apostles and San Nazaro. Left of the altar is the small cruciform chapel of San Lino, with traces of 10th – 15th-century frescoes. In the transepts are a fine *Last Supper* by Bernardino Lanino (right) and *Passion of Jesus* by Luini (left). The Chapel of St Catherine (1540) has Lanino's *Martyrdom of St Catherine* and a 16th-century stained-glass window depicting the *Life of St Catherine.*

The remains of San Nazaro, found by Sant'Ambrogio in AD 396

Ca' Granda ❹

17th-century window

The "Casa Grande", or Ospedale Maggiore, was built for Francesco Sforza from 1456 on with the aim of uniting the city's 30 hospitals. The "large house" was designed by Filarete, who built only part of it, and was finished in stages in the 17th and 18th centuries. In 1939 the hospital moved to a new site, and since 1952 the Ca' Granda has housed the liberal arts faculties of the Università Statale, Milan's university. The hospital was modern for its time: there were separate wings for men and women – each with a central infirmary – and a large courtyard between them.

VISITORS' CHECKLIST

Via Festa del Perdono 5. **Map** 8
D2. **Tel** 02-503 11. 🅼 3 Missori.
🚊 12, 15, 16, 24, 27. 🚌 54,
77, 94. ☐ 7:30am–7:30pm
Mon–Fri; 8am–noon Sat (first 3
weeks of Aug: 7:30am–3:30pm
Mon–Fri). ● Sun & hols (open
in morning pre-hols). 🅱 🚫
Chiesa dell'Annunciata **Tel**
02-58 30 77 19. ☐ 8am–7pm
(when University is open).

The church of the Annunciata (17th-century) contains a 1639 canvas by Guercino.

The Neo-Classical Macchio Wing, seat of the Faculty of Letters, Philosophy and Jurisprudence, housed the benefactors' art gallery, with portraits by leading artists.

★ Fifteenth-century Façade
The brick façade has round arches and is richly decorated. There were workshops and warehouses at ground level.

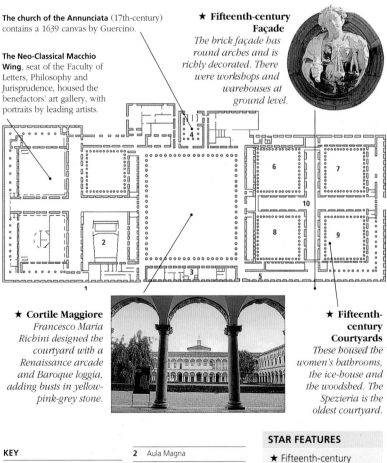

★ Cortile Maggiore
Francesco Maria Richini designed the courtyard with a Renaissance arcade and Baroque loggia, adding busts in yellow-pink-grey stone.

★ Fifteenth-century Courtyards
These housed the women's bathrooms, the ice-house and the woodshed. The Spezieria is the oldest courtyard.

KEY

☐	15th-century section
▦	17th-century section
☐	18th–19th-century section
1	Entrance to the Faculties of Liberal Arts, Philosophy and Jurisprudence

2	Aula Magna
2	Courtyard entrance
2	Chiesa dell'Annunciata
2	Porticoes, 15th-century wing
6-9	Courtyards, 15th-century wing
10	Crociera, formerly the infirmary

STAR FEATURES

★ Fifteenth-century Façade

★ Cortile Maggiore

★ Fifteenth-century Courtyards

The fish pond in the Giardino della Guastalla, near Via Sforza

Giardino della Guastalla **❺**

Via Francesco Sforza, Via S Barnaba, Via Guastalla. **Map** 8 D2. 🚃 *12, 23, 27.* 🚌 *60, 73, 77, 84, 94.* ⏰ *daily. Mar: 7am–8pm; Apr & Oct: 7am–9pm; May–Sep: 7am–10pm; Nov–Feb: 7am–7pm.*

This garden – Milan's oldest – was laid out in 1555 by Countess Ludovica Torelli della Guastalla, next to the college of the same name for the daughters of impoverished aristocrats. In the early 1600s it was transformed into an Italian-style garden, and a goldfish pond on two communicating terraces was added. There is also a 17th-century shrine representing Mary Magdalen attended by angels and a Neo-Classical temple by Luigi Cagnola. In 1939 the garden was separated from the adjacent Sormani park and opened to the public. At the Via Guastalla exit (at No. 19) you can visit the Synagogue, designed by Luca Beltrami (1890–92) and, at the corner of Via San Barnaba, the church of Santi Barnaba e Paolo, which is part of the nearby Chierici Regolari di San Paolo college. It is a prototype of 16th-century Lombard churches, founded in 1558 and then modified by Galeazzo Alessi. Inside are paintings by Aurelio Luini, son of Bernardino, Camillo Procaccini and Moncalvo.

Santo Stefano Maggiore and San Bernardino alle Ossa **❻**

Piazza Santo Stefano. **Map** 8 D1. Ⓜ *1, 3 Duomo.* 🚃 *12, 23, 27.* 🚌 *54, 60, 73, 77.* **Archivio Storico Diocesano** *Via San Calimero 13.* **Map** 8 D2. **Tel** *02-58 49 98 01.* ⏰ *9:15am–12:15pm Mon–Fri.* ⚫ *Aug.* **San Bernardino alle Ossa** *Tel 02-76 00 71 87.* ⏰ *7:30am–noon, 1–6pm Mon–Fri; 7:30am–noon Sat; 9am–noon Sun.* ↑ *8:30am Mon–Sat; 11am hols.* 🚫 ♿

Statue on the façade of San Bernardino alle Ossa

Santo Stefano dates back to the 5th century. It was rebuilt in 1075 after being destroyed by a fire and was again rebuilt in its present form in 1584 by Giuseppe Meda. The Baroque bell tower was built in 1643–74 by Carlo Buzzi: the pilaster at the base is all that remains of the quadriporticus that once faced the medieval basilica. The church was used as the Diocesan Archive, which has now moved. Next door are San Bernardino alle Ossa, originally medieval but since rebuilt many times, and the ossuary chapel (with a concave façade) built in 1210 and altered in 1695. The latter is small and covered with human bones and skulls. The dim light and dark walls contrast with the bright colours of the fresco on the vault by Sebastiano Ricci (1695): *The Triumph of Souls among Angels.*

Largo Augusto and Via Durini **❼**

Map 8 D1. Ⓜ *1, 3 Duomo.* 🚃 *12, 15, 23, 27.* 🚌 *54, 60, 61, 73, 77, 84, 94.*

The Verziere Column, commissioned by Carlo Borromeo to celebrate the end of the 1576 plague, has stood in Largo Augusto since 1580. It is one of the few votive columns to survive the late 18th century. Many were lost after the suppression of the monastic orders that owned them, or sacrificed to make room for new buildings. This square marks the beginning of Via Durini, which is dominated by the concave façade of Santa Maria della Sanità (1708). No. 20 is Casa Toscanini, the great conductor's house, and No. 24 is Palazzo Durini, built in 1648 by Francesco Maria Richini and now the headquarters for Inter Milan. On nearby Corso Europa is 16th-century Palazzo Litta Modignani, where a Roman mosaic was found.

Palazzo Sormani Andreani **❽**

Corso di Porta Vittoria 6. **Map** 8 E1. **Tel** *02-88 46 33 97.* **Fax** *02-76 00 65 88.* 🚃 *12, 23, 27.* 🚌 *54, 60, 73, 77, 84, 94.* ⏰ *9am–7:30pm Mon–Sat.* ⚫ *public hols, Aug.*

The palazzo, constructed in the 18th century, was enlarged in 1736 by Francesco Croce, who made it into one

Façade of Palazzo Sormani, the Municipal Library since 1956

For hotels and restaurants in this area see p162 and p175

of the most lavish residences of the time. Croce also designed the characteristic late Baroque curved façade. Reconstructed after World War II, the palazzo became the home of the Municipal (or Sormani Andreani) Library, the largest in Milan. It has over 580,000 works, including Stendhal's private library, a newspaper library with about 19,500 Italian and foreign publications, and a record and CD collection. A catalogue of all the Milan libraries is also here, as is the regional periodicals catalogue.

The Neo-Classical back opens onto a garden, part of the larger original one, which is used for small exhibitions. Nearby, at No. 2 Via Visconti di Modrone, is one of Milan's excellent traditional *pasticcerie*, the Taveggia pastry shop *(see p187)*.

Palazzo di Giustizia ⑨

Corso di Porta Vittoria. **Map** 8 E1.
🚊 *12, 23, 27.* 🚌 *60, 73, 77, 84.*

The centre of attention in the early 1990s because of the Mani Pulite (clean hands) corruption inquests and trials that changed much of the face of Italian politics, the Milan Law Courts were designed in typical Fascist style (1932–40) by Marcello Piacentini. The building also houses the Notarial Acts Archive, formerly in the Palazzo della Ragione *(see p54)*. The Palazzo has 1,200 rooms and 65 law courts with works by contemporary artists, including Mario Sironi's fresco in the Assize Court.

The Palazzo di Giustizia (1932–40), a typical example of Fascist architecture

Detail from *The Legend of the Virgin*, San Pietro in Gessate

San Pietro in Gessate ⑩

Piazza San Pietro in Gessate.
Map 8 E1. **Tel** 02-54 10 74 24.
🚊 *12, 23, 27.* 🚌 *60, 73, 77, 84.*
⏰ *Jul–mid-Sep: 8am–noon Mon–Fri, 8:30am–noon, 5–8pm Sat & Sun; mid-Sep–Jun: 7:30am–6pm Mon–Fri, 7:30am–noon, 2:30–6pm Sat & Sun.*
✝ *1:15pm Mon & Fri, 8am Tue & Thu, 8:30am Wed, 7pm Sat, 9am, noon, 7pm Sun.*

This church was built in 1447–75 by the Solari school and financed by the banker Pigello Portinari, whose emblem is on the outer wall of the apse. In the middle of the façade, rebuilt in 1912, is a portal with an effigy of St Peter, which was added in the 1600s. The Gothic interior has a three-aisle nave with ribbed vaulting and pointed arches and has preserved some original painting. The church was damaged during World War II, in particular the right-hand chapels, where there are traces of frescoes by Antonio Campi, Moncalvo and Bergognone (whose *Funeral of St Martin* is in the fifth chapel). The third and fifth chapels on the left have fine frescoes by Montorfano: *Life of St John the Baptist* (1484) and *The Legend of St Anthony Abbot*. The eight choir stalls were rebuilt with the remains of the 1640 ones by Carlo Garavaglia, damaged in 1943 and partly used as firewood during the war. The left-hand transept has frescoes of the *Life of Sant'Ambrogio* (1490) commissioned by the Sforza senator Ambrogio Grifi from Bernardino Butinone and Bernardino Zenale. In the lunettes under the vault, next to *Sant'Ambrogio on Horseback*, you can see the figure of a hanged man whose rope "drops" into the scene below, down to the hangman. These frescoes were discovered in 1862.

The arcade in the Rotonda di Via Besana

Rotonda di Via Besana ⓫

Via San Barnaba, corner of Via Besana. **Map** 8 F2. **Tel** 02-545 50 47. 🚊 9. 🚌 77, 84. ⏰ *for exhibitions and summer cultural events only.*

The Rotonda was the cemetery of the nearby Ca' Granda Hospital, designed in 1695 by Francesco Raffagno on present-day Viale Regina Margherita. About 150,000 dead were buried in the crypts under the arcades. When it was closed in 1783, viceroy Eugène de Beauharnais tried to change it into the Pantheon of the Regno Italico (1809), but the project fell through and the round brick building first housed patients with infectious diseases and then, up to 1940, was the hospital laundry. It is now used for temporary exhibitions and as an outdoor cinema in summer.

In the middle is the deconsecrated San Michele ai Nuovi Sepolcri, built in 1713. It has a Greek cross plan with a central altar, visible from all sides. The small skulls sculpted on the capitals are a reminder of the original function of this complex.

On Via San Barnaba is Santa Maria della Pace, designed by Pietro Antonio Solari in 1466, the property of the Order of Knights of the Holy Sepulchre. In 1805 the church was suppressed and the paintings removed (some are now in the Brera), but some 17th-century frescoes by Tanzio da Varallo remain.

The nearby monastery is the home of the Società Umanitaria, founded in 1893 to educate and aid the poor.

It has a library devoted to labour problems. The only remaining part of the monastery is the refectory, with a *Crucifixion* by Marco d'Oggiono. Returning to Corso di Porta Vittoria, you come to Piazza Cinque Giornate, with a monument by Giuseppe Grandi (1895) commemorating the anti-Austrian insurrection of 1848 *(see p24)*. The female figures symbolize the Five Days, whose dead are buried in the crypt below.

Conservatorio di Musica Giuseppe Verdi ⓬

Via Conservatorio 12. **Map** 8 E1. **Tel** 02-762 11 01. 🚊 54, 61, 77. ⏰ *for concerts only.* **Library Tel** 02-762 110 219. ⏰ *8am–8pm Mon–Fri, 8am–2pm Sat.*

Milan's Conservatory was founded by viceroy Eugène de Beauharnais in 1808. Important musicians and composers have studied here – but the young Verdi was refused admission. There is a chamber music hall and a large auditorium for symphonic music. The library boasts over 35,000 books and 460,000 pieces of written music, scores, etc, including works by Mozart, Rossini, Donizetti, Bellini and Verdi, as well as a small museum of precious stringed instruments.

Santa Maria della Passione ⓭

Via Conservatorio 14. **Map** 8 E–F4. **Tel** 02-76 02 13 70. 🚊 54, 61, 77. 🚌 94. ⏰ 7:45am–noon, 3:30–6:15pm Mon–Fri; 9am–12:30pm, 3:30–6:30pm Sat & Sun. ✝ 8:15am, 5:30pm Mon–Fri; 5:30pm pre-hols; 10am, 11:15am, 5:30pm hols.

The second largest church in Milan, after the Duomo, was built under the patronage of the prelate Daniele Birago, who had donated the land to the Lateran Canons. Work began in 1486 to a design by Giovanni Battagio. Originally the church had a Greek cross plan but it was lengthened with a nave and six semi-circular chapels on each side in 1573 by Martino Bassi. The façade of the church – and the nearby convent, now the home of the Conservatory – was added in 1692 by Giuseppe Rusnati, who kept it low so that visitors could appreciate the majestic octagonal covering of the dome designed by Cristoforo Lombardo (1530). To enhance this view and link the church with the Naviglio, Abbot Gadio had the Via della Passione laid out in front of the entrance in 1540. The interior, with a frescoed barrel vault, is very atmospheric. Fourteen early 17th-century portraits of the saints of the Lateran Order, attributed to Daniele Crespi and his school, are on the piers. In the right-hand chapels, two works worth seeing are *Christ at the Pillar*

The Giuseppe Verdi Conservatory, housed in a former monastery

The octagonal dome of Santa Maria della Passione (17th century)

by Giulio Cesare Procaccini, on the altar of the third chapel, and the *Madonna di Caravaggio*, a fresco attributed to Bramantino, in the sixth chapel. The presbytery still has its original Greek cross structure. The paintings hanging from the piers, mostly the work of Crespi, narrate the Passion and include *Christ Nailed to the Cross*. Behind the Baroque high altar is a wooden choir (16th-century) with mother of pearl inlay. The church became a place of intense musical activity in the 16th and 17th centuries, when two organs were built opposite each other, on either side of the choir. The instrument on the right was created by the famous Antegnati, and the left one by Cristoforo Valvassori, who was involved in building the organ in the Duomo. The doors of the left instrument have scenes from the Passion painted by Crespi. Frequent classical music concerts for organs pieces composed for four hands are still held here.

There are remarkable Cinquecento paintings in the transepts: the artwork on the right-hand side has a *Deposition* altarpiece by Bernardino Ferrari (after 1514) with the *Legend of the Cross* in the predella; and on the altar to the left is Gaudenzio Ferrari's *Last*

Santa Maria della Passione: one of the saints of the Lateran Order

Supper (1543), with a *Crucifixion* by Giulio Campi (1560) alongside.

The chapels on the left-hand side of the nave contain fine works by Camillo Procaccini, Vermiglio and Duchino. The first chapel is noteworthy because of the impressive realism of Crespi's *St Charles Fasting*, and the vault frescoed by Giulio Campi (1558) is also impressive.

The 15th-century Chapter House was designed and painted by Bergognone: saints and doctors are in a false peristyle.

On the right-hand wall is Christ with the Apostles. In Via Bellini you can see the left side of the church and the dome. At No. 11 is the Art Nouveau Casa Campanini (1904), with wrought iron work by Alessandro Mazzucotelli.

Palazzo Isimbardi ⑭

Corso Monforte 35. **Map** 4 E5. *Tel* 02-774 01 (Lombardy Province PR Office). Ⓜ 1 San Babila. 🚊 9, 23, 29, 30. 🚍 54, 61, 94. ⬜ apply to IAT (see p209).

The seat of the Milan provincial government since 1935, this palazzo dates from the 15th century but was enlarged by the noble families who lived in it, among whom were the Isimbardi, who purchased it in 1775. The 18th-century façade on

Corso Monforte leads to the porticoed court of honour (16th century), which still has its original herringbone pattern paving. The garden behind this boasts an admirable Neo-Classical façade designed by Giacomo Tazzini (1826).

The palazzo is open to the public and features many interestingly decorated rooms and fine works of art, such as the wooden 17th-century globe by Giovanni Jacopo de Rossi. The most important room is the Giunta (Council Chamber), which in 1954 became the home of Tiepolo's masterful *Triumph of Doge Morosini*, which came from Palazzo Morosini in Venice. The Sala dell'Antegiunta has a lovely 18th-century Murano glass chandelier, while the Sala degli Affreschi boasts 17th-century frescoes taken from the villa of Cardinal Monti at Vaprio d'Adda. The Studio del Presidente is decorated with a Neo-Classical ceiling, partly in fine gold. In 1940 the Province of Milan enlarged the palazzo. The new façade on Via Vivaio was decorated with bas-reliefs sculpted by Salvatore Saponaro depicting the activities of the Milanese. At No. 31 Corso Monforte is the Palazzo della Prefettura, rebuilt in its present state in 1782. It has frescoes by Andrea Appiani. It is not open to the public.

The 18th-century façade of Palazzo Isimbardi, in Corso Monforte

Abbazia di Chiaravalle ⓯

French Cistercian monks began constructing this church in 1150–60 and it was dedicated to the Virgin Mary in 1221. The complex is a combination of French Gothic and Lombard Romanesque, resulting in a delightful example of Cistercian architecture. The bell tower was added in 1349. The entrance is in the 16th-century tower flanked by two small churches. In 1798 Napoleon suppressed the monastic order, the monks were forced to leave and the abbey deteriorated so much that in 1861 Bramante's 15th-century cloister was demolished to make room for a railway line. Restored and given back to the monks, the abbey has regained its former splendour and is again an oasis of peace.

★ Frescoes
The 14th-century frescoes on the dome narrate The Legend of the Virgin. *Those in the transept (above), represent among other things the genealogical tree of the Benedictine monks.*

★ Wooden Choir
The 44 stalls have carvings of the Life of St Bernard *by Carlo Garavaglia (1645), who according to legend took refuge in the abbey to expiate the murder of his brother.*

The interior had no paintings because this would have distracted the monks from their prayers. The 17th-century frescoes tell the story of the order.

Entrance

The top of the façade, made of brick, is what remains of the original. The porch was added in 1625. The 16th-century main portal has figures of Cistercian saints, including St Bernard holding the church in his hand.

THE MONKS' LAND RECLAMATION

The Cistercian monasteries were based on the rule of *ora et labora* – prayer and labour – and played a crucial role in reclaiming the marshy Milanese terrain, which thanks to the monks became extremely fertile. They used the new water meadow technique, which consisted in flooding the meadows with water from an adjoining stream (kept at a constant temperature of 12° C/54° F) so that the grass would grow quickly and could be harvested even in winter.

A Cistercian monk at work in the garden

★ Bell Tower (ciribiciaccola)
Eighty small marble columns adorn the bell tower designed by Francesco Pecorari in 1329–40. Called ciribiciaccola *(clever contraption) by the Milanese, its bells accompanied the farmers' and monks' working day. The tower bell rope still hangs in the church.*

VISITORS' CHECKLIST

Via Sant'Arialdo 102, Chiaravalle Milanese. **Tel** 02-57 40 34 04. M 3 Corvetto, then bus 77. 77. 9am–noon, 2:30–5:30pm Tue–Sat; 2:30–5pm Sun. 8, 9:15 (Gregorian chant) & 11am, 5:30pm hols; 8am, 5:30pm Mon–Sat. (no flash). 4pm Sun.

The many windows (double, triple and quadruple lancet) lend movement to the tower structure.

Madonna della Buonanotte
Painted in 1512 by Bernardino Luini at the top of the steps leading to the dormitory, this picture is known as the Madonna della Buonanotte *because she "said goodnight" to the monks going to bed.*

The chapter house, designed in the late 15th century by Bramante, has three graffiti from that period depicting Santa Maria delle Grazie, the Duomo and Castello Sforzesco.

Refectory

★ Cloister
Rebuilt in 1952 by using the one surviving side as a model, the cloister has a plaque commemorating the founding of the church, next to which is a stork, the symbol of Chiaravalle.

STAR FEATURES

★ Wooden Choir

★ Cloister

★ Bell Tower (ciribiciaccola)

★ Frescoes

NORTHEAST MILAN

Elegant Via Manzoni is the heart of a vast area stretching from the Brera quarter to Via Montenapoleone and Corso Venezia. Brera is known for its characteristic winding streets, some of which still have their 18th-century paving. The fashion district around Via Montenapoleone is the domain of the designer shops. Starting from Piazza San Babila and continuing

Logo of the Museo Bagatti Valsecchi

through Corso Venezia, with its many aristocratic palazzi, you will come to the Giardini Pubblici and the Villa Reale, home of the Modern Art Gallery. The area extending beyond the ramparts, which was undeveloped up to the early 19th century, includes the Cimitero Monumentale, the Stazione Centrale (main railway station) and the Pirelli building, Milan's tallest.

KEY

▨	Street-by-Street map See pp106–107
▨	Street-by-Street map See pp110–111
M	Metro station
R	Railway station
S	Passante Ferroviario station
i	Tourist information
🚖	Taxi

GETTING THERE

Metro line 3 (Montenapoleone) and tram 1 go to the fashion area and Brera quarter, which is also served by metro line 2 (Lanza), bus 61 and trams 2, 4, 12 and 14. The Cimitero Monumentale is served by bus 37 and trams 4, 7, 12 and 14, while metro lines 2 and 3 stop at the Stazione Centrale.

SIGHTS AT A GLANCE

Churches
San Marco **6**
San Simpliciano **10**
Sant'Angelo **11**
Santa Maria del Carmine **9**
Santa Maria Incoronata **12**

Streets, Squares and Historic Buildings
Archi di Porta Nuova **5**
Bastioni di Porta Venezia **16**

Corso Venezia see pp122–3 **21**
Palazzo Cusani **8**
Pirelli Building **14**
Stazione Centrale **15**
Via Manzoni **1**

Museums and Galleries
Museo Bagatti Valsecchi **3**
Museo di Storia Naturale **18**
Museo Poldi Pezzoli **2**

Palazzo Morando – Costume Moda Immagine **4**
Pinacoteca di Brera see pp114–17 **7**
Planetarium **17**
Villa Belgiojoso Galleria d'Arte Moderna **20**

Gardens and Cemeteries
Cimitero Monumentale **13**
Giardini Pubblici **19**

◁ **Statue of Napoleon by Canova (1809), in the middle of the Brera art gallery courtyard**

Street-by-Street: the Fashion District

Versace logo

Via Montenapoleone represents the elegant heart of Milan and is one of the four sides of the so-called *quadrilatero* or fashion district (the other three sides are Via Manzoni, Via Sant'Andrea and Via della Spiga). When strolling through this district, besides the shops of some of the top Italian and international fashion designers, you will see grand Neo-Classical aristocratic residences such as Palazzo Melzi di Cusano, at No. 18 Via Montenapoleone, built in 1830. Via Bigli, on the other hand, is lined with 16th- and 17th-century palazzi with porticoed courtyards.

Archi di Porta Nuova
This city gate, once part of the medieval walls, is decorated with copies of 1st-century AD Roman tombstones. Left, a stele representing a family ❺

VALENTINO

GIORGIO ARMANI

Via Manzoni
This broad street is lined with aristocratic palazzi ❶

Grand Hotel et de Milan

Under the Portico del Lattèe (milkman's arcade) is the wall of the demolished church of San Donnino alla Mazza.

★ **Museo Poldi Pezzoli**
The Portrait of a Young Lady (15th century), attributed to Antonio Pollaiolo, is the symbol of this museum created by Gian Giacomo Poldi Pezzoli. Besides paintings by Mantegna, Piero della Francesca and Bellini, it has rugs, armour and precious ceramics ❷

VIA DELLA SPIG

VIA BORGOSPESSO

VIA SANTO SPIRITO

VIA MANZONI

STAR SIGHTS

★ Museo Poldi Pezzoli

★ Museo Bagatti Valsecchi

0 metres	50
0 yards	50

★ Museo Bagatti Valsecchi
This Neo-Renaissance palazzo was built as the family residence by the Bagatti Valsecchi brothers. It still has 16 rooms with their original 19th-century furnishings and many works of art belonging to the owners, who were art collectors ❸

LOCATOR MAP
See Street Finder, map 4

DOLCE & GABBANA

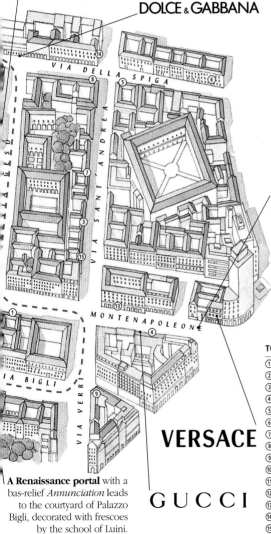

Via Montenapoleone follows the course of the ancient Roman walls. It gets its name from a bank that once stood here called "Monte Napoleone". Designer shops line the street.

KEY

– – – Suggested route

TOP FASHION DESIGNERS

① **A Ferretti** Via Montenapoleone 18.
② **Byblos** Via della Spiga 33.
③ **Chanel** Via Sant'Andrea 10.
④ **Etro** Via Montenapoleone 5.
⑤ **Fendi** Via Sant'Andrea 16.
⑥ **Genny** Via della Spiga 30.
⑦ **Gianfranco Ferrè** Via Sant'Andrea 15.
⑧ **Hermès** Via Sant'Andrea 21.
⑨ **Jil Sander** Via P Verri 6.
⑩ **Krizia** Via della Spiga 23.
⑪ **Laura Biagiotti** Via Borgospesso 19.
⑫ **Marni** Via della Spiga 50.
⑬ **Missoni** Via Montenapoleone 8.
⑭ **Prada** Via Sant'Andrea 21.
⑮ **Trussardi** Via Sant'Andrea 5.

VERSACE

GUCCI

A Renaissance portal with a bas-relief *Annunciation* leads to the courtyard of Palazzo Bigli, decorated with frescoes by the school of Luini.

The inner garden of a palazzo
in Via Manzoni

Via Manzoni ❶

Map 4 D4. Ⓜ 1 Duomo,
3 Montenapoleone. 🚋 1. 🚌 61, 94.
Palazzi not open for visitors.

Once known as "Corsia del
Giardino" (Garden Lane)
because of its many parks,
this street acquired its present
name in 1865, when the great
Italian novelist Manzoni died.
Its aristocratic appearance is
created by the patrician
palazzi and Teatro alla Scala
(see pp52–3), which stimula-
ted the opening of chic cafés
attracting a smart clientele. At
No. 6 is 19th-century Palazzo
Brentani, decorated with
medallions with busts of
illustrious persons, and
No. 10 is Palazzo Anguissola
(1775–8), which now houses
the historic archive of the
Banca Commerciale Italiana.
No. 12, another 19th-century
building, is the home of the
famous Museo Poldi Pezzoli,
and No. 29 is the Grand Hotel
et de Milan (1865), where
Giuseppe Verdi died in 1901.

Near the end of Via Montenapoleone stands Aldo Rossi's
monument to former Italian
President Sandro Pertini
(1990) and, next to this,
Palazzo Gallarati Scotti (No.
30), built in the early 1700s.
Opposite, Via Pisoni takes
you to the remains of the
15th-century cloister of the
Umiliate di Sant'Erasmo monastery, now part of a modern
building. In the last stretch is
18th-century Palazzo Borromeo d'Adda, which was a
haunt for literati and artists,
including Stendhal.

Museo Poldi Pezzoli ❷

Via Manzoni 12. **Map** 4 D5. **Tel** 02-
79 48 89. Ⓜ 3 Montenapoleone.
🚋 1. 🚌 61, 94. ◷ 10am–6pm
Wed–Mon (last adm: 5:30pm). ◐ 1
Jan, Easter, 25 Apr, 1 May, 15 Aug,
1 Nov, 8, 25 & 26 Dec. 🎟 📷 (no
flash). ♿ 📖 Lecture hall, Library.
🌐 www.museopoldipezzoli.it

This private museum was
established by nobleman Gian
Giacomo Poldi Pezzoli and
opened to the public in 1881.
The museum, a singular
example of a late 19th-century
aristocratic Milanese
residence, contains Poldi
Pezzoli's fine collection of
paintings,
sculpture, rugs,
armour, glass,
watches and
textiles. The
ground floor
houses arms
and armour from
the 14th to the 19th
century in a setting designed
by artist Arnaldo Pomodoro.
The Fresco Room, named
after The Apotheosis of Bartolomeo Colleoni frescoed by
Carlo Innocenzo Carloni,
boasts a Tabriz carpet with
hunting scenes (Persia, 1542–3).
In the adjoining room is the
museum's collection of lace.

The staircase, decorated
with landscapes by Magnasco,
leads to the first floor. In the
Lombard Rooms is
15th–16th-century
Lombard painting,
with works by
Bergognone, Luini,
the Leonardo-
esque painters,
a Polyptych by
Cristoforo Moretti,
and Vincenzo
Foppa's Portrait of
Giovanni Francesco
Brivio. The portraits
of Martin Luther
and his wife by
Lucas Cranach
(1529) are in the
Foreign Artists
Room. A showcase
of precious
porcelain separates
the next room from
the Golden Room,
where masterpieces
are on display.

Poldi Pezzoli
Museum logo

These include St Nicholas of
Tolentino by Piero della
Francesca, Botticelli's
Madonna and Child and
Lamentation, a Madonna and
Child by Andrea Mantegna,
Giovanni Bellini's Pietà and
the Portrait of a Young
Woman attributed to Piero
del Pollaiolo. Three small
rooms house the Visconti
Venosta collection, the
portraits by Fra Galgario,
including The Gentleman
with the Tricorn and a very
important collection of clocks
from the 16th to the 19th
century. The Murano Glass
Room has fine specimens of
Venetian glasswork, and the
Dante Study features two
stained-glass
windows
celebrating
Dante's life. The
last rooms
house paintings
by Tiepolo,
Guardia, Canaletto
and 14th-century
panels. Lastly, the Jewellery
Room hosts a collection of
precious jewellery and
goldsmithery from antiquity to
the 19th century.

On some Wednesdays the
museum organizes a "happy
hour" between 6 and 9pm.
The €9 fee includes admission
to the museum and a drink to
enjoy while taking in the
exhibits. Check the museum
website for further details.

Botticelli's Pietà (1495), Museo Poldi Pezzoli

A cradle from the Camera Rossa in the Museo Bagatti Valsecchi

Museo Bagatti Valsecchi ❸

Via Gesù 5. **Map** 4 D5.
Tel 02-76 00 61 32. Ⓜ 3 Monte-napoleone. 🚊 1. 🚌 94.
🕐 1–5:45pm Tue–Sun. ● 1 & 6 Jan, Easter, 25 Apr, 1 May, 2 Jun, 15 Aug, 7, 8, 25 & 26 Dec. 🏷️ 🚻 ground floor only. 📷 by appt. 🏠 www.museobagattivalsecchi.org

Opened in 1994 in the prestigious late 19th-century residence of the two Bagatti Valsecchi brothers, Fausto and Giuseppe, this fascinating museum is an important record of art collectors' taste in that period. The building was designed in Neo-Renaissance style, with an elegant façade and two well proportioned courtyards, and was furnished with works of art and imitation Renaissance furniture. It was seen as a private house and not a museum, and was furnished with every possible comfort. The rooms feature tapestries, ivory work, ceramics and arms, as well as important paintings such as the elegant *Santa Giustina* by Giovanni Bellini (c.1475; kept in what was Giuseppe Bagatti Valsecchi's bedroom), Bernardo Zenale's panels and a *Polyptych* by Giampietrino. The library, with its valuable 15th-century parchments and a series of 16th–17th-century porcelain pharmacy vases, is also worth a look.

The intriguing Valtellinese bedroom has a magnificent 16th-century bed with Christ ascending Calvary and scenes from the Old Testament carved in the bedstead.

The Sala della Stufa Valtellinese is also interesting, with its marvellous 16th-century wood panelling with an elegant sculpted frieze and a piece of furniture ingeniously concealing a piano. The Camera Rossa contains a delightful small collection of 15th–17th-century furniture for children that includes a high chair, a baby walker and a cradle. The dining room has a collection of kitchenware, tapestries and sideboards.

Palazzo Morando – Costume Moda Immagine ❹

Via Sant'Andrea 6. **Map** 4 D5.
Tel 02-88 46 59 33. Ⓜ 1 San Babila, 3 Montenapoleone. 🚊 1, 2. 🚌 94.
🕐 9am–1pm, 2–5:30pm Tue–Sun.
● 1 Jan, 1 May, 25 Dec. **www.** costumemodaimagine.it

Appropriately located in the Fashion District (Quadrilatero della Moda), Milan's Museum of Costume can be found in an 18th-century aristocratic townhouse that displays the elegant style of the time with its original furnishings.

The collection illustrates the history of Milanese fashion from the 18th to the 20th century, combining the costumes and accessories of the Municipal Collections of Applied Arts, (which used to be stored at the Castello Sforzesco) with the contents of the former Museum of Milan. The paintings and artifacts displayed alongside the costumes on the first floor reveal the extensive heritage of the city's art in its various forms.

On the ground floor are temporary exhibits connected with the history of Milan's fashion. Documentaries are screened at the museum, and concerts are also held here.

Archi di Porta Nuova ❺

Map 4 D4. Ⓜ 3 Montenapoleone. 🚊 1. 🚌 61, 94.

This city gate, restored in 1861, is one of two surviving ones forming part of the medieval wall system. Construction began in 1171, and the gate was probably modelled on the corresponding Porta Romana, some of whose building materials it used. The inner side on Via Manzoni is decorated with copies of 1st-century AD Roman tombstones, while the outside facing Piazza Cavour bears a tabernacle decorated with a *Madonna and Child with Saints Ambrose, Gervase and Protasius* (1330–39).

Facing the piazza is Palazzo dei Giornali (No. 2), built in 1942 as the main office of the newspaper *Il Popolo d'Italia* and decorated with bas-reliefs by Mario Sironi. The square is framed by the Giardini Pubblici, in front of which is a monument to Cavour by Odoardo Tabacchi (1865).

The Porta Nuova arches seen from Via Manzoni

Street-by-Street: the Brera Quarter

The name of Milan's traditional Bohemian quarter derives from the Germanic word *braida,* which denoted a grassy area. The presence of art students at the Accademia di Belle Arti and the world-famous Brera art gallery has contributed to the lively feel of this quarter, which is reinforced by the many cafés, restaurants, galleries, antique shops and night-clubs established here. In summer the narrow streets are enlivened even more by street stalls and fortune tellers. An antiques market is held on the third Saturday of each month in Via Brera.

The Indian Café is one of the most popular spots in the area.

The Museo Minguzzi has 100 pieces by the Bolognese sculptor.

The Naviglio della Martesana canal flowed from the Adda river and along present-day Via San Marco. It was used for transporting foodstuffs and building materials. At the end of the street is the Tombone di San Marco, a wooden canal lock that regulated the water flow.

★ **San Simpliciano**
This church was one of the four basilicas founded by Sant'Ambrogio and has preserved most of its original Early Christian architecture ⑩

Inside the Jamaica café, in Via Brera

CAFE LIFE IN THE BRERA

The cafés and bars of the Brera quarter are lively and atmospheric, many with live music. The Tombon de San Marc (Via San Marco) was once the haunt of the stevedores from the nearby Naviglio and now welcomes customers of all kinds. The famous Jamaica café (Via Brera) has jazz sessions on Mondays. Other atmospheric spots are Sans Égal, in the pedestrian precinct of Via Fiori Chiari and the Indian Café (Corso Garibaldi), which turns into a disco-pub in the evening *(see pp186–7 and pp198–9).*

| 0 metres | 100 |
| 0 yards | 100 |

STAR SIGHTS

★ Pinacoteca di Brera

★ San Simpliciano

★ San Marco

★ San Marco

The façade of this church, founded in 1254, was rebuilt in 1871 in Neo-Gothic style. The only remaining part of the original is the stone doorway, which has a relief of Christ between two saints and among symbols of the Evangelists ❻

LOCATOR MAP
See Street Finder, maps 3, 4

The Civico Museo del Risorgimento, opened in 1896, is in Neo-Classical Palazzo Moriggia.

★ Pinacoteca di Brera

The nucleus of one of Italy's top art galleries consists of works taken from churches that were suppressed in the late 1700s. The Brera boasts masterpieces by great artists such as Piero della Francesca, Mantegna, Raphael and Caravaggio ❼

Palazzo Cusani

This building with a late Baroque façade (1719) is the headquarters of the Third Army Corps. On the first floor is the Officers' Club ❽

Santa Maria del Carmine

The 15th-century church was built with material taken from the nearby Castello Sforzesco when it was partly demolished ❾

VIA FATEBENEFRATELLI
VIA BORGONUOVO
VIA BRERA
CHIARI
VIA MADONNINA
VIA PONTE VETERO
VIA DELL' ORSO

EY
– – – Suggested route

The lunette over the entrance to San Marco

San Marco ❻

Piazza San Marco 2. **Map** 3 C4.
Tel 02-29 00 25 98. 🚌 61, 94.
🕐 7am–noon, 4–7pm daily.
⛪ 7:45, 9:30am, 6:30pm Mon–Fri;
6:30pm pre-hols; 9:30am, noon,
6:30pm hols.

This church was begun in
1254 by the Augustine monk
Lanfranco Settala. It was built
on the site of an older church,
dedicated by the Milanese to St
Mark, patron saint of Venice,
to thank the Venetians for help
in the struggle against Emperor Frederick Barbarossa. In
1871 Carlo Maciachini built a
new, Neo-Gothic façade
around the Campionese school
ogival portal and tabernacle.

The church has a Latin
cross plan and nine patrician
chapels, which were added
to the right-hand aisle in the
14th–19th century. They
con-tain 16th–17th-century
paintings, including some by
Paolo Lomazzo. In the right-
hand transept is the
*Foundation of the Augustine
Order* by the Fiammenghino
brothers, Settala's sarcophagus
by Gio-vanni Balduccio
(1317–49), and fragments of
late Gothic frescoes found
during the 1956 restoration.
The presby-tery is decorated
with large canvases by
Camillo Procaccini and
Cerano depicting the Legend
of St Augustine, and the
Genealogical Tree of the Order
by Genovesino (17th century),
who also painted the *Angels'
Backs* on the cupola. The left-
hand transept leads to the
Chapel of the Pietà, with *The
Ascent to Calvary* by Ercole
Procaccini. The left-hand aisle
has canvases by Camillo and
Giulio Cesare Procaccini and
Palma il Giovane, and a

Leonardoesque fresco found in
1975. From outside the Romanesque transept the 13th-century
bell tower is visible.

Pinacoteca di Brera ❼

See pp114–17.

Palazzo Cusani ❽

Via Brera 15. **Map** 3 C4.
Ⓜ 2 Lanza. 🚋 2, 12, 14.
🚌 61. 🕐 to the public.

Originally built in the
1500s, this palazzo was
rebuilt in 1719 by Giovanni
Ruggeri, who designed the
late Baroque façade with its
ornate windows and balco-
nies, while the Neo-Classical
façade facing the garden
was designed by Piermarini.
Tradition has it that the
Cusani brothers ordered
twin entrances so that each
could have independent yet
equal access. In the drawing
room is an allegorical
Tiepolo-like fresco (1740).
The palazzo was the seat of
the Ministry of War in the
19th century.

Santa Maria del Carmine ❾

Piazza del Carmine 2. **Map** 3 B4.
Tel 02-86 46 33 65. 🚋 1, 2, 12,
14. 🚌 57, 61. 🕐 7:15–11:30am,
3:30–7pm daily. ⛪ 8am (except Sat),
9:30am, 6:30pm Mon–Sat; 5pm
(Eng) Thu; 8:30am (Eng and Tagalog),
10:30am (Eng), 11:30am, 4:30pm &
6:30pm (Eng and Tagalog) Sun.

Santa Maria del Carmine was
built in Gothic style in 1447
over a Romanesque church

and was then rebuilt in the
Baroque period, while the
present-day façade was
designed by Carlo Maciachini
in 1880. The spacious interior
has a three-aisle nave covered
by cross vaulting. The
inclination of the first piers
is due to the absence of a
façade for a long period
and the subsequent gradual
settling of the building.

The right-hand transept
contains part of the tomb of
the Ducal Councillor Angelo
Simonetta, above which are
two paintings by Carlo
Francesco Nuvolone and
Fiammenghino; the
opposite transept
is decorated with
a painting by
Camillo Landriani.

The statues
in the wooden
choir (1579–85)
are the original
plaster models
created for the
spires of the
Duomo by
19th-century artists.
The Cappella del
Rosario, built on
the right of the
choir (1673) by
Gerolamo Quadrio, has
marble dressing and is
decorated with canvases by
Camillo Procaccini depicting
The Legend of Mary.

On the left-hand side of
the church is the monastery
cloister, with remains of
noble tombs and ancient
tombstones, and a Baroque
sacristy, with furniture made
by Quadrio in 1692.

A statue in
the choir

Part of the Baroque sacristy, Santa
Maria del Carmine

Angel Musicians by Aurelio Luini (16th century), in the church of San Simpliciano

San Simpliciano ⑩

Piazza San Simpliciano 7. **Map** 3 B4.
Tel 02-86 22 74. Ⓜ 2 Lanza. 🚋 2, 4, 12, 14. 🚌 43, 57, 61. ⃝ 9am–noon, 2:15–7pm Mon–Fri; 9:30am–7pm Sat & Sun. ✝ 7:30am (Sep–Jun), 6pm Mon–Fri; 6pm pre-hols; 8am (Sep–Jun), 8 (except Jul & Aug), 10 & 11:30am, 6pm hols.

The church was founded by Sant'Ambrogio in the 4th century as the *Basilica Virginum* and completed in 401. It is preceded by a porch and once had open galleries on either side where penitents and new converts could take part in Mass. The façade, decorated with glazed plates, was added in 1870 by Maciachini, who retained the main portal. The capitals have 12th-century carvings of the processions of the Wise and Foolish Virgins. Fourteenthcentury frescoes have been discovered in the first chapel on the right, and in the fourth is Enea Salmeggia's *Miracle of St Benedict* (1619). The apse is frescoed with the *Coronation of the Virgin* by Bergognone (1508). The Neo-Classical altar covers

the wooden choir (1588), and on either side are two organ pedestals frescoed by Aurelio Luini in the 1500s. The transept leads to the Early Christian Sacellum of San Simpliciano (closed), built to house the remains of San Simpliciano and of martyrs.

Sant'Angelo ⑪

Piazza Sant'Angelo 2. **Map** 4 D3.
Tel 02-63 24 81. 🚋 43. 🚌 94. ⃝ 6:30am–8pm daily. ✝ 7, 8, 10am & 7pm Mon–Sat; 10, 11am, 12:15 & 7pm hols.

Built in 1552 by Domenico Giunti to replace the older Franciscan church outside the Porta Nuova, which had been demolished to make room for the Spanish ramparts, Sant'Angelo is an important example of 16th-century Milanese architecture. The nave is separated from the presbytery by a triumphal arch with the *Assumption of Mary* by Legnanino (17th century). There are many 16th- and 17th-century paintings in the chapels. The first one on the right has canvases by Antonio Campi (1584) and a copy of

the *Martyrdom of St Catherine of Alexandria* by Gaudenzio Ferrari (the original is in the Brera); the second has Morazzone's *St Charles in Glory*.

Santa Maria Incoronata ⑫

Corso Garibaldi 116. **Map** 3 C2.
Tel 02-65 48 55. Ⓜ 2 Garibaldi. 🚌 43, 70, 94. ⃝ 7:15am–1:30pm, 4–7pm Mon–Fri, 8am–12.30pm, 4–7:30pm Sat–Sun. ✝ 7:30 & 9:30am, 6:30pm Mon–Fri, 9:30am–6:30pm Sat; 8:30, 10 & 11:30am, 6:30pm hols.

This church consists of two buildings designed by Guiniforte Solari, which were merged in 1468. The left one was built for Francesco Sforza in 1451 and the other was built soon afterwards for his wife. The brick façade is double, as is the nave, which has two apses with 15th and 17th-century frescoes. In the right-hand chapels are plaques in memory of Sforzesco court personages. The chapels opposite have frescoes by Montalto and Bernardino Zenale (the fresco in the first chapel is attributed to Zenale).

Lunette over one of the doors of San Simpliciano

SAN SIMPLICIANO, THE THREE MARTYRS AND THE CARROCCIO

St Ambrose asked the young Sisinius, Martirius and Alexander to go to Anaunia (today Val di Non) in northern Italy to spread Christianity. In 397 they were martyred and the bodies were given to Bishop Simpliciano, who buried them in the *Basilica Virginum*.
According to legend, the martyrs were decisive in leading the Milanese to victory in the battle of Legnano against Barbarossa (1176). On that occasion three white doves flew out of the basilica and landed on the Carroccio (cart), the symbol of Milan, waiting to be blessed before the battle. On 29 May the city commemorates this event with a solemn ceremony.

Pinacoteca di Brera ❼

The Brera art gallery holds one of Italy's most important art collections, featuring masterpieces by leading Italian artists from the 13th to the 20th centuries, including Raphael, Mantegna, Piero della Francesca and Caravaggio. The Pinacoteca is housed in the late 16th–early 17th-century palazzo built for the Jesuits in place of the Santa Maria di Brera Humiliati monastery. The Jesuits made this into a cultural centre by establishing a prestigious school, a library and the astronomical observatory – all activities supported by Empress Maria Theresa of Austria, who founded the Accademia di Belle Arti after the Jesuit order was suppressed (1773).

Portrait of Moisè Kisling
Amedeo Modigliani painted this work in 1915, reflecting his interest in African sculpture. (Room 10

Finding the Body of St Mark
The bold perspective and almost super-natural light in the room where the saint's body is found make this canvas (1562–6) one of Tintoretto's masterpieces. (Room 9)

Mocchirolo Chapel

Twin staircases lead to the entrance to the gallery on the first floor.

KEY

- ☐ Jesi Collection (20th-century art)
- ☐ 13th–15th-century Italian painting
- ☐ 15th–16th-century Venetian painting
- ☐ 15th–16th-century Lombard painting
- ☐ 15th–16th-century Central Italian painting
- ☐ 17th–18th-century Italian, Flemish and Dutch painting
- ☐ 18th–19th-century Italian painting

The Kiss
This canvas by Francesco Hayez (1859) is one of the most reproduced 19th-century Italian paintings – a patriotic and sentimental work epitomizing the optimism that prevailed after Italy's unification. (Room 37)

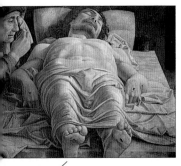

★ **Dead Christ**
This masterpiece by Mantegna (c.1480) is striking for its intense light and bold foreshortening. The work was among the artist's possessions at the time of his death. (Room 6)

VISITORS' CHECKLIST

Via Brera 28.
Map 3 C4. **Tel** *02-72 26 31.*
Info 02-89 42 11 46.
🅜 *1, 3 Duomo, 2 Lanza.*
🚎 *1, 4, 12, 14, 27.* 🚌 *61.*
⏱ *8:30am–7:15pm Tue–Sun*
(last adm: 45 mins before closing). ⬤ *Mon, 1 Jan, 1 May, 25 Dec.* 🔲 🚫 ♿ 🅿
www.brera.beniculturali.it

Room 15 has works by painters active in Lombardy from the late 15th to the mid-16th century, including Bergognone, Luini, Bramantino and Vincenzo Foppa.

★ **Montefeltro Altarpiece**
Piero della Francesca painted this great work in 1475 for Federico da Montefeltro, the Duke of Urbino, who is portrayed dressed in a Milanese suit of armour. (Room 24)

The courtyard with twin columns is the work of Richini (17th century).

GALLERY GUIDE
The Brera Gallery has 38 rooms, with works arranged in chronological order. The only exception is Room 10, where the Jesi and Vitali collections are on display. It includes 20th-century works which will be exhibited elsewhere in future. The paintings are also grouped together by schools of painting (Venetian, Tuscan, Lombard, etc.). The Sala della Passione on the ground floor is used for temporary exhibitions.

STAR PAINTINGS

★ Dead Christ

★ The Marriage
  of the Virgin

★ Montefeltro
  Altarpiece

Entrance

★ **The Marriage of the Virgin**
Raphael signed and dated (1504) his masterful altarpiece on the temple in the background. Some scholars say the young man breaking the staff is a self-portrait of the artist. (Room 24)

Exploring the Pinacoteca di Brera

The original nucleus of the Brera Gallery consisted mainly of plaster casts and drawings used as models for the art students of the Accademia di Belle Arti (founded in 1776). This collection was augmented with works from suppressed churches in Northern Italy and was officially opened in 1809, the paintings being arranged in rows on the wall, from floor to ceiling. The Pinacoteca became independent from the Accademia in 1882, and its fine collection further expanded through 19th- and 20th-century donations. The gallery has always suffered from lack of space, but there are plans to use the adjacent Palazzo Citterio.

The City Rises (c.1910) by Umberto Boccioni

JESI COLLECTION

The 72 works donated by Emilio and Maria Jesi in 1976 and 1984 are on show in room 10. The collection, mostly by Italian artists, covers the 1910–40 period. Key works include *Portrait of Moisè Kisling* by Modigliani, Umberto Boccioni's *Brawl in the Galleria* (1911) and *The City Rises* (a study for the canvas now in the New York MOMA), Carlo Carrà's *The Metaphysical Muse* (1917) and still lifes by Giorgio Morandi, as well as sculpture by Medardo Rosso, Arturo Martini and Marino Marini.

13TH–15TH-CENTURY ITALIAN PAINTING

The section given over to 13th–15th-century Italian art (rooms 2–4) includes frescoes from the Oratory at Mocchirolo, painted by an unknown Lombard master in around 1365–70. Among the gold-background works are the *Santa Maria della Celestia Polyptych* by Lorenzo Veneziano (14th century), Ambrogio Lorenzetti's *Madonna and Child* and *Christ the Judge* by Giovanni da Milano. A fine example of the International Gothic style is the *Valle Romita Polyptych* by Gentile da Fabriano, flanked by Stefano da Verona's *Adoration of the Magi* (1435), in which the viola and carnation at the feet of Jesus symbolize his humility and the Passion.

15TH–16TH-CENTURY VENETIAN PAINTING

Rooms 5 and 6 feature works by 15th–16th-century artists active in the Veneto such as Giovanni d'Alemagna and Antonio Vivarini, who painted the *Praglia Polyptych* (1448). Room 6 also has Mantegna's masterpieces *Dead Christ* and *St Luke Altarpiece* (1453–4). Giovanni Bellini is represented by two Madonnas with Child and a *Pietà* (c.1470), and Carpaccio by *Legend of the Virgin*. There are portraits by Titian, Lotto and Tintoretto in room 7. *St Mark Preaching in Alexandria* (room 8) was painted for the Scuola Grande in St Mark's in Venice by Giovanni and Gentile Bellini.

The following room has works by Titian and Paolo Veronese, as well as the *Finding of the Body of St Mark*, which Tintoretto painted for Tommaso Rangone, who is portrayed as the kneeling man in the middle of the scene.

15TH–16TH-CENTURY LOMBARD PAINTING

A large collection of 15th–16th-century Lombard paintings is exhibited in rooms 15, 18 and 19. The leading figure, Vincenzo Foppa, is represented by the *Polittico delle Grazie* (c.1483). An unknown master contributed the *Sforzesca Altarpiece* (1494), showing Lodovico il Moro and his family worshipping the Madonna. This room also has works by Bergognone, Gaudenzio Ferrari – an artist with a marked narrative vein, as can be seen in *Martyrdom of St Catherine* – and Bramantino's *Crucifixion*. Works influenced by Leonardo

Gentile da Fabriano's *Valle Romita Polyptych*

Supper at Emmaus, **painted by Caravaggio in 1606**

da Vinci include the small paintings for private chapels by De Predis and Luini (*Madonna del Roseto*), while the Cremona area is represented by names such as Boccaccino, Campi and Piazza.

15TH–16TH-CENTURY CENTRAL ITALIAN PAINTING

Rooms 20–23 illustrate artistic movements in the regions of Emilia and Marche. The Ferrara school is represented by its leading artists, Cosmè Tura, Francesco del Cossa and Ercole de' Roberti (whose *Madonna and Child among Saints* was painted around 1480). Correggio's *Nativity* is a major Emilian school work, while painting in Le Marche is documented by the works of Carlo Crivelli, including his *Madonna della Candeletta* (1490–91), rich in symbols.

Room 24 houses the two best-known masterpieces in the Brera. Piero della Francesca's *Montefeltro Altarpiece* (c.1475), was commissioned by Federico da Montefeltro. The egg suspended from its shell is a symbol of the Creation and of the Immaculate Conception. Next is Raphael's splendid *Marriage of the Virgin (see p115).*

Christ at the Pillar is a rare painting by Bramante, while works by Bronzino and Genga represent Mannerism.

17TH–18TH-CENTURY ITALIAN, FLEMISH AND DUTCH PAINTING

Room 28 features works by the Bolognese school, founded by the Carracci, including Guido Reni and Guercino. The next room boasts a masterpiece by Caravaggio, *Supper at Emmaus* (1606), in which the appearance of Christ occurs in a setting illuminated only by the light emanating from Jesus's face. Lombard artists shown here are Cerano, Morazzone and Giulio Cesare Procaccini, who painted the *Martyrdom of Saints Rufina and Secunda* together. Baroque painting is represented by Pietro da Cortona and the still lifes of Baschenis. Among the non-Italian artists are Rubens (*Last Supper,* 1631–2), Van Dyck, Rembrandt (*Portrait of the Artist's Sister,* 1632), El Greco and Brueghel the Elder (*The Village*).

18TH–19TH-CENTURY ITALIAN PAINTING

The following rooms cover various genres in 18th-century Italian art. Large-scale religious paintings are displayed in room 34 with works by the Neapolitan Luca Giordano and two Venetians: Giovan Battista Tiepolo's *Madonna del Carmelo* (1721–7), intended to be viewed from the side, and Piazzetta's *Rebecca at the Well.*

Giacomo Ceruti (Il Pitochetto) represents "genre painting", which was popular in the 18th century. This is followed by Venetian *vedutismo,* views by Bernardo Bellotto, Guardi and Canaletto. The works of Bellotto and Canaletto are characterized by their bright light and precision of detail (the latter even used a camera obscura to help him render this "photographic" effect).

Portraiture is best exemplified by Fra Galgario (*Portrait of a Gentleman*).

A representative 19th-century painting is Andrea Appiani's Neo-Classical *Olympus,* while the Macchiaioli movement is on display with works by Silvestro Lega and Giovanni Fattori, among others. The Brera also has paintings by the leading exponent of Lombard Romanticism, Francesco Hayez: his famous *The Kiss* and several portraits. The gallery closes with Divisionist Giuseppe Pelizza da Volpedo's *The Flood* (1895–7), a hymn to the struggle of the working class, and an early version of his *Fourth Estate,* now on display at the Museo del Novecento (*see p54*).

Madonna della Candeletta by Crivelli

Cimitero Monumentale  🔞

Piazzale Cimitero Monumentale.
Map 3 A1. **Tel** 02-88 46 56 00.
🚊 3, 12, 14. 🚌 43, 70.
⭘ 8am–6pm Tue–Sun (to 1pm
hols; last entry 5:30pm). Free
map of the cemetery
available at the entrance.

Extending over an
area of 250,000
sq m (300,000 sq
yds), the Cimi-
tero Monumentale
was begun by
Carlo Maciachini in 1866.
The eclectic taste of the
time dictated the use of
various styles for the
cemetery, from mock-
Lombard Romanesque
to Neo-Gothic, with
touches of Tuscan
thrown in. The
linchpin of the
structure is the
Famedio *(Famae Aedes)*,
or House of Fame, a sort
of pantheon of illustrious
Milanese and non-Milanese
buried here. Author Alessandro
Manzoni, Luca Beltrami, the
architect who oversaw
restoration of the Castello
Sforzesco, the patriot Carlo
Cattaneo and the Nobel
Prize-winning poet Salvatore
Quasimodo all have tombs in
this cemetery. There are also
busts of Garibaldi, Verdi and
Cavour. The Romantic painter
Hayez lies in the crypt. A visit

**Sculpture by Fontana,
Cimitero Monumentale**

to the Cimitero Monumentale,
which is a kind of open-air
museum of art from the late
19th century to the present,
begins at the large square
inside, which contains the
tombs of important Milanese
figures. Around the square
are monumental shrines
and the Civico Mausoleo
Palanti, an enormous
mausoleum with a
crypt, used as an air
raid shelter in 1943.
Among its tombs
are those of
comic actor
Walter Chiari and
Hermann Einstein,
Albert's father. On the
terraces, to the left are
the Elisi (sculpted by
Francesco Penna, 1916)
and Morgagni tombs,
and an epigraph
by Mussolini
commemorating
a disastrous
aeroplane crash. In the
central avenue are two tombs
designed and sculpted by
Enrico Butti: that of Isabella
Casati, *Young Woman
Enraptured by a Dream,* a
typical Lombard realist work
(1890), and the Besenzanica
shrine with *Work* (1912). On
your right, you will come to
the monumental Toscanini
tomb (Bistolfi, 1909–11), built
for the conductor's son.

Among other monumental
tombs for major figures in
Milanese life are those of
Carlo Erba, Bocconi, Campari
and Falck. Many
famous sculptors
made pieces
for this place:
Leonardo Bistolfi,
Giacomo Manzù,
Odoardo Tabacchi,
Adolfo Wildt and
Lucio Fontana.
The two enclosures
beside the Famedio
are for Jews and
non-Catholics,
with the remains
of sculptor
Medardo Rosso,
publishers Arnoldo
Mondadori and
Ulrico Hoepli and
Jules Richard,
founder of the
Richard-Ginori
ceramics industry.

**The Pirelli Building, symbol of
Milan's postwar reconstruction**

Pirelli Building 🔞

Piazzale Duca d'Aosta-Via Pirelli.
Map 4 E1. Ⓜ 2, 3 Centrale. 🚊 2,
9, 33. 🚌 60, 82. ⬤ to the public.

The symbol of postwar
reconstruction in Milan, the
Pirelli Building, affectionately
called "Pirellone" (big Pirelli)
by the Milanese, was built in
1955–60. It was designed by
a group of leading architects
and engineers: Gio Ponti,
Antonio Fornaroli, Alberto
Rosselli, Giuseppe Valtolina,
Egidio Dell'Orto, Pier Luigi
Nervi and Arturo Danusso.
At 127.10 m (417 ft) high, it
was the largest reinforced
concrete skyscraper in the
world until the 1960s. The
slender, elegant edifice
occupies only 1,000 sq m
(1,200 sq yds) and stands
on the site where, in 1872,
Giovan Battista Pirelli built
his first tyre factory. The
skyscraper was constructed as
the Pirelli company's main
offices. Among the many
records established by the
"Pirellone" was that it was the
first building in Milan taller
than the Madonnina on the
Duomo (108.50 m, 356 ft). As
a token of respect, a small
statue of the Virgin Mary was
placed on the Pirelli roof.
Since 1979 the building has
been the headquarters of
the regional government of
Lombardy. Next door is the
luxurious Excelsior Hotel
Gallia, opened in the 1930s.

**The Cimitero Monumentale, with tombs and
shrines produced by famous sculptors**

The Stazione Centrale, with its spectacular iron and glass roof

Stazione Centrale ⓯

Piazzale Duca d'Aosta. **Map** 4 E1.
Ⓜ *2, 3 Centrale.* 🚊 *2, 5, 9, 33.*
🚌 *42, 60, 82, 90, 91, 92.*

Milan's main railway station is one of the largest and perhaps the most monumental in Europe. Ulisse Stacchini's project design was approved and ready in 1912, but construction work proved so slow that the building was not opened until 1931. The new railway station replaced one located in present-day Piazza della Repubblica.

The building is dressed in Aurisina stone, and was clearly inspired by the late Art Nouveau style in vogue in the early 20th century, in marked contrast with the austere 1930s architecture of the surrounding buildings.

The façade is 207 m (679 ft) wide and 36 m (118 ft) tall and is crowned by two winged horses. The large arcades link up with the Galleria dei Transiti, a gallery decorated with four medallions by Giannino Castiglioni representing Labour, Commerce, Science and Agriculture. In the large ticket office hall, flights of steps lead up to the huge departures and arrivals lobby, with tile panels representing the cities of Milan, Rome, Turin and Florence.

The massive building is a landmark in Milan and second only to the cathedral in size. There are numerous shops inside, and some are open 24 hours a day.

Bastioni di Porta Venezia ⓰

Map 4 E3. Ⓜ *1 Porta Venezia, 3 Repubblica.* 🚊 *5, 9, 29, 30.*

What is today a major road was once part of the walls built to defend the city in 1549–61 by the Spanish governor Ferrante Gonzaga. In 1789 the walls became a tree-lined avenue for walking and coach parking. The Porta Venezia ramparts, flanked by the Giardini Pubblici, link Piazza della Repubblica and Piazza Oberdan. The former was laid out in 1931 when the 19th-century railway station was demolished and rebuilt 800 m (2,624 ft) away and greatly enlarged to cope with increasing traffic resulting from the opening of the St Gotthard (1882) and Simplon (1906) passes through the Alps.

Not far from the piazza, in Via Turati, is the Palazzo della Permanente, designed by Luca Beltrami in 1885 as the home of the Permanent Fine Arts Exhibition and now used for temporary exhibitions.

Piazza Oberdan is dominated by Porta Venezia, the city gate rebuilt in 1828 on the site of the Spanish gate of the same name and used as a customs toll station. The two buildings are decorated with statues and reliefs concerning the history of Milan. Porta Venezia separates Corso Venezia and Corso Buenos Aires, a major commercial thoroughfare.

In 1488–1513, Lazzaro Palazzi chose a site beyond the gate to build the *lazzaretto*, a hospital for plague victims commissioned by Lodovico il Moro. The few remains from the 1880 demolition can be seen in Via San Gregorio. A slight detour from Piazza Oberdan towards Viale Piave will take you past some interesting Art Nouveau style buildings: Casa Galimberti, designed by Giovan Battista Bossi in 1903–4, decorated with wrought iron and panels of ceramic tiles, and the Hotel Diana Majestic.

Plaque commemorating the *lazzaretto*

Casa Galimberti, decorated with wrought iron and tile panels

Planetarium ⑰

Corso Venezia 57. **Map** 4 E4.
Tel 02–88 46 33 40. Ⓜ 1 Porta
Venezia-Palestro. 🚊 9. ⭕ Shows
9pm Tue & Thu; 3 & 4:30pm Sat &
Sun. 🈂️ 🗓️ ♿ **www.**
comunemilano.it/planetario

Donated to the city by the
publisher Ulrico Hoepli,
the Planetarium was built
in 1930 in Classical style
by Piero Portaluppi. The
projection hall features a
large hemispherical dome
(20 m (65 ft) in diameter),
with the skyline outlined
just as it was when the
Planetarium first opened,
and 300 swivelling seats to
gaze at the movements of
the stars in absolute comfort.
The multimedia projection
system reproduces the stars
as seen from any point on
Earth, whether in the past,
present or future.

In addition to the shows,
the Planetarium offers
guided tours aimed at
different levels of knowledge,
including tours for students of
the subject, and a lively
programme of scientific and
popular-level lectures on
astronomy. There are also
special events for students
on Sundays.

Museo di Storia Naturale ⑱

Corso Venezia 55. **Map** 4 E4.
Tel 02–88 46 33 37.
Ⓜ 1 Porta Venezia-Palestro.
🚊 9. ⭕ 9am–5:30pm (last adm:
5pm) Tue–Sun. 🌑 1 Jan, Easter,
1 May, 15 Aug, 25 Dec. 📷 ✏️ 🛍️
♿ Lecture hall, library.

The Giardini Pubblici, a rare area of greenery in Milan

The museum of Natural
History was founded in
1838 with the donation of
the Giuseppe de Cristoforis
and Giorgio Jan collections.
The building was constructed
in Neo-Romanesque style and
with terracotta decoration
in 1893 by Giovanni Ceruti.
The museum has a specialist
library holding more than
30,000 volumes, including
sections on mineralogy and
zoology. On the ground floor
are the mineralogy and
entomology collections, and
part of the Museo Settala,
which was created by a
canon named Manfredo. It
features a series of scientific
instruments and natural
history specimens of varied
provenance. In the
palaeontology halls there are
reconstructions of dinosaurs
such as the Triceratops and a
large Allosaurus skeleton. The
ground floor also has displays
of molluscs and insects. The
upper floor is reserved for
reptiles, cetaceans and
mammals. There are also
several reconstructions of

animal habitats and an area
dedicated specifically to
Italian fauna and protected
nature reserves in Italy.

Giardini Pubblici ⑲

Corso Venezia, Via Palestro,
Via Manin, Bastioni di Porta
Venezia. **Map** 4 E4. Ⓜ 1 Porta
Venezia-Palestro, 3 Repubblica-Turati.
🚊 1, 2, 9, 11, 29, 30. 🚌 94.
⭕ 6:30am–sunset daily.

The public gardens extend
for about 160,000 sq m
(192,000 sq yds) and form
the largest city park in Milan.
They were designed by
Piermarini in 1786 and
enlarged in 1857 by Giuseppe
Balzaretto, who annexed
Palazzo Dugnani and its
garden. Further changes were
made by Emilio Alemagna
after the international
exhibitions held in 1871–81.

The gardens are home to
a wide range of tree species,
including fir, beech, linden,
elm and an ancient plane
tree. In June, the gardens
play host to Orticola, an
annual plant and flower
market (see p37). Between
July and early September,
there are open-air screenings
of recent films.

The park is home to the
Padiglione del Caffè (1863),
now a nursery school, the
Museo di Storia Naturale and
the Planetarium. Also immersed
in the gardens is the popular
Bar Bianco. This Milan
institution has plenty of
outside seating and is open
daily from 8am to 7pm.

Reconstruction of a dinosaur skeleton, Museo di Storia Naturale

For hotels and restaurants in this area see pp162–3 and pp175–8

Villa Belgiojoso – Galleria d'Arte Moderna ⑳

Milan's modern art gallery is housed in a splendid Neo-Classical villa built by the Austrian architect Leopold Pollack in 1790 for Count Lodovico Barbiano di Belgioioso. It was lived in by Napoleon in 1802 and later by Marshal Radetzky. Furnishings and frescoes decorate the main floor; the top attraction here is the dining room, with a *Parnassus* by Appiani. The gallery is devoted to 19th-century art movements in Italy, from the Romanticism of Francesco Hayez and Il Piccio to Scapigliatura, and from Divisionism to Macchiaioli, with artists like Fattori and Lega.

VISITORS' CHECKLIST

Via Palestro 16. **Map** 4 E4.
Tel *02-88 44 59 57.* Ⓜ *1
Palestro.* 🚋 *1.* 🚌 *61, 94.*
⬜ *9am–1pm, 2–5:30pm Tue–
Sun (last adm: 5pm).* ● *1 Jan,
Easter, 1 May, 15 Aug, 25 Dec.*
♿ 📷 **www**.gam-milano.com
**Giardini di Villa Belgiojoso
Bonaparte** ⬜ *only to adults
accompanying children. 9am–
noon, 2–7pm daily (Mar, Oct: to
6pm, Nov–Feb: to 4pm).*

★ **Grassi Collection**
In 1956 Nedda Grassi donated this fine collection to the city in memory of her son Gino. It comprises rugs, Oriental objects d'art and 135 paintings, including foreign and Italian 19th- and 20th-century artists such as Van Gogh, Cézanne, Corot and Gauguin, Fattori, Lega, Balla, Boccioni and Morandi.

KEY

⬜ Vismara Collection

⬜ Romantic Art

⬜ Neo-Classical Art

⬜ Grassi Collection

Antonio Canova's
bronze of Napoleon
is displayed here.

Hebe by Canova
Inspired by ancient sculpture while reflecting contemporary ideals of beauty, this marble statue by Antonio Canova represents Hebe, goddess of youth.

The Reader
Federico Faruffini was a member of the bohemian Scapigliatura movement of the 19th century. This work displays modern flair, especially in the pose of the sitter, who is smoking a cigarette with her back towards the viewer.

STAR EXHIBIT

★ Grassi Collection

Corso Venezia ㉑

Formerly called Corso di Porta Orientale, this famous and popular street was named after the gate in the medieval walls corresponding to present-day Via Senato. The same name was given to the quarter, whose emblem is the lion on the column in front of the church of San Babila. Corso Venezia was lined with relatively few buildings and bordered by kitchen gardens and orchards until the mid-18th century, when the reforms carried out by Maria Theresa of Austria led to the construction of the numerous patrician palazzi that make this one of Milan's most elegant streets.

LOCATOR MAP
See Street Finder map 4

Three inner courtyards lead to the garden.

On the balustrade are statues of the *Dei Consenti* (the 12 chief Roman gods) by Pompeo Marchesi and Grazioso Rusca.

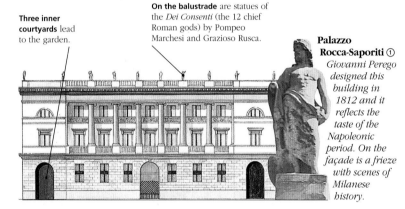

Palazzo Rocca-Saporiti ①
Giovanni Perego designed this building in 1812 and it reflects the taste of the Napoleonic period. On the façade is a frieze with scenes of Milanese history.

Palazzo Castiglioni ②
This palazzo was built by Giuseppe Somma-ruga in 1904. There were once two female nudes on the façade (later removed), hence its name Ca' di Ciapp (House of Buttocks).

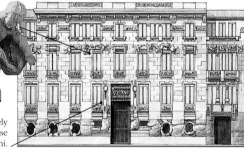

On the first floor is a lovely three-flight staircase and the Sala dei Pavoni.

A loggia with Ionic columns emphasizes the central section.

The side facing Via San Damiano has retained its original 17th-century features.

Palazzo Serbelloni ③
Completed in 1793 by Simone Cantoni, this palazzo played host to Napol-eon and Vittorio Emanuele.

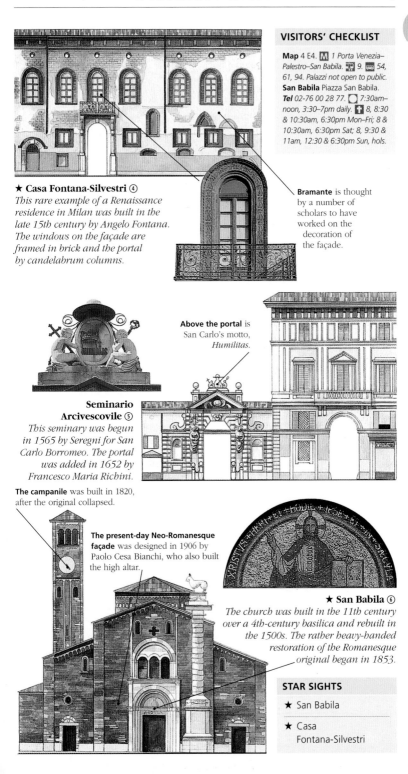

VISITORS' CHECKLIST

Map 4 E4. **M** 1 Porta Venezia–
Palestro–San Babila. 9. 54,
61, 94. Palazzi not open to public.
San Babila Piazza San Babila.
Tel 02-76 00 28 77. 7:30am–
noon, 3:30–7pm daily. 8, 8:30
& 10:30am, 6:30pm Mon–Fri; 8 &
10:30am, 6:30pm Sat; 8, 9:30 &
11am, 12:30 & 6:30pm Sun, hols.

★ **Casa Fontana-Silvestri** ④
*This rare example of a Renaissance
residence in Milan was built in the
late 15th century by Angelo Fontana.
The windows on the façade are
framed in brick and the portal
by candelabrum columns.*

Bramante is thought
by a number of
scholars to have
worked on the
decoration of
the façade.

Above the portal is
San Carlo's motto,
Humilitas.

**Seminario
Arcivescovile** ⑤
*This seminary was begun
in 1565 by Seregni for San
Carlo Borromeo. The portal
was added in 1652 by
Francesco Maria Richini.*

The campanile was built in 1820,
after the original collapsed.

**The present-day Neo-Romanesque
façade** was designed in 1906 by
Paolo Cesa Bianchi, who also built
the high altar.

★ **San Babila** ⑥
*The church was built in the 11th century
over a 4th-century basilica and rebuilt in
the 1500s. The rather heavy-handed
restoration of the Romanesque
original began in 1853.*

STAR SIGHTS

★ San Babila

★ Casa
  Fontana-Silvestri

TWO GUIDED WALKS IN MILAN

Most visitors travel around by Metro and come away with the impression that Milan offers little more than the Gothic-spired Duomo, the famed *Last Supper* and some chillingly expensive fashion boutiques. But by strolling around at a slower pace, you can find a Milan of great art, deep history and glorious monuments. The first walk investigates the hidden heart of Milan's historic centre, from church gems to fantastical façades tucked just off busy modern thoroughfares, and from designer boutiques to the elegant townhouses of Milan's 19th-century elite. The second walk examines the ages of Milan, from its Roman roots to Palaeochristian basilicas rich in mosaics and frescoes, and from the medieval Castello Sforzesco to Renaissance masterpieces by the likes of Bellini, Mantegna and Leonardo da Vinci. In fact, Leonardo pops up frequently on this walk in all his guises, from artist to inventor to engineer. The walk ends at the Navigli, a thriving restaurant and nightlife district based around the remnants of a canal system that the multi-talented Leonardo helped design.

A painting of La Scala

CHOOSING A WALK

The Two Walks
This map shows the location of the two guided walks in relation to the main sightseeing areas of Milan.

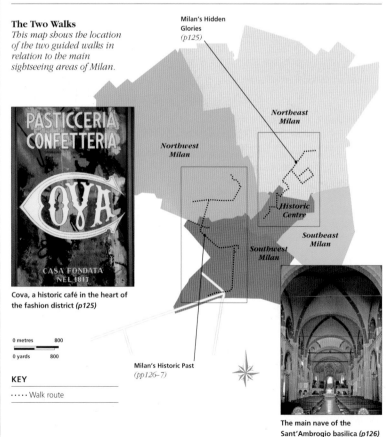

Milan's Hidden Glories *(p125)*

Northeast Milan

Northwest Milan

Historic Centre

Southeast Milan

Southwest Milan

PASTICCERIA CONFETTERIA
COVA
CASA FONDATA NEL 1817

Cova, a historic café in the heart of the fashion district *(p125)*

0 metres   800
0 yards   800

Milan's Historic Past *(pp126–7)*

KEY

····· Walk route

The main nave of the Sant'Ambrogio basilica *(p126)*

A 90-Minute Walk Around Milan's Hidden Glories

Milan's beauty is not immediately obvious. With a few exceptions, such as the Duomo and the Galleria, the city's glories are hidden. This walk takes in stunning Baroque façades lost amid bland buildings, and tours the fashion boutiques in the "Golden Rectangle".

Around the Duomo
Begin at the jewel-box church of Santa Maria presso San Satiro ① *(see p55)*, which is encased by modern buildings making it hard to find (it is down a short alley off Via Torino). A right down Via Speronari leads to its 10th-century bell tower. Leave the church, turn left up Via Mazzini into Piazza del Duomo ② *(see pp44–5)* and ascend to the cathedral's roof ③ *(see pp46–9)* for panoramic views. Descend and stop for a drink at the renowned Caffè Zucca ④ *(see p187)*, which lies near the entrance to the Galleria Vittorio Emanuele II ⑤ *(see p50)*, an imposing 19th-century shopping arcade. Stroll through its glass-roofed atrium, ensuring good luck by stomping on the testicles of the mosaic bull near the centre. Emerge at Piazza della Scala ⑥, for the splendid Teatro alla Scala opera house ⑦ *(see pp52–3)* and pay your respects to Verdi in the attached Museo Teatrale.

Cross the square and walk behind Palazzo Marino ⑧ *(see p50)* to the Counter-Reformation church of San Fedele ⑨ *(see p50)*. Head northeast along its left flank past the surreal Casa degli Omenoni ⑩ *(see p51)*. Turn left on Via Morone at the 18th-century Palazzo

Belgioioso ⑪ and turn right onto Via Manzoni ⑫ *(see p108)*, lined with grand palazzi.

The shopping district
Admire the magnificent Grand Hotel et de Milan ⑬, where Giuseppe Verdi died in 1901,

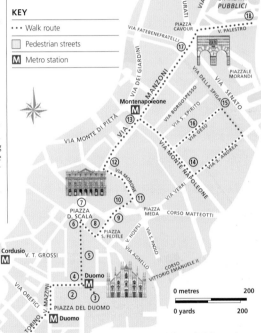

The Theatre Museum, part of the La Scala opera house ⑦

KEY
••• Walk route

▢ Pedestrian streets

Ⓜ Metro station

then turn right onto Via Montenapoleone, the heart of the fashion district. Versace, Gucci and Prada all have boutiques here. Continue along the road until you reach Cova ⑭ *(see p187)*, an elegant café famous for its *panettone*.

Turn left and left again onto Via della Spiga, home to Dolce & Gabbana ⑮. Turn left onto Via Gesù and half way down is Museo Bagatti Valsecchi ⑯ *(see p109)*, a refined town-house filled with 15th- to 17th- century furnishings. At the end of the road

turn right and right again onto Via Manzoni. Walk through Archi di Porta Nuova ⑰ *(see p109)*, a medieval gate with Roman funerary reliefs, and head to Giardini Pubblici ⑱ *(see p120)*, a welcome respite from the urban streetscape.

Cova, a Milanese must for an elegant coffee break since 1817 ⑭

TIPS FOR WALKERS

Starting point: Santa Maria presso San Satiro, off Via Torino.
Length: 2.8 km (1.7 miles)
Getting there: Duomo station.
Best time for walk: Morning.
Stopping-off points: Historic cafés such as Zucca and Cova.

A Two-Hour Walk around Milan's Historic Past

Milan is a city that tends to keep its history largely buried under a modern, business-oriented veneer. The following walk seeks out the remnants of Roman, medieval and Renaissance Milan while paying homage to the city's most famous adopted son, Leonardo da Vinci. The Renaissance master has left a distinctive stamp on the city. Examples of his genius are scattered all around town, from the *Last Supper* fresco to models of his inventions in the Museo della Scienza e della Tecnica, not to mention the surviving canals that were once part of a vast and intricate waterway system Leonardo helped plan.

Santa Maria delle Grazie, home to Leonardo's famous *Last Supper* ④

From the Castello Sforzesco to Leonardo's *Last Supper*

Begin at Milan's splendid 15th-century castle ① *(see pp64–7)*, which houses archaeological artifacts, paintings and sculptures. From the front gate, head towards Largo Cairoli and then turn right into Via San Giovanni sul Muro. At the junction with Via Meravigli turn right into Corso Magenta. Follow it west, and across

The cloistered entrance to the basilica of Sant'Ambrogio ⑦

TIPS FOR WALKERS

Starting point: Castello Sforzesco.
Length: 4.9 km (3 miles).
Getting there: Cairoli metro station.
Best time for walk: Morning.
Stopping-off points: Not far from the Castello Sforzesco is the genteel Marchesi pastry shop (see p178), or you can stop at the Art Nouveau Bar Magenta in Via Carducci (see p178). The walk ends in Milan's best district for wine bars and eateries.

from the Rococo Palazzo Litta ② *(see p74)*, you will see the Museo Archeologico ③ *(see p74)* – its cloisters preserve a bit of the city's Roman-era walls. Keep moving west on Corso Magenta to the church of Santa Maria delle Grazie ④ *(see p71)*, where you will find Leonardo's *Last Supper (see pp72–3)*. (Tickets to see this fresco should be booked at least six weeks in advance.)

Roman and medieval Milan

Trace your steps back along Corso Magenta and turn right at Via Carducci. At the bottom of this street is the Pusterla di Sant'Ambrogio ⑤ *(see p86)*, a remnant of the medieval city gates. Turn right into Via San Vittore for the Museo della Scienza e della Tecnologia Leonardo da Vinci ⑥ *(see p88)*, which contains models of Leonardo's inventions built to the master's sketches.

Double back along Via San Vittore to visit Sant'Ambrogio ⑦ *(see pp84–7)*, a 4th-century basilica with Palaeochristian mosaics, medieval carvings, and Renaissance frescoes. Head down Via de' Amicis, angling left at Piazza Resistenza Partigiana to continue along Via GG Mora ⑧. This street curves slightly since it follows the track of the interred Olona River. In ancient times this stream joined with the

Leonardo-designed wooden model

Nirone, Seveso and Vetra rivers at Corso di Porta Ticinese. The Vetra used to run south through what is now Piazza della Vetra and the Parco delle Basiliche ⑨. Head up Via Pio IV and turn left on Corso di Porta Ticinese for the church of San Lorenzo alle Colonne ⑩ *(see pp80–81)*. This magnificent 4th-century church is preceded by a set of free-standing Roman columns ⑪, probably the portico to a 2nd-century pagan temple, dismantled and moved here when the church was built.

Continue south along Corso di Porta Ticinese and go through the medieval Porta Ticinese ⑫ *(see p82)*, built as part of the city's 12th-century walls and modified in the 1860s. Keep following the road until you

(map labels:)
CORSO   GENOV
VIA C. FERRARI
VIA G. SIMONETTA
VIA M. D'OGGIONO
VIA A M. CONCA DEL NAVI
VIALE GORIZIA
VIA ALESSI
VIALE D'ANNUNZIO
VIA RONZONI
VIA ARENA
Ⓜ
Porta Genova
250m (230 yds)
Naviglio Grande ⑱
RIPA DI PORTA TICINESE ⑰
Darsena
⑮
⑯
PIAZZA XXIV MAGGIO
PIAZZA ⑬ S. EUSTORGIO
⑭
VIA SAMBU
CORS

reach Sant'Eustorgio ⑬ (see p90), a 4th-century church hiding behind an insipid 19th-century façade. Beyond the main church and behind the altar lies the Cappella Portinari, a masterpiece of early Renaissance architecture gorgeously frescoed with the story of St Peter Martyr by Vincenzo Foppa. The church houses a vast marble arch carved in the 1330s.

Along the Navigli

One more road south, past the confusingly named Porta Ticinese ⑭ (see p82) (unlike its medieval

The façade of Sant'Eustorgio hides a 4th-century church ⑬

namesake up the street, this Neo-Classical pile dates from 1801–14), and you are in the Piazza XXIV Maggio. This marks the intersection of the last

filled in. West of Piazza XXIV Marzo stretches the main "port", the 1603 Darsena ⑮, an artificial basin at the confluence of the underground Olona River and two canals.

The canal closest to the square is the Naviglio Pavese ⑯, running 33 km (20.5 miles) south to the Ticino River, near Pavia. Once the busiest canal in the entire system, since 1978 it has served as a very long irrigation ditch.

To the southwest of the Darsena is the Naviglio Grande ⑰ (see p89), a 50-km (31-mile) waterway connecting

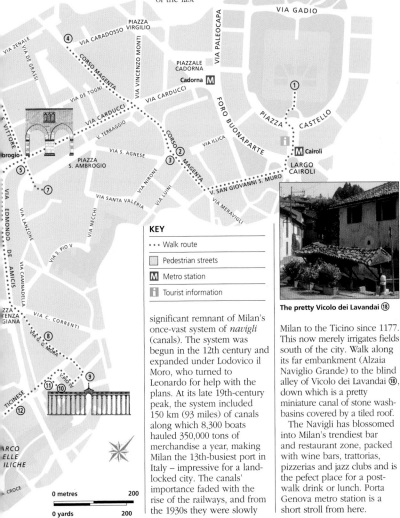

KEY

••• Walk route

☐ Pedestrian streets

Ⓜ Metro station

ℹ Tourist information

The pretty Vicolo dei Lavandai ⑱

significant remnant of Milan's once-vast system of *navigli* (canals). The system was begun in the 12th century and expanded under Lodovico il Moro, who turned to Leonardo for help with the plans. At its late 19th-century peak, the system included 150 km (93 miles) of canals along which 8,300 boats hauled 350,000 tons of merchandise a year, making Milan the 13th-busiest port in Italy – impressive for a land-locked city. The canals' importance faded with the rise of the railways, and from the 1930s they were slowly

Milan to the Ticino since 1177. This now merely irrigates fields south of the city. Walk along its far embankment (Alzaia Naviglio Grande) to the blind alley of Vicolo dei Lavandai ⑱, down which is a pretty miniature canal of stone wash-basins covered by a tiled roof.

The Navigli has blossomed into Milan's trendiest bar and restaurant zone, packed with wine bars, trattorias, pizzerias and jazz clubs and is the pefect place for a post-walk drink or lunch. Porta Genova metro station is a short stroll from here.

Exterior of Villa Balbianello in Lenno, Lake Como ▷

THE LAKES OF NORTHERN ITALY

THE LAKES OF NORTHERN ITALY

*A*ppreciated by the ancient romans for their beautiful location and mild climate, the lakes of Northern Italy – most of which are in Lombardy – are deservedly renowned for the fascinating and unique combination of magnificent scenery and historic and artistic heritage that characterizes the lakeside towns.

Besides Lake Maggiore, Lake Como and Lake Garda, there are smaller and less well-known bodies of water such as the lakes of Orta, Varese, Iseo and Idro. All these lovely lakes are the result of glaciation in the Pleistocene era, which enlarged clefts already in the terrain. The lake shores were inhabited during the prehistoric period – traces of ancient civilizations have been found almost everywhere – and for the most part were colonized by the Romans, as can be seen in the grid street plans of many towns and in the villas at Lake Garda. Churches, sanctuaries and castles were built here in the Middle Ages. In the winter the shores of the lakes can be battered by winds from Central Europe, but the climate remains quite mild thanks to the water. Typical Mediterranean vegetation can be seen everywhere: vineyards, olive trees, oleanders and palm trees. The many splendid villa gardens along the lakes' shores enhance the environment, and nature reserves have been established to protect some stretches.

In the 18th century a visit to the lake region was one of the accepted stages on the Grand Tour, the trip to Europe considered essential for the education of young people of good birth. These shores were also favourites with writers, musicians and artists such as Goethe, Hesse, Klee, Toscanini, Hemingway, Stendhal, Byron and Nietzsche. The numerous vantage points, connected to the shore by funiculars, narrow-gauge trains and cable cars, offer truly spectacular views over the landscape.

The peaceful shores of Lake Como, southwest of Bellagio

◁ Torre di San Marco at Gardone Riviera, on the western shore of Lake Garda

Exploring the Lakes

The larger lakes offer the best facilities for visitors, with hotels, restaurants and cafés lining the lake front. The lake shores are dotted with pretty villages, castles (Sirmione sul Garda), villas and gardens such as Villa Taranto or the Vittoriale, the residence of the poet D'Annunzio at Lake Garda, as well as a number of small local museums. In summer, you may be able to participate in cultural events such as the famous Settimane Musicali di Stresa music festival at Lake Maggiore. Although the smaller lakes offer fewer facilities, they are very peaceful, unspoilt places.

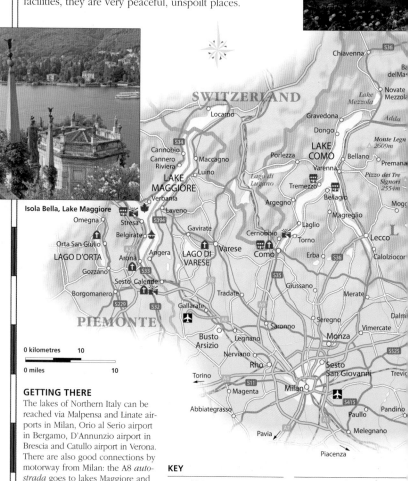

Isola Bella, Lake Maggiore

GETTING THERE

The lakes of Northern Italy can be reached via Malpensa and Linate airports in Milan, Orio al Serio airport in Bergamo, D'Annunzio airport in Brescia and Catullo airport in Verona. There are also good connections by motorway from Milan: the A8 *autostrada* goes to lakes Maggiore and Varese, the A9 to Lake Como, and the A4 to Iseo and Garda. Traffic on the major and minor roads is often heavy, so make allowances when planning. Boat services on the three major lakes are quite efficient; they go to the islands and are an enjoyable way of getting about.

0 kilometres   10
0 miles   10

KEY

═══	Motorway
═══	Major road
───	Secondary road
┄┄┄	Minor road
▬▬▬	Main railway

───	Minor railway
▪▪▪▪	International border
▫▫▫▫	Regional border
△	Summit

For additional map symbols *see back flap*

LOCATOR MAP

The pretty, colourful harbour of the town of Bellagio, on Lake Como

Looking over Lago d'Iseo

12th-century castle clings to the rock face above the town of Malcesine, on Lake Garda

The Lakes

Lake Maggiore

Villa statue, Isola Madre

With borders in Piedmont, Lombardy and the Ticino canton in Switzerland, Lake Maggiore, or Verbano, is the second largest lake in Italy (212 sq km, 82 sq miles) and has a maximum depth of 372 m (1,220 ft). For the most part it is fed and drained by the Ticino river, and is also fed by the Toce. The towns were embellished with churches and paintings from 1449 on, thanks to the wealthy Borromeo family, and with villas and gardens in the 18th–19th centuries. The opening of the Simplon pass and the introduction of ferry services (1826) helped trade to develop in the area.

★ **Isole Borromee**
Of the three islands, the best known is Isola Bella, named after Isabella d'Adda, wife of Charles III Borromeo ❺

The two castles of Malpaga, built in the 13th–14th century on two islets at the foot of Mount Carza, belonged to the Mazzardites, the pirates who raided the lake.

Magaduno

Vira

Locarno

San Nazzaro

Ascona

Gerra-Gambarogno

Porto Ronco

Sant' Abbondio

Isola di Brissago

Brissago

Maccagno

Luino ❾

Cannobio ❽

Gannero Riviera

Pieggio

Veltrava

Ghiffa

Stresa
This old fishermen's village began to become a tourist attraction thanks to the descriptions of famous writers such as Stendhal, Byron and Dickens ❹

Intra

Verbania ❼

Isola Madre

★ **Villa Taranto**
One of Italy's best-known botanic gardens was founded here in 1931 by an Englishman called McEacharn in an area of about 16 ha (40 acres). Many examples of species of plants from all over the world, including Victoria amazonica, are grown here (see p138).

★ Santa Caterina del Sasso Ballaro
Perched on a rocky spur near Laveno, this monastery is one of the most enchanting sights on Lake Maggiore. It was built by a local merchant in the 12th century to fulfil a vow made when he was saved from a storm ⑪

VISITORS' CHECKLIST

🛈 Local tourist bureau.
🚉 FS Stazione Centrale (89 20 21); Ferrovie Nord Milano Cadorna Station (800 500 005). 🚌 SAFduemila (0323-55 21 72); Autolinee Varesine (0332-73 11 10).
⛴ Navigazione Lago Maggiore (800-55 18 01).
www.navlaghi.it

★ Rocca di Angera
The imposing medieval fortress of the Borromeo family has 14th- and 15th-century frescoes. It now houses the Doll Museum ⑫

Arona
The huge 17th-century statue of San Carlo Borromeo was placed in Arona in honour of its illustrious citizen. A 35-m (115-ft) stairway leads to the top, from where there is a fine panoramic view ②

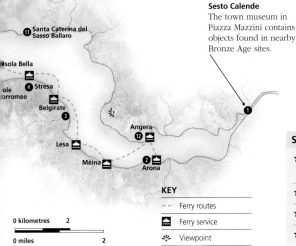

Sesto Calende
The town museum in Piazza Mazzini contains objects found in nearby Bronze Age sites.

⑩ Laveno
⑪ Santa Caterina del Sasso Ballaro
Isola Bella
④ Stresa
ole orromee
Belgirate
③
Lesa
Mèina
Angera
⑫
② ⑤ Arona
①

KEY

- - - Ferry routes
⛴ Ferry service
☼ Viewpoint

0 kilometres   2
0 miles   2

STAR SIGHTS

★ Santa Caterina del Sasso Ballaro

★ Rocca di Angera

★ Villa Taranto

★ Isole Borromee

Sesto Calende ❶

Varese. 🏛 10,800. 🗜 IAT (mid-Mar–Oct only), Viale Italia 3 (0331-92 33 29). www.prosestocalende.it

The town at the southern tip of Lake Maggiore marks the end of two motorways leading to the Verbano region. The road to Arona goes to **San Donato**, known as "La Badia" or abbey, a 9th-century basilica rebuilt in the 11th–12th century. The capitals have sculpted figures of animals and humans. There are frescoes from the 15th and 16th centuries in the nave and from the 18th century in the crypt. South of Sesto, near Golasecca, are Iron Age tombs (9th–5th century BC), part of the civilization named after the place. State road 33 to Arona will take you to the **Lagoni di Mercurago Regional Park**, with varied bird species and the remains of ancient villages.

🏛 Abbazia San Donato
Via San Donato 6. **Tel** 0331-92 42 71. ◯ 8am–noon, 4–7pm daily.

🏞 Lagoni di Mercurago Regional Park
Via Gattico 6, Mercurago.
Tel 0322-24 02 39.
www.parchilagomaggiore.it

Arona ❷

Novara. 🏛 15,000. 🗜 Largo Duca d'Aosta (0322-24 36 01).
🛋 antiques, 3rd Sun of month.

Arona once occupied an important trading position between Milan and the lake and mountain regions of Northern Italy. Because of its strategic location, a Rocca or fortress (the twin of the one at Angera; see p139), was built here; it was enlarged by the Borromeo and dismantled by Napoleon. Corso Marconi has a view of the Rocca at Angera, and leads to Piazza del Popolo. Here are the 15th-century Casa del Podestà, with an arched portico, and the 16th-century Madonna di Piazza church. Santi Martiri has 15th-century paintings by Bergognone, and Santa Maria Nascente has an altarpiece by Gaudenzio Ferrari (1511).

Just north of the centre is a massive **statue of San Carlo**. It was designed by Cerano in 1614 and finished in 1697. In the church of San Carlo there is a reconstruction of the room where San Carlo was born.

Villa Ponti is a mid-18th-century villa with Baroque and Art Deco decoration. It stands in a garden with a nymphaeum and a fountain.

🏛 Statue of San Carlo
Piazza San Carlo. **Tel** 0322-24 96 69. ◯ Mar: 9am–12:30pm, 2–4:30pm Sat & Sun; Apr–Sep: 9am–12:30pm, 2–6:30pm daily; Oct: 9am–12:30pm, 2–6:30pm Sat & Sun; Nov & Dec: 9am–12:30pm, 2–4:30pm Sat & Sun except 1 Nov, 8, 25 & 26 Dec. Children under eight are not allowed inside the statue. ◯ Jan, Feb. 🖼

🏛 Villa Ponti
Via San Carlo 63. **Tel** 0322-446 29. ◯ to the public

The square in Arona with the huge statue of San Carlo Borromeo

Lesa and Belgirate ❸

Lesa (Novara). 🏛 2,400. Belgirate (Verbania). 🏛 600. 🗜 IAT, Via Portici, Lesa (0322-77 20 78).

Lesa lies on a particularly charming stretch of the lake between Arona and Stresa, and has been popular as a resort for noble Lombard families since the 18th century. The **Museo Manzoniano di Villa Stampa** has mementos of author Alessandro Manzoni, who was a guest here. The hamlet of Villa boasts the Romanesque church of San Sebastiano.

Once past Lesa, continue to Belgirate and its charming historic centre, whose houses have porticoes and porches. This village also commands a panoramic view of the lake. It was a haunt of philosopher Antonio Rosmini and poet Guido Gozzano.

On the hills 4 km (2 miles) from Belgirate is the 13th-century **Castello Visconteo**, decorated with frescoes of the period. Nearby is the Romanesque church of San Michele, with a leaning bell tower.

🏛 Museo Manzoniano di Villa Stampa
Via alla Fontana 18, Lesa.
Tel 0322-764 21. ◯ Aug only: 10am–noon Thu, 5–9pm Sat & Sun.

🏛 Castello Visconteo
Via Visconti 1, Massino Visconti.
Tel 329-475 37 83 ◯ by arrangement only.

Looking over the lakeside town of Arona

Stresa ❹

Verbania. 🏙 *5,200.* 🛈 *IAT, Piazza Marconi 16 (0323-301 50 or 0323-31 308).*

The origins of medieval Strixia, dating from before 1000, are partially hidden by the palazzi and villas built for the aristocracy in the late 19th–early 20th century, partly because of the opening of an electric rack-railway (the first in Italy), which goes to the top of Mount Mottarone. The town is now a centre for conferences and tour groups, attracted by the easy access to the Borromean islands. On the lakefront are 19th-century villas, Sant'Ambrogio (18th century) and the **Villa Ducale** (1770), with mementos of 19th-century philosopher Antonio Rosmini, who died here (the villa is now the Rosmini Study Centre). Mount Mottarone (1,491 m, 4,890 ft), a ski resort, has a view from the Alps to the plain.

🏛 **Villa Ducale**
Centro di Studi Rosminiani
Corso Umberto I 15. **Tel** 0323-300 91. ⏲ *10am–noon, 3–6pm Mon–Fri.*

ENVIRONS

🌳 **Parco di Villa Pallavicino**
State road 33.
Tel 0323-324 07. ⏲ *Mar–Oct: 9am–5pm Mon–Fri.* ♿ 🚻 🛈 www.parcozoopallavicino.it

This villa near Stresa is famous for its gardens. The luxuriant English garden has centuries-old plants as well as exotic creatures such as llamas and pelicans.

A fountain at Villa Pallavicino

The garden of the 18th-century palazzo on Isola Madre

Isole Borromee ❺

Verbania. 🚤 *from Arona, Laveno, Stresa, Baveno, Pallanza. To Isola Madre and Isola Bella: tel. 0322-23 32 00 or 800 55 18 01.* ⏲ *late Mar–mid-Oct: 9am–5:30pm daily.* 🔴 *Nov–Mar.* 📷 🎟 *by appt.* 🛈 www.borromeoturismo.it

These three islands, which can be reached easily from Stresa, became famous thanks to the Borromeo family, who built elegant palazzi and magnificent gardens there. The loveliest is **Isola Bella**, an old fishing village transformed from 1632 to 1671 by the Borromeo family into a lovely complex consisting of a Baroque palazzo and a terraced Italian-style garden with rare plants. Inside are a music room (where Mussolini met British and French officials in 1935), the Sala di Napoleone (where Napoleon stayed in 1797), a ballroom, throne room and bedroom with 17th-century decoration and furnishings and paintings by Carracci, Cerano and Tiepolo. The six grottoes are decorated with shells and pebbles.

Isola Madre, the largest island, boasts an 18th-century villa with a garden where white peacocks roam freely; it has rare plants as well as azaleas, rhododendrons and camellias. The villa has period furnishings and a collection of 18th- and 19th-century puppet theatres.

Tiny **Isola dei Pescatori**, once the leading fishing village, has retained its quaint atmosphere and architecture.

Baveno ❻

Verbania. 🏙 *5,000.* 🛈 *IAT, Piazza della Chiesa 8 (0323-92 46 32).*

Made famous by its pink granite quarries, which among other things supplied the stone for the Galleria in Milan (*see p50*), Baveno became a fashionable resort in the mid-19th century, entertaining guests such as Queen Victoria, who stayed in the Villa Clara (now Villa Branca) in 1879. A major attraction is Santi Gervasio e Protasio, with its 12th-century facade and 15th-century octagonal baptistery with Renaissance frescoes. Going towards Verbania, take the turn-off for San Giovanni at Montorfano, one of the loveliest churches in the area.

The garden at Villa Pallavicino, the home of many species of animals

Verbania ❼

🏚 *31,000.* ℹ️ *IAT, Corso Zanitello 6–8 (0323-55 66 69); Pro Loco, Viale delle Magnolie 1 (0323-55 76 76).* 🏺 *antiques, Jul & Aug: 8pm–midnight Fri.*

Pallanza and Intra were merged in 1939 to create the town of Verbania (capital of the Verbano-Cusio-Ossola province established in 1992). The former, facing the Borromeo gulf, is the seat of the municipal government and has retained its medieval aspect and atmosphere. The latter dominates the promontory of Castagnola and has a Baroque and Neo-Classical flavour. Intra, the main port of call on the lake and one of its major industrial centres, was the regional leader in textile manufacturing in the 18th century. Pallanza was the only town in Lake Maggiore not under Borromeo dominion, and it has some of the most important monuments. These include Romanesque Santo Stefano, the parish church of San Leonardo and 18th-century Palazzo Viani Dugnani, home to the **Museo del Paesaggio**, which has an exhibit of 16th–20th-century landscape paintings, sculpture by Arturo Martini and Giulio Branca and a plaster cast gallery. Isolino di San Giovanni was a favourite refuge of Arturo Toscanini. In the environs is 16th-century Madonna di Campagna,

with a small Romanesque campanile and frescoes by Gerolamo Lanino and Camillo Procaccini (16th–17th centuries).

🏛 Museo del Paesaggio

Via Ruga 44.
Tel 0323-55 66 21.
◻ *Apr–Oct: 10am–noon, 3:30–6:30pm Tue–Sun.*

ENVIRONS

🌺 Giardini di Villa Taranto

Via Vittorio Veneto, Pallanza. **Tel** 0323-55 66 67. ◻ *mid-Mar–Oct: 8:30am–6:30pm (to 5pm Oct).*
🅿️ ♿ 🏪

In 1931 a Scottish captain named Neil McEacharn created one of the outstanding botanic gardens in Europe on the Castagnola promontory, using the lake water for irrigation. He is buried in the small park church. McEacharn exploited the valley terrain, creating terraced gardens, a winter garden and a marsh garden among small falls and water lily ponds. He donated the Villa Taranto garden to the Italian state and it was opened to the public in 1952. It has a range of exotic plants, including *Victoria amazonica* in the glasshouses. Azaleas, dahlias and rhododendrons (over 300 varieties) look wonderful in full flower.

Cannobio ❽

Verbania. 🏚 *5,300.* ℹ️ *IAT, Via Antonio Giovanola 25 (0323-712 12).* **www**.procannobio.it

This pleasant tourist resort is the last Italian town on the Piedmontese side of the lake. It still retains its old medieval character, exemplified in the Palazzo della Ragione or Palazzo Parrasio, the town hall with a 12th-century Commune Tower. The Santuario della Pietà, which was rebuilt by San Carlo Borromeo in 1583, contains a fine altarpiece by Gaudenzio Ferrari.

Effigy of McEacharn, who created the Villa Taranto gardens

The Orrido di Sant'Anna, in Val Cannobina

In nearby Val Cannobina, the Orrido di Sant'Anna is worth a visit. This deep gorge was carved out of the rock by the Cannobino river.

Luino ❾

Varese. 🏚 *14,400.* ℹ️ *IAT, Via Chiara 1 (0332-53 00 19).*

Luino, which occupies a cove on the eastern side of the lake, is a town dating from ancient Roman times. Its name may have derived from the Luina torrent or perhaps from the local term *luina* (landslide). In the Middle Ages it was contested by the leading Como and Milanese families and became famous when Garibaldi landed here in 1848 with a group of volunteers and routed an entire Austrian detachment.

The large railway station (1882) shows how important the town was when it linked Italy with Central Europe, a position that declined when railway traffic shifted to Chiasso. Luino's market was founded by an edict of Charles V in 1541 and is still a tourist attraction. San Pietro in Campagna has frescoes by Bernardino Luini and a lovely Romanesque bell tower; the oratory of the Chiesa del Carmine dates back to 1477. A must is a visit to the town's symbol, the 17th-century oratory of San Giuseppe.

Laveno ⑩

Varese. 🚂 8,800.
ℹ️ IAT, Piazza Italia 2
(0332-66 87 85).

**The natural harbour of Laveno,
once an Austrian naval base**

The name of this town goes back to Titus Labienus, the Roman general who was Caesar's legate in Cisalpine Gaul. Laveno was important strategically because of its port, the only natural harbour on Lake Maggiore. During their period of rule, the Austrians moored the gunboats controlling the lake here. Today the town is the main ferry point to the Piedmontese shores. The Ferrovie Nord railway linked Laveno to Varese and Milan, fostering commercial development, especially in the field of ceramics with the founding of well-known Società Ceramica Italiana Richard-Ginori, in 1856. In the town centre, the garden in the Villa Frua (18th century) is worth visiting.

A cable car goes up to Sasso del Ferro, at 1,062 m (3,483 ft), behind Laveno with fine views of the lake, Monte Mottarone and Monte Rosa.

Santa Caterina del Sasso Ballaro ⑪

Via Santa Caterina 13, Leggiuno.
Tel 0332-64 71 72. 🕐 Apr–Oct:
8:30am–noon, 2:30–6pm daily;
Nov–Mar: 9am–noon, 2–5pm Sat
& Sun (except Mar & 23 Dec–6 Jan:
daily). 🚌 4:30pm hols. ♿

To get to this small monastery perched on a steep rock 18 m (59 ft) above the lake, you can either climb the 240 steps near Leggiuno or take the boat and enjoy the lovely views. The place was founded in the mid-12th century by a local merchant. The Dominicans arrived in 1230 and after numerous changes in fortune have since returned. Over the centuries the original building was enlarged and rebuilt, as can be seen by the different architectural styles. The chapter at the entrance has important 14th–15th-century frescoes, including a *Crucifixion with Armigers*. In the second portico the 17th-century fresco, only partly preserved, represents a *Dance of Death*. The frescoes inside the church were executed in the 16th century, and the *Madonna and Child with Saints* on the high altar dates from 1612. By the entrance porticoes there is a large wine press made in 1759.

**14th–15th-century frescoes,
Rocca di Angera**

Rocca di Angera ⑫

Fortress and museum Via Rocca,
Angera. **Tel** 0331-93 13 00.
🕐 Apr–Oct: 9am–5:30pm daily.
📷 ♿ 🚻 🍴

A majestic fortress, probably built over the ruins of an ancient Roman fortification, the Rocca once belonged to the archbishops of Milan. In the 13th century it was taken over by the Visconti family and in 1449 was granted as a fief to the Borromeo family, who still own it. The Visconti building has single and double lancet windows and partly lies against the earlier castle tower. The frescoes in the halls are well worth a look, especially those in the Salone Gotico, with a cycle of the *Battles of Ottone Visconti against the Torriani* (14th century). The vaults in this hall are decorated with the Visconti coat of arms, while those in the other rooms have geometric patterns and signs of the Zodiac. The Borromeo wing has frescoes removed from Palazzo Borromeo in Milan in 1946, with *Aesop's Fables* by the school of Michelino da Besozzo (15th century). The Rocca is used for art shows and is also home to the **Museo della Bambola** (Doll Museum) in the Visconti wing, one of the best of its kind in Europe, created with the collection of Princess Bona Borromeo. Besides dolls and doll's houses, it contains books, games and children's clothing.

Santa Caterina del Sasso Ballaro, built on a cliff overlooking the lake

Lake Como

This lake, which is also known as Lario, is the third largest in Italy and the deepest (410 m, 1,345 ft). It is shaped like a sprawling upside-down Y, with the arms of Como, Lecco and Colico. The Como shore is the most developed, with numerous restaurants and hotels, as well as a scenic road that follows the ancient Strada Regina, lined with elegant villas and aristocratic gardens. The Lecco area has more stark scenery and small coves.

Decoration in Villa d'Este, at Cernobbio

You may spot the typical "Lucia" boats, named after the heroine in Manzoni's *The Betrothed*, which was partly set here.

★ Bellagio
Its position at the junction of the arms of the lake and the spectacular view from the Spartivento point make this one of the most popular spots on Lake Como ⑫

The bell tower on Santa Maria Maddalena at Ossuccio is one of the symbols of the lake.

Menaggio ⑥

★ Como
Construction of Como's Duomo began in 1396 and ended in 1740 with the huge dome. Next to it is the elegant 13th-century Broletto, the old town hall ❶

Sala Comacina
Lenno   Tremezzo   Cadena
❹   ❺
Argegno
Isola Comacina ❸
Lake Como
Lezzeno

STAR SIGHTS

- ★ Bellagio
- ★ Como
- ★ Tremezzo

Nesso

Careno

Torrigia

Ùrio

Moltrasio

Pognana Lario

Cernobbio ❷

Torno ⑬

Belvio

Travernola

Como ❶   Brunate

KEY

─ ─ ─ Ferry routes

🛥 Ferry service

☀ Viewpoint

Cernobbio
The 16th-century Villa d'Este in Cernobbio, now a famous hotel, is surrounded by beautiful landscaped gardens with many fountains ❷

Gravedona

Santa Maria del Tiglio in Gravedona is the most famous Lombard Romanesque construction in the Alto Lario region. Its main features are the layers of black and white stone and the unusual octagonal bell tower set into the façade **7**

VISITORS' CHECKLIST

ℹ Local information bureaus.
🚉 FS: Milan–Chiasso line (89 20 21); Ferrovie Nord Milano: (031-30 48 00 or 800 500 005). 🚌 ASF Autolinee, Piazza Matteotti, Como (031-24 72 47). ⛴ Navigazione Lago di Como (800-55 18 01 (freefone) or 031-57 92 11). www.navlaghi.it

Stazzona •

Domase

Gravedona **7**

Dongo

Musso

Abbazia di Piona **8**

Colico

Lake Mezzola, separated from the Lario region by silt from the Adda river, is a natural reserve inhabited by grey herons.

Pianello del Lario

Lake Como

The "crotti" are typical mountain caves in the upper Lario region, used as wine cellars since the 19th century.

Dèrvio
Siro

Bellano **9**

Varenna **10**

The medieval Vezio castle, built on the site of a Roman tower, is a 20-minute walk from Varenna and offers a stunning panoramic view.

Lierna

monta

Lake Lecco

Sala ssena

Mandello del Lario

Onno

Abbadia Lariana

Lecco **11**

agio

Varenna
Some of the paths in this village, one of the best preserved on the lake, consist of steps and raised boardwalks perched over the water **10**

★ **Tremezzo**
The Villa Carlotta in Tremezzo was a wedding gift for Carlotta of Prussia (1843). Inside there is a copy of Canova's Cupid and Psyche **5**

Como ❶

🏠 85,200. ℹ️ IAT, Piazza Cavour 17 (031-26 97 12). www.lakecomo.org

Comum was founded by the Romans in 196 BC and in the 12th century fought against Milan as an ally of Barbarossa, who built the medieval walls. In 1335 Como came under Visconti rule and in 1451 under Sforza rule. The town shared Milan's fate under Spanish and Austrian domination, becoming part of the Kingdom of Italy in 1859.

Como's many Romanesque churches include the 12th-century San Fedele and the jewel of the Comacine masters, 11th-century Lombard–Romanesque Sant' Abbondio.

The **Duomo**, begun in 1396, is dominated by Filippo Juvarra's Baroque dome. The sculpture on the Gothic façade and the Porta della Rana door were executed by Tommaso and Jacopo Rodari (c.1500). The nave and side altars are decorated with 16th-century tapestries and canvases by Ferrari and Luini. Next to the Duomo is the Romanesque-Gothic Broletto (1215).

The **Tempio Voltiano** (1927) contains relics of the physicist Alessandro Volta from Como, who gave his name to "voltage". The Casa del Fascio (1936) exemplifies Italian Rationalist architecture. **Villa Olmo**, designed by Simone

Piazza del Duomo in Como, the birthplace of Pliny the Elder

Cantoni in 1797, has frescoed rooms and a park. A funicular goes up to **Brunate**, with spectacular views of Como and popular hiking trails.

🔒 Duomo
Piazza Duomo. **Tel** 031-26 52 44.
⏱️ 8am–noon, 3–7pm daily.

🏛️ Tempio Voltiano
Viale Marconi. **Tel** 031-57 47 05.
⏱️ 10am–noon, 3–6pm (2–4pm Nov–Mar) Tue–Sun. 📷

🏛️ Villa Olmo
Via Cantoni 1. **Tel** 031-57 61 69.
⏱️ 9am–noon, 3–6pm Mon–Sat.
⏱️ hols. 📷 📷

Cernobbio ❷

Como. 🏠 7,000. ℹ️ Via Regina 33b (031-51 01 98) (open Apr–Sep); P.za Cavour 17, Como (031-26 97 12).

Cernobbio marks the beginning of a series of splendid villas that have made the western side of the lake famous. **Villa d'Este**, built by Pellegrino Tibaldi in 1570 for the Gallio family, became a luxury hotel in 1873, frequented by princes and actors. The rooms have period furnishings and are used for conferences. The villa stands in an Italianate garden with a nympheum. The 18th-century **Villa Erba** (now a

conference centre) is known for its interior (visits by request): the Salone da Ballo, chapel and Sala delle Nozze, decorated by architect Giocondo Albertolli, are lovely.

🏨 Hotel Villa d'Este
Via Regina 40. **Tel** 031-34 81.
◑ Nov–Mar.

🏨 Villa Erba
Largo Visconti 4. **Tel** 031-34 91. ◑ to the public. The Luchino Visconti rooms can be booked for group visits.

Isola Comacina ❸

Como. ℹ️ IAT, Piazza Cavour 17, Como (031-26 97 12). 🚌 (as far as Sala Comacina, then by boat).

The only island on Lake Como has been inhabited since

FROM MULBERRY TO SILK

Como produces about 80 per cent of Europe's silk. Silk worms were imported in the 14th century and production thrived in the 17th century with the large-scale cultivation of mulberries, the worms' food. Silk thread was woven and sent on the "silk route" in Austria and Bavaria. Competition from Chinese silk now forces Como to concentrate on quality silk, as shown in the Museo della Seta (Silk Museum) in Como.

Cocoons

The Villa d'Este in Cernobbio, once host to the Duke of Windsor and Mrs Simpson

Roman times. It was fortified by the Byzantines and enjoyed a period of splendour in the Middle Ages. The people of Como conquered the fortress in 1169 and destroyed the seven churches on the island. The ruins, along with those of a mosaic-decorated baptistery, were found after World War II and are now being studied. Sala Comacina, where boats depart for the island, has an 18th-century church with a fresco by Carlo Carloni, and the villa of Cesare Beccaria, where Manzoni was a guest.

Villa Carlotta, built in the 18th century by Marchese Giorgio Clerici

Lenno ❹

Como. 🏠 1,800. 🛈 IAT, Piazza Cavour 17, Como (031-26 97 12).

This town is famous for the **Villa del Balbianello**, built by Cardinal Durini in the 17th century onto a 16th-century building attributed to Pellegrini. The magnificent garden has a loggia with a view of Isola Comacina on one side and the Tremezzina bay on the other. Access to the villa is by boat from Sala Comacina.

Also worth a visit are the octagonal baptistery and church of Santo Stefano, built in the 11th century over a Roman building and decorated with frescoes by Luini. Above the town is the Cistercian abbey of Acquafredda, rebuilt in the 17th century, with frescoes by Fiammenghino. At nearby Giulino di Mezzegra, the Fascist dictator Benito Mussolini and his mistress Claretta Petacci were executed on 28 April 1945.

🏛 Villa del Balbianello
Balbianello. **Tel** 0344-561 10 (FAI).
Garden ⬜ mid-Mar–mid-Nov: 10am–6pm Thu–Tue.
Villa ⬜ by appt only.

Tremezzo ❺

Como. 🏠 1,300. 🛈 IAT, Via Regina 3 (0344-404 93) (open Apr–Sep); Piazza Cavour 17, Como (031-26 97 12).

This lakeside town is a major tourist resort and home to the 18th-century **Villa Carlotta**. The residence, surrounded by a terraced garden with landscaped staircases, was converted in the 1800s into a Neo-Classical villa. It houses paintings by Hayez, furniture by Maggiolini and sculpture pieces by Canova, including a copy of *Cupid and Psyche* and *Terpsichore*. Among the rooms decorated with stuccowork is one with Appiani's

frescoes taken from the Palazzo Reale in Milan. The villa is famous for its garden, with over 150 species of rhododendrons and azaleas.

🏛 Villa Carlotta
Via Regina 2b. **Tel** 0344-404 05.
⬜ Apr–Oct: 9am–6pm daily;
Nov: 10am–5pm daily. 🌐
www.villacarlotta.it

Menaggio ❻

Como. 🏠 3,200. 🛈 IAT, Piazza Garibaldi 8 (0344-329 24).
www.menaggio.com

The name Menaggio supposedly derives from two Indo-European words: *men* (mountain) and *uigg* (water), referring to the mouth of the Sanagra river on which the town lies. Menaggio is the leading commercial centre in the upper Lario region and a popular tourist resort. It is dominated by the ruins of a castle and has preserved some of its medieval layout. Of note are the parish church of Santo Stefano, the Baroque architecture of which conceals its Romanesque origin and 17th-century San Carlo, with a fine painting by Giuseppe Vermiglio (1625). The lakeside promenade, with arcaded houses and villas, is a must. Past Menaggio, at Loveno, is the Neo-Classical Milyus-Vigoni villa with family portraits by Francesco Hayez. Around it is a lovely park, designed by Balzaretto in 1840.

Menaggio, a lakeside town especially popular with British visitors

Gravedona ❼

Como. 🏠 2,800. 🛈 Piazza Trieste
(0344-850 05); IAT, Piazza Cavour 17,
Como (031-26 97 12).

A fortified town of some
importance in Roman times,
Gravedona was destroyed by
the people of Como in the
13th century because it was
allied with Milan. It later
became capital of the small
Tre Pievi republic. The town
then declined and was ceded
to Cardinal Tolomeo Gallio,
who in 1583 asked Tibaldi to
build Palazzo Gallio. Gravedona is known for the church
of **Santa Maria del Tiglio** (12th
century). The aisled nave
with tall galleries houses a
12th-century wooden Crucifix,
a floor mosaic dating from
the 6th century and various
12th–14th-century frescoes.
Santi Gusmeo e Matteo was
frescoed by Fiammenghino,
while Santa Maria delle Grazie
(1467) contains 16th-century
frescoes. Nearby Dongo is an
ancient village known for the
Falck steelworks, responsible
for building the metal parts of
the *Italia* and *Norge* airships.
Above Gravedona, at Peglio,
is the Sant' Eusebio complex,
with fine 17th-century
frescoes in the church. The
Spanish fort in the outskirts
was built in 1604 to guard
the Adda river plain.

🏛 **Santa Maria del Tiglio**
Piazza XI Febbraio. **Tel** 0344-852 61.
🕐 9am–6pm daily.

The Cluniac Piona abbey, founded in the 11th century

Abbazia di Piona ❽

Via Santa Maria di Piona 1, Colico.
Tel 0341-94 03 31. 🕐 9am–noon,
2:30–5pm daily. 📷

A promontory on the north–
eastern shore of the lake
conceals this extraordinary
abbey built by Cluniac
monks in the 11th century.
The exterior of Romanesque
San Nicolao is adorned with
small arches and pilasters.
The bell tower dates from
1700 and the cloister (1252–7)
has sculpted capitals with
fantastic figures. There are
13th-century frescoes here
as well as in the apse.

Bellano ❾

Lecco 🏠 3,400. 🛈 IAT, Via Nazario
Sauro 6, Lecco (0341-29 57 20).

In the middle ages
Bellano was the
summer residence
of Milanese bishops
and it has preserved
its medieval charac-
ter. Among houses
with wrought-iron
coats of arms is
the church of Santi
Nazaro, Celso e
Giorgio, the work of
Campionese masters
(14th century). Santa
Marta houses a *Pietà*
executed in 1518.
However, the main
appeal of Bellano is
the Orrido, a deep
gorge created by the
Pioverna torrent.

🔺 **Orrido**
Tel 0341-82 11 24. 🕐 Apr–Jun &
Sep: 10am–1pm, 2:30–7pm daily;
Jul–Aug: 8:45–10pm Sat & Sun;
Oct–Mar: 10am–12:30pm, 2:30–
5pm Sat & Sun. 📷

Varenna ❿

Lecco. 🏠 800. 🛈 Pro Loco
(Aug only), Via IV Novembre 3
(0341-83 03 67).

This splendid village of
Roman origin, with a perfectly
intact medieval layout, was a
haven for the inhabitants of
Isola Comacina when the
citizens of Como burned the
island (1169). The 14th-century
church of San Giorgio has an
altarpiece by Pietro Brentani
(1467), while Santa Marta
houses the parish art gallery.
Varenna is famous for **Villa
Cipressi**, with its terraced
garden, and **Villa Monastero**,
built over a Cistercian
monastery. All around the
town were quarries for the
black Varenna marble used in
the Milan Duomo. Since 1921
Mandello del Lario has housed
the **Moto Guzzi factory**, with
a Motorcycle Museum.

🏛 **Villa Cipressi**
Via IV Novembre 18. **Tel** 0341-83 01
13. 🕐 (garden) Mar–Oct: 9am–6pm
daily. 🌙 Nov–Feb. 📷

🏛 **Villa Monastero**
Via Polvani 2. **Tel** 0341-29 54 50.
🕐 (garden) May–Sep: 9am–7pm
(6pm Mar–Apr & Oct) daily. 🌙 Nov–
Feb. 📷 **www**.villamonastero.eu

Palazzo Gallio, designed by architect
Pellegrino Tibaldi in 1583

🏛 **Museo Moto Guzzi della Motocicletta**
Via Parodi 57, Mandello del Lario.
Tel 0341-70 91 11. ⭕ *3–4pm Fri.*
⚫ *hols.* **www**.motoguzzi.it

Lecco ⓫

🏃 *46,000.* ℹ️ *IAT, Via Nazario Sauro 6 (0341-29 57 20).*
www.aptlecco.com

Lecco lies on the southern tip of the arm of the lake of the same name. It was inhabited in prehistoric times and fortified in the 6th century AD. In the 1300s it was taken over by Azzone Visconti, who built the Ponte Vecchio.

Manzoni set his novel *I Promessi Sposi (The Betrothed)* here. Mementos of his life can be found in his childhood home, the **Casa Natale di Manzoni** at Caleotto, which also houses the Galleria Comunale d'Arte. In the centre are the Teatro della Società (1844) and San Nicolò, whose baptistery chapel has 14th–15th-century frescoes. The **Museo di Storia Naturale** in the 18th-century **Palazzo Belgioioso** is also of interest. Sites described by Manzoni in his novel have been identified, including the castle of the Unnamed at Vercurago, and Lucia's home at Olate. Near Civate is Romanesque **San Pietro al Monte** (12th century), with frescoes and reliefs depicting the Passion. A turn-off on the road to Bellagio leads to the Madonna del Ghisallo sanctuary.

The Italian writer Manzoni, author of *The Betrothed*

A drawing room in Villa Serbelloni overlooking the lake

⛪ **Casa Natale di Manzoni**
Via Guanella 1. *Tel 0341-48 12 47.*
⭕ *9:30am–5:30pm Tue–Sun.* 🎫 ♿

⛪ **Palazzo Belgioioso and Museo di Storia Naturale**
Corso Matteotti 32. *Tel 0341-48 12 48.* ⭕ *9:30am–2pm Tue–Sun.* ⚫ *1 Jan, Easter, 15 Aug, 1 May, 25 & 26 Dec.* ♿

🔒 **San Pietro al Monte**
Civate. *Tel 0341-55 07 11.*
⭕ *Tue–Sat; call ahead for opening times.* **www**.amicidisanpietro.it

Bellagio ⓬

Como. 🏃 *3,050.*
ℹ️ *Piazza Mazzini (031-95 02 04).* **www**.bellagiolakecomo.com

Known since antiquity for its fine climate and scenery, Bellagio still has its medieval layout, with stepped alleyways. It became the site of splendid noble villas in the 1700s and then became a famous resort town in the 19th century. Among the attractive residences, the loveliest are **Villa Serbelloni** and **Villa Melzi d'Eril**. In 1870 the former became a hotel that numbered Winston Churchill and JF Kennedy among its guests. The Neo-Classical Villa Melzi was built in 1810 by Giocondo Albertolli. The interior is not open to the public, but the Museo Archeologico, the chapel and the gardens are. Near the town are the

One of the statues at Villa Melzi d'Eril

18th-century Trivulzio and Trotti villas. Do not miss the 12th-century San Giacomo, with its pulpit decorated with symbols of the Evangelists.

⛪ **Villa Serbelloni**
Piazza della Chiesa.
Tel 031-95 15 55. ⭕ *for guided visits only, mid-Mar–mid-Nov: 11am and 3:30pm Tue–Sun.* 🎫 🎫 *for groups of up to 30 people (book ahead).*

⛪ **Villa Melzi d'Eril**
Lungolario Marconi.
Tel 031-95 02 04.
⭕ *9:30am–6:30pm end Mar–Oct.* 🎫

Torno ⓭

Como. 🏃 *1,200.* ℹ️ *IAT, Piazza Cavour 17, Como (031-26 97 12).*

The village of Torno boasts the churches of Santa Tecla, which has a beautiful marble portal dating from 1480, and the 14th-century San Giovanni, with its remarkable Renaissance door. However, Torno is best known for the Villa Pliniana, built in 1573 (and attributed to Tibaldi) for Count Anguissola, the governor of Como. The villa is surrounded by a park and stands right by the lake. The writers Foscolo, Stendhal and Byron, and composer Rossini were all guests here.

Lake Garda

Remains of mosaics in the Roman villa at Desenzano del Garda

Italy's largest lake was created by glaciation. The scenery is varied, with steep, rugged cliffs at the northern end and softer hills southwards, where the basin widens and Mediterranean flora prevails. Over the centuries the praises of Lake Garda have been sung by such greats as Catullus, Dante and Goethe, and today it caters for luxury holidays and tour groups alike. Garda is an ideal spot for windsurfing and sailing, and it hosts famous regattas such as the Centomiglia.

★ **Desenzano del Garda**
This is one of the liveliest and most popular towns on Lake Garda. Above, one of the mosaics in the Roman villa, built in the 4th century and discovered in 1921 ❷

Villa Bettoni in Bogliaco (1756) has elegant frescoed rooms with masterpieces by Reni and Canaletto, as well as a garden with a nymphaeum.

★ **Gardone Riviera**
In this pleasant tourist resort is the Vittoriale degli Italiani, where the writer Gabriele D'Annunzio lived from 1921 to 1938. It embodies the decadence of which this poet and novelist was the last exponent ❺

Toscolano Maderno ❻

Gardone Riviera ❺   Fasano

Salò ❹

The Valtènesi and San Felica del Benaco ❸   Isola di Garda

Manerba

Moniga del Garda

Desenzano ❷

Sirmione ❶

San Pietro in Mavino

★ **Sirmione**
This Roman villa, which extends over a large area and was once thought to be the residence of the Latin poet Catullus, is one of the most impressive examples of an ancient Roman dwelling in Northern Italy ❶

KEY

‑ ‑ ‑ Ferry routes

⛴ Ferry service

❉ Viewpoint

🚉 Railway station

0 kilometres   5

0 miles   5

For hotels and restaurants in this region see pp166–7 and pp181–3

Limone sul Garda
The abundance of citrus trees grown here is supposedly the reason why the locals have the longest life expectancy in Italy **7**

VISITORS' CHECKLIST

Local information bureau. FS Milan–Venice line (89-2021). Azienda Provinciale Trasporti di Verona (045-805 78 11) or Società Italiana Autoservizi (840-62 00 01). Navigazione Lago di Garda (freefone 800-55 18 01). **www.**navlaghi.it

Riva del Garda **8**

Torbole

Limone sul Garda **7**

Campione del Garda

Malcesine **9**

gnano

Isola di Trimelone

Porta di Brenzone

Castelletto de Brenzone

Pai

At Torbole, now a surfers' paradise, Venetian ships – which defeated the Visconti in 1440 – were reassembled after being transported along the Val d'Adige.

Punta San Vigilio was named after the bishop from Trent who brought Christianity to the area in the 4th century.

10 Torri del Benaco

The Camaldolite Hermitage (16th century), which only relatively recently allowed women visitors, has a splendid panoramic view.

11 Garda

Bardolino **12**

Lazise

SIGHTS AT A GLANCE

14 Gardaland

13 Peschiera del Garda

Torri del Benaco
The economy of this small town, which thanks to its strategic position controls access to the upper lake region, is based on tourism and fishing. The townspeople have enjoyed special fishing privileges since the 1400s **10**

STAR SIGHTS

★ Sirmione

★ Gardone Riviera

★ Desenzano del Garda

Sirmione ❶

Brescia. 🏛 8,200.
ℹ Viale Marconi 8 (030-91 61 14).
www.comune.sirmione.bs.it

Roman Sirmio lay in the hinterland and only the villa quarter faced the lake. In the 13th century the Scaligeri lords of Verona turned it into a fortress to defend Lake Garda. In 1405 Sirmione was taken over by Venice, which then ruled until the 18th century. The main focus of the town is the **Rocca Scaligera**, a castle built by Mastino I della Scala (13th century), the inner basin of which served as shelter for the Veronese boats. Roman and medieval plaques are in the entrance arcade.

Fifteenth-century Santa Maria Maggiore, built over a pagan temple, has a Roman column in its porch, while the campanile was a Scaligera tower. The interior has 15th- and 16th-century frescoes and a 15th-century Madonna.

The **spas** use the water from the Boiola spring, known since 1546. San Pietro in Mavino, re-built in 1320, boasts fine 13th– 16th-century frescoes. Sirmione is also famous for the so-called **Grotte di Catullo**, a huge Roman residence built in the 1st centuries BC–AD. The most evocative rooms are the Grotta del Cavallo, the Cryptoporticus and the pool. The Sala della Trifora del Paradiso and Sala dei Giganti overlook the lake. The Antiquarium has finds from the villa, including a mosaic of a seascape and a portrait of Catullus (1st century BC).

⚓ Rocca Scaligera
Piazza Castello **Tel** 030-91 64 68. ◯
8:30am–7pm Tue–Sun. ◉ hols. 🔲

Terme Catullo (Spa)
Piazza Castello **Tel** 030-990 49 23
(for bookings).

🏛 Grotte di Catullo
Via Catullo **Tel** 030-91 61 57.
◯ Mar–14 Oct: 8:30am–7pm Tue–
Sat, Sun am only; 15 Oct–Feb:
8:30am–4:30pm Tue–Sun. ◉ Mon
(Tue if Mon is hol). 🔲

Christ Enthroned with Angels and Saints, San Pietro in Mavino

Desenzano del Garda ❷

Brescia 🏛 27,000. ℹ Via Porto Vecchio 34 (030-374 87 26).
🔲 (antiques, 1st Sun of month (except for Jan & Aug).

Probably founded by the Romans on a site inhabited since prehistoric times, Desenzano was taken over by Venice in the 15th century, when it became the leading lakeside town. Since the 19th century it has been a tourist resort. The heart of the town centre is Piazza Malvezzi, home to an antiques market known for its silverware and prints. The 16th-century town hall and Provveditore Veneto buildings are also here. In the **Duomo** (16th century) is a fine *Last Supper* by Tiepolo. The **Museo Civico Archeologico**, in the cloister of Santa Maria de Senioribus, contains displays of Bronze Age finds and the oldest known wooden plough (2000 BC).

The **Villa Romana** was built in the 4th century AD and rediscovered in 1921. It had been covered by a landslide, which preserved some lovely mosaics with geometric motifs such as the *Good Shepherd* and *Psyche and Cupids*. Finds from the villa are in the Antiquarium.

🏠 Duomo
Piazza Duomo. **Tel** 030-914 18 49.
◯ 9:30am–noon, 3:30–6pm daily
(to 6:30pm May–Sep).

🏛 Museo Civico Archeologico
Via Anelli 7. **Tel** 030-914 45 29 or
030-999 42 75. ◯ 3–7pm Tue–Sun.

🏛 Villa Romana
Via Crocifisso 2. **Tel** 030-914 35 47.
◯ Mar–14 Oct: 8:30am–7pm Tue–
Sun; 15 Oct–Feb: 8:30am–5pm Tue–
Sun. ◉ Mon (Tue if Mon is hol). 🔲

The Valtènesi and San Felice del Benaco ❸

Brescia 🏛 3,400. ℹ Via Porto-vecchio 34, Desenzano del Garda (030-374 87 26).

The area between Desenzano and Salò, called Valtènesi, is rich in medieval churches and castles. At Padenghe, the Rocca (9th–10th century) is reached by a drawbridge. Nearby is 12th–century Sant'Emiliano. The houses in Moniga del Garda are protected by a 10th-century wall with turrets. Here stands Santa Maria della Neve, built in the 14th century. The Rocca di Manerba del Garda (8th century) lies on a headland over the lake where a castle once stood. The ruins

The Rocca Scaligera at Sirmione, with its tower and battlements

For hotels and restaurants in this region see pp166–7 and pp181–3

Cappella del Santissimo Sacramento, Salò Duomo (18th century)

have become part of a regional park. At Solarolo, the 15th-century Santissima Trinità has a fresco cycle with the *Last Judgment*, while prehistoric finds from this area can be seen at the **Parco Archeologico Naturalistico della Rocca**. The bay between the Punta Belvedere and Punta San Fermo headlands is dominated by San Felice del Benaco. To the south is the Madonna del Carmine sanctuary (1452) containing outstanding 15th- and 16th-century frescoes. In the town centre the parish church has a *Madonna and Saints* by Romanino. Opposite Punta San Fermo is Isola di Garda. It is said that the Franciscans in the 13th-century monastery introduced citrus fruit cultivation to Lake Garda.

🌿 **Parco Archeologico Naturalistico della Rocca**
Via Rocca 20, Manerba del Garda. **Tel** 339 613 72 47. ☐ Apr–Sep: 10am–8pm daily; Oct–Mar: 10am–6pm Fri–Sun.

Salò ④

Brescia. 🏘 10,700. 🛈 Piazza San Antonio 4 (0365-214 23).

A former Roman town, in 1337 Salò became the seat of the Consiglio della Magnifica Patria, the governing body of 42 towns which met in the palazzo built by Sansovino in 1524 (now the Museo Archeologico). The late Gothic cathedral has a *Madonna and Saints* by Romanino (1529) and an altarpiece from 1476. Palazzo Fantoni is home to the Biblioteca dell'Ateneo di Salò and **Museo del Nastro Azzurro**, a military museum with items from 1796 to 1945. Palazzo Terzi-Martinengo at Barbarano was the seat of Mussolini's Salò puppet government.

🏛 **Museo del Nastro Azzurro**
Via Fantoni 49. **Tel** 0365-29 07 65. ☐ 10:30am–12:30pm, 2:30–5:30pm Sat & Sun. 📷

VINES, CHURCHES AND CASTLES

The Valtènesi area is known for its vineyards, where the rosé wine Chiaretto della Riviera del Garda is produced. A visit to the wineries here offers a chance to visit the inland region of this side of Lake Garda and also see the medieval fortresses of Soiano del Lago, Puegnago sul Garda and Polpenazze del Garda. In the cemetery of this last-mentioned village is the Romanesque church of San Pietro in Lucone, with its 15th-century frescoes depicting the lives of St Peter and the Apostles.

The medieval church of San Pietro in Lucone

Gardone Riviera ⑤

Brescia. 🏘 2,700. 🛈 Corso Repubblica 8 (0365-203 47).

Boasting the highest winter temperatures in Northern Italy, Gardone Riviera became a fashionable tourist resort in the late 19th century because of its mild dry climate, which is beneficial for those suffering from lung ailments. Two celebrated villas are Villa Alba and Villa Fiordaliso.

Gardone is also famous for the **Vittoriale degli Italiani**, Gabriele D'Annunzio's residence, where the poet collected over 10,000 objects including works of art, books and mementos, which he later donated to the state. In the garden are the Prioria, his residence, the Schifamondo with mementos, the Auditorium and the Mausoleum. On display are objects related to his exploits during and after World War I, such as his motor boat and aeroplane.

Another attraction is the **Giardino Botanico Hruska**, a fine botanic garden with over 2,000 Alpine, Mediterranean and subtropical species of plants.

D'Annunzio, who lived out his days at the Vittoriale degli Italiani

🏛 **Vittoriale degli Italiani**
Gardone. **Tel** 0365-29 65 11. ☐ Apr–Sep: 8:30am–8pm daily; Oct–Mar: 9am–5pm daily. 📷 **House** ☐ Apr–Sep: 9:30am–7pm Tue–Sun; Oct–Mar: 9am–1pm, 2–5pm Tue–Sun (last adm: 1 hour before closing). 📷 🖥 **www.vittoriale.it**

🌿 **Giardino Botanico Hruska**
Via Roma 2. **Tel** 0365-203 47 (IAT Gardone). ☐ 15 Mar–15 Oct: 9am–6pm daily. 📷

Canvas by Celesti in the Santi Pietro e Paolo parish church, Toscolano

Toscolano Maderno 6

Brescia. 🏛 8,100. 🛈 Via Sacerdoti, Maderno (0365-64 13 30).

This town is made up of the two villages of Toscolano and Maderno. Sights of interest at Maderno are the Romanesque church of Sant'Andrea, with a panel by Paolo Veneziano, and the parish church of Sant'Ercolano, with paintings by Veronese and Andrea Celesti. Here the Gonzaga family built the Palazzina del Serraglio (17th century) for Vincenzo I's amorous assignations. Toscolano, ancient Benacum, was the largest town on Lake Garda in Roman times. At Santa Maria del Benaco, with 16th-century frescoes, archaeologists found Roman and Etruscan objects and the ruins of a mosaic-decorated villa (1st century AD). The parish church of Santi Pietro e Paolo has 22 canvases by Andrea Celesti. Gargnano boasts San Giacomo di Calino (11th–12th century) and San Francesco (1289), whose cloister has Venetian arches. Another sight is Villa Feltrinelli, Mussolini's residence during the Republic of Salò.

Limone sul Garda 7

Brescia. 🏛 1,100. 🛈 Via Comboni 15 (0365-954 070).

Known for its mild climate, Limone may have been named after the lemon tree terraces (no longer used) typical of this area. Or the name may derive from *Limen* (border), since the Austrian frontier was here until 1918. In the town centre are the 15th-century church of San Rocco and a parish church (1685), with canvases by Celesti. Near Tignale is the **Montecastello Sanctuary** (13th–14th century) with a *Coronation of the Virgin* (14th century) and medallions by the school of Palma il Giovane. Towards Tremosine is the Brasa river gorge, in a panoramic setting.

Deposition (15th century), Malcesine parish church

🔒 **Montecastello Sanctuary**
Via Chiesa, Tignale. 🕐 9am–7pm daily mid-Mar–Oct. **Tel** 0365-730 19.

Riva del Garda 8

Trento. 🏛 16,000. 🛈 Largo Medaglie d'Oro (0464-55 44 44). **www**.gardatrentino.it

Situated at a strategic point on the northern tip of the lake, in the Trentino region, Riva was under Austrian rule until 1918. The Rocca and Torre Apponale (13th century) were built to defend the town; an angel, the town symbol, tops the tower. In the square opposite are Palazzo Pretorio (1370) and Palazzo del Provveditore (1482). The 12th-century Rocca is the home of the **Museo Alto Garda (MAG)**, with 14th–20th-century paintings. Santa Maria Assunta has two canvases by

Piazzetta, while the octagonal, richly frescoed Inviolata (1603) has works by Palma il Giovane. The impressive waterfalls of the Varone river, above Riva, are 80 m (262 ft) high.

Nearby Torbole was described by Goethe in *Italian Journey* and is a popular spot for sailing.

🏛 **Museo Alto Garda (MAG)**
Piazza Battisti 3. **Tel** 0464-57 38 69.
🕐 end Mar–Oct: 10am–noon, 1:30–6pm Tue–Sun. ⬤ Nov–Feb. ⬛

Malcesine 9

Verona. 🏛 3,700. 🛈 Seasonal office: Via Gardesana 238 (045-740 00 44).

One of the most fascinating towns along the lake shore, Malcesine stands on a stretch of impervious rock, hence the name *mala silex*, inaccessible rock. The 12th-century **Castello** was rebuilt by the Scaligeri of Verona in 1277. It houses the Museo di Storia Naturale del Garda e del Monte Baldo, the lake's natural history museum, which among other things shows how the Venetians transported ships to Torbole (1438–40). The parish church contains a 16th-century Deposition. Towering above Malcesine is Monte Baldo (2,218 m, 7,275 ft), accessible by cable car, with nature trails and stunning views.

The Legend of Maria (c.1614–20) by Martino Teofilo Polacco, in the Inviolata at Riva del Garda

The castle at Torri del Benaco, built in 1393

♠ **Castello Scaligero**
Via Castello. *Tel* 045-657 03 33.
◯ 7 Jan–mid-Mar: Sat & Sun; mid-Mar–Nov & 8 Dec–6 Jan: daily. ●
3 & 4 Jan; Nov; 25, 28 & 29 Dec. 🖼

Torri del Benaco ⑩

Verona. 🏛 2,500. 🛈 *Via Fratelli Lavanda (045-722 51 20).*

Roman Castrum Turrium was a major stop between Riva and Garda and has preserved the typical grid plan. Due to its strategic position, Torri was fortified and a castle was built; it is now a **museum**, with old farm tools and prehistoric finds. Santissima Trinità has some 15th-century frescoes.

🏛 **Museo del Castello**
Via Fratelli Lavanda. *Tel* 045-629 61 11. ◯ mid-Jun–mid-Sep: 9:30am–1pm, 4:30–7:30pm daily; mid-Sep–Oct & Apr–mid-Jun: 9:30am–12:30pm, 2:30–6pm daily.

Garda ⑪

Verona. 🏛 4,000. 🛈 *Piazzetta Donatori di Sangue (045-627 03 84).*

Built around a small bay, Garda was one of the major towns along the lake, controlling the southern basin. Its name, then given to the lake as well, comes from the German *Warten* (fortress), referring to the wall around the historic centre with its small port, accessible through the Torre dell'Orologio tower and gate. Among the historic buildings are the 15th-century Palazzo del Capitano, the Iosa,

the dock of Palazzo Carlotti designed by Sanmicheli, and **Santa Maria Maggiore** (18th century) with a painting by Palma il Giovane and a 15th-century cloister. At the new port is Villa Albertini, with an English-style park, while at Punta San Vigilio is Villa Guarienti (1542), designed by Sanmicheli, where the WWF offers a tour of the Bronze Age rock engravings.

🛈 **Santa Maria Maggiore**
Piazzale Roma. *Tel* 045-725 68 25.

Bardolino and Lazise ⑫

Verona. 🏛 6,800. 🛈 *Piazzale Aldo Moro (045-721 00 78).* 🛍 *antiques, 3rd Sun of month.*

The Cornicello and Mirabello headlands enclosing Bardolino made it a natural harbour. Originally it was a prehistoric settlement and then became a Roman camp. The historic centre has two early medieval churches, San Zeno and San Severo. The first still has its 9th-century Carolingian cruciform structure. Roman-esque San Severo was founded in the 9th century but rebuilt in the 12th. It has 12th–13th-century frescoes with battle scenes and biblical episodes, and a 10th-century crypt.

Among the civic buildings is the Loggia Rambaldi, in the Rambaldi family palazzo. Bardolino is also famous for its wine.

Lazise also boasted a prehistoric civilization. A castle was built in the 11th century and the lords of Verona erected the walls in the 1300s. The 16th-century Venetian Customs House is all that remains of the old harbour. Next to it is San Nicolò (12th century), with Giotto school frescoes.

♨ **Terme di Villa Cedri**
Piazza di Sopra 4, Località Colà di Lazise. *Tel* 045-759 09 88.
◯ 9am–9pm Mon–Thu, 9–2am Fri & Sat, 9am–11pm Sun. 🖼

Peschiera del Garda ⑬

Verona. 🏛 10,000. 🛈 *Piazzale Betteloni 15 (045-755 16 73).* **www**.tourism.verona.it

Peschiera has retained its military image more than any other town on Lake Garda. The old town lies on an island surrounded by a star-shaped wall – "a fortress beautiful and strong", says Dante. The walls were reinforced by the Scaligeri of Verona, rebuilt for the new Venetian rulers by Sanmicheli in 1556, and completed with two forts by the Austrians two centuries later. Besides the frescoed 18th-century San Martino, there is the 16th-century Madonna del Frassino sanctuary.

San Zeno in Bardolino, crowned by a tower, containing traces of its original frescoes

Gardaland ⓮

This theme park was opened in 1975 and is one of the largest in Italy (500,000 sq m, 600,000 sq yds). The 32 attractions range from the rollercoaster to reconstructions of the pyramids and a jungle, the Gardaland Theatre and the Fantasy Kingdom, all ideal for families with children. The fun park facilities are good, including a wide range of refreshments, theme shops and souvenir photos. At busy times queues are kept informed about the length of the wait.

The canoe safari, one of the many attractions

Gardaland Theatre
The park's actors take to the stage every day to provide entertainment for both adults and children.

Space Vertigo
There's a bacteriological alarm in the space station – everyone must escape! The only hope is to jump into space at top speed from a 40-m (131-ft) high tower. Thrills galore for everyone.

Ice Age 4D

Top Spin

Raptor *is a winged rollercoaster that takes you on a flight of near-misses at breathtaking speed.*

Ramses the Awakening
Lovers of ancient Egypt can enter the temple of Abu Simbel and explore the dark corridors while shooting laser guns.

Monorail station

The floating tree trunks of the Colorado Boat confront the canyon rapids.

Magic Mountain
This super-fast rollercoaster is one of the most famous rides of all, with two hairpin bends and two death-defying spins. Only for the most intrepid of visitors.

STAR FEATURES

★ Blue Tornado

★ Fantasy Kingdom

Jungle Rapids
Here you climb aboard a rubber dinghy and are taken over the rapids of a canyon, past a volcano, into the heart of mysterious and magical Southeast Asia with its temples.

VISITORS' CHECKLIST

Peschiera del Garda. *Tel* 045-644 97 77. ☐ Apr–mid-Jun & second week Sep–end Sep: 10am–6pm daily; mid-Jun–first week Sep: 10am–11pm daily; Oct: weekends only & 31 Oct; Dec–first week Jan: 10am–6pm weekends and Christmas hols. ● Nov, mid-Jan–end Mar. ☒ (free for ♿ and children under 1m tall). ☒ ⓘ www.gardaland.it

Escape from Atlantis

Mammoth

★ Blue Tornado
Even more exciting than the rollercoaster, this attraction offers you the chance to experience first-hand the thrills of piloting an American fighter plane.

★ Fantasy Kingdom
Children will love this! The talking trees, singing animals and puppet show will keep them entertained for hours.

Prezzemolo
Gardaland's mascot, Prezzemolo (Parsley) the dragon, is always at the park entrance to welcome all visitors.

0 metres   100

0 yards   100

The stepped Motta ascent, the setting for the Ortafiori festivities in April and May

Lago d'Orta

ℹ️ APTL, Via Panoramica, Orta–San Giulio (0322-90 56 14). 🚂 FS Novara-Domodossola line (848-88 80 88). ⛴ Nav. Lago d'Orta (0345-517 00 05).

Lake Orta, or Cusio, is the westernmost lake in the lower Alps region, characterized by soft hills and scenery. Villages are dotted around the lake, along the shore or perched among green terracing. The Mottarone, a ski resort, and the other mountains surrounding the lake offer attractive hiking trails.

As far back as the 1700s, Orta was a tourist attraction and many villas were built in large parks. The chief town is Orta San Giulio, on a promontory in the middle of the lake. The village alleyways wind around Piazza Motta, on which lies the Palazzetto della Comunità (1582) and where the stepped Motta ascent begins. Opposite the square is the island of San Giulio, converted to Christianity by the Greek deacon Julius, who built the 4th-century **basilica**. The church was restored in the 11th–12th centuries and has a 12th-century Romanesque marble pulpit and

Figure on the pulpit, San Giulio

15th-century frescoes. Next door is the Palazzo del Vescovo (16th– 18th century). The UNESCO World Heritage site of **Sacro Monte** is a sanctuary built in 1591 on the rise above Orta. Dedicated to St Francis, it consists of 20 chapels with 17th–18th-century terracotta statues and frescoes. Opposite, perched over a steep quarry, is the Madonna del Sasso sanctuary (1748).

On the northern tip of the lake is Omegna, whose medieval quarter boasts the late Romanesque collegiate church of Sant'Ambrogio.

At Quarna there is the **Museo Etnografico e dello Strumento a Fiato**, with displays of wind instruments, made in this village for centuries. Other interesting villages are Vacciago di Ameno, with the Calderara Collection of contemporary art, featuring 327 international avant-garde works of the 1950s and 1960s; Gozzano, with the church of San Giuliano (18th century), Palazzo Vescovile and the seminary; and, lastly, Torre di Buccione. San Maurizio d'Opaglio has a curious attraction: a museum devoted to the production of taps.

🔒 **Basilica di San Giulio**
Isola di San Giulio. APTL, ring road, Orta San Giulio (0322-90 56 14). ⏰ 9:30am–12:15pm Mon; 9:30am–12:15pm, 2–6:45pm Tue–Sun (5:45pm Oct–Mar).

🔒 **Sacro Monte**
Via Sacro Monte. **Tel** 0322-91 19 60. **Chapels** ⏰ summer: 8:30am–6:30pm daily; winter: 9am–4:30pm daily (5pm hols). ● 1 & 6 Jan, 25, 26 & 31 Dec.

🏛️ **Museo Etnografico e dello Strumento Musicale a Fiato**
Via Roma, Quarna Sotto. **Tel** 0323-82 63 68. ⏰ Jul–Aug: 2:30–6:30pm Tue–Fri, 10:30am–12:30pm, 2:30–6:30pm Sat & Sun.

Lago di Varese

ℹ️ IAT, Via Romagnosi 9, Varese (0332-28 19 13). 🚂 Ferrovie Nord Milano, Milan–Laveno line to Gavirate (02-202 22). ⛴ Autolinee Varesine (0332-73 11 10).

This lake basin was created by glacial movement during the Quaternary era. It offers pleasant scenery, with rolling hills and the Campo dei Fiori massif. In prehistoric times it was inhabited by a prehistoric civilization, the important remains of which were found on the island of Isolino Virginia (which can be reached from Biandronno), where they are on display at the **Museo Preistorico**, a UNESCO heritage site.

Part of the lake shore is now protected as the Brabbia marsh nature reserve. Not far away, at Cazzago Brabbia, are ice-houses used to conserve fish in the 18th century. On

Fishing boats along the shores of the Lago di Varese

For hotels and restaurants in this region see p167 and p183

the northern tip of the lake, at Voltorre di Gavirate, the **Chiostro di Voltorre** is worth a visit. It was part of a 12th-century Cluniac monastery and is now used for exhibitions. On the slopes of Campo dei Fiori you can see the lake of the UNESCO site **Sacro Monte** di Varese, a sanctuary made up of 14 17th-century chapels with frescoes and life-size statues.

🏛 **Museo Preistorico**
Isolino Virginia. *Tel 0332-25 54 82 (Musei Civici di Varese).* ☐ *Apr–Sep: 2–6pm Sat & Sun (Oct: 2–6pm Sun).* 🖼 🗺 *(book in advance).*

🏠 **Chiostro di Voltorre**
Voltorre di Gavirate. *Tel 0332-73 14 02.* ☐ *10am–5pm Tue–Sun.* www.museoartemoderna.it

🏠 **Sacro Monte**
Varese. *Tel 0332-22 92 23.* ☐ *daily.*

Lago d'Iseo

ℹ️ *IAT, Lungolago Marconi 26, Iseo (030-98 02 09).* 🚆 *FS to Brescia, then Ferrovie Nord Milano (02-20 222).* 🚌 *SAB (west side, 035-28 90 11); SIA (east side, 030-377 42 37).* 🚢 *Navigazione Lago d'Iseo (035-97 14 83).* www.lagodiseo.org

Lake Iseo, also known as Sebino, extends between the provinces of Bergamo and Brescia. It is the seventh-largest lake in Italy and the fourth in Lombardy, created by a glacier descending from the Val Camonica. The chief towns here are Iseo, Sarnico, Lovere and Pisogne. The historic centre of Iseo has kept its medieval character, with the church of Sant'Andrea (1150), the Neo-Classical interior of which contains a painting by Hayez. Next to this is the tomb of the feudal landowner Giacomo Oldofredi and, on a hill at the entrance to the town, the Castello degli Oldofredi (both built in the 14th century), which in 1585 became a Capuchin monastery. At Provaglio d'Iseo there is the San Pietro in Lamosa Cluniac monastery, founded in 1030. Its 11th–12th-century Romanesque church has frescoes by the school of Romanino. Sarnico, at the southern end of the lake, was an important commercial and industrial town. Among the Art Nouveau houses built here by Giuseppe Sommaruga is Villa Faccanoni (1912), one of the best examples of this style.

The road that follows the western side of the lake rounds the Corno headland, which has fine views of Monte Isola, the largest lake island in Europe, with its typical villages, dominated by the Madonna della Ceriola sanctuary and the 15th-century Rocca Oldofredi. At the northern end of the lake is Lovere, which has medieval tower-houses.

On the lakeside is the **Galleria dell'Accademia Tadini**, featuring fine works of art ranging from the 14th to the 20th century, including Jacopo Bellini, Strozzi, Tiepolo, Hayez and Canova. The church of Santa Maria in Valvendra (1483) has paintings by Floriano Ferramola and

The Piramidi di Zone pinnacles, some reaching 30 m (98 ft)

Moretto and a 16th-century wooden altarpiece on the high altar. At Pisogne is Santa Maria della Neve (15th century), with scenes of the Passion frescoed by Romanino (1534). From here you can go to the Val Camonica rock engravings park. The lake is also famous for its lovely scenery, including the Piramidi di Zone, pinnacles protected from erosion by the rock massif above them, and the Torbiere d'Iseo, a marshy area with peat bogs.

🏛 **Galleria dell'Accademia Tadini**
Via Tadini 40, Lovere. *Tel 035-96 27 80.* ☐ *May–Sep: 3–7pm Tue–Sat, 10am–noon, 3–7pm Sun & hols; Apr & Oct: 3–7pm Sat, 10am–noon, 3–7pm Sun & hols.* 📷 *Nov–Mar.* 🖼 ♿

Lago d'Idro

ℹ️ *Pro Loco, Via Trento 16, Idro (0365-832 24).* 🚌 *SIA (030-377 42 37).*

The highest large lake in Lombardy (368 m, 1,207 ft above sea level) was turned into an artificial basin in 1932 to provide irrigation and hydroelectricity. It is dominated by the Rocca di Anfo, a fortress with a splendid panoramic view that was built over older fortifications by the Venetians in 1450, and then rebuilt many times. From here you can reach Bagolino, with its charming stone houses and San Rocco (1478), which contains a fresco cycle by Giovan Pietro da Cemmo.

Rocca Oldofredi, Monte Isola, the Martinengo residence since the 1500s

TRAVELLERS' NEEDS

WHERE TO STAY

It is not easy to find atmospheric hotels or charming guesthouses in Milan because the city caters mostly to businessmen and women and the majority of hotels are therefore geared to their needs, with working facilities in the rooms and public areas. This type of accommodation comes in the medium–high price range and usually offers either private parking or nearby garage facilities. The four-star hotels not only have prestigious restaurants that are among the best in the city, but may also have lovely inner gardens not seen from the street. It is best to book accommodation well in advance, especially during the international fashion shows (held in March and October) and the many top trade fairs. At the lakes, on the other hand, the choice ranges from guesthouses to fascinating historic hotels, which have drawn visitors and celebrities from all over the world since the 19th century. The most luxurious are in charming 17th- and 18th-century villas, with flower-filled terraces, health clubs and heated pools. For more detailed information regarding accommodation in Milan and at the lakes, *see pages 160–167*.

Porter, Westin Palace, Milan (see p163)

CHOOSING A HOTEL

The Italian for hotel is *albergo*. A *pensione* or *locanda* theoretically indicates a more modest guesthouse, but in practice the distinctions are quite blurred.

Most of the hotels in Milan are concentrated in the Buenos Aires-Stazione Centrale area, near the Fieramilanocity and in the Città Studi district. The first group is situated for the most part in Piazza della Repubblica and near the main railway station, which is practical for visitors on a short stay. Some of the more interesting hotels are the five-star **Westin Palace** *(see p163)*, the **Sanpi** *(see p162)*,

The elegant Four Seasons Hotel in Milan *(see p163)*

which features a charming inner courtyard filled with flowers – and the **Principe di Savoia** *(see p163)*, which is decorated in the 1930s style. Around the Fiera, large hotels cater for professional and business visitors. The **Regency** *(see p161)* is smaller, with a warm atmosphere. At Città Studi you can find clean, inexpensive two-star hotels and an example is the **San Francisco** *(see p162)*.

In the historic centre a few charming, small hotels remain. The **Antica Locanda Solferino** *(see p163)* has an intimate, family atmosphere. The **Grand Hotel et de Milan** *(see p163)* and the **Four Seasons** *(see p163)* are both elegant, historic hotels.

At the lakes, hotels are more geared to holiday-makers and families. Some of Italy's most famous luxury hotels are sited around the lake shores. The **Des Iles Borromées** *(see p164)* at Lake Maggiore was once a royal residence. Lake Como boasts famous luxury hotels such as the **Grand Hotel Villa d'Este** *(see p165)* at Cernobbio, and the **Grand Hotel Villa Serbelloni** *(see p165)* at Bellagio.

BOOKING

Accommodation can be booked by phoning or sending a fax. The hotel will probably ask for a credit card number in advance. Almost all Milanese hotels have e-mail facilities and some, usually the luxury ones, have websites where you can book directly

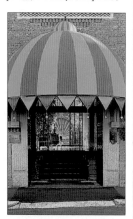

Entrance to the Hotel Regency *(see p161)* in Milan

◁ **Pavement cafés near Castello Sforzesco, Milan**

The Grand Hotel Villa Serbelloni *(see p165)* at Lake Como

online. Milan is a busy commercial city so it is best to book well in advance.

GRADING

Along with the rest of Italy, hotels in Milan and at the lakes are classified by a star system, from one (the lowest) to five stars. Luxury hotels are graded five-star "L". It is best to avoid one-star hotels in Milan (unlike the rest of Italy).

Two-star hotels usually offer bed and breakfast, and rooms may not have private bathrooms. Three-star hotels offer en-suite bathrooms, TV and sometimes a mini-bar; room service is usually available.

Four-star hotels, besides the above facilities, usually provide a laundry service, services for business travellers and (in Milan) a shuttle service to and from the airports. Five-star hotels are luxurious and offer exclusive restaurants and facilities for conferences.

At the lakes, accommodation ranges from luxury hotels to family-run guesthouses. There are also youth hostels and campsites with tents and caravans (RVs). Some have self-catering (efficiency) apartments.

PRICES

Accommodation in Milan is generally expensive. Because Milan is primarily a business destination, there is little seasonal variation in pricing; in fact, tariffs usually increase when the fashion shows are held and when there are major trade shows at the Fiera, which is quite often. Some of the larger hotels may also require you to take half-board (MAP) during your stay. For a hotel bargain, visit Milan in August. This is when most Italians leave the city to go on holiday – so, as well as cheaper accommodation, you will have Milan to yourself.

At the lakes, prices vary according to the season: in spring and summer, the peak tourist seasons, prices are higher. August is the busiest time. Many hotels expect you to take full board, especially in the summer months. Some hotels close for part of the year, usually in winter.

By law, prices have to be displayed in every hotel bedroom. Beware of extras: mini-bar drinks will be expensive. A view and air conditioning will add to costs, and hotel phone charges are higher than standard rates. By law, the hotel must issue you with a receipt when you pay, and the receipt should be kept until you leave Italy.

CHILDREN

In general, children are welcomed everywhere in Italy, but hotels may not go out of their way to provide special facilities. Some of the cheaper hotels may not be able to provide cots. However, most hotels, from the simplest to the most grand, will put a small bed or two into a double room for families travelling together. The price is usually an additional 30–40 per cent of the double room rate per bed. Hotels around the lakes tend to be better equipped for children than the business hotels of Milan. Babysitting services are offered by some large hotels at the lakes.

PETS

For those travelling with their dog or other pet, some hotels actively welcome animals and provide special facilities for them, especially at the lakes. In Milan it is more difficult to find hotels and guesthouses that accept pets, but some of the larger hotels have rooms specially furnished for clients and can even offer dog-sitting services. However, if you mean to travel with pets it is always a good idea to check these details when booking.

Four-poster bed in a room at the Villa Crespi *(see p167)*, Lake Orta

Choosing a Hotel

The hotels in this guide have been selected across a wide price range for the quality of service, decor and facilities. Hotels within the same price category are listed alphabetically. All the hotels listed accept credit cards unless otherwise stated. For Milan map references, see pages 224–37 and the inside back cover.

PRICE CATEGORIES
The price ranges are for a standard double room and taxes per night during the high season. Breakfast is not included, unless specified.

€ under €120
€€ €120–€160
€€€ €160–€210
€€€€ €210–€275
€€€€€ over €275

MILAN

CITY CENTRE Hotel Sempione   €

Via Finocchiaro Aprile 11, 20124 **Tel** *02 657 03 23* **Fax** *02 657 53 79* **Rooms** *46*   *Map 4 E2*

Located halfway between the train station and Piazza del Duomo, this hotel is close to the shopping and entertainment hub of Corso Buenos Aires. The airy, simple rooms offer all modern comforts, and they all have en-suite bathrooms. Wi-Fi is available in the public areas. Breakfast is included. **www.hotelsempionemilan.com**

CITY CENTRE Gran Duca di York   €€€

Via Moneta 1, 20123 **Tel** *02 87 48 63* **Fax** *02 869 03 44* **Rooms** *33*   *Map 7 B1*

This 18th-century palazzo is close to Piazza del Duomo and the best designer shops. It has retro bathrooms and ochre-coloured rooms that are quite compact in size. A small bar adjacent to the lobby serves hot and cold drinks. Parking is available nearby for a daily fee. Closed two weeks mid-Aug, 22–26 Dec. **www.ducadiyork.com**

CITY CENTRE Spadari al Duomo   €€€€

Via Spadari 11, 20123 **Tel** *02 72 00 23 71* **Fax** *02 86 11 84* **Rooms** *40*   *Map 7 C1*

A cosy, friendly hotel just steps from the Duomo, the famous Peck delicatessen and restaurant, and some of Milan's great shops. The blue-themed rooms are decorated with art and designer furniture; the best ones have balconies and even views from the bathroom. There is a small bar with Internet access. Closed 22–26 Dec. **www.spadarihotel.com**

CITY CENTRE Straf   €€€€

Via San Raffaele 3, 20121 **Tel** *02 80 50 81* **Fax** *02 89 09 52 94* **Rooms** *64*   *Map 7 C1*

Behind the 1883 Neo-Classic façade, the Straf has an ultra-modern interior. Luxurious natural materials set the minimal design tone. It boasts five unique chromatherapy and aromatherapy rooms. Straf's cosy lounge bar next door is very popular with the fashion and design set. An excellent central location. There is free Wi-Fi access. **www.straf.it**

CITY CENTRE The Gray   €€€€€

Via San Raffaele 6, 20121 **Tel** *02 720 89 51* **Fax** *02 86 65 26* **Rooms** *21*   *Map 7 C1*

Each room here has completely different decor, layout and focus, such as split levels, fitness facilities or a steam room. It is Milan's ultimate upmarket design hotel, with a fabulous restaurant and a central location just a stone's throw from the Duomo. Breakfast not included. Wi-Fi available at extra cost. Closed Aug. **www.sinahotels.com**

CITY CENTRE Hotel de la Ville   €€€€€

Via Hoepli 6, 20121 **Tel** *02 879 13 11* **Fax** *02 86 66 09* **Rooms** *109*   *Map 4 D5*

This hotel is located within walking distance of fashionable Via Montenapoleone. The decor is reminiscent of an English country house, with a stunning wood-panelled hall. The bedrooms have silk tapestries and marble bathrooms. The in-house bar is popular for pre-dinner drinks. There is a fee for Wi-Fi access. **www.delavillemilano.com**

CITY CENTRE Park Hyatt Milano   €€€€€

Via Tommaso Grossi 1, 20121 **Tel** *02 88 21 12 34* **Fax** *02 88 21 12 35* **Rooms** *106*   *Map 7 C1*

An elegantly designed hotel occupying a former bank. The luxurious modern decor in muted tones and the high level of service are synonymous with the global Hyatt group. The hotel's restaurant is excellent and the bathrooms are very spacious. Breakfast not included. Free Wi-Fi available. **www.milan.park.hyatt.com**

NORTHWEST MILAN Antica Locanda Leonardo   €€€

Corso Magenta 78, 20123 **Tel** *02 48 01 41 97* **Fax** *02 48 01 90 12* **Rooms** *16*   *Map 3 A5*

This hotel is a short walk from the church housing Leonardo da Vinci's *Last Supper*. Period furniture, brocade, bows and lace feature in the cosy rooms. There is also a leafy garden with cobblestones and wrought-iron furniture. A brief tram ride takes you directly to the city centre. **www.anticalocandaleonardo.com**

NORTHWEST MILAN Antica Locanda dei Mercanti   €€€

Via San Tomaso 6, 20121 **Tel** *02 805 40 80* **Fax** *02 805 40 90* **Rooms** *15*   *Map 3 B5*

A peaceful and pleasant inn in a pedestrian area near La Scala, Piazza del Duomo, the Castello Sforzesco and the shops. Some suites have kitchenettes, four rooms have a terrace and relaxed, Mediterranean-style decor, but some are rather compact. Wi-Fi and broadband access are available throughout the hotel. **www.locanda.it**

Key to Symbols *see back cover flap*

NORTHWEST MILAN Enterprise €€€

*Corso Sempione 91, 20154 **Tel** 02 31 81 81 **Fax** 02 31 81 88 11 **Rooms** 123*   **Map** 2 D1

This contemporary hotel built in a former radio factory is within walking distance from Fieramilanocity. It is also close to some popular nightspots. It features modern design throughout and a first-class restaurant, Sophia's, with a red dining room. All rooms have a sophisticated digital multimedia system and soundproofing. **www.enterprisehotel.com**

NORTHWEST MILAN Hotel Fiera Congressi €€€

*Via Spinola 9, 20149 **Tel** 02 48 54 72 **Fax** 02 48 00 84 94 **Rooms** 29*   **Map** 1 C3

This hotel is located right at Fieramilanocity, ideal for business guests. It is also near the famous San Siro stadium for football and concerts, and Corso Vercelli for shops. Simple in style, it has clean, spacious rooms, mostly overlooking the garden. Non-smoking rooms are available, as is Wi-Fi (at extra cost). **www.hotelfieracongressi.com**

NORTHWEST MILAN Johnny €€€

*Via Prati 6, 20145 **Tel** 02 34 18 12 **Fax** 02 33 61 05 21 **Rooms** 31*   **Map** 2 D3

This hotel is close to Fieramilanocity in a quiet side street. The colourful decor is understated, with a brick-vaulted breakfast room and a lounge like a winter garden. The metro is nearby and will take you to the Duomo and shops in ten minutes. A small, friendly, family-run hotel. **www.hoteljohnny.com**

NORTHWEST MILAN Ariosto €€€€

*Via Ariosto 22, 20145 **Tel** 02 481 78 44 **Fax** 02 498 05 16 **Rooms** 49*   **Map** 2 E5

Close to Conciliazione metro station, near the shops on Corso Vercelli and not far from Leonardo's famous *Last Supper*, this Art Nouveau building has a grand staircase, a detailed façade and wrought-iron railings. The bathrooms have modern frosted-glass doors and there are contemporary mosaics in the courtyard. **www.aristo.com**

NORTHWEST MILAN King €€€€

*Corso Magenta 19, 20123 **Tel** 02 87 45 45 **Fax** 02 89 01 07 98 **Rooms** 48*   **Map** 3 A5

This hotel is close to the Castello Sforzesco – and to Cadorna station, for the Malpensa Express train. The style is chintzy, with reproduction tapestries, Regency furniture and a grand old façade. Some rooms have views over the rooftops and castle towers. Bikes available for hire. There is a fee for Wi-Fi access. **www.hotelkingmilano.com**

NORTHWEST MILAN Regency €€€€

*Via G Arimondi 12, 20155 **Tel** 02 39 21 60 21 **Fax** 02 39 21 77 34 **Rooms** 71*

The Regency is rich in character, style and taste. It is housed in the 19th-century home of a famous nobleman, with a spectacular façade, open fire and marble bathrooms. The rooms are floral in design, while the lounge has chequered walls. Wi-Fi access is subject to extra cost. Closed 3 wks in Aug, 23 Dec–6 Jan. **www.regency-milano.com**

SOUTHWEST MILAN Hotel dei Fiori €€

*Via Privata Renzo e Lucia 14, 20142 **Tel** 02 843 64 41 **Fax** 02 89 50 10 96 **Rooms** 53*   **Map** 7 A5

Hotel dei Fiori is easily accessible from the motorway and close to the Navigli area, which is great for nightlife. The nearby road is busy, but the clean and comfortable rooms all have soundproofing. They are basic in design, with wooden furnishings. The hotel also offers an Internet point and Wi-Fi for a fee. **www.hoteldeifiori.com**

SOUTHWEST MILAN Marriott €€€

*Via Washington 66, 20146 **Tel** 02 485 21 **Fax** 02 481 89 25 **Rooms** 321*   **Map** 5 C2

The Marriott is corporate in style and particularly convenient for visitors to the Fiera, for whom there is a complimentary shuttle service. The hotel offers reliable standards of service, with very large public areas and spacious rooms. Decor is a mix of stripes, florals and chintz. Wi-Fi is charged at an hourly rate. **www.marriott.com**

SOUTHWEST MILAN Liberty €€€€

*Viale Bligny 56, 20136 **Tel** 02 58 31 85 62 **Fax** 02 58 31 90 61 **Rooms** 52*   **Map** 8 D4

A classic, elegant hotel with a nice courtyard close to the Bocconi university. Tastefully decorated with spacious comfy rooms and Art Nouveau touches, it is spread over six floors. The lobby is filled with light from the stained-glass roof, while the marble bathrooms have a Jacuzzi. Wi-Fi costs extra. Closed Aug. **www.hotelliberty-milano.com**

SOUTHWEST MILAN Regina €€€€

*Via C Correnti 13, 20123 **Tel** 02 58 10 69 13 **Fax** 02 58 10 70 33 **Rooms** 43*   **Map** 7 B2

A short tram ride away from Piazza del Duomo is this cosy, pleasant hotel in a converted 18th-century residence. The colonial-style lobby has palms, pillars and a domed glass roof. Some rooms have small balconies. In summer you can breakfast outdoors on the cobblestoned terrace. Free Wi-Fi is available. **www.hotelregina.it**

SOUTHWEST MILAN Zurigo €€€€

*Corso Italia 11/a, 20122 **Tel** 02 72 02 22 60 **Fax** 02 72 00 00 13 **Rooms** 42*   **Map** 7 C2

The Zurigo is centrally located a ten-minute walk from Piazza del Duomo. The hotel offers single occupancy rooms, making it a good option for sole travellers. Snacks are available from the bar and the restaurant is open on weekdays. Bike hire is free, but Wi-Fi access is subject to an additional charge. **www.brerahotels.com**

SOUTHWEST MILAN Carrobbio €€€€€

*Via Medici 3, 20123 **Tel** 02 89 01 07 40 **Fax** 02 805 33 34 **Rooms** 56*   **Map** 7 B2

This original 1930s-style hotel has pleasant rooms, decorated in a simple style favouring muted colours and plaids or stripes. Rooms look on to the street or an internal courtyard. Suites have a private garden, and some rooms feature large terraces. A communal room has Internet access; Wi-Fi is available for a fee. **www.hotelcarrobbiomilano.com**

SOUTHEAST MILAN Hotel 22 Marzo   €

Piazza Santa Maria del Suffragio 3, 20129 **Tel** *02 70 10 70 64* **Rooms** *15*   **Map** *8 F1*

A good budget option, the Hotel 22 Marzo is a friendly, family-run place conveniently located just east of the city centre, in the Vittoria district. Rooms are clean and simply furnished, and they vary in size. Triples and quads are available, and groups are welcome. Breakfast is included in the price. **www.hotel22marzo.com**

SOUTHEAST MILAN Hotel del Sud   €€

Corso Lodi 74, 20139 **Tel** *02 57 40 99 18* **Fax** *02 569 34 57* **Rooms** *27*   **Map** *8 F4*

Hotel del Sud is a small, homely one-star hotel on Corso Lodi, a busy street with easy access to Porta Romana train station. There are a few bars and pizzerias nearby. The metro station Brenta is opposite the hotel, so access to the city centre is quick and easy. Rooms are small and simple, all with bathroom and TV. **www.hoteldelsud.com**

SOUTHEAST MILAN Townhouse 31   €€€

Via Goldoni 31, 20129 **Tel** *02 701 56* **Fax** *02 71 31 67* **Rooms** *20*   **Map** *4 F5*

With only 20 rooms, this hotel feels very cosy, with a warm, relaxing, friendly atmosphere. The emphasis is on well-being, with tasteful decor, artifacts from the owners' travels, a large communal breakfast table and a cosy lobby. In summer the garden bar is very popular for apéritifs and cocktails. **www.townhouse.it**

SOUTHEAST MILAN Vittoria   €€€

Via Pietro Calvi 32, 20129 **Tel** *02 545 65 20* **Fax** *02 55 19 02 46* **Rooms** *40*   **Map** *8 F1*

This fairly central hotel has a modern façade. The compact rooms are decorated in a light, classic style, and the staff are friendly. It is a family-owned hotel on a residential street, not far from the Duomo. In summer, breakfast can be taken in the little garden at the back. Wi-Fi access is available for a fee. **www.hotelvittoriamilano.it**

NORTHEAST MILAN Ibis Milan Centro   €€

Via Finocchiaro Aprile 2, 20124 **Tel** *02 631 51* **Rooms** *437*   **Map** *4 E2*

Close to the Stazione Centrale, the Ibis offers contemporary, no-frills style at low prices. Compact rooms are attractive and functional, with laminate flooring and rich colour tones. Business visitors are well catered for, with a restaurant, private parking and a 24-hour bar. Wi-Fi access is available on payment of a fee. **www.ibishotel.com**

NORTHEAST MILAN Lombardia   €€

Viale Lombardia 74–76, 20131 **Tel** *02 289 25 15* **Fax** *02 289 34 30* **Rooms** *78*   **Map** *4 F3*

Housed in an old palazzo with a lovely façade, the Lombardia has a welcoming feel with classic marble and oriental rugs in the lobby. Some of the clean and pleasant rooms look on to a small courtyard garden. Apartments with kitchenette are also available weekly. Wi-Fi costs extra. Closed 2 wks mid-Aug. **www.hotellombardia.com**

NORTHEAST MILAN Mediolanum   €€

Via Mauro Macchi 1, 20124 **Tel** *02 670 5312* **Rooms** *51*   **Map** *4 F2*

A stylish, contemporary design hotel with an emphasis on colour and clever lighting. Rooms and bathrooms are not spacious, but they are individual. Staff are friendly and breakfast is included in the price. Wi-Fi access is available at an hourly rate. Closed 2 wks Aug, 23 Dec–2 Jan. **www.mediolanumhotel.com**

NORTHEAST MILAN Ritter   €€

Corso Garibaldi 68, 20121 **Tel** *02 29 00 68 60* **Fax** *02 657 15 12* **Rooms** *89*   **Map** *3 B3*

Ritter is located in Brera, the bohemian quarter of the city. The decor is rather old, but the hotel offers comfort and a good base from which to explore Milan, being close to Parco Sempione and the Castello Sforzesco. There is a garden terrace, solarium and Internet access for a fee. **www.ritter-hotel.com**

NORTHEAST MILAN San Francisco   €€

Viale Lombardia 55, 20131 **Tel** *02 236 10 09* **Fax** *02 26 68 03 77* **Rooms** *28*   **Map** *4 F3*

Located in the academic area of town, this family-run hotel is small, affordable and only six metro stops from the Duomo and three from Central Station. Rooms are adequate, if sparse. Ask for one overlooking the pretty little garden with its pergola, roses, lawn and paved terrace. Internet point for guests' use. **www.hotel-sanfrancisco.it**

NORTHEAST MILAN Andreola Central   €€€

Via Domenico Scarlatti 24, 20124 **Tel** *02 670 9141* **Rooms** *85*   **Map** *4 F1*

An attractive 19th-century hotel located close to the Stazione Centrale. The pillared lobby is spacious and elegant, with marble floors and a large reading area. Double rooms are a good size and classically furnished. A plus are the views from the panoramic restaurant on the top floor. Wi-Fi access is available at a charge. **www.andreolahotel.it**

NORTHEAST MILAN Hermitage   €€€

Via Messina 10, 20154 **Tel** *02 31 81 70* **Fax** *02 33 10 73 99* **Rooms** *131*   **Map** *3 A1*

Situated between Garibaldi station and Corso Sempione, next to the Cimitero Monumentale, this classic, spacious hotel offers good amenities, such as a garden, spa and fitness facilities. The restaurant is renowned for great fish and seafood. There is also a sun terrace and garage. Wi-Fi is available for a fee. Closed Aug. **www.monrifhotels.it**

NORTHEAST MILAN Sanpi   €€€

Via Lazzaro Palazzi 18, 20124 **Tel** *02 29 51 33 41* **Fax** *02 29 40 24 51* **Rooms** *79*   **Map** *4 E3*

With a modern façade and simple, sophisticated decor, Sanpi offers easy access to the shops on Corso Buenos Aires, the public gardens and a metro station. Pick a room overlooking the pretty little garden. Some rooms have balconies, suites have Jacuzzis; the hotel also has Wi-Fi access for a fee. **www.hotelsanpimilano.it**

Key to Price Guide *see p160* **Key to Symbols** *see back cover flap*

NORTHEAST MILAN Sheraton Diana Majestic
€€€

Viale Piave 42, 20129 **Tel** *02 205 81* **Fax** *02 20 58 20 58* **Rooms** *106* **Map** *4 F4*

A majestic hotel boasting one of the loveliest gardens in the city. Built in 1908 on the site of Milan's first public baths, the Diana is close to some great shops, art galleries and restaurants. Milan's *beau monde* gathers at the hotel bar at happy hour. Breakfast not included; Wi-Fi costs extra. Closed Aug, 25 Dec–6 Jan. **www.sheratondianamajestic.com**

NORTHEAST MILAN Antica Locanda Solferino
€€€€

Via Castelfidardo 2, 20121 **Tel** *02 657 01 29* **Fax** *02 657 13 61* **Rooms** *11* **Map** *3 C3*

Old-world charm reigns at this upmarket B&B, which is more stylish and affordable than most conventional hotels. Located in the heart of bohemian Brera, it features antique and retro details such as tiny wrought-iron balconies, traditional floorboards and narrow corridors. **www.anticalocandasolferino.it**

NORTHEAST MILAN Baviera
€€€€

Via Panfilo Castaldi 7, 20124 **Tel** *02 659 05 51* **Fax** *02 29 00 32 81* **Rooms** *50* **Map** *4 E3*

This hotel has a spacious lobby and a design mix of stripes and chintz. It is situated a couple of streets behind Piazza della Repubblica, where there is a metro station. There are restaurants nearby, secure parking and a shuttle to and from the main train station. Bike hire is available, as is Internet access; Wi-Fi costs extra. **www.hotelbaviera.com**

NORTHEAST MILAN Cavour
€€€€

Via Fatebenefratelli 21, 20121 **Tel** *02 62 00 01* **Fax** *02 659 22 63* **Rooms** *113* **Map** *3 C4*

Close to Villa Reale and the public gardens, the Cavour is also near Brera, the lively quarter with art galleries and bars. The impressive lobby has an elegant villa style, with columns and staircases, and the rooms are clean and contemporary. The hotel restaurant Conte Camillo is excellent. Closed Aug. **www.hotelcavour.it**

NORTHEAST MILAN Holiday Inn Garibaldi Station
€€€€

Via Ugo Bassi 1a, 20158 **Tel** *02 607 68 01* **Rooms** *129* **Map** *3 F1*

This Holiday Inn is situated in a very busy area of the city with good tram links to the centre; the nearest metro is 10 minutes walk away. The hotel offers standard, but very clean and comfortable, rooms decorated in light, neutral tones. Wi-Fi is available only in the reception area, and there is a charge. **www.himilangaribaldi.com**

NORTHEAST MILAN Manin
€€€€

Via Manin 7, 20121 **Tel** *02 659 65 11* **Fax** *02 655 21 60* **Rooms** *118* **Map** *4 D4*

The Manin sits in a quiet side street, facing the public gardens of Via Palestro. Part of the Tulip group, it features all the amenities one would expect of such a chain. It has a restaurant, American bar and pretty garden with pergola. Large painted scenes decorate the bedheads. Wi-Fi is available at extra cost. Closed Aug. **www.hotelmanin.it**

NORTHEAST MILAN Bulgari
€€€€€

Via Privata Fratelli Gabba 7b, 20122 **Tel** *02 805 80 51* **Fax** *02 805 80 52 22* **Rooms** *58* **Map** *3 C4*

The luxury you would expect from Bulgari, one of Italy's high-class designers, in a peaceful setting, a few minutes' walk from the best shops and next to the Botanical Gardens. Rooms are decorated with the finest natural materials. Exclusive spa and treatment room and an innovative restaurant. Breakfast not included. **www.bulgarihotels.com**

NORTHEAST MILAN Carlton Baglioni
€€€€€

Via Senato 5, 20121 **Tel** *02 770 77* **Fax** *02 78 33 00* **Rooms** *89* **Map** *4 D4*

This hotel is in an ideal location for the shops, just off the boutique-laden Via della Spiga. The excellent restaurant, Il Baretto, a bar in summer on the roof terrace, a cosy library with an open fireplace and spacious rooms are just some of its charms. Three rooms have a modern, sleek design. Breakfast not included. **www.baglionihotels.com**

NORTHEAST MILAN Four Seasons
€€€€€

Via Gesù 8, 20121 **Tel** *02 770 88* **Fax** *02 77 08 50 00* **Rooms** *118* **Map** *4 D5*

The setting of the Four Seasons is a former monastery, with rooms overlooking the 15th-century cloistered garden. Service is faultless (there is 24-hour room service) and the spacious rooms exude luxury through rich fabrics, hand-crafted lampshades and extremely comfortable beds. Wi-Fi available at extra cost. **www.fourseasons.com/milan**

NORTHEAST MILAN Grand Hotel et de Milan
€€€€€

Via Manzoni 29, 20121 **Tel** *02 72 31 41* **Fax** *02 86 46 08 61* **Rooms** *95* **Map** *4 D4*

The Grand is steeped in history. Hemingway and Callas stayed here, and Giuseppe Verdi called it his home for 27 years. It offers luxury and elegance, with 19th-century furniture throughout and Art Nouveau skylights in the bar. The rooms have large marble bathrooms. Breakfast not included. Wi-Fi available for a fee. **www.grandhoteletdemilan.it**

NORTHEAST MILAN Principe di Savoia
€€€€€

Piazza della Repubblica 17, 20124 **Tel** *02 623 01* **Fax** *02 659 58 38* **Rooms** *404* **Map** *4 D2*

A Milanese landmark, this hotel set in a charming 19th-century building is known for its elegance and high level of service (24-hour room service is available). The top-floor fitness and spa club with beauty centre offers sauna, Jacuzzi and indoor pool. Breakfast not included; Wi-Fi is available at extra cost. **www.hotelprincipedisavoia.com**

NORTHEAST MILAN Westin Palace
€€€€€

Piazza della Repubblica 20, 20124 **Tel** *02 633 61* **Fax** *02 65 44 85* **Rooms** *228* **Map** *4 E3*

The Westin Palace is a minutes walk away from the Duomo and the designer shops. Palatial touches include marble pillars, wood panelling and chandeliers. Enjoy cocktails in the lounge bar, dine in one of the three restaurants or work out in the state-of-the-art gym. Breakfast not included; Wi-Fi available for a fee. **www.westinpalacemilan.com**

LAKE MAGGIORE

BAVENO Lido Palace
Strada del Sempione 30, 28831 **Tel** *0323 92 44 44* **Rooms** *82*

This 19th-century villa near the lake once hosted a newly married Winston Churchill. The Lido Palace is a family-run hotel that sits in its own park a short distance from the centre of Baveno and enjoys stunning lake views. Rooms are bright, elegant and classically furnished. Wi-Fi access costs extra. Closed Nov–mid-Mar. **www.lidopalace.com**

BELGIRATE Villa Carlotta
Via Mazzini 121–125, 28832 **Tel** *0322 764 61; 800 82 00 80 (within Italy)* **Fax** *0322 767 05* **Rooms** *129*

Set in private parkland on the lush banks of Lake Maggiore, Villa Carlotta is a splendid three-storey villa. The classic decor of the compact rooms exudes an old-fashioned charm. As well as extensive grounds, the hotel offers bike hire, horse riding, tennis and golf facilities nearby. Wi-Fi available for a fee. **www.villacarlottalagomaggiore.it**

CANNOBIO Hotel Cannobio
Piazza Vittorio Emanuele III 6, 28822 **Tel** *0323 73 96 39* **Fax** *0323 73 95 96* **Rooms** *18*

A lovely hotel in a grand building facing the lake. The rooms are clean and pleasant, with elegant decor in rich colours. The painted antique bedheads add a striking touch. Modern facilities, friendly staff and a lovely restaurant with a summer terrace over the lake complete the experience. Wi-Fi costs extra. **www.hotelcannobio.com**

CANNOBIO Hotel Pironi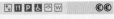
Via Marconi 35, 28822 **Tel** *0323 706 24; 0323 70 87* **Fax** *0323 721 84* **Rooms** *12*

This hotel is housed in a former Franciscan monastery and original touches include frescoes, antiques and vaulted ceilings. Decor is tasteful and intimate. Some rooms have views, others small balconies. There is an open fire in the first-floor lobby and a tavern in the cellar. Closed Nov–Mar. **www.pironihotel.it**

GHIFFA Castello di Frino
Via C Colombo 8, 28823 **Tel** *0323 591 81* **Fax** *0323 597 83* **Rooms** *11*

The former residence of Cardinal Morigia (1623–1701) has been architecturally restored to its former glory. It boasts ornamental details and parkland with a formal garden, pool and lake. The period furniture and simplicity of decor set a sober, quasi-religious tone. Good restaurant with terrace. Closed mid-Oct–mid-Mar. **www.castellodifrino.com**

GHIFFA Hotel Ghiffa
Corso Belvedere 88, 28823 **Tel** *0323 592 85* **Fax** *0323 595 85* **Rooms** *39*

Ghiffa offers its guests lots of sporting opportunities, plus a large pool, sun terrace with loungers, private beach and landing stage for boats. The elegant villa-like hotel has simple decor and the rooms with lake views have floor-to-ceiling windows. Ask for one with a balcony or terrace. Wi-Fi available for a fee. **www.hotelghiffa.com**

ISOLA DEI PESCATORI, STRESA Verbano
Via Ugo Ara 2, 28838 **Tel** *0323 304 08; 0323 325 34* **Fax** *0323 331 29* **Rooms** *12*

Hotel Verbano has an idyllic setting on an island in the lake, overlooking Isola Bella and Palazzo Borromeo. It has charming rooms named after flowers. Enjoy breakfast on the terrace, listen to the waves lapping on the shore and take in the lake views. There is a shuttle boat service from Stresa. Closed Nov–Mar. **www.hotelverbano.it**

PALLANZA Grand Hotel Majestic
Via V Veneto 32, 28922 **Tel** *0323 50 97 11* **Rooms** *80*

In an idyllic setting on the shore of the lake, this palatial hotel offers splendid original 19th-century features with contemporary facilities and comfort. There are great views from most rooms, and a tiny private beach. Room decor is elegantly subdued. Breakfast included. Closed mid-Oct–end Mar. **www.grandhotelmajestic.it**

RANCO Il Sole di Ranco
Piazza Venezia 5, 20120 **Tel** *0331 97 65 07* **Fax** *0331 97 66 20* **Rooms** *14*

Located amid verdant parkland leading to the shores of Lake Maggiore, this hotel boasts a private garden, views from the excellent restaurant where you can dine alfresco in the summer and even a helicopter landing area. Facilities include a pool, sauna and *hammam*. Wi-Fi access costs extra. Closed mid-Oct–end Jan. **www.ilsolediranco.it**

STRESA La Palma
Lungolago Umberto I 33, 28838 **Tel** *0323 324 01* **Fax** *0323 93 39 30* **Rooms** *120*

Luxury living at relatively moderate prices. Rooms are spacious, and they come equipped with big marble bathrooms and Jacuzzis. Take in the beautiful lake views from the balconies. The hotel has a pool that overlooks the lake and its own private beach. Breakfast is included. Wi-Fi is available but at extra cost. Closed Dec–Feb. **www.hlapalma.it**

STRESA Grand Hotel des Iles Borromées
Corso Umberto I 67, 28838 **Tel** *0323 938 938* **Fax** *0323 324 05* **Rooms** *170*

This imposing *belle époque* hotel features palatial decor as well as lake and alpine views. The facilities are excellent, ranging from sports amenities to beauty and fitness, piano bar, extensive lush gardens, pools, tennis courts and a great restaurant. Stunning setting and great service. Wi-Fi is available for a fee. **www.borromees.it**

Key to Price Guide *see p160* **Key to Symbols** *see back cover flap*

STRESA Villa Aminta

Via Sempione Nord 123, 28838 **Tel** *0323 93 38 18* **Fax** *0323 93 39 55* **Rooms** *67*

North of Stresa, this beautiful villa is set in its own park, with great views of the lake. It has elegant decor throughout, including chandeliers and *trompe-l'oeil* paintings. There is a piano lounge, refined restaurant, pool and tennis court. Cookery lessons available. Breakfast not included. Closed Dec–Mar. **www.villa-aminta.it**

LAKE COMO

ARGEGNO Villa Belvedere

Via Milano 1, 22010 **Tel** *031 82 11 16* **Rooms** *16*

Located right on the lake, this 18th-century villa is a family-run place with bags of charm. Some rooms have beautiful painted ceilings, and many enjoy stunning views across Lake Como. Dine on the terrace or fall asleep with a book in the adjoining garden. Closed Nov–Mar. **www.villabelvedere-argegno.it**

BELLAGIO Florence

Piazza Mazzini 46, 22021 **Tel** *031 95 03 42* **Fax** *031 95 17 22* **Rooms** *30*

In a great location on the shores of Lake Como, this stylish hotel has elegant modern decor, with canopy beds, roll-top baths, a bar and a gourmet restaurant. A shady terrace offers guests wonderful views of the lake. Extra facilities include a spa with sauna, Turkish bath and Jacuzzi. Closed end Oct–Easter. **www.hotelflorencebellagio.it**

BELLAGIO Belvedere

Via Valassina 31, 22021 **Tel** *031 95 04 10* **Rooms** *64*

In the same family since 1880 and set in luxuriant grounds 400 metres (1,300 ft) above the village, this 19th-century hotel enjoys fantastic views across the lake. Rooms are elegantly furnished, bright and attractive. Most have views of the lake, and some have balconies. Wi-Fi access costs extra. Closed end Oct–Easter. **www.belvederebellagio.com**

BELLAGIO Grand Hotel Villa Serbelloni

Via Roma 1, 22021 **Tel** *031 95 02 16* **Fax** *031 95 15 29* **Rooms** *95*

Set in a breathtaking position on a headland between two branches of the lake, Villa Serbelloni was once the holiday home of Milanese aristocracy. Frescoes, Italianate gardens, marble staircases and crystal echo the prestige of this Neo-Classical villa. Ask for a large room with a lake view. Wi-Fi costs extra. Closed Nov–Mar. **www.villaserbelloni.com**

CERNOBBIO Grand Hotel Villa d'Este

Via Regina 40, 22012 **Tel** *031 34 81* **Fax** *031 34 88 44* **Rooms** *154*

A sumptuous, luxurious *grande dame* of a hotel, with elegantly appointed rooms. Period furniture, fine paintings, chandeliers and marble fireplaces add to the old-world charm and feeling of a private palatial villa. The hotel is steeped in history but not lacking in modern services and facilities. Closed mid-Nov–end Feb. **www.villadeste.it**

COMO Borgovico

Via Borgovico 91, 22100 **Tel** *031 57 01 07* **Rooms** *13*

A small, friendly hotel in Como town, near the San Giovanni train station. There are no views, but it is just a short walk to the lake. Most rooms have subtle decor in cream and ochre, with beamed ceilings or exposed stone walls giving the place bags of cosy character. Breakfast included. **www.hotelborgovico.it**

COMO Hotel Firenze

Piazza Volta 16, 22100 **Tel** *031 30 03 33* **Fax** *031 30 01 01* **Rooms** *44*

This Neo-Classic hotel sits in a pedestrianised square in the town centre, a short walk from the lakeside, with a terrace on which to enjoy an apéritif. The rooms have a basic contemporary design, though some retain original beams or parquet flooring. Ask for one looking onto the inner courtyard. **www.hotelfirenzecomo.it**

COMO Terminus

Lungo Lario Trieste 14, 22100 **Tel** *031 32 91 11* **Fax** *031 30 25 50* **Rooms** *50*

Before being converted into a hotel, this was the 19th-century home to Lombard aristocracy. It is full of atmosphere, with Art Nouveau details, beautiful frescoes and tapestries. The decor is colourful, with precious fabrics and floral bedspreads. There are also formal gardens, a lovely terrace and a small restaurant. **www.albergoterminus.com**

COMO Metropole Suisse

Piazza Cavour 19, 22100 **Tel** *031 26 94 44* **Fax** *031 30 08 08* **Rooms** *71*

Located in the heart of Como, this hotel commands great lake views. The façade by architect Comasco Terragni dates back to 1892 and incorporates wrought-iron balconies for most rooms. Boat trips leave from the pier in front of the hotel. Choose between formal or informal dining. Closed mid-Dec–mid-Jan. **www.hotelmetropolesuisse.com**

LENNO San Giorgio

Via Regina 81, 22019 **Tel** *0344 404 15* **Fax** *0344 415 91* **Rooms** *33*

A calm hotel with large gardens facing Lake Como. The 1920s building has period-style rooms with modern facilities and bathrooms. A lovely terrace, tennis courts and a good restaurant add to its charm. Ask for a room with lake views. Breakfast not included. Wi-Fi costs extra. Closed Nov–Mar. **www.sangiorgiolenno.com**

TREMEZZO Grand Hotel Tremezzo 🄵 🎙️ 🎚 🅿️ 🌐 €€€€€
Via Regina 8, 22019 **Tel** *0344 424 91* **Fax** *0344 402 01* **Rooms** *98*

This prestigious lakeside hotel built in Art Nouveau style in 1910 is surrounded by gardens and terraces with lake views. The grand hotel feel is echoed in ornate gilt and antiques. There is also a floating pool on the lake. Sauna, gym, tennis courts and golf facilities are available, as is Wi-Fi (for a fee). Closed Nov–Feb. **www.grandhoteltremezzo.com**

VARENNA Hotel du Lac 🄵 🎙️ 🎚 🅿️ 🌐 €€€
Via del Prestino 11, 23829 **Tel** *0341 83 02 38* **Fax** *0341 83 10 81* **Rooms** *16*

A smallish hotel at the water's edge with enchanting views from the lake-facing rooms. Enjoy the terrace restaurant under vines at the side of hotel, looking out over the lapping water. Charming features include marble columns, wrought-iron balustrades and the floral names given to every room. Closed Nov–Mar. **www.albergodulac.com**

LAKE GARDA

DESENZANO DEL GARDA Piroscafo 🄵 🎙️ 🎚 🅿️ 🌐 €€
Via Porto Vecchio 11, 25015 **Tel** *030 914 11 28* **Fax** *030 991 25 86* **Rooms** *32*

Located at the old dock of the town in a historic building. The terrace on the ground floor is housed in an arched portico. Pick a room looking out on to the dock or watch the boats from the terrace restaurant, which serves a simple menu of fish and international dishes. Parking is available nearby. Closed Nov–mid-Mar. **www.hotelpiroscafo.it**

DESENZANO DEL GARDA Tripoli 🄵 🎚 🌐 €€
Piazza Matteotti 18, 25015 **Tel** *030 914 13 05* **Fax** *030 914 43 33* **Rooms** *24*

This pleasant and relatively quiet hotel overlooking the harbour in Desenzano sits on the pretty pedestrianised promenade overlooking the lake. The basic bedrooms are comfortable and pleasant; be aware that you need to book well ahead for a room with a balcony and lake view. Wi-Fi available. **www.gardalake.it/hotel-tripoli**

DESENZANO DEL GARDA Park Hotel 🄵 🎙️ 🎚 🅿️ 🛗 🌐 €€€
Lungolago Cesare Battisti 19, 25015 **Tel** *030 9143494* **Rooms** *52*

On the lake promenade and close to Desenzano's town centre, this family-run hotel is furnished with a mix of contemporary fabrics and antique furniture. Public areas feature marble floors, rich wood and fresh flowers. A classic hotel with modern facilities. A rooftop pool adds glamour. Wi-Fi access costs extra. **www.parkhotelonline.it**

GARDONE RIVIERA Villa Capri 🄵 🎚 🎙️ 🅿️ 🛗 🌐 €€€
Via Zanardelli 172, 25083 **Tel** *0365 215 37* **Fax** *0365 227 20* **Rooms** *45*

Located between Fasano and Gardone, Villa Capri exudes old world charm. This family-run hotel has great views and setting; the grounds are breathtaking, with lawns, ancient trees, a pool and a bathing jetty in the lake. Rooms are standard, simply furnished and compact. Closed Oct–Easter. **www.hotelvillacapri.com**

GARDONE RIVIERA Grand Hotel Fasano 🄵 🎙️ 🎚 🎙️ 🅿️ 🌐 €€€€€
Corso Zanardelli 190, 25083 **Tel** *0365 29 02 20* **Fax** *0365 29 02 21* **Rooms** *75*

This former Austrian imperial hunting lodge set in private parkland with semi-tropical vegetation is now a luxurious and romantic hotel. The rooms are fairly small, but some have four-poster beds, classic Italian-style decor and balconies. The Fasano also boasts the fine restaurant, Il Fagiano and an Aveda spa. Closed Oct–Easter. **www.ghf.it**

GARDONE RIVIERA Villa Fiordaliso 🎙️ 🎚 🌐 €€€€€
Corso Zanardelli 132, 25083 **Tel** *0365 201 58* **Fax** *0365 29 00 11* **Rooms** *5*

This beautiful four-story villa overlooking Lake Garda is situated ten minutes walk from the centre of Gardone. All rooms are named after flowers and the eclectic decor reflects the name. The hotel also boasts a lovely garden. Try the regional specials in the restaurant, especially the fresh catch of lake fish. Closed end Oct–Feb. **www.villafiordaliso.it**

GARDONE RIVIERA Villa del Sogno 🄵 🎙️ 🎚 🎙️ 🅿️ 🌐 €€€€€
Via Zanardelli 107, 25083 **Tel** *0365 29 01 81* **Fax** *0365 29 02 30* **Rooms** *33*

This splendid Neo-Classical villa boasts a peaceful panoramic position. It is set in a large park not far from the town centre. Enjoy facilities such as tennis and a great pool, or hire a car to explore the surrounding countryside and towns before dining on the creative Italian cuisine in the villa's restaurant. Closed Nov–Mar. **www.villadelsogno.it**

GARDONE SOPRA Locanda Agli Angeli 🄵 🎙️ 🎚 🎙️ 🅿️ 🌐 €€
Piazza Garibaldi 2, 25083 **Tel** *0365 208 32* **Fax** *0365 207 46* **Rooms** *16*

This hotel is a short walk from the lake, between the Botanical Gardens and the Vittoriale. The rooms are located in two houses above the popular eponymous trattoria. Rooms are spacious and stylish, and both the hotel and restaurant are decorated with furniture from Bali. There is also a lovely sun veranda. Closed Nov–Feb. **www.agliangeli.biz**

LIMONE SUL GARDA Capo Reamol 🄵 🎙️ 🎚 🎙️ 🎚 🅿️ 🎙️ €
Via IV Novembre 92, 25010 **Tel** *0365 95 40 40* **Fax** *0365 198 08 00* **Rooms** *58*

The hotel sits on the lakeside in a verdant area 3 km (1.8 miles) from Limone – take the bus or use the hotel's bikes. Boasting a private beach, pool, and balconies with lake views for all the rooms, plus an excellent surf school, it is ideal for families keen on sport. Closed mid-Oct–mid-Apr. **www.hotelcaporeamol.com**

Key to Price Guide *see p160* **Key to Symbols** *see back cover flap*

RIVA DEL GARDA Feeling Hotel Luise

€€€

Viale Rovereto 9, 38066 **Tel** *0464 55 08 58* **Fax** *0464 55 42 50* **Rooms** *68*

This hotel is close to the centre of Riva del Garda and the lakeside. It has a well-kept garden and swimming pool, and welcomes cyclists and mountain-bike enthusiasts. A good family hotel with a restaurant and a miniclub for children in high summer. Closed Feb. **www.hotelluise.com**

RIVA DEL GARDA Du Lac et du Parc

€€€€

Viale Rovereto 44, 38066 **Tel** *0464 56 66 00* **Fax** *0464 56 65 66* **Rooms** *226*

This large resort is set in luxurious parkland and splendidly situated on the lake. In addition to traditional rooms, it offers suites, bungalows and studios. A range of sports and activities are available, including a sailing school. Popular too for congresses and weddings. Closed Nov–Mar. **www.dulacetduparc.com**

SALÒ Laurin

€€€€

Viale Landi 9, 25087 **Tel** *0365 220 22* **Fax** *0365 223 82* **Rooms** *30*

An Art Nouveau gem of a hotel, set in lovely gardens and a short walk to the lake. Great attention to historic detail throughout, while contemporary facilities include an outdoor pool and gourmet restaurant. Rooms vary in size, all with old-world charm and some with lake views. Breakfast included. Closed Oct–Easter. **www.laurinhotelsalo.com**

SIRMIONE Villa Cortine

€€€€€

Via Grotte 6, 25019 **Tel** *030 990 58 90* **Fax** *030 91 63 90* **Rooms** *54*

A huge, luxurious Neo-Classical villa in a tranquil setting of lush, immaculate gardens. Enjoy the meandering paths through parkland, ponds, mythological fountains, a cypress grove by the lake, statues and a jetty with loungers. The lakeside terrace offers summer lunches of barbecued meat and fish. Closed Oct–Easter. **www.hotelvillacortine.com**

LAGO D'ISEO

ERBUSCO L'Albereta

€€€€€

Via Vittorio Emanuele 23, 25030 **Tel** *030 776 05 50* **Fax** *030 776 05 73* **Rooms** *57*

This country mansion was converted to a luxurious hotel and restaurant run by chef Gualtiero Marchesi. The setting of the hotel is inland from Lago d'Iseo, surrounded by vineyards and beautiful countryside. Excellent food and wines, and a wellness beauty spa. High-quality design and fine furnishings. Breakfast not included. **www.albereta.it**

ISEO I Due Roccoli

€€€

Via Silvio Bonomelli, Strada Per Polaveno, 25049 **Tel** *030 982 29 77* **Fax** *030 982 29 80* **Rooms** *19*

Housed in a charming patrician home, this fine rustic residence has a country setting but still offers panoramic views over the lake from its rooms and terrace. The converted farmhouse has a good restaurant with regional cuisine, hotel facilities also include a swimming pool and tennis court. Wi-Fi costs extra. Closed Nov–Mar. **www.idueroccoli.com**

RIVA DI SOLTO Albergo Ristorante Miranda

€

Via Cornello 8, 24060 **Tel** *035 98 60 21* **Fax** *035 98 00 55* **Rooms** *25*

A peaceful panoramic setting on a hillside overlooking Lago d'Iseo. This simple family-run *pensione* offers comfortable rooms, all with balconies. There is an outdoor pool in an olive grove and a play area for kids. Good fresh fish dishes are offered in the terrace restaurant by the lake. Wi-Fi is available at extra cost. **www.albergomiranda.it**

LAGO D'ORTA

ORTA SAN GIULIO Aracoeli

€€

Piazza Motta 34, 28016 **Tel** *0322 90 51 73* **Rooms** *7*

A fun and quirky design hotel in the heart of the town, alongside popular bars and restaurants. Contemporary styling includes some in-room showers, so this is not a place for the shy. Some rooms enjoy breathtaking lake and island views. Breakfast is lavish and included in the price. **www.orta.net/aracoeli**

ORTA SAN GIULIO Hotel San Rocco

€€€€

Via Gippini 11, 28016 **Tel** *0322 91 19 77* **Fax** *0322 91 19 64* **Rooms** *80*

A splendid hotel overlooking Lago d'Orta, with stunning terraces to lounge in and soak up the views. Converted from a 17th-century convent, it still retains the tranquillity of former days. Facilities include a spa with sauna and massage, and a private boat for tours round the lake. Wi-Fi access is available for a fee. **www.hotelsanrocco.it**

ORTA SAN GIULIO Villa Crespi

€€€€€

Via G. Fava 18, 28016 **Tel** *0322 91 19 02* **Fax** *0322 91 19 19* **Rooms** *14*

Surrounded by woodland, this unique fairytale hotel is located within an Islamic villa with murals, minarets and precious fabrics, reminiscent of *Arabian Nights*. Luxurious marble and mosaics are everywhere. It has a first-class restaurant and a wellness centre. Its elaborate design makes it unique. Closed Jan–Feb. **www.villacrespi.it/**

WHERE TO EAT

Milan is a cosmopolitan city and offers a wide range of restaurants in all price categories. As well as Milanese and Tuscan cooking (the latter has become a real speciality of the city), ethnic cuisine has recently come to the fore – from North African to Oriental and even South American, reflecting the city's multicultural character. The fish restaurants are excellent, offering skilfully prepared fish and seafood.

The Barchetta chef, Bellagio *(see p180)*

Restaurants are at their most crowded at the weekend, and it is often best to book in advance. Sunday brunch has become part and parcel of the Milanese life style, and a number of cafés offer this late morning meal. At the lakes there are restaurants with terraces overlooking the water, and cafés with tables outside. Menus are dominated by fish dishes and local specialities. For more detailed information, see the chart on pages 172–83, with a selection of 122 restaurants.

CHOOSING A RESTAURANT

In Milan the Brera and Navigli districts are filled with both trendy restaurants and inexpensive eateries. Around the Brera quarter, the fashion crowd congregate at the hip **Rigolo** *(see p177)*, while vegetarians head for **Joia** *(see p178)*, which also serves some fish dishes. Those on a budget will find many options around the Navigli, such as the Neapolitan-inspired **Pizzeria Tradizionale con Cucina di Pesce** *(see p174)* and **Premiata Pizzeria** *(see p174)*. Near Porta Genova is **Osteria dei Binari** *(see p174)*, serving Lombard and Piedmontese dishes. The **Raw Fish Café, Centro Ittico** *(see p178)* and **Malavoglia** *(see p177)*, near the fish market, have excellent fresh fish.

Classic restaurants in the city centre include **Boeucc**

The Premiata Pizzeria sign, Milan *(see p174)*

(see p172) and the historic **Savini** *(see p172)*, both of which specialize in traditional Milanese cuisine. Also popular are **Aimo e Nadia** *(see p175)*, in the Bande Nere district, and **I Sapori del Mare** *(see p178)*, near the Città Studi.

Some of Italy's best restaurants are in beautiful locations near the lakes. At Lake Maggiore, **Il Sole di Ranco** *(see p179)* is one of Italy's finest, while at Lake Como good places include **Barchetta** *(see p180)* at Bellagio and **Raimondi del Villa Flori** *(see p181)*, a hotel/restaurant near Como. Lake Garda also boasts excellent restaurants, such as **Villa Fiordaliso** *(see p182)*, at Gardone. At Erbusco (Lake Iseo), is **Gualtiero Marchesi** *(see p183)*, the restaurant of Italy's most famous chef.

To prevent disappointment, book a table ahead if there is a restaurant you are particularly keen on trying.

The entrance to Barchetta, in Bellagio, on Lake Como *(see p180)*

ETIQUETTE

Not surprisingly, the Milanese are very dress-conscious: they like to dress up for dinner, and indeed looking smart will also ensure better (and speedier) service.

In 2005 regulations came into force in Italy, and now restaurants and bars must provide separate no-smoking areas or face a fine. Smokers who light up in no-smoking areas are also liable to a fine. At cafés and restaurants that do not provide sealed-off areas, smoking is limited to outside tables.

TYPES OF RESTAURANTS

Milan offers an unusually wide range of types of cuisine for an Italian city. Alongside traditional Italian cooking you can also find Asian, North African and Mexican food of all kinds. Classic Milanese cooking survives in the traditional

EATING HOURS

Lunch is generally served between 1 and 2:30pm. Dinner is usually at about 8pm and goes on until about 11pm (or later in summer). Most restaurants close during the month of August.

The refined interior of Boeucc, in the centre of Milan *(see p172)*

restaurants of the centre. International cuisine is found in places frequented by business people. Italian regional cooking, from Tuscan to Piedmontese, Neapolitan and Sicilian, is increasingly popular in Milan.

There are several different types of restaurant. Traditionally, a *ristorante* is smarter and more expensive than an *osteria* or a *trattoria,* but the divisions are increasingly blurred. A pizzeria is usually an inexpensive place to eat and many serve pasta, meat and fish dishes as well as pizza. Those with wood-fired ovens (*forno a legna*) are the most highly rated. Milan's pizzerias tend to be more expensive than in the rest of Italy but the quality is excellent thanks to the many Neapolitan pizza chefs in the city. An *enoteca* or *vineria* is a place to taste wine and sample snacks.

Genuine small trattorias still abound as well as the increasingly rare *latterie* (dairies), which are small, crowded kitchens.

The Milan fish market is one of the best in Italy, and the city's excellent seafood restaurants guarantee superfresh fish.

At the lakes, much use is made of local fish such as carp, tench and shad, and you will also find regional specialities – in particular, Piedmontese, Valtellinese and Veneto cooking.

Gualtiero Marchesi's restaurant at Erbusco, Lago d'Iseo *(see p183)*

Raimondi del Villa Flori, Lake Como *(see p181)*

The wine cellar in the famous Il Sole di Ranco restaurant, Lake Maggiore *(see p179)*

READING THE MENU

A classic Italian dinner begins with an *antipasto* or starter. The first course (*il primo*) is likely to be pasta or risotto but may be a hearty soup. The main course (*il secondo*) consists of meat or fish served with a side dish of vegetables (*contorno*). Dessert (*il dessert*) follows and may consist of fruit, ice cream or pastries. Coffee (*il caffè*) comes next, and maybe a digestif.

A typical Milanese dinner might consist of *nervetti*, or *nervitt* (calf cartilage with oil, vinegar and onions), followed by *risotto alla milanese*, and then a veal cutlet (*cotoletta*). Other classic dishes are *ossobuco* (a cut of veal including the bone and its marrow) and *cassoeûla* (a dish of pork and cabbage served with polenta).

Vegetarians will find that many pasta dishes are meat-free. Autumn is good for non-meat eaters, as wild mushrooms and pumpkins start to appear on the menu. Cheeses are also a good option.

PAYING

Menus are usually posted outside restaurants, with prices. An unavoidable extra is the cover charge (*coperto*), which is charged per person. In general Milanese restaurants accept major credit cards, except for some of the smaller, family-run trattorias, where you will need cash. Commonly accepted cards include Visa and MasterCard. Even restaurants in the smaller villages around the lakes now increasingly accept credit cards. When paying for a meal (the Italian for the bill is *il conto*), it is normal to leave a small tip.

WHEELCHAIR ACCESS

Unfortunately, not all Milanese restaurants have facilities for the disabled. Wheelchair access may be even more of a problem at the lakes, with restaurants often sited at the top of long slopes or paths with steps. Do telephone the restaurant beforehand for advice.

CHILDREN'S FACILITIES

Less expensive places such as trattorias and pizzerias are ideal for children. They may be less welcome in Milan's sophisticated restaurants. Restaurant owners at the lakes are more accustomed to families with children, and can often provide smaller portions if required.

The Flavours of Milan and the Lakes

As a powerhouse of industry, finance and fashion, Milan, more than any other Italian city, has embraced international cuisine. The Milanese are quick to adopt new culinary trends and food fads come and go. But there has also been a long-standing interest in rediscovering the historic cuisine of the region. Like the prosperous city itself, this traditional food is rich. Milanese risottos are laced with butter and Parmesan, and even the local asparagus is likely to arrive at the table topped with an egg and grated cheese. Increasingly chefs are now scaling down the fats and substituting olive oil to suit today's health-conscious palates.

Asparagus

Selection of salami at a delicatessen, Cremona

MILAN

The city is surrounded by vast agricultural plains that provide an abundance of fresh produce, including meat, cereals, cheese and vegetables. The Milanese are great meat-eaters – pork, veal and game are all very popular. The region's typical hearty casseroles were once the staples of the local peasant diet, combining whatever meat, grains and vegetables happened to be available. Filling *minestre* soups with added rice or pasta stem from the same tradition. A more elaborate cuisine also developed at the courts of the ruling Visconti and Sforza families. Recipes created there are still being prepared by Milanese chefs today. Spanish rule in the 16th century led to rice being grown with other crops along the Po valley. This was used to make risotto – a direct descendant of paella. Saffron, cultivated locally, was added to flavour Milanese risottos, giving them their characteristic yellow hue. Again, the grain was cooked with anything that was in season to make a filling meal –

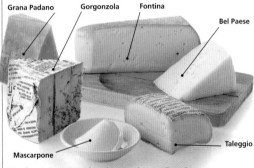

Grana Padano   Gorgonzola   Fontina   Bel Paese   Taleggio   Mascarpone

Mouthwatering range of northwest Italy's excellent cheeses

LOCAL DISHES AND SPECIALITIES

Rich dishes with meat and offal are traditional Milanese fare. Meals often start with slices of cured meats or the fine-grained *salame di Milano*. Popular main courses include *cassoeûla*, a rich stew of pork, cabbage and sausage, served with polenta; *busecca alla Milanese*, tripe with onion, carrot, sage and celery; and *fritto misto alla Milanese*, fried mixed offal coated in breadcrumbs. Seasonal specialities are *fagiano alla Milanese*, braised spiced pheasant, and *rise spargitt*, rice and asparagus. From the lakes come *alborelle fritte*, tiny fish, floured and deep-fried, and *missoltini*, shad, air-dried then salted and flavoured with bay leaves. A selection of regional cheeses is usually served at the end of a meal.

Panettone

Risotto alla Milanese *Rice is cooked slowly with onion, stock, wine, butter, grated Parmesan and golden saffron.*

Fresh vegetables on sale at a Milanese greengrocer

vegetables, freshwater fish, meat and game. Milanese risottos still tend to have a seasonal twist. In the autumn, locally grown pumpkin is often added and, in summer, wild strawberries.

During the 18th century, maize (corn) was introduced into the region and polenta – made from maize flour and water – soon became an important staple food. Today, even though pasta is hugely popular, it is just as likely that polenta and rice will be found on the table in Milan.

Rule by Austria in the late 18th century has also left its mark on the Milanese diet. The popular bread-crumbed veal *costoletta Milanese* is a version of *Wiener Schnitzel*, and *panettone* is based on the rich yeast cakes of Central Europe.

THE LAKES

Although fishing on the region's deep glacial lakes is no longer a major industry, it still plays a central role in shaping the local diet. Pike, perch, trout, tench, bleak, shad, sardines and eel are

Shad, part of a catch of fish from the clear waters of Lake Como

plentiful, while carp is more elusive and prized. The catch served at lakeside restaurants is often simply fried, grilled or poached, although it is also popular marinated and is used in risottos, soups, pâtés and as a ravioli filling.

The land around Lake Garda is particularly suited for growing vines and olive trees. Light and delicate, Garda extra virgin olive oil is perfect in salad dressings and can be bought direct from oil mills. Other regional products include capers and a delicious honey sold by local bee-keepers.

WHAT TO DRINK

Franciacorta wines The reds and whites from the Lago d'Iseo area are held in high esteem by the Milanese, especially the *spumante*.

Oltrepo Pavese wines More than 20 different varieties, both still and sparkling, are produced in ancient vineyards to the south-west of Milan.

Valtellina wines From the Swiss border, north of Lake Como, these include reds and the unusual raisin-like *sforzato* made from semi-dried grapes.

Garda wines Made from a wide variety of grapes, the reds, whites and rosés from the area around Lake Garda include a light red Bardolino, Garda Classico Groppello and Garda Classico Chiaretto. The white Lugana goes particularly well with lake-fish dishes.

Minestrone *The Milanese add beef marrow and rice to their version of this hearty bean and vegetable soup.*

Ossobuco *Veal shanks are braised very slowly in white wine. The bone marrow is considered a delicacy.*

Trota Ripiena *Lake trout are stuffed with mushrooms, onion and parsley, then poached in red wine.*

Choosing a Restaurant

The restaurants in this guide have been selected across a wide price range for the high quality of their service, decor, value and location. They have been divided into six areas and listed by price category. Milan restaurants are further subdivided according to city areas. For Milan map references, see pages 224–37 and the inside back cover.

PRICE CATEGORIES
The price ranges are for a three-course meal for one, including a half-bottle of house wine, tax and service.

€ under €30
€€ €30–€45
€€€ €45–€65
€€€€ €65–€90
€€€€€ over €90

MILAN

CITY CENTRE Serendib
Via Pontida 2, 20121 **Tel** 02 659 21 39   🛈📖   €
Map 3 B2

This Sri Lankan restaurant is one of Milan's best ethnic eateries. Choose from a variety of delicate curry dishes. Serendib soup is a must, with meat broth, vegetables and mixed spices, as are the spicy fried artichokes and coconut milk, or try the chicken in spicy sauce. The decor is a combination of Italian and Sri Lankan styles. Closed lunch.

CITY CENTRE Hostaria Borromei
Via Borromei 4, 20123 **Tel** 02 86 45 37 60   🛈📅📖   €€
Map 7 B1

In the heart of Milan's business quarter is this unpretentious family-run tavern. It has a romantic courtyard setting in an old palazzo and in summer you can sit outside under the vines. Typical dishes include home-made pumpkin-filled pasta and a platter of boiled meats served with various spicy sauces. Closed Sat & Sun lunch; 1 wk mid-Aug.

CITY CENTRE La Rinascente Food Market
Via San Raffaele 2, 20121 **Tel** 02 885 24 71   🛈📅📖   €€
Map 7 C1

Located at the top of the famous department store La Rinascente, the Food Market boasts an unbeatable view. It is a great place for a cappuccino or snack while shopping or for a full evening meal. In summer it opens a terrace that faces the spires of the cathedral.

CITY CENTRE Osteria Artidoro
Via Camperio 15, 20123 **Tel** 02 805 73 86   🛈📖   €€
Map 3 B5

A laid-back, rustic-looking *osteria* close to the Castello Sforzesco. Contemporary cuisine meets classic fare here. The place is run by a young crew who add their own twist to dishes from Lombardy and Emilia Romagna. Expect rich meat dishes like *culatello*, cured hams and salami, and fresh pasta. Closed Sat & Sun lunch; 2 wks Aug.

CITY CENTRE Al Cantinone
Via Agnello 19, 20121 **Tel** 02 86 30 15   📖🍷   €€€
Map 8 D1

Located in a 17th-century former residence on a quiet backstreet between the Duomo and Piazza Scala, Al Cantinone offers a Lombard-Tuscan menu. The *ossobuco* (veal shank) is famous; also try the *raspadüra noci e pere* (thinly sliced Parmesan cheese served with pears and nuts). The bar has a large selection of wines and spirits. Closed 1 wk mid-Aug.

CITY CENTRE Alla Collina Pistoiese
Via Amedei 1, 20123 **Tel** 02 86 45 10 85   📖🍷   €€€€
Map 7 C2

Still run by the same family who founded it in 1938, Alla Collina Pistoiese offers robust Tuscan dishes, including pasta with beans and Florentine steak, in a traditional *osteria*-type setting. Centrally located, it is a favourite with the local population. Closed Fri & Sat lunch; Easter, 1 wk mid-Aug, 23 Dec–2 Jan.

CITY CENTRE Boeucc
Piazza Belgioioso 2, 20121 **Tel** 02 76 02 02 24   🛈📖🍷📅   €€€€
Map 4 D5

This is possibly Milan's oldest restaurant, dating back to 1696. It is located near La Scala, on the ground floor of an old palazzo. Its name, pronounced "butch", is old Milanese for *buco* (hole). It offers classic Milanese dishes such as *cassoeüla* (a pork, cabbage and salami stew). Closed Sat & Sun lunch; Easter, Aug, 1 wk at Christmas.

CITY CENTRE Le Noir
Via San Raffaele 6, 20121 **Tel** 02 720 89 51   🛈📅📖🍷   €€€€
Map 7 C1

The refined restaurant of The Gray hotel (*see p160*), Le Noir is famous for its style. The wenge wood tables contrast with the Rosenthal porcelain tableware and are set off by the subtle changes of coloured lighting. The food is to as high a standard as the design. The menu offers creative Mediterranean and international cuisine. Closed 3 wks Aug.

CITY CENTRE Savini
Galleria Vittorio Emanuele II, 20121 **Tel** 02 72 00 34 33   🛈📅📖🍷📅   €€€€
Map 7 C1

This elegant restaurant is favoured by older clients and business people. It is full of *belle époque* charm. The fare is high quality, with prices to match. The specials are typically Milanese dishes: ox muzzle fried with sweet red onions, balsamic vinegar and raisins, and *ossobuco* (veal shank). Closed Sat lunch, Sun dinner; 2 wks Aug.

Key to Symbols *see back cover flap*

CITY CENTRE Cracco

Via Victor Hugo 4, 20121 **Tel** *02 87 67 74*

€€€€€

Map *7 C1*

One of Milan's best restaurants, this is led by Carlo Cracco, one of the first Italian chefs to be awarded three Michelin stars. The innovative cuisine is a fusion of the traditional and the contemporary. Delights include saffron risotto with coriander juice, and spaghetti with parsley sauce and shrimps. Closed Sun (Sat & Sun in Jun & Jul); Aug, Christmas.

CITY CENTRE La Cupola

Via Tommaso Grossi 1, 20121 **Tel** *02 88 21 12 34*

€€€€€

Map *7 C1*

In the luxurious surroundings of the Park Hyatt hotel, the stylish La Cupola is a chic establishment. Breakfast is served until late morning, plus there's an impressive Sunday brunch and an all-day menu. A muted, sophisticated colour scheme, subtle lighting and an impressive glassed dome set the tone. Open until midnight daily.

CITY CENTRE Trussardi alla Scala

Piazza della Scala 5, 20121 **Tel** *02 80 68 82 64*

€€€€€

Map *3 C5*

Enjoy the view of Piazza della Scala from the stylish first-floor dining room in the Palazzo Trussardi. The fashion designer's shop is on the ground floor, alongside a more casual bistro, which is always busy at lunchtimes. On the menu is a refined Mediterranean cuisine rich in fish and vegetables. Excellent wines. Closed Sat lunch, Sun.

CITY CENTRE Vun

Via Tommaso Grossi 1, 20121 **Tel** *02 88 21 12 34*

€€€€€

Map *7 C1*

Elegance, attention to detail and sophisticated cuisine make dining at the Park Hyatt hotel's restaurant a delight. The fare is modern Italian with Mediterranean flavours and regional dishes with a twist. Choose from a list of good wines. Fine glassware and Limoges china, leather seating and beige tones. Closed Sat lunch, Sun; 3 wks Aug.

NORTHWEST MILAN Tagiura

Via Tagiura 5, 20146 **Tel** *02 48 95 06 13*

€

Map *5 C2*

Known locally as *Il Bar Bello* (the beautiful bar), this pleasant bar-cum-restaurant is a great spot for lunch, or a coffee and pastry during the day. In the evening it is open only on Thursdays and Fridays, so booking is essential. They serve traditional food from Piacenza, including meat and pasta, plus a wide choice of cured meats. Closed Sun; 3 wks Aug.

NORTHWEST MILAN Taverna della Trisa

Via Ferrucci 1, 20145 **Tel** *02 34 13 04*

€€

Map *2 E2*

This typical trattoria specializes in Trentino cuisine. Close to Fieramilanocity with a garden for summer dining. Good regional wines accompany the hearty Italian food, such as cured ham, dumplings and mushrooms. It has a homely and intimate atmosphere, subtle lighting and dark wood interior. Closed Mon, alternate Sun; Aug.

NORTHWEST MILAN La Veneta

Via Giusti 14, 20154 **Tel** *02 34 28 81*

€€€

Map *3 A2*

At this quiet, family-run restaurant in the centre of Chinatown, near Corso Sempione, carefully chosen ingredients are turned into high-quality Venetian-style dishes, including tender braised liver and onions, and home-made pastas and desserts. A good selection of wines and spirits are available. Closed Mon; Aug.

NORTHWEST MILAN Alfredo Gran San Bernardo

Via Borgese 14, 20154 **Tel** *02 331 90 00*

€€€€

Map *2 D1*

A traditional Milanese restaurant opened by veteran chef Alfredo Valli in 1964 in a residential area of the city, east of Piazza Firenze. Valli's breaded veal cutlet is legendary. Other dishes include risotto with sea salt, tagliatelle in meat sauce and beef in red wine. The dining rooms are smart. Closed lunch, Sun (Jun & Jul).

NORTHWEST MILAN Primo Novecento

Via Ruggero di Lauria 17, 20100 **Tel** *02 33 61 16 43*

€€€€

Map *2 D1*

This cosy restaurant serves classic Italian cuisine, mainly fish. Early 20th-century black-and-white photos line the walls. Specialities include linguine with scampi in ginger and sherry, mixed fried seafood, and chocolate fondue Bourguignonne. Closed Sat lunch; 2 wks Aug; 26 Dec–Jan.

NORTHWEST MILAN Quattro Mori

Largo Maria Callas 1, 20121 **Tel** *02 87 84 83*

€€€€

Map *3 B5*

Quattro Mori specializes in fish but also offers delicious grilled meats, vegetable and pasta dishes. The owners are friendly and welcoming, the pasta is home-made and the classic antipasti are a treat. Make sure you leave some room for the chef's fine desserts. In summer you can dine on the garden terrace. Closed 2 wks Aug.

NORTHWEST MILAN Trattoria Franca, Paola e Lele

Viale Certosa 235, 20151 **Tel** *02 38 00 62 38*

€€€€

Map *2 D1*

This is an excellent family-run trattoria in the northern outskirts of the city. The seasonal produce is carefully sourced throughout Italy and transformed into great Lombard dishes. Ask about the daily specials and try the excellent wine. This cosy and well-designed restaurant gets pretty busy, so book well ahead. Closed Sat, Sun.

SOUTHWEST MILAN L'Oca Giuliva

Viale Bligny 29, 20136 **Tel** *02 58 31 28 71*

€

Map *7 C4*

"The happy goose", as this restaurant is called, has a lively atmosphere and lots of goose-related images and ornaments. The popular Puglian cuisine has Mediterranean influences. Try the prawns in saffron or gnocchi made with chestnuts and cheese. The pizzas are good too. The kitchen stays open until 11pm. Closed Mon; 2 wks Aug.

SOUTHWEST MILAN Pizzeria Tradizionale con Cucina di Pesce   €

Ripa di Porta Ticinese 7, 20144 **Tel** *02 839 51 33*   **Map** *6 D4*

This traditional pizzeria serves excellent Neapolitan-style wood-oven baked pizzas, plus pasta dishes with seafood and fish. The fresh fish dishes vary daily. The interior is styled in old Milanese fashion, and in the summer months you can sit outside by the canal. Book ahead. Closed Wed lunch.

SOUTHWEST MILAN Premiata Pizzeria   €

Via Alzaia Naviglio Grande 2, 20144 **Tel** *02 89 40 06 48*   **Map** *7 A4*

A great, affordable pizzeria in a central location near the canals. Tables are available in a lovely courtyard at the back when the weather is warm. Service can be hurried and the seating is communal on long tables, but they do serve good pizzas and pasta dishes. Alternatively, try the Parma ham focaccia or the rocket (arugula) salad.

SOUTHWEST MILAN Osteria dei Binari   €€

Via Tortona 1, 20144 **Tel** *02 89 40 94 28*   **Map** *6 E3*

Located behind Porta Genova station in a *casa ringhiera* (a traditional Milanese dwelling with an open terrace), this informal restaurant offers genuine Lombard cuisine, from *ossobuco* (veal shank) to a wide range of cold meats. The service is friendly and efficient. Closed lunch.

SOUTHWEST MILAN Osteria di Via Pre   €€

Via Casale 4, 20144 **Tel** *366 159 7478*   **Map** *6 F4*

A simple, historic tavern serving Ligurian seafood specials that harness the delicate flavours of the coast. Try the stuffed vegetable antipasti, swordfish *carpaccio* (thin, raw slices), organic pesto from Albenga, *pansotti* (pasta filled with ricotta, lemon and herbs) with nut sauce or the fish ravioli. Excellent for seafood.

SOUTHWEST MILAN Osteria Grand Hotel   €€

Via Ascanio Sforza 75, 20136 **Tel** *02 89 51 15 86*   **Map** *7 A4*

Owner Fabrizio is head of one of Milan's Slow Food groups and he practises what he preaches. The ingredients are fresh, and the food is excellent. Try the gnocchi with smoked ricotta or the venison cutlet in apple and cheese sauce. Competent and courteous service, good wine list and old-tavern setting. Closed lunch; Mon (winter); 2 wks mid-Aug.

SOUTHWEST MILAN Pace   €€

Via G Washington 74, 20146 **Tel** *02 46 85 67*   **Map** *5 C1*

An honest and unpretentious Tuscan trattoria with wood-panelled walls and white linen tablecloths. The menu focuses on traditional cuisine based on meat and fish. Specials include ravioli in broth, mushroom and bean soup and, on Mondays, *bollito* (boiled meats with spicy mustard). Closed Wed, Sat lunch; Easter, Aug Christmas.

SOUTHWEST MILAN Rifugio Pugliese   €€

Via Costanza 2, 20144 **Tel** *02 48 00 09 17*   **Map** *6 D2*

Rifugio Pugliese is a lively and pleasant restaurant just outside the centre of Milan, in the Universtiy district. Sample Puglian specialities like pasta with turnip tops, home-made *orecchiette* (a small, ear-shape pasta) with a variety of sauces or mozzarella served with cherry tomatoes. Book ahead. Closed Sun; Aug.

SOUTHWEST MILAN Trattoria Aurora   €€

Via Savona 23, 20144 **Tel** *02 89 40 49 78*   **Map** *5 B4*

Aurora serves Piedmontese cuisine in the heart of Milan. This local favourite offers specials such as wafer-thin veal in a creamy sauce, stuffed ravioli tossed in butter and sage and roast meat on skewers. In summer take advantage of the lovely vine-covered shady garden and in winter enjoy the cosy turn-of-the-century dining room. Closed Mon.

SOUTHWEST MILAN Al Pont de Ferr'   €€€

Ripa di Porta Ticinese 55, 20143 **Tel** *02 89 40 62 77*   **Map** *6 D4*

Typical Milanese tavern on the Navigli blending traditional cuisine with modern flair. Good antipasti include courgette flower flans, salamis and bean soups. The restaurant is renowned for its great variety of cheeses, from taleggio to gorgonzola. Also recommended is the Argentine beef fillet. Good selection of wines. Closed mid-Aug, Christmas.

SOUTHWEST MILAN Chic 'n' Quick   €€€

Via Ascanio Sforza 77, 20141 **Tel** *02 89 50 32 22*   **Map** *7 A4*

This is the relaxed, but still sophisticated, sister restaurant to neighbouring Sadler, both owned by top chef Claudio Sadler. Choose from a range of nine types of dishes, from superb salads and grilled food to exceptional gourmet cuisine. There's an impressive wine list with a good selection by the glass. Closed Mon lunch, Sun; first 2 wks Jan, Aug.

SOUTHWEST MILAN Osteria Porta Cicca   €€€

Ripa di Porta Ticinese 51, 20143 **Tel** *02 837 27 63*   **Map** *6 D4*

This typical *osteria* (tavern) in Milan's canal district gives traditional Italian cuisine a creative slant. The menu offers good-quality meat and fish dishes and home-made pastas. Small but not over-crowded, with a pleasant, welcoming ambience. Booking is advisable. Closed lunch, Mon; 2 wks end Aug.

SOUTHWEST MILAN Al Porto   €€€€

Piazzale Generale Cantore **Tel** *02 89 40 74 25*   **Map** *6 F3*

One of Milan's most popular seafood restaurants, Al Porto has been around since 1907. The fish dishes include sea bass in white wine and olives, seafood risotto and the traditional *fritto misto*, a platter of mixed fried fish and seafood. The warm antipasti are good, as is the selection of Friulian wines. Closed Mon lunch, Sun; Aug, 25 Dec–3 Jan.

SOUTHWEST MILAN L'Assassino ©©©©
Via Cornaggia, corner of Via Amedei, 20123 **Tel** *02 805 61 44*   **Map** *7 C2*

This place has a very stylish, contemporary interior, with splashes of rich colour. Mouth-watering dishes on the menu include veal shank and golden and crispy suckling pig. There's also a bistro menu, which offers splendid cheeses, seafood and cured meats. A laid-back place popular with celebrities. Closed Sun; 1 wk mid-Aug, Christmas.

SOUTHWEST MILAN L'Ulmet ©©©©
Via Disciplini, corner Via Olmetto, 20123 **Tel** *02 86 45 27 18*   **Map** *7 B2*

L'Ulmet serves traditional Milanese fare, such as *ossobuco* (veal shank), risotto with asparagus and morels, or steak in a rich red wine sauce with shallots, in a formal, elegant dining room. Friendly ambience and pleasant decor, including wooden ceilings, matt green walls and an open fire. Closed Mon lunch, Sun; Aug, 10 days at Christmas.

SOUTHWEST MILAN Aimo e Nadia ©©©©©
Via Raimondo Montecuccoli 6, 20147 **Tel** *02 41 68 86*   **Map** *5 A5*

Expect creative pan-Italian cuisine here. Perfect pasta dishes and game in autumn, such as guinea fowl. The finest ingredients, from seafood to vegetables, are blended into superb culinary delights. Worth the trip out to the suburbs for the truffle risotto at this two-Michelin-starred restaurant. Closed Sat lunch, Sun; Easter, first 3 wks Aug, Christmas.

SOUTHEAST MILAN Pizzeria Napoletana La Taverna ©
Via F Anzani 3, 20135 **Tel** *02 59 90 07 93*   **Map** *8 F1*

Southern hospitality in the heart of Milan. This pizzeria's reputation is clear by the number of Neapolitans who favour it. The pizzas are the authentic thin and crispy variety. Neapolitan-style meat and fish dishes are also served. There is a convivial and popular atmosphere, so book ahead. Seating outdoors in summer. Closed Sun lunch, Mon; 1 wk Aug.

SOUTHEAST MILAN Al Merluzzo Felice ©©
Via L Papi 6, 20135 **Tel** *02 545 47 11*   **Map** *8 F4*

This tiny restaurant specializes in Sicilian-style seafood and desserts. The owner rattles off the names of daily specials, created using the freshest ingredients – clams, prawns, garlic, lobster, ginger and fish. A simple, cosy atmosphere and a rich cuisine full of flavour and colour. Closed Mon lunch, Sun; 3 wks Aug.

SOUTHEAST MILAN Dongio ©©
Via Corio 3, 20135 **Tel** *02 551 13 72*   **Map** *8 F4*

Dongio is a typical simple trattoria, where the food is the highlight. The rustic, comfortable and intimate atmosphere is perfect for a romantic meal. Calabrian and Piacenza cuisines are both on offer, with plenty of salami, pasta, cheese and paprika. Try the Calabrian home-made gnocchi. Booking recommended. Closed Sat lunch, Sun; 3 wks Aug.

SOUTHEAST MILAN Taverna degli Amici ©©
Via Spartaco 4, 20135 **Tel** *02 55 19 40 05*   **Map** *8 F2*

A laid-back *trattoria*, where the cuisine is simple but prepared with good-quality ingredients. Salami, cheeses, salads, pastas and great desserts are on offer, but most people come here for the grilled meat, the restaurant's signature dish. There are two fixed price menus in addition to the regular menu. Good wine list. Closed Sat lunch, Sun; 3 wks Aug.

SOUTHEAST MILAN Da Giacomo ©©©
Via Sottocorno 6, corner Via B Cellini, 20129 **Tel** *02 76 02 33 13*   **Map** *4 F5*

A popular haunt for the well-heeled and fashionable Milanese. The stylish dining room is decorated with Art Deco lamps and photos of famous faces. House specialities include fish, such as swordfish steak *alla Giacomo*. The wine list offers a wide choice of quality vintages and desserts are a must. Closed Aug.

SOUTHEAST MILAN Masuelli San Marco ©©©
Viale Umbria 80, 20135 **Tel** *02 55 18 41 38*   **Map** *8 F3*

Milanese cuisine is the pride of this trattoria, which has been in the same family since 1921. It has a contemporary feel, with terracotta floor tiles, a black ceiling and Murano glass chandeliers. Excellent antipasti, risottos, soups, pasta with beans, veal, meat stews and desserts. Good wines too. Closed Mon lunch, Sun; 3 wks Aug, 25 Dec–6 Jan.

SOUTHEAST MILAN Mauro ©©©
Via Colonnetta 5, corner Via Cesare Battisti, 20122 **Tel** *02 546 13 80*   **Map** *8 E1*

Expect classic modern Italian cuisine with some great seafood at Mauro. This family-run affair serves smoked salmon with *scamorza* cheese, grilled fish, spaghetti with clams, and *pappardelle* with scampi in a curry sauce. The selection of wines and the service are good. Parking available. Closed Sat lunch.

SOUTHEAST MILAN Trattoria del Pescatore ©©©
Via Vannucci 5, 20135 **Tel** *02 58 32 04 52*   **Map** *8 E4*

As the name suggests, this restaurant specializes in fish and seafood. It may not be directly in the centre, located in the Porta Romana zone, but the dishes are of high quality, and it is necessary to book ahead. The food is full of great flavours and scents. Try the Catalan lobster, or the spaghetti with squid and mullet roe. Closed Sun; Aug.

NORTHEAST MILAN Da Rino Vecchia Napoli ©
Via Chavez 4, 20131 **Tel** *02 261 90 56*   **Map** *4 F1*

Vecchia Napoli is all about pizza. It gets popular and crowded, since the prices are low and the pizzas delicious. The restaurant's creations have won awards, and you can enjoy delightful toppings such as fried aubergine (eggplant) with Parmesan flakes, sweet pizzas laden with fruit or gluten-free soya-flour pizzas. Closed Mon, Sun lunch; Aug.

NORTHEAST MILAN Geppo
Via GB Morgagni 37, 20100 **Tel** *02 29 51 48 62*

A fairly small classic pizzeria with more than 50 varieties of pizza to choose from. A speciality is the local Milanese-style pizza, with rocket, saffron and porcini mushrooms. The convivial atmosphere makes this a good destination if you're on a budget. Parallel to Corso Buenos Aires, the busy shopping street. Closed Sun; 2 wks Aug.

NORTHEAST MILAN Il Doge di Amalfi
Via Sangallo 41, 20133 **Tel** *02 73 02 86*   **Map** *4 F5*

Warm and welcoming, this restaurant offers a real Neapolitan experience, from the pizzas and typical dishes, to the slightly chaotic ambience. Photos of Naples and fishing paraphernalia decorate the walls. Expect dishes such as linguine with lobster, Sicilian pasta specials and lots of *limoncello* (a traditional lemon liqueur). Closed Mon; Aug.

NORTHEAST MILAN Massawa
Via Sirtori 6, 20129 **Tel** *02 29 40 69 10*   **Map** *4 F4*

Massawa, with its typical Eritrean cuisine, lies on the streets behind Corso Buenos Aires which are rich in African smells and flavours. Choose between the affordable, Eritrean fixed menu or Italian dishes à la carte. Specials include *zighini* (meat with spicy vegetables and sourdough) and fish on Fridays. Closed Sat & Sun lunch; 2 wks Aug.

NORTHEAST MILAN Pizzeria Piccola Ischia
Via Gian Battista Morgagni 7, 20124 **Tel** *02 204 76 13*

Great Neapolitan pizza can be found at this place with a fun, fantasy interior. Pizzas come in three sizes – large is huge – and there's a range of other Neapolitan dishes, plus salads and baked breads. Service is friendly and efficient, the place is very popular and prices are low. One of three in the city. Closed Wed; Sat & Sun lunch; Aug.

NORTHEAST MILAN Princi
Largo La Foppa, 20154 **Tel** *02 659 90 13*   **Map** *3 C2*

This designer bakery is part of a popular chain in Milan. It is highly sophisticated and full of the *beau monde*, with a sleek, stylish atmosphere. It is perfect for a light snack, coffees and pastries and bread-based lunches, with pizza slices, tartlets and flans. You can also sit in and watch the bakers at work.

NORTHEAST MILAN 10 Corso Como
Corso Como 10, 20154 **Tel** *02 29 01 35 81*   **Map** *3 C2*

Carla Sozzani's designer empire 10 Corso Como is still a firm favourite in fashion circles. The Zen restaurant here is found on the ground floor, with a leafy and tranquil courtyard. The menu offers a selection of healthy dishes for those who are watching their figure. Fusion cuisine and a bistrot-style atmosphere.

NORTHEAST MILAN Amaltea
Via Guglielmo Pepe 38, 20159 **Tel** *02 60 63 40*   **Map** *3 B1*

Close to Garibaldi station, this restaurant serves regional Italian dishes and historic classics in a refined and elegant environment. The decor is light and sophisticated, with paintings covering the walls. Service is attentive, but tables are few. Closed 1 wk mid-Aug.

NORTHEAST MILAN Be Bop Pizzeria
Via Col di Lana 4, 20136 **Tel** *02 837 69 72*   **Map** *4 F4*

One of Milan's most popular pizza restaurants, this attractive place is located close to the Navigli district. Diners looking for non-wheat or gluten-free, vegan and vegetarian pizzas are well catered for. In addition, Be Bop also serves Mediterranean-inspired fare. Open daily. Closed Aug.

NORTHEAST MILAN Fortunio
Via del Carmine 3, 20121 **Tel** *02 72 00 31 85*   **Map** *3 B4*

Fortunio offers a seasonal menu that changes on a monthly basis, featuring innovative, international cuisine. The decor is simple and stylish, with contemporary red leather seating but the food is the main attraction. Specials include pumpkin flowers stuffed with ricotta and pesto. Great value for money. Closed Sat lunch, Sun.

NORTHEAST MILAN Hong Kong
Via Schiaparelli 5, 20125 **Tel** *02 670 19 92*

A well-regarded restaurant, close to Sondrio metro station, serving Cantonese and Sichuan cuisine over two floors (locals recommend the second). The interior is elegant and richly decorated. The menu isn't extensive, and there are few surprises for Chinese food fans, but the quality is good and the service kind and attentive. Closed Mon lunch.

NORTHEAST MILAN Matarel
Corso Garibaldi 75, 20121 **Tel** *02 65 42 04*   **Map** *3 B3*

Traditional Milanese cuisine with lots of veal and saffron risotto is the order of the day at Matarel. The house special is *cassoeûla*, a classic pork stew. This charming, homely restaurant does not look much from outside, but it is always packed with tables squeezed close together. A great choice in the heart of the city. Closed Tue, Wed lunch; Jun, Jul.

NORTHEAST MILAN Osteria del Treno
Via San Gregorio 46, 20124 **Tel** *02 670 04 79*   **Map** *4 E2*

Located in an old railway workers' club, this restaurant specializes in Italian cuisine with an innovative touch. Influenced by the Slow Food philosophy, the chef creates dishes such as gnocchi made with cocoa and gorgonzola in a thyme and pecorino sauce. Closed Sat & Sun lunch; Easter, 2 wks mid-Aug.

Key to Price Guide *see p172* **Key to Symbols** *see back cover flap*

NORTHEAST MILAN Ran

€€

Via Antonio Bordoni 8–10, 20124 **Tel** *02 669 69 97*

Map *4 D1*

Ran is a great choice for Japanese food in Milan. The tasting menu is one option; alternatively, the chefs and kimono-clad waitresses can prepare sushi in front of you. Specialities include sushi, *sashimi*, *tempura*, soups, and *sukiyaki* (cooked vegetables, meat, soya and noodles). A favourite of the local Japanese community. Closed lunch, Sun.

NORTHEAST MILAN Rigolo

€€

Largo Treves, corner Via Solferino, 20121 **Tel** *02 86 46 32 20*

Map *3 C3*

Rigolo is centrally located, near Milan's pretty bohemian district of Brera. It serves a predominantly Tuscan menu to the fashionable set. Choose from wild boar with *pappardelle*, rich local sausages, and steaming boiled meat (*bollito*), which is served on Thursdays. The service is excellent. Closed Mon; Aug.

NORTHEAST MILAN Da Bimbi

€€€

Viale Abruzzi 33, 20131 **Tel** *02 29 52 61 03*

Classic Italian cuisine at this small, relaxed trattoria close to the polytechnic. Food is seasonal, with an extensive menu where both fish and meat lovers are well catered for. Decor is fresh and simple, with white-washed walls, old photos of the city on the walls and a terracotta-tiled floor. Closed Mon lunch, Sun; 3 wks Aug.

NORTHEAST MILAN Da Ilia

€€€

Via Lecco 1, 20124 **Tel** *02 29 52 18 95*

Map *4 E3*

A classic north Italian restaurant with an ample antipasti buffet. Choose from delicious Tuscan cheeses and salamis, various meat dishes with *porcini* (cep) mushrooms, grilled monkfish with rosemary or ravioli with ricotta cheese and spinach in melted butter. All dishes are excellent and home-made. Closed Fri & Sat lunch; Aug, 1 wk at Christmas.

NORTHEAST MILAN Giglio Rosso

€€€

Piazza Luigi di Savoia 2, 20124 **Tel** *02 669 41 74*

Map *4 F1*

A few steps from the main train station, this elegant place, decorated in contemporary neutral shades, is a firm favourite with the locals. It offers high-quality, Tuscan-inspired cuisine, with a menu of traditional and innovative pasta, fish and meat dishes. Vegetarians are also well looked after. Closed Sat & Sun lunch; Aug, 23 Dec–6 Jan.

NORTHEAST MILAN Il Coriandolo

€€€

Via dell'Orso 1, 20121 **Tel** *02 869 32 73*

Map *3 C5*

Located in the heart of Brera, Milan's artistic quarter, this is an elegant place for dinner, with a tastefully decorated, if a little spartan, room. It is not far from La Scala opera house, and one of few restaurants to open in August. The emphasis is on excellent food and wine; dishes include a wonderful Milanese-style risotto. Closed Christmas.

NORTHEAST MILAN Il Giorno Bistrot dell'Hermitage

€€€

Hotel Hermitage, Via Messina 10, 20154 **Tel** *02 31 81 70*

Map *3 A2*

Located in the Hotel Hermitage, this restaurant with a literary salon-style decor serves modern Milanese and Mediterranean cuisine in a relaxed setting. The menu includes meat, fish, seafood, and gluten-free dishes. Diners can enjoy an apéritif in the hotel's Caesar's Bar beforehand and, in summer, terrace dining is an enticing option.

NORTHEAST MILAN Le Langhe

€€€

Corso Como 6, 20154 **Tel** *02 655 42 79*

Map *3 C2*

Just a few doors down from the fabulous designer store 10 Corso Como is this restaurant with two rooms – the upstairs one for informal meals, and the one downstairs for more elegant dining. The menu comprises of classic Piedmont dishes including Barolo risotto and *tomini alle erbe* (goat's cheese flavoured with herbs). Closed Sun; 3 wks Aug.

NORTHEAST MILAN Malavoglia

€€€

Via Lecco 4, 20124 **Tel** *02 29 53 13 87*

Map *4 E3*

This restaurant has been run by a Sicilian couple since 1973: she runs the kitchen and he is front of house. The seafood menu has Sicilian origins with a modern twist. Specials include spaghetti with tuna, pasta with swordfish and spicy tuna steak. There is a good wine list and booking is essential. Closed Mon lunch & Sun; Easter, Aug, Christmas.

NORTHEAST MILAN Mykonos

€€€

Via Tofane 5, 20217 **Tel** *02 261 02 09*

Map *4 F1*

This traditional Greek taverna is located in the Buenos Aires area, not far from Central Station, and overlooks the Martesana canal. It is advisable to book in advance. Among the classics are the starters and *tiropita*, a delicious goat's cheese quiche. The kitchen is open until 1am, which is rare in Milan. Closed lunch.

NORTHEAST MILAN Piccola Cucina

€€€

Viale Piave 17, 20129 **Tel** *02 76 01 28 60*

Map *4 F4*

This tiny restaurant is colourful and unpretentious, but still chic and favoured by local architects, design and fashion people. The specials range from octopus and squid on chickpeas to a chocolate sponge filled with hot chocolate sauce. The small number of tables ensures an intimate ambience. Closed lunch, Sun; 3 wks Aug, 24 Dec–6 Jan.

NORTHEAST MILAN Piero e Pia

€€€

Piazza Aspari 2, 20219 **Tel** *02 71 85 41*

Map *4 F4*

Piero e Pia is a small, family-run establishment in the Città Studi, the smart area near Milan's polytechnic. Expect typical cuisine from the Piacenza area of Emilia-Romagna: fresh pasta parcels, roast pork and boiled meats. Cordial and informal ambience and good wine list. Closed Sun; 3 wks Aug, Christmas.

NORTHEAST MILAN Valtellina
Via Taverna 34, 20134 **Tel** *02 756 11 39* €€€

A refined restaurant offering Valtellina specialities. These rustic dishes include salamis, local hams, good meat and game with mushrooms and polenta. Also recommended are the antipasti and home-made pasta dishes. Finish with a home-made dessert. Parking is available nearby. Book ahead. Closed 2 wks mid-Aug, 1 wk at Christmas.

NORTHEAST MILAN Bulgari Restaurant
Via Privata Fratelli Gabba 7b, 20122 **Tel** *02 805 80 52 33* €€€€

Map *3 C4*

Join the stylish Milanese for an elegant dining experience, worth the expense. Bulgari is in a tranquil location at the edge of the Botanical Gardens, in a curvaceous space on two levels with an outdoor courtyard. A typical dish is lemon risotto with vanilla flowers accompanied by an excellent choice of wines. Sunday brunch is sublime.

NORTHEAST MILAN Da Giannino
Via Vittor Pisani 6, 20135 **Tel** *02 66 98 69 98* €€€€

Map *8 F1*

The place to go for a classic Italian meal with excellent service. The sophisticated atmosphere in the smart *belle époque* dining rooms is preferred by the city's influential figures. Giannino's veal cutlet is one of the best in the city, but also recommended are saffron rice, home-made pasta dishes, seafood and desserts. Closed Sat & Sun lunch.

NORTHEAST MILAN Il Baretto al Baglioni
Via Senato 7, 20121 **Tel** *02 78 12 55* €€€€

Map *4 E5*

Il Baretto al Baglioni is more a bar-cum-dining-room than a restaurant proper, though it offers traditional Italian fare of the finest quality. Try the truffle risotto or the seafood salad. Attentive service, extensive wine list and a sophisticated ambience. Closed 3 wks Aug.

NORTHEAST MILAN I Sapori del Mare
Via Nullo 14, corner Via Goldoni, 20129 **Tel** *02 70 12 34 76* €€€€

Map *4 F5*

A formal place with a reputation for good service. The typical setting for great seafood and fish specials includes a huge buffet display of hors d'oeuvres, an aquarium tank, sea-related decor and murals of old fishing scenes. Choose from Catalan prawns, mixed seafood platter, tuna, swordfish, sea bass, scampi and more. Closed Mon; 2 wks Aug.

NORTHEAST MILAN Joia
Via Panfilo Castaldi 18, 20124 **Tel** *02 204 92 44* €€€€

Map *4 E3*

A gourmet restaurant close to the Porta Venezia metro station. The dining room is minimalist and well lit. The food on offer is mostly vegetarian and includes vegetable foie gras with truffle sauce, greens layered with fontina cheese and herbs, and tuna and beans with balsamic vinegar and ginger oil. Closed Sat lunch, Sun; 3 wks Aug, 24 Dec–7 Jan.

NORTHEAST MILAN Raw Fish Café Centro Ittico
Via Martiri Oscuri 19, 20125 **Tel** *02 28 04 03 96* €€€€

Map *4 F1*

This exceptional seafood restaurant is located right next to the fish market, so the freshest produce and excellent shellfish are always ensured for the creative dishes produced here. Centro Ittico is contemporary in design, with neon-lights shining through a long glass-tiled bar. Booking is essential. Closed Mon lunch; Sun; Aug.

NORTHEAST MILAN Il Teatro (Four Seasons)
Four Seasons Hotel, Via Gesù, 20121 **Tel** *02 770 88* €€€€€

Map *4 D5, 10 E2*

This award-winning restaurant treats guests like royalty, with excellent service, sophisticated table settings and a wonderful menu. Try the dried salt cod with artichokes and spinach infused with onions and wine or the medallion of veal with foie gras, black truffle and green vegetables. Sunday brunch is served 11:45am–3pm. Closed lunch.

NORTHEAST MILAN Nobu/Armani
Via Gastone Pisoni 1, 20121 **Tel** *02 62 31 26 45* €€€€€

Map *4 E2*

Within the white Armani megastore on Via Manzoni you can find Japanese master chef Nobuyuki Matsuhisa's famous Nobu restaurant. The menu is exquisite, unique and worth the expense. Enjoy the famous house special of black cod in miso sauce and sip saké with added gold leaf, all in a stylish, low-lit designer environment. Closed Sun lunch.

LAKE MAGGIORE

ARONA Del Barcaiolo
Piazza del Popolo 23, 28041 **Tel** *0322 24 33 88* €€

In an ancient palazzo in the main square of Arona, under the medieval arches, is this cosy restaurant specializing in Piedmontese cuisine. It offers a rustic menu of good antipasti, chargrilled meats and fish and other hearty fare from the northern region. Seating outdoors in summer. Closed Wed (winter), Thu lunch; 12–20 Dec.

ARONA La Vecchia Arona
Lungolago Marconi 17, 28041 **Tel** *0322 24 24 69* €€€

Welcoming restaurant on the lakeside with imaginative Piedmontese cuisine. The atmosphere is comfortable, intimate and favoured by couples. Home-made pâtés, pasta with cheese or meat sauces, or Mediterranean fish dishes are all delicious. Leave room for the excellent desserts and cheeses. Good regional and international wines. Closed Fri.

ARONA Taverna del Pittore

€€€€

Piazza del Popolo 39, 28041 **Tel** *0322 24 33 66*

This is one of the region's best restaurants, located in the main square in Arona. Spectacular lake views from the terrace only enhance the excellent menu. Simple Tuscan cuisine is mixed with more elaborate dishes using game, or fish caught on the lake. Sample the multicoloured pasta and excellent-quality fish. Closed Mon; 23 Dec–23 Jan.

CANNOBIO Osteria Vino di Vino

€€

Strada della Valle Cannobina 1, 28822 **Tel** *0323 719 19*

Housed in a former stable block and with a pretty courtyard, this youthful and relaxed trattoria serves classic Italian dishes with a contemporary twist. Cheese is a speciality, with over 120 seasonal varieties, and there's an extensive wine list with more than 350 labels. Closed lunch, Wed (except mid-Jun–end Aug); Nov–mid-Mar.

CANNOBIO Del Lago

€€€

Casali Carmine Inferiore 2, Località Carmine Inferiore, 28822 **Tel** *0323 705 95*

The refined Italian and international cuisine and the views of Lake Maggiore are the main draws for the faithful followers to this restaurant. The freshest ingredients are used to produce imaginative simple dishes, enhancing aromas and flavours. There is a lovely summer terrace surrounded by verdant gardens. Closed Wed lunch, Tue; Nov–Feb.

CANNOBIO Porto Vecchio

€€€

Piazza Vittorio Emanuele III 6, 28822 **Tel** *0323 73 96 39*

Hotel Cannobio's lovely restaurant has a central, peaceful location on the promenade. The stylish intimate interior has a warm atmosphere, with large lamps, creamy decor, striped walls and rattan chairs. Excellent fish, seafood, salads and pasta. No reservations taken for the spectacular terrace at the lakeside. Closed lunch, Tue; Nov–Mar.

LAVENO Il Porticciolo

€€€€

Via Fortino 40, 21014 **Tel** *0332 66 72 57*

The owner provides his guests with creatively cooked fish from the lake, while his wife will suggest a complementary wine. In summer the veranda overlooking the Laveno Gulf is open. Try the trout ravioli with prawns, thyme and mushrooms or whitefish with lemon sauce, capers and tomatoes. Closed Wed lunch, Tue; end Jan–Feb, 1 wk Nov.

PALLANZA Il Torchio

€

Via Manzoni 20, 28048 **Tel** *0323 50 33 52*

Located within a stylish provicial setting, Il Torchio is a small but popular restaurant. The cuisine is regional but creative and accompanied by a good selection of local wines. Lake Maggiore fish is served alongside other traditional Piedmontese meat dishes. Book ahead. Closed Wed, Thu lunch, but open daily mid-Jun–Sep.

PALLANZA Dell'Angolo

€€

Piazza Garibaldi 35, 28048 **Tel** *0323 55 63 62*

Located in a small square, Dell'Angolo is a typical regional tavern offering a variety of refined fish dishes, a mix of Piedmontese and Lombardy cuisine and good value for money. In the summer months, tables are also available outside on the square. There is limited space, so book ahead. Closed Mon; Nov.

PALLANZA Milano

€€€€

Corso Zanitello 2, 28048 **Tel** *0323 55 68 16*

Milano is located in a Neo-Gothic building in the centre of Pallanza. It has a lovely terrace with views across Lake Maggiore and serves great fish from the lake, including perch and char accompanied by home-grown seasonal organic vegetables and great wines. Closed Tue; mid-Nov–Feb.

RANCO Il Sole di Ranco

€€€€€

Piazza Venezia 5, 20120 **Tel** *0331 97 65 07*

This excellent restaurant is surrounded by parkland and offers great panoramic views. Chef Carlo Brovelli uses only the freshest ingredients for his dishes, without smothering them with sauces or added flavours. In the summer months you can also eat alfresco. Closed Mon lunch, Tue lunch (mid-Oct–mid-Apr); mid-Nov–mid-Jan.

SESTO CALENDE La Biscia

€€€

Piazza de Cristoforis 1, 21028 **Tel** *0331 92 44 35*

A light, airy restaurant in the centre of town, Biscia offers a menu based around regional dishes from the surrounding countryside and the lake, as well as some seafood. A speciality is white bream cooked in rocket (*arugula*) or linguine with Sicilian red prawns. Excellent desserts complete the menu. Closed Sun dinner, Mon; first 2 wks Jan, 2 wks end Aug.

STRESA Piemontese

€€

Via Mazzini 25, 28838 **Tel** *0323 302 35*

A good place for award-winning creative versions of traditional local cuisine. This intimate establishment in the centre of Stresa offers relaxed elegance and a pretty terrace under vines in the summer. An excellent selection of wines is also available. Try the spaghetti with chilli and onions, or the foie gras pâté with fondue. Closed Mon; Dec–Jan.

VERBANIA Boccon di Vino

€

Via Troubetzkoy 86, 28900 **Tel** *0323 50 40 39*

An elegant tavern with reliably good food. A local special of pasta with leeks is offered here and the desserts are also fine. Enjoy the lake views over other dishes, including home-made pastas, smoked fish or Piedmontese meat specials. The owner knows his wines, so just ask and he will pick the best. Closed Tue lunch, Wed lunch (winter); Nov.

VERBANIA (BÈE) Chi Ghinn €€€
Via Maggiore 21, 28900 **Tel** *0323 563 26*

In the tiny village of Bèe, above Verbania, chef Adolfo Porta serves local and regional dishes such as risotto with lake shrimp and suckling pig. The dining room is elegant and decorated in rich creams with crisp white linen. Guests can enjoy views over the lake from the garden. Car/taxi needed. Closed Tue; Wed (Oct–Mar); Jan–Feb.

LAKE COMO

BELLAGIO Silvio €€
Via Paolo Carcano 12, 22021 **Tel** *031 95 03 22*

This restaurant's owner and his son are professional fishermen providing an abundant catch of fresh lake fish for their patrons. The catch ranges from perch, served with rice, Parmesan and sage, to lake trout, served in a fine parsley sauce. Visitors can even arrange a fishing trip with them. The views over Lake Como are enchanting. Closed Mon–Fri; Jan–Feb.

BELLAGIO Barchetta €€€
Salita Mella 13, 22021 **Tel** *031 95 13 89*

Fish fills the menu, and the home-made cakes come highly recommended. Local ingredients form the basis of the food here, which the chef deftly works into a creative Lombard and Mediterranean mixed menu. Established in 1887, Barchetta offers a lovely terrace in summer and nearby parking. Booking advisable. Closed Tue; Nov–Easter.

BRIENNO Crotto dei Platani €€€
Via Regina 73, 22010 **Tel** *031 81 40 38*

The setting is the draw: bang on the lake, with a terrace under a canopy of trees and stunning views. The menu offers fresh takes on national dishes made with top-quality ingredients. Try buffalo mozzarella wrapped in crispy Parma ham or tureen of perch with aged balsamic and grapes. Booking highly advisable.

CERNOBBIO La Terrazza Asnigo €€
Via Noseda 2, 22012 **Tel** *031 51 00 62*

Housed in the Hotel Asnigo, this well-regarded gourmet restaurant serves contemporary European and Italian cuisine. Try the risotto with new peas and roasted calamari, or the pasta with wild boar and cocoa bean sauce. Guests can also enjoy panoramic views over the lake and an excellent wine list. Closed Mon; Jan.

CERNOBBIO Ristorante Pizzeria Giardino €€
Via Regina 73, 22012 **Tel** *031 51 11 54*

This restaurant with views of the lake is situated within a delightful garden filled with palm trees and flowers. The menu is simple and with few surprises, but everything is prepared with high-quality ingredients. There is a dedicated pizza menu for children. After 10:30pm, they serve only pizzas. Booking is advisable. Closed Wed (winter).

CERNOBBIO Trattoria del Vapore €€
Via Garibaldi 17, 22012 **Tel** *031 51 03 08*

This trattoria in the town centre has a pleasant atmosphere and plenty of local dishes. Try the house special of risotto with carp and perch from the lake. The cosy atmosphere is partly due to the decor, which includes antique furniture, old stone walls and an open fire. There is also an excellent wine cellar. Closed Tue (winter); 20 Dec–20 Jan.

CERNOBBIO Gatto Nero €€€€
Via Monte Santo 69, Località Rovenna, 22012 **Tel** *031 51 20 42*

Il Gatto Nero offers a stunning view over Lake Como, from the road to Monte Bisbino above Canobbio. The menu is kept to a few high-quality dishes, with such delicacies as tagliatelle with fresh truffles and chopped kidneys cooked in brandy. All dishes are regional specialities. Booking essential. Closed Mon, Tue lunch; Nov–Jan.

COMO Al Giardino €€
Via Monte Grappa 52, 22100 **Tel** *031 26 50 16*

This family-run restaurant serves local and regional specialities. The range of cured meats and cheeses is particularly fine. The fresh interior is a delight, and the service is friendly and relaxed. A garden makes this place family-friendly – as the popular Sunday lunch proves. Book ahead. Closed Sun dinner, Mon; 2 wks Aug.

COMO Locanda dell'Oca Bianca €€
Via Canturina 251, 22100 **Tel** *031 52 56 05*

Housed in a renovated 17th-century farmhouse with a warm, intimate atmosphere, this restaurant is located outside Como, in the village of Trecallo. It offers a variety of Italian dishes with a French twist. Choose from lake fish, vegetable soups, meat dishes, cheeses and home-made desserts. The garden is open in summer. Closed Mon; lunch Tue–Sat; Jan.

COMO Sant'Anna 1907 €€
Via Turati 3, 22100 **Tel** *031 50 52 66*

Creative local food is served at this traditional restaurant split into four elegant, soberly designed rooms. Typical fare includes veal in an olive crust, fillet of red tuna with chicory shoots and olives and risotto with fish and saffron. Artichokes and polenta also feature heavily on the menu. Closed Sat lunch, Sun.

Key to Price Guide *see p172* **Key to Symbols** *see back cover flap*

COMO L'Osteria l'Angolo del Silenzio
Viale Lecco 25, 22100 **Tel** *031 337 21 57*

A locals' favourite, this attractive, elegant restaurant is situated in the heart of Como, just a few minutes walk from the cathedral. The menu is extensive, featuring regional and national cuisine, and it is evenly split between fish and meat dishes. Booking compulsory. Closed Mon & Tue lunch; 2 wks Aug.

COMO Raimondi del Villa Flori
Via Cernobbio 12, 22100 **Tel** *031 338 20*

Raimondi is a romantic and refined restaurant with a splendid setting in a grand 19th-century hotel with lovely views of the lake and the gardens. Enjoy the elegant terrace in summer. The classic Italian regional cuisine offers a selection of Lombardy specials and excellent freshwater fish from the lake. Closed Mon, Sat lunch; Dec–Feb.

ISOLA COMACINA Locanda dell'Isola Comacina
Sala Comacina, 22010 **Tel** *0344 550 83*

A unique experience on an island that is deserted except for this restaurant, which is reached by boat (pay on board). The same set menu of fish has survived since 1947 and still thrives today as a set-price option. However, chicken is also served. It is necessary to book ahead. Wonderful at any time of the year. Closed Tue (in spring); 2 Nov–1 Mar.

LECCO Antica Osteria Casa di Lucia
Via Lucia 27, Località Acquate, 23900 **Tel** *0341 49 45 94*

This superb gourmet restaurant with a good reputation and loyal clientele is housed in a characteristic 17th-century house that also holds photographic exhibitions. Lake fish specialities, game, pasta dishes and a delicious home-made nut tart are some of the traditional Slow Food specials. Closed Sat lunch, Sun.

LECCO Al Porticciolo
Via Fausto Valsecchi 5–7, 23900 **Tel** *0341 49 81 03*

This restaurant serves high-quality fish and shellfish, with home-made pastas as well as excellent antipasti. The well-spaced room is welcoming, with an open fire in winter and outdoor terrace in summer. It is advisable to book in advance. Parking available. Closed lunch (except Sun & hols); Mon, Tue; 2 wks Jan, 1 wk Jun, 3 wks Aug.

MANDELLO DEL LARIO Riva Granda
Piazza XXV Aprile 5A, 23826 **Tel** *0341 70 03 36*

Located in the town centre, just metres from the harbour, this small, friendly restaurant offers local dishes made with fresh fish from Lake Como, such as a delicious combination of rice and perch, home-made pasta and gnocchi, and exquisite desserts. In summer, diners can enjoy eating on the veranda on the square.

MOLTRASIO Imperialino
Via Antica Regina 26, 22010 **Tel** *031 34 61 11*

The restaurant is part of the Imperial hotel, a splendid villa overlooking Lake Como. The food served is regional, sourced from local ingredients and with a leaning towards seafood. There are three dining rooms with plenty of tables, but it is best to book ahead. Try the prawns and cannelloni. Closed Mon; Jan.

SALA COMACINA La Tirlindana
Piazza Matteotti, 22010 **Tel** *0344 566 37*

This elegant restaurant sits in a picturesque square overlooking the lake and the landing stage where the boats leave for Isola Comacina. The menu offers fish from the lake, some meat dishes and a French slant. The house special is ravioli stuffed with a local lemon-flavoured cheese. Sit outside in summer. Closed Wed (winter); Nov–Feb.

VARENNA Vecchia Varenna
Contrada Scoscesa 10, 23828 **Tel** *0341 83 07 93*

This restaurant is right on the lake, near a tiny harbour, with terrace dining in summer. The menu mixes regional surf and turf. Some of the best dishes include rainbow trout baked with olives, capers and anchovies; lasagne with lake fish sauce and beef with rosemary and madeira. Closed Mon; Jan.

LAKE GARDA

DESENZANO Cavallino
Via Gherla 30, corner Via Murachette, 25015 **Tel** *030 912 02 17*

Set in a courtyard, Cavallino serves a high-class menu of fish from the lake and the sea. A fine special is caviar risotto whisked with Franciacorta wine. The main dining room is light and pleasantly decorated and a smaller, more intimate room can also be booked. In the summer months, tables are set up on the terrace. Closed Sun dinner, Mon; Nov.

DESENZANO Esplanade
Via Lario 3, 25015 **Tel** *030 914 33 61*

With sweeping views across the lake, this elegant gourmet restaurant has won accolades for its innovative cuisine specializing in fish (though there are meat options too). Choose from dishes such as roasted cod with spinach, pine nuts and grapes, or roasted saddle of mountain goat. The superb wine list has more than 1,500 labels. Closed Wed.

GARDONE Locanda Agli Angeli €€

Piazza Garibaldi 2, 25083 **Tel** *0365 208 32*

Within the narrow streets of Gardone Riviera, this cosy restaurant is a short walk from the lake. It is part of a charming hotel with arches and wooden beams on the ceiling. It serves homely Italian and Mediterranean cuisine. Try the risotto with trout from the lake and pumpkin or the sea bass with *porcini* (cep) mushrooms. Closed Tue; mid-Nov–Feb.

GARDONE Villa Fiordaliso €€€€€

Corso Zanardelli 132, 25083 **Tel** *0365 201 58*

Excellent-quality ingredients and fine flavours make the cuisine of Fiordaliso stand out. The Art Nouveau-style restaurant offers a creative menu of meat, seafood and fish from the lake. *Tagliolini neri ai crostacei* (black pasta with shellfish) is one of the chef's specials. The villa boasts wonderful grounds and a lovely terrace. Closed Mon; Nov–Feb.

GARGNANO Tortuga €€€€

Via XXIV Maggio 5, 25084 **Tel** *0365 712 51*

A light, imaginative cuisine is offered at this refined, intimate lakeside restaurant. Despite serving dishes with foie gras, lobster and pasta, the meals are still light and delicate in flavour. The fish is excellent and the wine list superb. Guests travel here from miles around, so it is best to book ahead. Closed lunch; Tue; mid-Nov–Feb.

MANERBA Capriccio €€€€

Piazza San Bernardo 6, 25080 **Tel** *0365 55 11 24*

A sophisticated establishment with splendid views of Lake Garda and the surrounding hills. A high-quality cuisine with such delicacies as sea bass with scallops on fennel cream with a grapefruit sauce and medallions of *ricciola* (greater amberjack fish). A highlight among the desserts is the passion-fruit sorbet. Closed Tue (except Jul & Aug); Jan–Feb.

PESCHIERA DEL GARDA Trattoria al Combattente €€

Strada Bergamini 60, Località San Benedetto, 37019 **Tel** *045 755 04 10*

Situated in the village of Bergamini, between Sirmione and Peschiera, this popular trattoria serves local specials, including a wide variety of Lake Garda fish. The true flavours of the ingredients, such as the simple grilled lake sardines or pike, are not hidden by rich extras. The antipasti are delicious. Closed Mon; 1 wk Feb, 2 wks Nov.

RIVA DEL GARDA Restel de Fer €€

Via Restel de Fer 10, 38066 **Tel** *0464 55 34 81*

Moments walk from the lake, this historic inn with low vaulted ceilings has been in the same family for over 600 years. Seasonal food is served, with an emphasis on freshness and quality. There's an excellent choice of fresh pasta, meat, and lake and river fish dishes. There are also two well-priced tasting menus. Closed Wed (except summer); Nov.

SALÒ La Campagnola €€

Via Brunati 11, 25087 **Tel** *0365 221 53*

Angelo del Bon, of Slow Food fame, has made this one of the best-known restaurants in Lombardy. He uses fresh ingredients to produce refined regional, national and international dishes. He also offers some 600 wines. One of the oldest restaurants around Lake Garda, this is a popular spot, so book well ahead. Closed Mon, Tue lunch; Feb.

SALÒ Osteria dell'Orologio €€

Via Butturini 26, 25087 **Tel** *0365 29 01 58*

An old, beautifully restored inn in Salò's historic centre. It is always busy, so book in advance for delicious local specialities. The home-made dishes include game, such as partridge with *pappardelle* pasta. Great variety of wines by the glass or bottle and a young, informal atmosphere. Closed Mon–Fri (Nov only), Wed; 1 wk end Jan.

SALÒ Antica Trattoria Alle Rose €€€

Via Gasparo da Salò 33, 25087 **Tel** *0365 432 20*

A young clientele flocks here for the innovative lakeside cuisine. This old trattoria offers local seasonal fresh produce from the market, freshwater fish from the lake and dishes such as *carpaccio* (wafer-thin slices) of *porcini* (cep) mushrooms, rabbit or delicious spaghetti with rocket (*arugula*), tomatoes and langoustines. Closed Wed; 2 wks Nov.

SAN VIGILIO Locanda San Vigilio €€€€

Località San Vigilio, 37016 **Tel** *045 725 66 88*

A noble tavern dating back to 1500, with medieval arches and spectacular views. As well as a romantic setting in a lovely garden by the lake, the restaurant offers regional specialities from the land and the lake. On Fridays and Saturdays, from June to August, there is a candlelit supper with a grand buffet. Book well ahead. Closed Nov–Feb.

SIRMIONE Al Porticciolo €€

Porto Galeazzi, Via XXV Aprile 83, 25019 **Tel** *030 919 61 61*

This lakeside trattoria, located outside the town of Sirmione, is very popular. On the menu is a wide variety of dishes: fresh salads, seafood, lake fish and great pastas, all served in ample portions. Pick a table in the cosy indoor room, under the roof outdoors or on the open terrace under parasols. Closed Sun evening (Nov–Feb).

SIRMIONE La Rucola €€€€

Via Strentelle 7, 25019 **Tel** *030 91 63 26*

Located in the historic centre of Sirmione, with ancient brick walls adding a certain charm, La Rucola serves innovative Mediterranean cuisine using both meat and fish. Specials include calamari in squid ink with potato cakes and prosciutto, or lamb cutlets in onion glaze with potato purée. Compulsory booking at lunchtime. Closed Thu; Jan.

Key to Price Guide *see p172* **Key to Symbols** *see back cover flap*

SIRMIONE Signori
Via Romagnoli 17, 25019 **Tel** *030 91 60 17*

This elegant restaurant close to the Castello Scaligero is the ideal destination for an intimate dinner. Get there a little early to enjoy the views of the sunset over the lake. The modern decor is highlighted by large artworks on the walls and the menu relies heavily on locally sourced products, reflecting seasonal variations. Closed Mon; Nov–Feb.

SOIANO DEL LAGO Aurora
Via Ciucani 1, 25080 **Tel** *0365 67 41 01*

A good, simple restaurant with a warm country feel to it. It is housed in an elegant villa decorated with taste and originality and features a lovely covered veranda in summer. House specials include pasta filled with squid and spinach, marinated smoked salmon and pasta with a ragout of fresh lake fish. Good value for money. Closed Wed.

LAGO D'ISEO

ERBUSCO Mongolfiera dei Sodi
Via Cavour 7, 25030 **Tel** *030 726 83 03*

An excellent, cosy artisan restaurant offering local traditional game, meat, fish and vegetables, as well as rich, innovative cuisine. Try the famous Florentine steak, home-made pasta with pigeon sauce, baked lamb with sheep's cheese and prawns with a hot curry sauce. The drinks list includes local Franciacorta wines. Closed Thu; 1 wk Jan, 3 wks Aug.

ERBUSCO Gualtiero Marchesi
Via Vittorio Emanuele II 23, 25030 **Tel** *030 776 05 62*

This place is run by one of Italy's most famous chefs, Gualtiero Marchesi, under the Relais gastronomy banner. It is also a wine estate in the heart of the Franciacorta region with exceptional food. For a taste of the house specials, try the saffron risotto, *porcini* (cep) casserole or roast turbot. Lovely views and stylish, luxurious decor. Closed Sun lunch; Mon.

ISEO Osteria Il Volto
Via Mirolte 33, 25049 **Tel** *030 98 14 62*

Il Volto is one of the lesser-known addresses around Lake Iseo. The interior is rustic, and the menu is regional and simple, but excellent quality. The best ingredients are cooked to perfection, unadulterated by fancy blends of flavours. Highlights include pasta with a lake fish ragout, caviar in potato pastry and beef in olive oil. Closed Wed, Thu.

MONTE ISOLA La Foresta
Località Pescheria Maraglio 174, 25050 **Tel** *030 988 62 10*

What makes this a popular spot at the water's edge is the excellent menu, laden with fish from Lake Iseo. Good wines too, especially the sparkling Franciacorta. Salted pressed fish, dried in the sun and marinated in olive oil is a speciality, and is often prepared on the shore in front of the restaurant. Closed Wed; 20 Dec–Feb.

SARNICO Al Desco di Puledda Mario
Piazza XX Settembre 19, 24067 **Tel** *035 91 07 40*

In summer, expect Al Desco's terrace to be packed. People return to this elegant restaurant again and again – for the lakeside view, but also for the great choice of dishes. In addition to fresh fish, the menu has local and international meat dishes and home-made pastas. Good wine list. Book ahead. Closed Mon (except summer); Jan.

LAGO D'ORTA

ORTA SAN GIULIO Ai Due Santi
Piazza Motta 18, 28016 **Tel** *0322 901 92*

This elegant restaurant is located right in the middle of town, and it offers a breathtaking view of the island of San Giulio. On the menu, diners will find a varied selection of traditional Italian and local fare. The fish, meat and vegetable dishes are paired with wines from all over the country, with an emphasis on Piedmont. Closed Wed; Nov.

ORTA SAN GIULIO Villa Crespi
Via G Fava 18, 28016 **Tel** *0322 91 19 02*

The gourmet and regional menus available at this ornate Moorish villa offer highly acclaimed, innovative Mediterranean dishes, and the wines include some of the world's best. Try the lobster medallions with cheese and pepper sauce, or the pasta with crayfish, sea urchins and apples. Closed Mon & Tue (Mar–Dec except evenings Jan-Feb, Apr–Oct).

SORISO Al Sorriso
Via Roma 18, 28018 **Tel** *0322 98 32 28*

A fine gourmet restaurant with three Michelin stars, sober decor, high-quality cuisine and a fabulous wine cellar. The chef offers an imaginative menu of seasonal, fragrant Piedmontese dishes. Specials include egg and potato gratin with white truffles and saffron risotto with courgettes and San Remo prawns. Closed Mon & Tue; 10 days Jan, 10 days Aug.

BARS AND CAFES

In general, Milanese bars and cafés are places to go for lunch or an aperitif. Breakfast for most Milanese office workers tends to consist of a cappuccino with a croissant, usually consumed at the bar counter. In the Brera quarter, cafés are lively and full of atmosphere. In the early evening they are popular places to relax in with colleagues and friends. Fashions come and go and a café that is "in" one month may be suddenly empty a few months later. To counteract such swings, many Milanese bars have initiated a "happy hour",

Logo of Bar Jamaica (see p187)

when drinks are cheaper. Cafés are usually more crowded during the lunch break, when office workers stop for a quick salad or panino. As well as cafés, Milan also has excellent cake shops or *pasticcerie*, where you can sample pastries and cakes. For a more formal afternoon tea there are tea rooms (*sala da thé*), which are also packed at lunchtime. Many are historic places with period furniture. At the lakes, some of the more enterprising bars and cafés offer entertainment in the evening, either with a piano bar area or a small band.

WHERE TO LOOK

In Milan, there are plenty of places to choose from, whether you are going out for an aperitif or to eat snacks, and the choice will vary from area to area. In the atmospheric Brera quarter the bars usually have tables outside in summer. These places are popular with the fashion set and art students. **Jamaica** *(see p187)* is one established institution, an ideal place for a cocktail before dinner as well as for a chicken salad for lunch or an after-dinner drink. **Sans Égal** *(see p187)* is equally popular; on Sunday afternoons they show football (soccer) live on television, and in the evening the place is filled with young rock music buffs.

Around the Navigli, which is a pedestrian precinct, from 8pm in summer all the bars and cafés have tables set out outside, and it is possible to forget that Milan is a bustling commercial city altogether.

The Conca del Naviglio area is always busy. There are numerous places to try such as the **Caffè della Pusterla** *(see p187)*, located in the renovated medieval walls of the city, **Julep's New York** *(see p186)*, which is a good place to try for Sunday brunch, and the **Colonial Fashion Café** *(see p186)*, deservedly famous for its aperitifs.

In the Ticinese quarter **Coquetel** *(see p186)* is a popular place, especially during happy hour, when the young Milanese get together for an early evening drink.

For those with a sweet tooth who like croissants

Sans Égal business card (see p187)

and pastries for breakfast, the place to go is **Angela** *(see p186)*, near Fieramilanocity, or **Sissi** *(see p186)*, where you can enjoy cream pastries. If you like brunch, a habit that is increasingly popular in Milan, you can choose from among **Refeel** *(see p186)*, an American bar that looks like a living room, **Speak Easy** *(see p186)*, which also serves good salads, and the **Orient Express** *(see p186)*, with its appealingly old-fashioned look.

HISTORIC CAFES AND BARS

Some of Milan's most frequented cafés and pastry shops have a long tradition, and are housed in old palazzi with fine interiors. One interesting historic pasticceria is **Sant'Ambroeus** *(see p187)*, famous for its traditional panettone. Another ornate setting for breakfast and an aperitif is **Taveggia** *(see p187)*, which has been a favourite with the Milanese since 1910. Don't miss **Zucca**

Watching life go by at a café in Piazza del Duomo

in Galleria *(see p187)*, (formerly Camparino), a historic, old-fashioned bar and the place where the world-famous Campari drink was invented. Another must is **Cova** *(see p187)*, a café-pastry shop in Via Montenapoleone in business since 1817. In the heart of the fashion district, it is perfect for a cup of mid-afternoon hot chocolate or an evening aperitif. Lastly, the **Bar Magenta** *(see p186)* has been popular year in and year out and is now an evening haunt for the young Milanese crowd.

WHAT TO ORDER

A vast selection of beers, wines, aperitifs, excellent cocktails and non-alcoholic drinks is served in Milanese bars. A wide range of international beers is available as well as the Italian brands Peroni and Moretti. The current fashion is for Latin-American cocktails, which are gradually replacing classics like the Alexander and Bloody Mary. Almost every bar produces its own house aperitif.

A tray of savouries served with aperitifs

Italy is a wine-producing country and the regions of Piedmont, Lombardy and the Veneto all have extensive areas under vine. Piedmont is best known for its red wines, Barolo and Barbaresco, and the more affordable Barbera and Dolcetto. Good reds are also made in Franciacorta in Lombardy, in the Valtellina and near Verona, where Bardolino and Valpolicella are made. These regions' white wines include Gavi, Soave, Bianco di Custoza and Lugana, and there are some very good sparkling wines.

The historic Cova pastry shop in Via Montenapoleone (see p187)

Most bars provide snacks to go with early evening drinks. These may be simple, such as peanuts, or more elaborate. For generous snacks, try **Honky Tonks** *(see p186)*, where they serve Ascoli olives and pasta salad, as well as the classic *pinzimoni* dips with raw vegetables and canapés, during happy hour.

USEFUL HINTS

It is best to get around by public transport as parking is notoriously difficult in Milan and popular bars are likely to be surrounded by scooters, motorbikes and cars. Most bars and cafés operate two price tariffs, with higher prices charged for sitting down at a table. Ordering and con–suming at the bar counter is the most economical option, but you may prefer to linger and "people-watch".

Many bars operate a "happy hour" from 6:30 to 9:30pm, when drinks such as cocktails are sold at half-price. As a result these places become extremely crowded. At bars attracting younger people the music can be very loud, so if peace and quiet are needed, "happy hour" may not suit.

BARS IN HOTELS

Unlike the other bars in town, those in the large hotels are mostly used as venues for business meetings. Splendidly furnished and usually quiet, they exude discretion and privacy, creating the ideal conditions for discussing business matters.

Among the most distin-guished are the Lounge Bar in the **Westin Palace** *(see p163)*, which hosts art exhibitions, and the Foyer, in the **Hotel Four Seasons** *(see p163)*. The latter is decorated with theatre set designs. Extra charm is added by an antique fireplace, recreating the plush atmosphere of old Milanese palazzi.

The Foyer in the Hotel Four Seasons (see p163)

HAPPY HOUR

Colonial Fashion Café
Via De Amicis 12. **Map** 7 A2.
Tel 02-89 42 04 01.
◻ 5pm–2am.

Fitted out with furniture and objects from all over the world, many reminiscent of the colonial style, this café is very popular for its aperitifs and also offers a wide range of delicious snacks.

Coquetel
Via Vetere 14. **Map** 7 B3.
Tel 02-39 54 85 01. ◻ 8am–2am Mon–Sat; 6pm–2am Sun.

For years this establishment has been popular with young Milanese. It is especially busy in the summer, when people stroll around the grassy stretches of the adjacent Piazza della Vetra, and drop in for a beer and a chat. The cocktails are very good. Happy hour is from 6:30 to 8:30pm.

Honky Tonks
Via Fratelli Induno, corner of Via Lomazzo. **Map** 2 F1. **Tel** 02-345 25 62. ◻ 6pm–2am daily.

This establishment in a converted garage is famous for the variety and sheer quantity of the snacks offered during happy hour. The counter is laden with heaps of Ascoli olives, croquettes, stuffed *focaccia* (flat bread) and cured meats of every kind. A good choice of traditional and Caribbean cocktails.

Magenta
Via Carducci 13. **Map** 3 A5 & 7 A1.
Tel 02-805 38 08. ◻ 7am–3am Tue–Sun.

This historic café is ideal for a light lunch snack or a beer in the evening. Try an aperitif at the counter with delicious savouries and *bruschetta*. The good atmosphere attracts smart young Milanese, as well as students from the Università Cattolica and the San Carlo secondary school, both of which are nearby. Live music on Thursdays.

Makia
Corso Sempione 28. **Map** 2 E2.
Tel 02-33 60 40 12. ◻ 8am–3pm, 6pm–2am Mon–Sat. ● Aug.

This chic cocktail bar-restaurant offers tasty Italian/European dishes at lunch, dinner and Sunday brunch. There are also a great selection of snacks served to your table so you avoid the crush at the bar during cocktail hour.

BRUNCH

Julep's New York
Via Evangelista Torricelli 21.
Map 7 A5. **Tel** 02-89 40 90 29.
◻ 7pm–2am Mon–Sat; noon–4pm, 7pm–2am Sun.

Great atmosphere and excellent service await at this American bar-restaurant. The interior is done out in stylish 1930's decor and the cuisine is typical North American. On Sundays you can enjoy brunch with a Tex-Mex twist.

Orient Express
Via Fiori Chiari 8. **Map** 3 C4.
Tel 02-805 62 27.
◻ 11am–2am daily.

The decor, atmosphere and service are all reminiscent of the good old days, when the famous Orient Express was in its heyday. Bar, restaurant and Sunday brunch.

Refeel
Viale Sabotino 20. **Map** 8 E4.
Tel 02-58 32 42 27.
◻ 7am–2am Mon–Sat, noon–4pm Sun (for brunch). www.refeel.it

This American bar looks like a living room, with leather sofas and pot plants. A great brunch is served between noon and 4pm on Saturdays and Sundays. There's live jazz on Tuesday evenings.

Speak Easy
Via Castelfidardo 7. **Map** 3 C2. **Tel** 02-65 36 45. ◻ noon–3pm, 7pm–2:30am Mon–Sat; noon–5pm Sun.

"Eat as much as you like" is the motto in this place in the Brera quarter, which offers a tantalizing, varied buffet and fresh salads.

BREAKFAST

Angela
Via Ruggero di Lauria 15.
Map 2 D1. **Tel** 02-34 28 59.
◻ 8am–7:30pm Tue–Fri; 8.30am–1.30pm, 3–7pm Sat & Sun.

This small pastry shop near the Fiera has a counter where you can pause and enjoy breakfast. Go for the pastries with custard or whipped cream, the warm puff pastry with ricotta cheese and the fresh croissants with hot custard.

De Cherubini
Via Trincea delle Frasche 2.
Map 7 B3 & B4. **Tel** 02-54 10 74 86. ◻ 6:45am–11pm daily.

On the south side of Piazza XXIV Maggio, under a colonnade, lies this lovely café-cum-pastry shop. Good dishes at lunchtime, snacks with pre-dinner drinks and excellent croissants. Grab an outside table in good weather.

Leonardo
Via Aurelio Saffi 7. **Map** 2 F5.
Tel 02-439 03 02. ◻ 7:30am–9pm daily.

This ice cream parlour and pastry shop is famous for its crème patissière. The pastry rolls and cream puffs are delicious. Try the home-made yogurt or vanilla ice cream.

Marchesi
Via Santa Maria alla Porta 11a.
Map 7 B1. **Tel** 02-87 67 30.
◻ 7:30am–8pm Tue–Sat; 8:30am–1pm Sun.

This historic pastry shop, in the centre between Via Meravigli and Piazza Cordusio, offers croissants, savouries, salads, a vast assortment of cakes and delicious tartlets.

San Carlo
Via Matteo Bandello 1, corner of Corso Magenta. **Map** 6 E1.
Tel 02-48 12 227.
◻ 6:30am–8:30pm daily.

A stone's throw from Santa Maria delle Grazie, this pastry shop features delicious chocolate-based delicacies and irresistible cream-filled pastries.

Sissi
Piazza Risorgimento 6.
Map 4 F5 & 8 F1. **Tel** 02-76 01 46 64. ◻ 6:30am–noon Mon, 6:30am–8pm Wed–Sun.

A small pastry shop featuring a host of tempting morsels, including custard-filled croissants or raw ham savouries. The pretty courtyard with its pergola is ideal for Sunday afternoon tea.

SNACKS

Coin – The Globe
Piazza Cinque Giornate 1a.
Coin department store, 8th floor.
Tel 02-55 18 19 69.
◻ 11:30am–9:30pm Mon; 11:30am–2am Tue–Sat, noon–4pm (brunch), 6:30pm–1am Sun.

This restaurant, bar and food market, on the top floor of the Coin department store, is similar to those in Harrod's or Macy's. The restaurant offers light lunches and traditional dinners, both high quality. The bar offers fine aperitifs, and you will find delectable delicatessen specialities in the food market.

De Santis

Corso Magenta 9. **Map** 3 A5 & 6 F1.
Tel 02-87 59 68. ⬤ noon–4pm,
7pm–12:30am daily. ⬤ Christmas.

This compact place specializes in
filled rolls. On the walls are banknotes from all over the world and
signed photographs of celebrities
who have enjoyed choosing from
150 types of sandwich, made with
fresh, tasty ingredients.

El Tombon de San Marc

Via San Marco 20.
Map 3 C3. **Tel** 02-659 95 07.
⬤ 7am–3pm, 7pm–2am Mon–Sat.
⬤ Mon am, Aug.

A historic establishment that has
resisted passing fashions since the
1930s. A warm, intimate atmosphere. Sandwiches and salads
as well as excellent soups and
various hot and cold dishes.

Latteria di Via Unione

Via dell'Unione 6. **Map** 7 C1.
Tel 02-87 44 01.
⬤ noon–4pm Mon–Sat. ⬤ Aug.

This dairy in the heart of town
offers good vegetarian dishes.
Get there early, because it is
small and usually quite crowded.

Luini

Via Santa Radegonda 16.
Map 7 C1. **Tel** 02-86 46 19 17.
⬤ 10am–3pm Mon, 10am–8pm
Tue–Sat.

Since 1949 this baker's has
featured Puglian panzerotti
(ravioli) filled with tomatoes
and mozzarella.

Salumeria Armandola

Via della Spiga 50. **Map** 4 D4.
Tel 02-76 02 16 57.
⬤ 8:30am–7:30pm Mon–Sat
(to 10:30pm Thu & Fri). ⬤ 2 wks
mid-Aug.

People drop in here for a quick
bite at the counter. The chef's
specialities include baked pasta,
roasted meat and a range of
vegetable and side dishes.

BARS AND CAFES

Biffi

Corso Magenta 87.
Map 3 A5 & 6 F1.
Tel 02-48 00 67 02.
⬤ 6:30am–8:30pm daily.

This historic bar-pastry shop dates
from the end of the 19th century.
Biffi is famous for its milk rolls
with cured ham or butter and
anchovies. The home-made
panettone, made every year,
is one of the best in Milan.

Caffè della Pusterla

Via De Amicis 22. **Map** 7 A2.
Tel 02-89 40 21 46. ⬤ 7am–2am
Mon–Sat; 9am–2am Sun.

This charming café is located
in the former Pusterla, or minor
gate, in Milan's medieval walls.
A wide range of cocktails and a
fine wine list too. The savouries
served with the aperitifs are also
very good.

Cova

Via Montenapoleone 8.
Map 4 D5. **Tel** 02-76 00 05 78.
⬤ 8am–8:30pm Mon–Sat. ⬤ Aug.

Founded in 1817, this elegant
pastry shop is right in the heart
of the fashion district and is an
ideal place for a pause during
your shopping spree. Cova is
well-known for its chocolates
and stuffed panettone.

Jamaica

Via Brera 32. **Map** 3 C4.
Tel 02-87 67 23.
⬤ 9am–2am daily (to 9pm Mon,
to 1:30am Sun). ⬤ 2 wks Aug.

This historic Milanese café is the
haunt of artists and intellectuals,
who flock to this fascinating
corner of the Brera quarter. Busy
at all hours. Drinks as well as
good huge salads.

Sans Égal

Vicolo Fiori 2. **Map** 3 B4.
Tel 02-869 30 96.
⬤ 9am–2am daily.

In an alley in the Brera quarter,
this multi-faceted establishment
is a sports pub on Sunday, a small
lunch-time restaurant during the
week, a drinks bar in the evening
and a music pub at night.

Sant'Ambroeus

Corso Matteotti 7. **Map** 4 D5.
Tel 02-76 00 05 40.
⬤ 7:45am–8:30pm daily. ⬤ Aug.

The atmosphere in what is probably Milan's most elegant pastry
shop is plush, with sumptuous
window displays and slick service.
The tarts, pralines and cakes are
famous. There is a lovely tearoom
inside and tables outside under
the arcade opposite.

Taveggia

Via Visconti di Modrone 2.
Map 8 E1. **Tel** 02-76 28 08 56.
⬤ 7am–9pm Mon–Sat,
7:30am–8pm Sun
⬤ last 3 wks Aug.

Another historic Milanese pastry
shop, inaugurated in 1910. Great
rice pudding, many different
types of croissants and various
delicacies. Taveggia is also
popular for its aperitifs.

Victoria Café

Via Clerici 1. **Map** 3 C5. **Tel** 02-805
35 98. ⬤ 7:30am–2am Mon–Fri;
9am–2am Sat, 5–10pm Sun.

Behind Piazza della Scala is this
Parisian-style fin de siècle café with
red lamps on the tables, lace cur-
tains and red leather seats. Popular
for aperitifs and after dinner.

Zucca in Galleria

Piazza del Duomo 21.
Map 7 C1. **Tel** 02-86 46 44 35.
⬤ 7:15am–8:40pm Tue–Sun.

This famous bar (formerly
Camparino) in the Galleria has
period decor and tables outside.
The world-famous Campari drink
was created here in the late 1800s.

LAKE BARS & CAFES

Matella (Lake Maggiore)

Via Ruga 1, Pallanza.
Tel 0323-50 19 88.
⬤ 7:30am–8pm Wed–Mon
(to midnight in summer).
⬤ mid-Oct–mid-Nov.

Bar-pasticceria shop in the
19th-century arcades of Palazzo
Municipale featuring amaretti
(macaroons). Nice tables for a
drink outside.

Mimosa (Lake Garda)

Via RV Cornicello 1, Bardolino.
Tel 045-621 24 72. ⬤ 3–10pm
daily. ⬤ mid-Oct–May.

The barman at Mimosa is a true
cocktail "magician". There is also
a garden where you can listen to
the music while sipping your
drink or enjoying good home-
made ice cream.

Monti (Lake Como)

Piazza Cavour 21, Como.
Tel 031-30 11 65. ⬤ 7am–
midnight Wed–Mon. ⬤ Tue.

Bar-pastry shop in lovely Piazza
Cavour, with tables outside and
a view of the lake. Perfect for
sipping tea and tasting pastries
in tranquil surroundings.

Vassalli (Lake Garda)

Via San Carlo 84, Salò. **Tel** 0365-
207 52. ⬤ 8am–9pm Wed–Mon
(Jun–Sep: to 11pm daily).

This historic bar-pastry shop in
Salò has been popular for over a
century. The aperitifs and cocktails
are good, but Vassalli is most well-
known for its desserts, such as the
exquisite bacetti di Salò chocolates
and the lemon mousse.

SHOPS AND MARKETS

Whether buying or just looking, shopping is a real leasure in Milan. As well as the window displays of the leading national and international fashion designers – whose outlets are all within the area between Via Manzoni, Via Montenapoleone, Via della Spiga and Via Sant'Andrea, the so-called "quadrilateral" – you can find small shops and stores throughout the city. Shops are generally smart and stylish, especially in the city centre, as good design is highly regarded in Italy, and Milan is one of the most affluent cities. For those who are interested in interior design there is plenty of choice among the specialist shops, while lovers of antiques will love the Brera and Navigli quarters, where regular outdoor antique markets are held. Milan also has some excellent *pasticcerie*, where you can purchase authentic delicacies and traditional Milanese confectionery. At the lakes the choice is widest in the bigger towns, and includes clothes shops, craft shops and wine shops selling local produce.

Shopping in Milan

OPENING HOURS

Shops in Milan are usually open from 9:30am to 1pm and then from 3:30 to 7:30pm. However, many shops in the city centre and the department stores stay open all day, without a break, and major bookshops stay open until 11pm.

Shops are closed on Sunday and Monday mornings, except over Christmas, when they are usually open every day of the week. Food shops, on the other hand, close on Monday afternoon, with the exception of supermarkets.

During the summer holiday period, shops generally close for most of August, apart from the department stores and shopping centres which remain open as normal, even during this rather inactive month.

Window shopping in fashionable Via Montenapoleone

The Coin department store in Piazza Cinque Giornate

DEPARTMENT STORES

There are not many department stores in Milan. One of the most central is **La Rinascente**, which is open seven days a week and stays open until 10pm. Opposite the Duomo, it is perhaps the most prestigious department store in the city, selling everything from clothing, perfumes, toys and stationery to food over eight floors. The restaurant has a view of the Duomo and an exhibition space.

In Piazza Cinque Giornate is the **Coin**, with quality products at medium-range prices, including clothes and household goods. **Oviesse**, in Via Spadari, is more downmarket and sells clothes and other articles at reasonable prices. The **Centro Bonola** is a huge shopping centre with a Coop supermarket and an Upim department store, as well as 60 shops and many bars and cafés. Lastly, there is **Il Portello**, a shopping centre with shops, boutiques and a large supermarket.

MARKETS

Italy's outdoor markets are always fun and Milan has some good specialist markets. The Mercatone dell'Antiquariato, held on the last Sunday of the month at the Alzaia Naviglio Grande, is an extensive antiques market with more than four hundred exhibitors offering antique objects and bric-a-brac. Every Saturday at the Darsena on Viale d'Annunzio there is the Fiera di Senigallia, where you can find almost anything, from clothing to records and ethnic handicrafts.

The Mercato dell'Antiquariato in the Brera area, between Via Fiori Chiari and Via Madonnina, is also worth a visit. Every third Saturday of

The Fiera di Senigallia along the Darsena

the month antiques, books, postcards and jewellery go on sale here. Lastly, don't miss the Mercato del Sabato on Viale Papiniano, which offers, great designer-label bargains, clothes, shoes and bags.

FOOD SHOPS

Gourmets will appreciate the well-stocked Milanese delicatessens and food shops. Perhaps the most famous is **Peck**, which since 1883 has been synonymous with fine food and delicacies. Besides the main delicatessen in Via Spadari, selling hams, salami and cheeses of all kinds, there is also a popular Peck *rosticceria* in Via Cantù where you can buy the best ready-made dishes in Milan.

Another top-quality establishment is **Il Salumaio** on Via Montenapoleone, which is both a delicatessen and a restaurant. The top floor of **La Rinascente** department

Corso Vittorio Emanuele, a popular street for shopping

store has an array of eateries and a terrace with spectacular views of the Duomo. There is also an excellent food and wine shop.

N'Ombra de Vin is one of Milan's most famous *enoteche*, where you'll find the best Italian wines. For those who love chocolate, **Neuhaus Maitre Chocolatier** is paradise. Its specialities are fresh praline and home-baked cakes – if you feel the need, Neuhaus will even deliver.

Garbagnati is the best-known baker in town, and is especially known for *panettone*. Garbagnati has been making this traditional Milanese cake with a natural leavening process since 1937. Go to **Fabbrica di Marroni Giovanni Galli** for sweet things; this shop has made the best marrons glacés in Milan since 1898. Equally famous is **L'Angolo di Marco**, in the Brera quarter, a delightful *pasticceria* (pastry shop) offering delectable treats of all kinds. At **Ranieri** they make a *panettone* with pineapple, and sweets and pastries with fresh fruit. Last but not least, **Marchesi** is the best place to go for meltingly good chocolates, both milk and dark.

SALES

In Milan, sales *(saldi)* are held twice a year: in early July and then in January, immediately after Epiphany. Discounts may even be as much as 70 per cent, but check goods carefully before you buy, especially if the discount looks overgenerous. Shop-owners may use the sales as an excuse to get rid of old stock or defective clothing. For all-year-round bargains, try the numerous outlet shops: Il Salvagente at Via Bronzetti 16 or Diffusione Tessile in Galleria San Carlo.

Clothing and Accessories

The clothes shops of Milan are known all over the world because of their associations with famous Italian fashion designers. The city centre fashion district is stormed each year by Italians and foreigners alike in search of the latest top fashion items. However, Milan is not just about expensively priced goods, and the true secret of pleasurable shopping can lie in discovering the less well-known shops which offer good prices and still work to high standards of quality.

CLASSIC CLOTHING

Women in search of impeccable classic clothing for themselves and their children should seek out the **Pupi Solari** shop, which also makes wedding dresses to order. Lovers of colourful sports clothes, on the other hand, will be more than satisfied at **Urrà**. Elegant children's apparel and shoes can be found at **Gusella**, while **Host** features men's sports and informal clothes. Elegant, stylish clothes for men can also be found at **Bardelli** or **Gemelli**, and **Ravizza** is an ideal shop for those who prefer classic wear with a casual touch. **Ermenegildo Zegna** is the place to go for stylish men's classic clothing made of the best quality fabrics. **Brian & Barry** offers both classic and sports clothes at reasonable prices. Lastly, **Neglia** has two floors filled with fashionable menswear, from clothing to accessories.

DESIGNER WEAR

Almost all the shops that feature the latest in top designer clothes are in or near the city centre (see pp106–7). **Hugo Boss** is a recently opened shop of some size, selling elegant clothes for men. **Giò Moretti**, an institution in Via della Spiga, features articles by the top names as well as pieces by up-and-coming fashion designers. **Marisa** is a shop specializing in Italian and foreign designers and there is always something new and interesting, while **Fay** has clothes for the young and sophisticated. **Biffi** is famous for its wide-ranging selection of top designer clothes.

Among non-Italian fashion designers **Jil Sander** is growing more and more popular. **Guess**, the well-known New York designer, is represented in the city and offers the latest lines.

The diffusion lines of the most famous designers can be found in the fashion district, where the main names have their own branches, from **Miu Miu** to **D&G** and **Emporio Armani**. Armani's Via Manzoni store also houses an art gallery and Nobu sushi bar. Lastly, **Antonio Fusco** attracts an enthusiastic clientele.

ACCESSORIES

For good quality sports shoes there is **Tod's**. Less well-known but equally good is the **Stivaleria Savoia**, which features classic styles that can also be made to measure. **Gallo** is proud of its stylish high-quality hosiery. **Ferragamo**, the Italian designer known all over the world for his top fashion styles, offers elegant classic shoes. More bizarre and unconventional articles can be found at **La Vetrina**, while **Camper** features original shoes known for their fine workmanship. **Garlando** offers a vast range of styles and colours that aim at the young people's market.

Crocodile, ostrich and leather handbags can be found at **Colombo**, while **Valextra** features high-quality

SIZE CHART

Children's clothing

Italian	2–3	4–5	6–7	8–9	10–11	12	14	14+	(age)
British	2–3	4–5	6–7	8–9	10–11	12	14	14+	(age)
American	2–3	4–5	6–6X	7–8	10		12	14	16	(size)

Children's shoes

Italian	24	25½	27	28	29	30	32	33	34
British	7½/	8	9	10	11	12	13	1	2
American	7½	8½	9½	10½	11½	12½	13½	1½	2½

Women's dresses, coats and skirts

Italian	38	40	42	44	46	48	50	52
British	6	8	10	12	14	16	18	20
American	4	6	8	10	12	14	16	18

Women's blouses and sweaters

Italian	40	42	44	46	48	50	52
British	30	32	34	36	38	40	42
American	6	8	10	12	14	16	18

Women's shoes

Italian	36	37	38	39	40	41
British	3	4	5	6	7	8
American	5	6	7	8	9	10

Men's clothing

Italian	44	46	48	50	52	54	56	58
British	34	36	38	40	42	44	46	48
American	34	36	38	40	42	44	46	48

Men's shirts

Italian	36	38	39	41	42	43	44	45
British	14	15	15½	16	16½	17	17½	18
American	14	15	15½	16	16½	17	17½	18

Men's shoes

Italian	40	41	42	43	44	45	46
British	7	7½	8	9	10	11	12
American	7½	8	8½	9½	10½	11	11½

suitcases and briefcases. For something original head for the **Atelier Anne Backhaus**, where they make handbags and accessories using different materials.

The **Mandarina Duck** shops have stylish sports bags, luggage, casual handbags and knapsacks. **Borsalino** is the place to go for top-quality classic hats. **Giusy Bresciani** has more original designs, as well as gloves and other highly stylish accessories. **Cappelleria Melegari** deals in hats imported from all over the world and they

can do hat alterations in their workshop if a customer requires. A wide range of ties and knitwear can be found at **Fedeli** and at **Oxford**, where you can also find good ranges of men's shirts.

JEWELLERY

Elegant, classic jewellery is featured at **Rocca 1872**, which has designed jewels for smart Milanese women since 1840, and **Cusi**, which has been in business since 1885. **Tiffany & Co** is known for high-class jewellery, while

Mario Buccellati has gold and silver pieces of elegant workmanship. Another historic shop is **Bulgari**, known for its beautiful jewellery and watches. **Mereú** features original and modern hand-crafted jewels. Jewellery dating from the 19th century to 1950 is to be found at **Mirella Denti**. For modern costume jewellery, you will find a good collection at **Donatella Pellini**, and **Sharra Pagano** also has a good choice of the latest costume jewellery and jewellery styles, made of original materials.

DIRECTORY

CLASSIC CLOTHING

Bardelli
Corso Magenta 13.
Map 3 A5.
Tel 02-86 45 07 34.

Brian & Barry
Via Durini 28. **Map** 8 D1.
Tel 02-76 00 55 82.

Ermenegildo Zegna
Via Montenapoleone 27.
Map 4 D5. *Tel* 02-76 00 64 37.

Gemelli
Corso Vercelli 16. **Map** 2 D5. *Tel* 02-48 00 00 57.

Gusella
Corso V Emanuele II 37b. **Map** 8 D1.
Tel 02-79 65 33.

Host
Piazza Tommaseo 2. **Map** 2 E5. *Tel* 02-43 60 85.

Neglia
Corso Venezia 2. **Map** 4 E4. *Tel* 02-79 52 31.

Pupi Solari
Piazza Tommaseo 2. **Map** 2 E5. *Tel* 02-46 33 25.

Ravizza
Via Hoepli 3. **Map** 4 D5.
Tel 02-869 38 53.

Urrà
Via Solferino 3. **Map** 3 C2. *Tel* 02-86 43 85.

DESIGNER WEAR

Antonio Fusco
Via Sant'Andrea 11.
Map 4 D5. *Tel* 02-76 00 18 88.

Biffi
Corso Genova 6. **Map** 7 A2. *Tel* 02-831 16 01.

D&G
Corso Venezia 7. **Map** 4 E4. *Tel* 02-76 00 40 91.

Emporio Armani
Via Manzoni 31. **Map** 3 C5. *Tel* 02-72 31 86 00.
www.armani-viamanzoni31.com

Fay
Via della Spiga 15. **Map** 4 D4. *Tel* 02-76 01 75 97.

Giò Moretti
Via della Spiga 4. **Map** 4 D4. *Tel* 02-76 00 31 86.

Guess
Piazza San Babila 4b. **Map** 4 D5. *Tel* 02-76 39 20 70.

Hugo Boss
Corso Matteotti 11. **Map** 4 D5. *Tel* 02-76 39 46 67.

Jil Sander
Via P Verri 6. **Map** 4 D5.
Tel 02-777 29 91.

Marisa
Via della Spiga 52. **Map** 4 D4. *Tel* 02-76 00 20 82.

Miu Miu
Via Sant'Andrea 21. **Map** 4 D5. *Tel* 02-76 00 17 99.

ACCESSORIES

Atelier Anne Backhaus
Corso di Porta Vigentina 10. **Map** 8 D3.
Tel 02-58 30 27 93.

Borsalino
Galleria Vittorio Emanuele II. **Map** 7 C1.
Tel 02-89 01 54 36.

Camper
Via Torino 15. **Map** 7 B1.
Tel 02-805 71 85.

Cappelleria Melegari
Via P Sarpi 19. **Map** 3 A2.
Tel 02-31 20 94.

Colombo
Via della Spiga 9. **Map** 4 D4. *Tel* 02-76 02 35 87.

Fedeli
Via Montenapoleone 8.
Map 4 D5.
Tel 02-76 02 33 92.

Ferragamo
Via Montenapoleone 3.
Map 4 D5.
Tel 02-76 00 00 54.

Gallo
Via Durini 26. **Map** 8 D1.
Tel 02-76 00 20 23.

Garlando
Via Madonnina 1. **Map** 3 B4. *Tel* 02-87 46 65.

Giusy Bresciani
Via del Carmine 9. **Map** 3 C4. *Tel* 02-89 01 35 05.

La Vetrina
Via Statuto 4. **Map** 3 B3.
Tel 02-65 42 78.

Mandarina Duck
Via Verri 8. **Map** 4 D5.
Tel 02-78 13 02.

Oxford
Via Verri 2. **Map** 4 D5.
Tel 02-76 02 34 04.

Stivaleria Savoia
Via Petrarca 7. **Map** 2 E4.
Tel 02-46 34 24.

Tod's
Via della Spiga 22.
Map 4 D4.
Tel 02-76 00 24 23.

Valextra
Via Manzoni 3. **Map** 4 D5. *Tel* 02-99 78 60 60.

JEWELLERY

Bulgari
Via Montenapoleone 2.
Map 4 D4.
Tel 02-77 70 01.

Cusi
Via Montenapoleone 21a.
Map 4 D5.
Tel 02-76 01 43 23.

Donatella Pellini
Corso Magenta 11. **Map** 3 A5. *Tel* 02-72 01 05 69.

Mario Buccellati
Via Montenapoleone 23.
Map 4 D5.
Tel 02-76 00 21 53.

Mereú
Via Solferino 3. **Map** 3 C3. *Tel* 02-86 46 07 00.

Mirella Denti
Via Montenapoleone 23.
Map 4 D5.
Tel 02-76 02 25 44.

Rocca 1872
Piazza Duomo 25.
Map 7 C1.
Tel 02-805 74 47.

Sharra Pagano
Corso Garibaldi 35. **Map** 3 B3. *Tel* 02-89 01 35 42.

Tiffany & Co
Via della Spiga 19a. **Map** 4 D4. *Tel* 02-76 02 23 21.

Design and Antiques

Milan is the acknowledged capital of modern design and a paradise for enthusiasts, who can spend their free time browsing in the numerous shops and showrooms throughout the city. Every spring the Salone del Mobile, the famous Milan furniture fair, attracts all the top designers and trade buyers. During the fair, many of Milan's interior design shops extend their opening hours and put on various events for trade experts and visitors.

INTERIOR AND INDUSTRIAL DESIGN

At **De Padova**, elegant, studiously avant-garde objects for the home, including furniture, are made of the finest materials. For stylish lighting there is **Artemide**, which is known for its superb modern designs, created by well-known names, and **Flos**, in Corso Monforte, which features sleek ultra-modern lighting of all kinds.

Fontana Arte is a kind of gallery and a leading light in the field of interior design. Founded in 1933, its displays include splendid lamps, mostly crystal.

Da Driade, located in the heart of the fashion district, features objects created in the last 30 years which have since become collectors' items. **Galleria Colombari**, on the other hand, offers modern antiques as well as a range of contemporary design objects.

Spazio Cappellini is a show room for informal and elegant furniture, while **Zani & Zani** features interior design accessories, displayed in a chessboard pattern to show off the individual objects at their best.

Kartell stocks various articles for the home and the office, while **Arform** specializes in Scandinavian design. **Venini** is an institution in the production of blown Venetian glass vases, while **Barovier & Toso** offers extremely high-quality chandeliers and vases, and **Cassina** features products by leading designers.

Spazio 900 has fabulous furniture and interior objects by top designers from the 1950s to the 1980s, as well as vintage and end-of-line pieces at discount prices.

Officina Alessi, in Corso Matteotti, specializes in interior design pieces and kitchenware in stainless steel and colourful plastic. **Kitchen** has everything a cook could need, including top quality utensils and a cookery school for those looking to expand their repertoire of recipes.

Those who love stylish period furniture should stop by **Dimorae**, where the furniture is beautifully and imaginatively displayed in welcoming settings.

MEGASTORES

The Megastore, where you can purchase almost anything under the sun, from the tiniest household article to a large piece of furniture, is now becoming the rage in Milan as well as in other Italian cities. These large establishments (empori) are usually open late in the evening and on Sunday and are frequently able to offer their customers various additional services.

High Tech was one of the first to offer this new mode of shopping. Come here for exotic furniture, fabrics and wallpaper for the home, kitchenware, perfume and accessories imported from all over the world.

Visit **Cargo Hightech's** warehouse store for beautiful Chinese laquered chests or ultra modern Italian design lighting. Alternatively, browse their clothing in fabulous cloth from India and bamboo furniture from the Philippines.

Emporio 31 is another interesting place built in the old industrial district near the Navigli. It offers everything for the interior designer, selected for the discerning eye. There are three spacious floors, often with design exhibitions thrown in for free.

10 Corso Como is an unusual place featuring designer articles and objects from the Middle and Far East. It has a gallery and an interesting café/bar.

The ultramodern and unconventional **Moroni Gomma** offers boots, raincoats, kitchenware and interior design and household articles, all made of plastic or rubber (gomma).

FABRICS AND LINEN FOR THE HOME

For elegance and high-class interior design, Milan cannot be beaten. There are many shops which specialize in fabrics and linen which can be made to order.

Etro, in Via Montenapoleone, is famous for its fabrics and stylish accessories. In the Brera area is **KA International**, a sales outlet for a Spanish chain of fabric shops, offering excellent value for money. Among the many other articles, **Lisa Corti** features original Indian cotton and cheesecloth fabrics with floral and stripe decorative patterns. **Mimma Gini** has characteristic fabrics from India, Japan and Indonesia; **Castellini & C** is known mostly for its linen articles.

Original and exclusive fabrics can be found at **Fede Cheti**. Among the shops featuring household linen, **Pratesi**, in the heart of the fashion district, is known for its classic and elegant ranges. **Zucchi** is a very well-known name in Italy for beautifully made fabrics.

Bed linen and table linen in both modern and practical styles are featured at **Mirabello**. Since 1860 **Frette** has been a guarantee of high quality bed linen, table linen and articles for the bathroom such as towels and bathrobes. They also offer delivery throughout the world as well as advice and help from an interior designer.

ANTIQUES

Milan has numerous antique shops and workshops. Subert, in Via della Spiga, specializes in 18th-century furniture and scientific instruments. In the same street is **Mauro Brucoli**, where they specialize in 19th-century furniture and objects as well as splendid jewellery dating from the same period. At Franco Sabatelli, which is also a furniture restorers, you can find picture frames of all periods, some even dating to the 16th century.

Lovers of 18th- and 19th-century British furniture must head for Old English Furniture, which also has a fine stock of medical and scientific instruments. If you prefer the unusual and even bizarre object, try **L'Oro dei Farlocchi**, a historic antique gallery in the Brera area.

Galleria Blanchaert is one of Milan's best-known shops for antique glass, with Murano chandeliers and Venini vases.

At **Antichità Caiati** you will find stunning 17th- and 18th-century Italian paintings, Valuable canvases are also sold at **Walter Padovani** as well as decorative art, sculpture and precious stones. **Carlo Orsi** has exclusive antiques, including bronze sculpture, splendid paintings, fine furniture, delicate ivory pieces and precious stones.

DIRECTORY

INTERIOR AND INDUSTRIAL DESIGN

Arform
Via della Moscova 22.
Map 3 B3.
Tel 02-655 46 91.

Artemide
Corso Monforte 19.
Map 4 E5.
Tel 02-76 00 69 30.

Barovier & Toso
Via Manzoni 40. **Map** 4 D5. **Tel** 02-76 00 09 06.

Cassina
Via Durini 16.
Map 8 D1.
Tel 02-76 02 07 58.

Da Driade
Via Durini 5.
Map 8 E1.
Tel 02-76 00 09 06.

De Padova
Corso Venezia 14. **Map** 4 E4. **Tel** 02-77 72 01.
www.depadova.it

Dimorae
Corso Magenta 56.
Map 3 A5.
Tel 02-481 84 66.

Flos
Corso Monforte 9.
Map 4 E5.
Tel 02-76 00 36 39.

Fontana Arte
Via Santa Margherita 4.
Map 3 C5.
Tel 02-86 46 45 51.

Galleria Colombari
Via Maroncelli 10. **Map** 3 B1. **Tel** 02-29 00 25 33.

Kartell
Via Turati (corner of Via Porta 1). **Map** 4 D3.
Tel 02-659 79 16.

Kitchen
Via De Amicis 45. **Map** 7 A2. **Tel** 02-58 10 28 49.

Magazzini Cappellini
Via S Cecilia 4.
Tel 02-76 00 38 89.

Officina Alessi
Corso Matteotti 9. **Map** 4 D5. **Tel** 02-79 57 26.

Spazio 900
Corso Garibaldi 42. **Map** 3 B2. **Tel** 02-72 00 17 75.
www.spazio900.com

Venini
Via Montenapoleone 9.
Map 4 D5.
Tel 02-76 00 05 39.

Zani & Zani
Corso Venezia 16. **Map** 4 E4. **Tel** 02-79 80 96.

MEGASTORES

10 Corso Como
Corso Como 10. **Map** 3 C2. **Tel** 02-29 00 26 74.

Cargo-Hightech
Via Meucci 39.
Tel 02-272 21 31.
www.cargomilano.it

Emporio 31
Via Tortona 31. **Map** 6 D3.
Tel 02-42 22 577.

High Tech
Piazza XXV Aprile 12.
Tel 02-624 11 01.

Mondadori Multicenter
Piazza Duomo. **Map** 1 C5. **Tel** 02-481 00 63.

Moroni Gomma
Corso Matteotti 14.
Map 4 D5.
Tel 02-76 00 68 21.
Via Giusti 10. **Map** 3 A2.
Tel 02-33 10 65 65.

FABRICS AND LINEN FOR THE HOME

Castellini & C
Via B Zenale. **Map** 6 F1.
Tel 02-48 01 50 69.

Etro
Via Montenapoleone 5.
Map 4 D5.
Via Bigli 2. **Map** 4 D5.
Tel 02-76 00 50 49.

Fede Cheti
Via Manzoni 23.
Map 3 C5.
Tel 02-86 46 40 05.

Frette
Via Montenapoleone 21.
Map 4 D5.
Tel 02-78 39 50.
Via Manzoni 11.
Map 3 C5.
Tel 02-86 44 43.
Via Belfiore 16.
Map 2 D5.
Tel 02-498 97 56.

KA International
Via Pontaccio 3. **Map** 3 B4. **Tel** 02-86 45 12 44.
Viale Piave 28. **Map** 4 F4. **Tel** 02-20 40 18 09.

Lisa Corti
Via Lecco 2. **Map** 4 E3.
Tel 02-29 40 55 89.

Mimma Gini
Via Santa Croce 21. **Map** 7 B3. **Tel** 02-89 40 07 22.

Mirabello
Via Balzan (corner of Via San Marco). **Map** 4 D3. **Tel** 02-65 48 87.

Pratesi
Via Giuseppe Verdi 6.
Map 3 C5.
Tel 02-80 58 30 58.

Zucchi
Via Cherubini 3. **Map** 2 D5. **Tel** 02-48 00 72 18.

ANTIQUES

Antichità Caiati
Via Gesà 17. **Map** 4 D5.
Tel 02-79 48 66.

Carlo Orsi
Via Bagutta 14.
Tel 02-76 00 22 14.

Galleria Blanchaert
Piazza Sant'Ambrogio 4.
Map 7 A1.
Tel 02-86 45 17 00.

L'Oro dei Farlocchi
Via Madonnina, opposite No. 5. **Map** 3 B4.
Tel 02-86 05 89.

Mauro Brucoli
Via della Spiga 17.
Map 4 D4.
Tel 02-76 02 37 67.

Walter Padovani
Via Santo Spirito 25.
Map 4 D4.
Tel 02-76 31 89 07.

Books and Gifts

Milan is well supplied with good bookshops, many offering foreign-language publications as well as books in Italian. The larger bookstores in the centre are usually open late in the evening and also on Sunday. They have plenty of space where you can quietly browse through the books on display at your leisure. In addition there are plenty of small bookshops, many stocking rare or out-of-print books. Around the University there are many specialist bookshops. Music fans can head for the megastores and the many music shops in town, while the specialist gift article shops will help those interested in buying presents to take home.

BOOKSHOPS

The **Mondadori Multicenter** is centrally located and open daily until 11pm. It stocks newspapers and periodicals (including international ones) along with new releases, both fiction and non-fiction, for visitors who read Italian. It also has a café on the first floor, Puro Gusto.

Computer buffs should head for **Mondadori Informatica**, which is a paradise for anyone who is interested in IT.

Another large, well-stocked and very popular bookstore is **Rizzoli** in the Galleria Vittorio Emanuele, which has a fine arts section.

Feltrinelli has six bookshops in Milan, which are open every day including Sunday. The main bookshop in Piazza del Duomo, almost 500 sq m (5,380 sq ft) in size, has more than 60,000 books and offers various services, such as wedding lists, to its customers.

Five-floor **Hoepli** is a serious bookstore steeped in tradition. It specializes in scientific publications and subscriptions to foreign periodicals. The **American Bookstore** and **English Bookshop** specialize in English-language literature and the **Libreria Francese Ile de France** has a good selection of publications in French.

For second-hand books, go to **Il Libraccio**, which has a number of branches. Besides school textbooks, it has various books, comic books and even CDs.

A small shop where opera fans can find interesting publications is **Il Trovatore**. Out-of-print editions, scores and libretti are offered together with valuable rarities such as facsimiles of scores by Donizetti or Verdi with the composers' signatures. This music store also provides a catalogue of its publications.

Books Import specializes in books on art, architecture, design and photography, almost all of which are published abroad. Their section on hobbies is particularly good. **Bookshop Armani**, on the first floor of the Armani complex in Via Manzoni, specializes in books on fashion, travel and hotels, and the arts.

L'Archivolto, which specializes mostly in architecture and design, also has a section on antiques with books from the 1500s to the present. This shop also has modern design objects on display. The **Libreria della Triennale** also deals mainly in books on architecture and design, but has a well-stocked children's book section as well.

Art lovers will also enjoy the **Libreria Bocca**, in the Galleria Vittorio Emanuele. The **Libreria dei Ragazzi** is the only bookshop in town entirely given over to children's books, with games and educational books. The **Libreria del Mare**, as its name suggests, offers a wide range of prints and books on the sea (*il mare*), while the **Libreria Milanese** has books (including photographic ones), prints, posters and gadgets concerning Milan. **Milano Libri**, always up with the latest trends, has a section on high fashion and another on photography. **Luoghi e Libri** specializes in travel books, novels, non-fiction and original language books. Comic-book fans should visit **La Borsa del Fumetto**, which also has rare and old editions.

Besides travel guides, the **Libreria dell'Automobile** stocks handbooks and illustrated books on cars and motorcycles. **Libreria dello Sport** features books and videos on all kinds of sport, and **Libreria dello Spettacolo** specializes in theatre and biographies of famous actors and actresses. **FNAC** is another great option for a wide variety of books (see Music, CDs & Records for address).

MUSIC, CDs & RECORDS

A good music shop in the city is the **Ricordi Media Store**, which has parts and scores as well as books on composers and their works. It is open even on Sunday (until 8pm), offers discounts on items at least once a month and also has a ticket office for concerts. Another good destination for music lovers is **Mondadori**. Located over three floors, it boasts a vast range of records, tapes and CDs, as well as a well-stocked section with books on music in various foreign languages.

The **Bottega Discantica** is a paradise for lovers of opera and church and symphonic music, while **Serendipity** is a shop with a British flavour: besides the latest trends in music, there are records that are almost impossible to find elsewhere and a wide range of Italian and foreign periodicals as well as rare music-themed T-shirts. **Buscemi Dischi** is one of the best-stocked and low-priced music shops and is especially recommended for jazz lovers.

FNAC, on Via Torino, has a large assortment of music,

computers and telephones, as well as a coffee shop and a ticket office for events.

GIFTS

Visitors in search of gifts would do well to try **MacKenzy Gadgets** in the Galleria for Italian branded merchandise or **Co Import** for household goods and funky items. For something special try **Penelopi 3**. If circumstances call for a more sophisticated gift, head for **Ca' Albrizzi**, a famous bookbinder's

dealing in quality note-books, albums and other handcrafted articles. Another good alternative in this field is **Tra le Pagine**, where visitors will find excellent handcrafted stationery, including writing paper and cardboard articles.

Smokers will love **Lorenzi** which, besides a vast assort-ment of knives, scissors and toilet and gift articles, has high-quality pipes and accessories for smokers. Again for the smoker, **Savinelli** is an institution in Milan. Since 1876 it has sold pipes of all

kinds, at all prices, up to unique and extremely expensive ones.

For toys or games, try the **Città del Sole**, which stocks Milan's largest assortment of traditional wooden toys, educational games and board games for both children and adults. **Movo**, in business since 1932, is the domain of model-making enthusiasts, while **Pergioco** specializes in more modern pursuits such as video games and DVDs, as well as computer games.

DIRECTORY

BOOKSHOPS

American Bookstore
Via Camperio 16. **Map** 3
B5. **Tel** 02-87 89 20.

Books Import
Via Maiocchi 11.
Tel 02-29 40 04 78.

Bookshop Armani
Via Manzoni 37. **Map** 3
C5. **Tel** 02-72 31 86 75.

English Bookshop
Via Mascheroni 12. **Map**
2 E4. **Tel** 02-469 44 68.
www.englishbookshop.it

Feltrinelli
Branches across Milan.
Megastore: Piazza
Piemonte 2. **Map** 1 C5.
Tel 02-43 35 41.
Via Manzoni 12. **Map** 3
C5. **Tel** 02-76 00 03 86.
Via Foscolo 1–3.
Tel 02-86 99 68 97.
Corso Buenos Aires 33.
Map 4 F3.
Tel 02-20 23 361.
Via MV Traiano 79
(Il Portello).
Tel 02-392 71 53.

Hoepli
Via Hoepli 5. **Map** 4 D5.
Tel 02-86 48 71.
www.hoepli.it

Il Libraccio
Via Arconati 16.
Tel 02-55 19 06 71.
Via Corsico 9. **Map** 6 F3.
Tel 02-837 23 98.
Via Santatecla 5.
Tel 02-87 83 99.
Viale Vittorio Veneto 22.
Map 4 E3.
Tel 02-655 56 81.

Il Trovatore
Via Carlo Poerio 3.
Tel 02-76 00 16 56.

L'Archivolto
Via Marsala 2. **Map** 3 C3.
Tel 02-659 08 42.

La Borsa del Fumetto
Via Lecco 16. **Map** 4 E3.
Tel 02-29 51 38 83.

Libreria Bocca
Galleria Vittorio Emanuele
II 12. **Map** 7 C1.
Tel 02-86 46 23 21.

Libreria dei Ragazzi
Via Tadino 53. **Map** 4 F2.
Tel 02-29 53 35 55.

Libreria del Mare
Via Broletto 28. **Map** 3
B5. **Tel** 02-89 01 02 28.

Libreria dell'Automobile
Corso Venezia 43. **Map** 4
E4. **Tel** 02-76 00 66 24.

Libreria della Triennale
Viale Alemagna 6. **Map** 2
F3. **Tel** 02-72 01 81 28.

Libreria dello Spettacolo
Via Terraggio 11. **Map** 7
A1. **Tel** 02-86 45 17 30.

Libreria dello Sport
Via Carducci 9. **Map** 3
A5. **Tel** 02-805 53 55.

Libreria Francese Ile de France
Via San Pietro all'Orto 10.
Map 4 D5.
Tel 02-76 00 17 67.

Libreria Milanese
Via Meravigli 18. **Map** 3
B5. **Tel** 02-86 45 31 54.

Luoghi e Libri
Via Vettabbia 3. **Map** 4
F5. **Tel** 02-58 31 07 13.
www.luoghielibri.it

Milano Libri
Via Verdi 2. **Map** 3 C5.
Tel 02-87 58 71.

Mondadori
Piazza Duomo. **Map** 7 C1.
Tel 02-454 41 10.
Corso Vittorio Emanuele
II 34. **Map** 8 D1.
Tel 02-76 05 51.

Mondadori Informatica
Via Berchet 2.
Tel 02-80 62 71.

Rizzoli
Galleria Vittorio Emanuele
II 79. **Map** 7 C1.
Tel 02-86 46 10 71.

MUSIC

Buscemi Dischi
Corso Magenta 31. **Map**
3 A5. **Tel** 02-80 41 03.

FNAC
Via della Palla 2 (corner
of Via Torino). **Map** 7 B1.
Tel 02-86 95 41.

La Bottega Discantica
Via Nirone 5. **Map** 7 A1.
Tel 02-86 29 66.

Mondadori
Galleria del Corso 2.
Tel 02-76 05 54 31.

Ricordi Media Store
Galleria Vittorio Emanuele
II. **Map** 7 C1.
Tel 02-86 46 02 72.

Serendipity
Corso di Porta Ticinese
100. **Map** 7 B2.
Tel 02-89 40 04 20.

GIFTS

Ca' Albrizzi
Corso Venezia 29. **Map** 4
E4. **Tel** 02-76 00 44 39.

Città del Sole
Via Orefici 13. **Map** 7 C1.
Tel 02-86 46 16 83.

Co Import
Piazza Diaz. **Map** 7 C1.
Tel 02-86 98 40 84.

Ferrari Store
Piazza Liberty 8.
Tel 02-76 01 73 85.

Lorenzi
Via Montenapoleone 9.
Map 4 D5.
Tel 02-76 02 28 48.

MacKenzy Gadgets
Galleria Vittorio Emanuele
II. **Map** 7 C1.
Tel 02-87 50 85.

Movo
Piazzale Principessa
Clotilde 8. **Map** 4 D2.
Tel 02-655 48 36.

Penelopi 3
Via Palermo 1. **Map** 3 B3.
Tel 02-72 00 06 52.

Savinelli
Via Orefici 2. **Map** 7 C1.
Tel 02-87 66 60.

Tra le Pagine
Via Palermo 11. **Map** 3
B3. **Tel** 02-86 11 13.

ENTERTAINMENT IN MILAN

The entertainment scene is lively in Milan and there is plenty of choice for those who love night life, given the hundreds of clubs that animate the Brera and Navigli quarters in particular. Pubs, discos and nightclubs with live music, as well as late-night bistros, are filled every evening with people who come from all corners of Italy. The theatres offer the public a rich and varied programme: La Scala represents the top in opera and ballet. Major music concerts are usually held in the Palavobis

**Javier Zanetti,
defender for Inter club**

arena (formerly PalaTrussardi) or at the Filaforum at Assago. Milan is equally generous to sports lovers. Every Sunday from September to May the San Siro stadium plays host to the matches of local football teams Inter and Milan. It also stages national and international championship matches. Sometimes matches are also scheduled during the week. Horse racing takes place all year round at the Ippodromo racecourse Milan's many sports and leisure clubs cater to those who like to play as well as watch sports.

INFORMATION

In order to find out the latest information on the many evening events in Milan, check the listings in *ViviMilano*, a Wednesday supplement to the newspaper *Corriere della Sera*. Every Thursday the daily paper *La Repubblica* publishes *Tutto Milano*, which is also full of useful information.

The IAT tourist offices in Piazza Castello and the Stazione Centrale (main railway station) provide free copies of the brochure *Milano Mese*, containing information on art shows, light and classical music concerts, jazz and other cultural events. Alternatively, pick up a copy of *Easy Milano*. You can also log on to the *Inmilano* or *Easy Milano* websites: (www.inmilano.it or www.

easymilano.it) for information on Milanese nightlife, exhibitions, plays and other forms of entertainment.

BUYING TICKETS

Tickets for the theatre and various concerts can be purchased in specialist booking offices such as **Ricordi Box Office**, **Ticket It** (telephone reservations and online www.ticket.it) or **Ticket One**. However, note that for performances at La Scala, you have to go in person to the box office in the Duomo metro station or book through the theatre's website (www. teatroallascala.org).

Tickets for football (soccer) matches can be purchased directly from the stadium box offices. Alternatively tickets for Inter matches

**Alcatraz, one of the trendiest
discos in Milan (see p199)**

can be bought from the Banca Popolare di Milano, Banca Briantea, Banca Agricola Milanese and Ticket One. Tickets for AC Milan matches are sold by Cariplo bank, various businesses (40 bars and shops) and Milan Point, whose listings are shown at the Milan Club.

Tickets for the annual Formula 1 Grand Prix, held in September at the Autodromo Nazionale in Monza, are sold at the **Automobile Club Milano**, **Acitour Lombardia** and **AC Promotion**. The Monza race track is usually open to visitors at weekends when there are no other events going on. Cars and motorbikes can be driven on the track when it is free. For more information, enquire at the **Autodromo Nazionale**.

The auditorium of La Scala, Milan's premier theatre

The Filaforum at Assago is a sports arena which is also used for concerts *(see p199)*

CHILDREN

Families visiting Milan with children should be warned that the city does not have extensive specialist entertainment available for them. However, some of the museums and galleries are quite child-friendly. To stimulate the young imagination and provide lots of interesting educational material, there are the Planetarium *(see p120)* and the Science and Technology Museum *(see p88)*, as well as the Civic Aquarium *(see p68)*.

As far as shows and spectacles are concerned, the **Teatro delle Marionette** is a popular children's puppet theatre that performs classic plays and famous novels.

If, on the other hand, you opt for pure entertainment, the amusement park at the **Idroscalo** is a good choice.

In the summer months (June to September), **Gardaland Water Park** is a popular place to take children: slides, pools and shows make this aquatic park a children's paradise that will entertain both the youngsters and adults alike.

Children over the age of 12 who are keen on video games can try out one of the numerous amusement arcades in the city.

A good place for entertaining smaller children only is the **Play Planet**. This is a recreation centre where the kids can let off some steam and use up a lot of energy or become involved in some of the creative workshops that are on offer. Play Planet is open all year round, and there are also two rooms in which birthday parties can be held.

In sunny weather there are always local public parks to take children to. The most suitable parks for children are the ones at Porta Venezia and Via Palestro, where theoretically no one is allowed to enter unless they are accompanied by a child. There is also a large play area with an electric train in Parco Sempione (between Piazza Castello and Piazza Sempione), near the Arco della Pace.

Young tourists enjoying an ice cream

DIRECTORY

TICKET AGENCIES

Acitour Lombardia
Corso Venezia 43.
Map 4 E4.
Tel 02-76 00 63 50.

ACP & Partners
Piazza E Duse 1.
Map 4 F4.
Tel 02-76 00 25 74.

Autodromo Nazionale
Parco di Monza.
Tel 039-248 21.
www.monzanet.it

Automobile Club Milano
Corso Venezia 43.
Map 4 E4.
Tel 02-77 451.

La Scala Box Office
Galleria del Sagrato
(inside Duomo metro station)
Tel 02-72 00 37 44.
www.teatroallascala.org

Ricordi Box Office
Galleria Vittorio Emanuele II.
Map 7 C1.
Tel 02-72 00 70 31.

Ticket It
Tel 02-542 71.
www.ticket.it

Ticket One
Tel 892 101.
www.ticketone.it

CHILDREN

Gardaland Water Park
Via G Airaghi 61.
Tel 02-48 20 01 34.

Idroscalo (Fun Park)
Via Rivoltana 64.
Tel 02-70 20 10 39.
www.idroscalo.info

Play Planet
Via Airolo 4.
Tel 02-668 88 38.
www.playplanet.it

Teatro delle Marionette
Via Oglio 18.
Tel 02-55 21 13 00.

Nightlife

One of the characteristics that distinguishes Milan from other Italian cities is the way in which the city really comes alive at night. From Tuesday to Saturday the city's pubs, bars, restaurants, cafés and discotheques are generally packed, though there are fewer Milanese and more people from outside the city on Saturdays. Monday and, to a certain extent, Sunday, are the quiet days, offering only rare occasions for entertainment. During the week clubs and discos organize theme evenings, and some of them operate a strict door policy. Places offering live music are also very popular; they often feature promising performers. The majority are located in the Navigli district, one of Milan's most vibrant areas.

DISCOS AND CLUBS

For the energetic on the lookout for new trends in music and dance, Milan is a great place to be. The many discos and clubs in town offer different types of music and are so popular that they attract young people from all over Italy. The scene is quite volatile and with rare exceptions – some places have become positive institutions – Milan discos change their name, management and style periodically. It is quite common for a wildly popular club to fall out of favour, only to return to popularity once again some time later.

Some places charge an entrance fee; others are free but you are obliged to pay for drinks. Prices vary quite a lot; the so-called drinkcard system, whereby you pay for your drinks at the entrance, is fairly common.

One disco that has adopted this method is **Alcatraz**, a former factory converted into a multi-purpose venue for concerts, fashion shows and even conventions. Friday is given over to 1970s and 1980s revival dance music.

Next door is a restaurant and also a private club called **De Sade**.

La Banque attracts a chic crowd to its good restaurant. The clientele stay on to dance to music mixed by hip DJs. **Colony Dine & Dance** has live music and a students' night on Mondays.

Sunday is cocktail evening with dancing.

Currently drawing in the fashion crowd is **Hollywood**. This is the place to go if you fancy celebrity spotting. The **Magazzini Generali**, which is also used for concerts and exhibitions, attracts a mixed crowd. The week opens on Wednesday and themed evenings include new musical trends and popular DJs. Friday is usually international night, with the latest music from around the world. Saturdays focus on the best of new dance, rock and contemporary pop music.

The **Shocking Club** is crowded every night from Monday to Saturday, and has become a Milanese institution just like **Nepentha**. There is a strict door policy. A trendy multi-purpose disco is the **Café Atlantique**, which is a café, bar, restaurant and disco in one. **Rolling Stone** is a historic address where rock music reigns supreme. Thanks to its size, concerts are often held here.

The **Old Fashion**, inside the Triennale, is a disco with popular theme evenings. (The restaurant is also a big draw, especially for Sunday brunch.)

One of the largest discos in Milan is **Limelight**. The place is also used for television programmes and music concerts.

For an alternative spot, try the **Rainbow**: it features rock and pop and on Friday and Saturday is mainly the haunt of teenagers. **Il Ragno d'Oro**, near the Spanish

walls overlooking Porta Romana, is jam-packed in the summer.

NIGHTSPOTS WITH LIVE MUSIC

Listening to live music is a popular activity in the city and the choice of venues is wide. **Scimmie** is one of the city's historic nightspots. In the 1980s it was the place to go for live jazz, but recently has concentrated more on rock, blues and ethnic music. The place gets very crowded and it can be difficult to find a table unless you go early.

In the Navigli area, **Grillo-parlante** is worth checking out for up-and-coming bands. **Ca' Bianca** is the place to hear jazz and cabaret. You can sit outside in the summer, and there is also a restaurant.

Nidaba is small, dark and smoky, but people love the atmosphere and it is always full. Promising young bands often perform here.

Lastly, concerts of current music are held at the **Tunnel**, a converted warehouse under the Stazione Centrale (main railway station). Tunnel also functions as a cultural centre, hosting shows and exhibitions as well as book launches for new publications.

DISCOPUBS

For those who want to dance without going to a disco there are so-called discopubs. In the early evening, these places are ideal for a relaxing drink and quiet conversation. Later in the evening, the atmosphere livens up considerably. **Loolapaloosa**, for example, is an Irish pub with a happy hour extending from 5 to 9pm. Late at night it transforms into a totally different creature: the volume is turned up and every available spot is used for dancing, including the tables and the counter.

The **Indian Café**, in the Brera area, has a happy hour from 6 to 8pm, and turns into a discopub in the evening. There are three floor levels, and concerts are put on for very reasonable prices. Music tends to be rock-oriented.

A great place for followers of fashion is the **Grand Café Fashion**, which is popular with celebrities and models. Happy hour runs from 6:30 to 9:30pm, after which you can dance downstairs. The house aperitifs are excellent.

Stonehenge is a bar and disco on two floor levels, inspired by Celtic culture. It is popular for theme evenings, live music and Latin-American dance courses. Happy hour extends from 6 to 9pm.

LATIN-AMERICAN

Latin-American dance is increasingly popular in Milan. The place to go for uninhibited dancing is the

Tropicana. It attracts mostly the over-thirty crowd and the best evenings to go are Thursday, Friday and Saturday.

If you find Cuban atmosphere intriguing and feel like trying out some Creole cuisine, the place to go is **Bodeguita del Medio**. Live music is on offer late at night and you can try salsa and merengue dancing.

A disco with Latin-American music only is **Etoile**, where entry is free but drinks are obligatory.

Oficina do Sabor, on the other hand, alternates rock and blues evenings with nights entirely given over to Latin-American music. They also offer courses in salsa-merengue dancing, and anyone who wants to celebrate a special occasion can rent the club.

El Tropico Latino is a great place to try Mexican food while listening to music

and sampling different types of tequila. Wednesday is the best evening to go.

MAJOR CONCERT VENUES

Milan's largest concerts are sometimes performed in places normally associated with football. The stadium San Siro *(see p202)* is sometimes used, but the usual venue is the **Filaforum**, an ultra-modern sports arena with a seating capacity of 12,000. Other venues are the **Palasharp**, the former Palavobis, which can hold 9,000 people, and the **Palalido**, with 5,000 seats Al-though space is limited at the **Leoncavallo** social centre, interesting concerts are put on. In the summer, concerts are also held at the Idroscalo or under the Arco della Pace. Sponsored by the Milan city council, entry is free.

DIRECTORY

DISCOS AND CLUBS

Alcatraz
Via Valtellina 21.
Tel 02-69 01 63 52.

Café Atlantique
Viale Umbria 42.
Tel 02-67 19 94 34.

Colony Dine & Dance
Piazza XXIV Maggio 8.
Tel 02-58 10 27 66.

De Sade
Via Valtellina 21.
Tel 02-688 88 98.

Hollywood
Corso Como 15.
Tel 02-659 89 96.

Il Ragno d'Oro
Piazzale Medaglie d'Oro.
Tel 02-54 05 00 04.

La Banque
Via Porrone 6.
Tel 02-86 99 65 65.

Lime Light
Via Castelbarco 11.
Tel 346 033 84 59.

Magazzini Generali
Via Pietrasanta 14.
Tel 02-539 39 48.

Nepentha
Piazza Diaz 1.
Tel 02-84 57 11 26.

Old Fashion
Viale Alemagna 6.
Tel 02-805 71 69.
www.oldfashion.it

Rainbow
Via Besenzanica 3.
Tel 02-404 83 99.

Rolling Stone
Corso XXII Marzo 32.
Tel 02-89 69 04 57.

Shocking Club
Bastoni di Porta
Nuova 12.
Tel 02-89 07 80 79.

NIGHTSPOTS WITH LIVE MUSIC

Ca' Bianca
Via Lodovico il Moro 117.
Tel 02-89 12 57 77.

Grilloparlante
Alzaia Naviglio
Grande 36.
Tel 02-89 40 93 21.

Indian Café
Corso Garibaldi 97–99.
Tel 02-29 00 03 90.

Nidaba
Via Gola 12.
Tel 339 347 75 12
(mobile).

Scimmie
Via Ascanio Sforza 49.
Tel 02-89 40 28 74.

Tunnel
Via Sammartini 30.
Tel 366 135 81 51
(mobile).

DISCOPUBS

Grand Café Fashion
Via Vetere 6.
Tel 02-89 40 29 97.

Loolapaloosa
Corso Como 15.
Tel 02-655 56 93.

Stonehenge
Viale Pasubio 3.
Tel 02-655 28 46.

LATIN-AMERICAN

Bodeguita del Medio
Viale Col di Lana 3.
Tel 02-89 40 05 60.

El Tropico Latino
Via San Caropoforo 7.
Tel 02-72 00 23 13.

Oficina do Sabor
Via Gaetana Agnesi 17.
Tel 02-58 30 49 65.

Tropicana
Viale Bligny 52.
Tel 02-58 43 65 25.

MAJOR CONCERT VENUES

Filaforum
Via Di Vittorio 6,
Assago.
Tel 02-48 84 48 98.

Leoncavallo
Via Watteau 7.
Tel 02-36 51 02 87.

Palalido
Piazza Stuparich.
Tel 02-39 26 61 00.

Palasharp
Via Elia 33.
Tel 02-33 40 05 51.
www.palasharp.it

Opera, Theatre and Cinema

The theatre season in Milan is undoubtedly one of the best and most varied in Italy. Visitors interested in a specific performance (especially if it is being put on in a well-known theatre such as the Scala or the Piccolo) should book well in advance, either directly through the theatre box office or by contacting one of the booking agencies in the city centre *(see p197)*.

For those who prefer films to the stage, Milan has a great number of cinemas. A bonus is that new releases are shown in Milan ahead of most other Italian cities. Many of the cinemas are multiplexes with plenty of screens, and the majority are concentrated in the city centre. Foreign-language films are also screened at some cinemas on specific days of the week.

OPERA, BALLET & THEATRE

It would be a shame to leave Milan without having seen an opera at **La Scala** *(see pp52–3)*. The opera season begins on 7 December, the feast day of Sant'Ambrogio, the city's patron saint. Lovers of ballet and classical music can also enjoy performances at the highest level from the theatre's ballet company and Filarmonica orchestra. It is important to book as far ahead of performances as possible, because, inevitably, there is much competition for seats at one of the world's most famous opera houses.

No less prestigious and world-famous is the **Teatro Grassi**. Founded just after World War II by Giorgio Strehler as "an arts theatre for everyone", its productions are known for their excellence. The **Teatro Strehler**, opened in 1998, was dedicated to the maestro, who had planned a state-of-the-art theatre worthy of his company's quality productions for over 40 years. The theatre, with a seating capacity of 974, hosts the major Piccolo Teatro productions.

The **Teatro Studio** was originally meant to be a rehearsal hall for the Piccolo Teatro, but later became an independent company. Though interesting from an architectural standpoint, it is not all that comfortable. The **Manzoni**, a favourite with the Milanese, presents a very eclectic programme,

ranging from musicals to drama and comedy, that always attracts top-level directors and actors.

Another historic theatre is the **Carcano**, first opened in 1803. It was restructured in the 1980s and has a capacity of 990 people. Its repertoire is classical, and dance is sometimes offered as well. For comedy, head for the **Ciak**, which usually stars leading comic actors.

For lovers of experimental and avant-garde theatre there are the **Teatro Elfo Puccini** and **Teatro Leonardo** theatres, which are dedicated to performing original works that are always fascinating and thought-provoking, and may sometimes shock. The **Out Off** is also dedicated to avant-garde productions. Milanese experimental theatre is performed at the **CRT Teatro dell'Arte**, which has a seating capacity of 800. The **San Babila** theatre offers a programme of more traditional theatre. Here the fame of the directors and actors attracts a large number of spectators, so that getting hold of a ticket may be hard.

The largest theatre in Milan is the **Smeraldo**, which can seat 2,100 people. Besides famous musicals, it plays host to dance performances, straight theatre and concerts.

The **Teatro Nazionale** always features famous actors and has been concentrating more and more in recent years on dance and operettas.

The **Litta**, in Corso Magenta, is an elegant theatre that

usually presents classic 20th-century plays. Another fascinating theatre is the **Teatro Franco Parenti**, which has a seating capacity of 500. The programme is quite varied, with particular attention being paid to new international works and music.

The small, intimate **Filodrammatici**, next to La Scala, presents a repertoire of classical works that also includes contemporary plays. The **Nuovo**, with its 1,020 seats, presents different kinds of theatrical productions, including musicals, comedies and dance, usually with famous actors. The **Teatro Dal Verme** is also worth checking out.

CINEMAS

Most of the leading cinemas in Milan are concentrated in the city centre, around Corso Vittorio Emanuele II. Most of these are multiplexes, which means there is plenty of choice. Ticket prices are reduced on Wednesday evening and in almost all cinemas on week-day afternoons as well. When popular new films are being shown there are always long queues, so be sure to go early.

Most non-Italian films are dubbed into Italian and presented without subtitles, so they will be difficult to follow for anyone unfamiliar with the language. Visitors who want to see a film with the soundtrack in the original language *(in lingua originale)* can try **Anteo Spazio Cinema** on Mondays, or **Arcobaleno** on Tuesdays, **Mexico** on Thursdays or the **Odeon The Space Cinema**, where they have all-day showings of films in the original language on Mondays.

The **Teatro alle Colonne**, with 170 seats, promotes various cultural events and programmes, such as the African Cinema Festival. The **Auditorium San Fedele** is the home of three film clubs which offer different screening schedules and subject matter. The **Odeon**

The Space Cinema, a multiplex, is the largest cinema in Milan, with ten screens. Near Corso Vittorio Emanuele II there is **Apollo Spazio Cinema**, with five screens. Another centrally located option is the **Eliseo**, which shows lesser-known films that do not benefit from high-budget publicity campaigns.

Another popular venue is the **Arlecchino** on Via San Pietro all'Orto. The **Anteo Spazio Cinema** houses three theatres and also presents children's films.

The **Plinius Multisala**, in Viale Abruzzi, is a multiplex with six screens, while the **Colosseo** has five theatres. The **Ducale**, in Piazza Napoli, is an old cinema that has been converted into a multiplex with four theatres. The **Orfeo Multisala**, near Porta Genova, features state-of-the art screening and sound equipment in a setting decorated with drawings of both Hollywood and Italian film stars.

The **UCI Cinemas Certosa** has a wide selection of films (to get there, take tram 12 or 19 from the Duomo). The **UCI Bicocca**, in the Bicocca Village shopping centre has 18 screens, as well as shops, restaurants and a Wi-Fi zone.

The renovated **Gloria** has two theatres (Garbo and Marilyn), huge screens and a good audio system. Fans of arthouse films can head for the **Ariosto**. At the **Nuovo Orchidea**, Milan city council organizes themed seasons of films, debates and film club showings. The **Palestrina** has a Cineforum on Thursday evenings in winter.

Every year the Milan city council organizes cinema festivals, one of the best of which is the Panoramica di Venezia, held in September, when previews of the films competing in the Venice Film Festival are shown.

Many cinemas in Milan do provide wheelchair access, but it is always a good idea to telephone the box office beforehand for advice.

DIRECTORY

THEATRES

Carcano
Corso di Porta Romana 65. **Map** 8 E3.
Tel 02-55 18 13 77.
www.teatro carcano.com

Ciak
Via Procaccini Giulio 4.
Tel 02-76 11 00 93.
www.teatrociak.it

CRT Teatro dell'Arte
Viale Alemagna 6. **Map** 2 F3. *Tel* 02-89 01 16 44.
www.teatrocrt.it

Filodrammatici
Via Filodrammatici 1.
Map 3 C5.
Tel 02-36 72 75 50.
www.teatrofilo drammatici.it

Litta
Corso Magenta 24. **Map** 3 A5. *Tel* 02-86 45 45 45.
www.teatrolitta.it

Manzoni
Via Manzoni 42. **Map** 4 D4. *Tel* 02-76 36 901.
www.teatromanzoni.it

Menotti-Tieffe
Via C Menotti 11.
Tel 02-36 59 25 44.
www.tieffeteatro.it

Nuovo
Piazza San Babila 37.
Map 4 D5.
Tel 02-76 00 00 86.
www.teatronuovo.it

Out Off
Via MacMahon 16.
Tel 02-34 53 21 40.
www.teatrooutoff.it

San Babila
Corso Venezia 2/a. **Map** 4 E4. *Tel* 02-79 54 69.
www.teatrosanbabila.it

Smeraldo
Piazza XXV Aprile 10.
Map 3 C2.
Tel 02-29 00 67 67.
www.teatrosmeraldo.it

Teatro Elfo Puccini
Corso Buenos Aires 33.
Map 4 F3.
Tel 02-00 66 06 06.
www.elfo.org

Teatro Franco Parenti
Via Pier Lombardo 14.
Tel 02-59 99 52 06.

Teatro Grassi
Via Rovello 2. **Map** 3 B5.
Tel 02-848 80 03 04.
www.piccoloteatro.org

Teatro Leonardo
Via Ampere 1. **Map** 7 C2.
Tel 02-26 68 11 66.
www.teatroleonardo.org

Teatro Nazionale
Piazza Piemonte 12.
Map 1 C5.
Tel 02-848 44 88 00.

Teatro alla Scala
Via Filodrammatici 2.
Tel 02-86 07 75
(automatic booking service).
Tel 02-72 00 37 44
(information).
www.teatroallascala.org

Teatro Strehler
Largo Greppi 1.
Tel 02-848 80 03 04.

Teatro Studio
Via Rivoli 6. **Map** 3 B4.
Tel 02-848 80 03 04.

Teatro Dal Verme
Via San Giovanni sul Muro. **Map** 3 B5.
Tel 02-87 905.
www.dalverme.org

CINEMAS

Anteo Spazio Cinema
Via Milazzo 9. **Map** 3 C2.
Tel 02-659 77 32.

Apollo Spazio Cinema
Galleria de Cristoforis 3.
Map 8 D1.
Tel 02-78 03 90.

Arcobaleno
Viale Tunisia 11. **Map** 4 E2. *Tel* 899 39 98 16.

Ariosto
Via Ariosto 16. **Map** 2 E4.
Tel 02-48 00 39 01.

Arlecchino
Via San Pietro all'Orto 9.
Map 4 D5.
Tel 02-76 00 12 14.

Auditorium S Fedele
Via Hoepli 3b. **Map** 4 D5.
Tel 02-86 35 22 31.

Colosseo
Viale Montenero 84.
Tel 02-59 90 13 61.

Ducale
Piazza Napoli 27.
Map 5 C3.
Tel 02-899 39 98 16.

Eliseo
Via Torino 64. **Map** 7 B2.
Tel 02-72 00 82 19.

Gloria
Corso Vercelli 18. **Map** 2 D5. *Tel* 02-48 00 89 08.

Mexico
Via Savona 57. **Map** 5 B3.
Tel 02-48 95 18 02.

Nuovo Orchidea
Via Terraggio 3. **Map** 7 A1. *Tel* 02-87 53 89.

Odeon The Space Cinema
Via Santa Radegonda 8.
Tel 02-89 21 11.

Orfeo Multisala
Viale Coni Zugna 50.
Map 6 E2.
Tel 02-89 40 30 39.

Palestrina
Via PL da Palestrina 7.
Tel 02-670 27 00.

Plinius Multisala
Viale Abruzzi 28–30.
Tel 02-29 53 11 03.

Teatro alle Colonne
Corso di Porta Ticinese 45. **Map** 7 B2.
Tel 02-58 11 31 61.

UCI Cinemas Bicocca
Viale Sarca 336.
Tel 02-89 29 60.
www.ucicinemas.it

UCI Cinemas Certosa
Via Stephenson 29.
Tel 02-89 29 60.
www.ucicinemas.it

Sports and Outdoor Activities

People visiting Milan on business may want to continue with a routine of practising a sport or exercising. If so, there are many facilities in the city, including health clubs and gymnasiums, that will suit the purpose. These centres often offer a range of activities under one roof so that you can make the most of your free time. Visitors preferring to spectate rather than participate can go and see the local football (soccer), basketball and hockey teams. All are in the first division and offer top-quality sport.

SPORTS FACILITIES

Football (soccer) fans should go to a match at the **Meazza** (or **San Siro**) **Stadium** *(see p203)* at least once in their lifetime. Called the "Scala of football", this stadium has a seating capacity of over 80,000. One particularly popular competition from both the sporting and the theatrical point of view is the local derby between the city's two teams, Inter and AC Milan. However, it is best to plan attendance in advance as tickets sell out pretty quickly.

For horse-racing fans there is the **Ippodromo**, where races are held all year long, except for December. Night races are held from June to September.

The Filaforum arena at Assago *(see p199)* is the home of the local basketball (Pallacanestro Olimpia) and volleyball (Gonzaga) teams. The arena also plays host to various tennis tournaments, first and foremost the Internazionale di Milano, which takes place in spring.

Ice-hockey buffs can follow the matches of the Vipers, who play at the **PalAgorà** arena. They have won the Italian championship for the last four years.

FIVE-A-SIDE FOOTBALL

One of the most popular sports at the moment in Milan is *calcetto* – five-a-side football (soccer). Those wishing to play should go to the **Centro Peppino Vismara**, where they play 11-, 7- and 5-a-side. Another good leisure facility is the **Palauno**, where there are five pitches.

GOLF

There are several golf courses in the Milan area. The closest one to the city is **Le Rovedine Golf Club–Sporting Mirasole**, which is about 7 km (4 miles) from the city centre. There is also a restaurant for the use of players at the club.

SWIMMING

For a relaxing swim, one good swimming pool is the **Piscina Solari**, which has five lanes. A good alternative is the **Piscina Giovanni da Procida**, which boasts a half-size Olympic pool with six lanes. There is also a gym at this site which is ideal for warming up.

The **Lido** is the city's most popular outdoor swimming pool. Visitors who are not daunted by large crowds and enjoy slides can come here to swim during the heat of the Milanese summer.

SKATING

Those keen on roller skating will enjoy themselves at the multi-purpose **Quanta Village**, which has rinks for roller skating, roller hockey and aerobic roller skating. They also offer facilities for many other sporting activities, including tennis, basketball, swimming and mountain biking. Ice-skaters can go to the **PalAgorà**, which has an indoor rink where people can skate at their leisure on Friday and Saturday nights (9:30pm–12:30am, from 10:30pm Sat) and Sunday mornings (10am–noon). It is also open in the afternoon at the weekends from 3 to 6pm. All the rinks have skates for rent. During the Christmas season (24 Dec–8 Jan) an ice-skating rink is usually set up near the Giardini Pubblica enabling people to skate by starlight. From 2–8pm performances, which range from ice hockey to figure skating, take place.

SQUASH

This sport is ideal for fitness, and players usually head to the **Mediolanum Forum Club**, where there are nine courts. Private and group lessons are available, and equipment can be hired. The centre is open every day, including the evening. Although this is a private club, visitors are welcome.

TENNIS

Tennis players can play in an ideal setting at the **Associazione Sporting Club Corvetto**. The Club does not operate a membership card scheme, and there are 13 indoor courts as well as a gymnasium, bar and restaurant and parking space reserved for customers.

The **Centro Sportivo Mario Saini** has 12 courts, either covered or open to the air, depending on the season. It is best to book ahead by telephone. Another place where it is possible to play in peace and quiet, in a sporting club reserved exclusively for this sport, is the **Tennis Club 5 Pioppi**, in Fiera-milanocity. There are four courts that can be used both in summer and winter.

JOGGING

The best and healthiest place for running is the Monte Stella park (also known as the "Montagnetta"), near the San Siro Stadium. This large area of greenery is a good place to jog, following marked paths, or even for cycling around on mountain bikes. In the summer the park is often filled with numbers of apartment-dwelling Milanese, catching some sun.

DIRECTORY

SPORTS FACILITIES

Ippodromo
Via Piccolomini 2.
Tel 02-48 21 61.
www.trenno.it

**Meazza Stadium
(San Siro)**
Piazzale A Moratti.
Tel 02-48 79 82 02.
www.sansiro.net

FOOTBALL

**Centro Peppino
Vismara**
Via dei Missaglia 117.
Tel 02-826 58 23.

Palauno
Largo Balestra 5.
Tel 02-423 54 48.
www.palauno.it

GOLF

**Le Rovedine Golf
Club – Sporting
Mirasole**
Via K Marx 16, Noverasco
di Opera. *Tel 02-57 60 64
20.* www.rovedine.com

SWIMMING

Lido
Piazzale Lotto 15.
Tel 02-39 27 91.

**Piscina Giovanni
da Procida**
Via Giovanni da Procida
20. **Map** 2 D2.
Tel 02-33 10 49 70.

Piscina Solari
Via Montevideo 20. **Map**
6 E2. *Tel 02-469 52 78.*

SKATING

PalAgorà
Via dei Ciclamini 23.
Tel 02-48 30 09 46.

Quanta Village
Via Assietta 19.
Tel 02-662 16 11.
www.quantavillage.com

SQUASH

**Mediolanum
Forum Club**
Via G Di Vittorio 6, Assago.
Tel 02-48 85 72 20.

TENNIS

**Associazione Sport-
ing Club Corvetto**
Via Fabio Massimo 15/4.
Tel 02-53 14 36.

**Centro Sportivo
Mario Saini**
Via Corelli 136.
Tel 02-756 27 41.

Tennis Club 5 Pioppi
Via Marostica 4. **Map** 5
A1. *Tel 02-404 85 93.*

SAN SIRO STADIUM

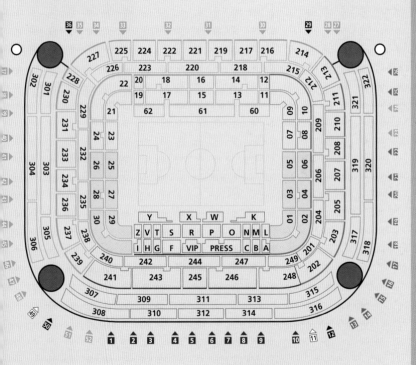

KEY

○ ticket office

■ stadium entrances

  area for Milan guests

  area for Inter guests

— block of seats

  block of seats

— block of seats

  block of seats

GETTING THERE
Avoid going by car, as parking space is very
hard to find. The best way to get there is to
take line 1 of the metro to the Lotto stop; from
there a shuttle bus goes to the stadium. At the
end of the match the No. 16 trams (under the
blue area) go to the city centre. Another option
is taking a taxi (from the Lotto metro as well).

ENTERTAINMENT AT THE LAKES

At the lakes it is possible to devote a considerable amount of leisure time to entertainment and sport. At Lake Garda in particular, you will be able to practise any type of aquatic sport, have a go at trekking in the hinterland and dance the night away at the discos. Of the lakes, Garda also has the liveliest nightlife and is the most popular with young people. Lake Como, Lake Maggiore and the smaller lakes still offer a variety of opportunities for entertainment. In recent years the enterprising local IAT tourist offices, sponsored by the town administrations, have been quite successful in promoting initiatives aimed at making holidays more interesting for visitors. Outdoor markets, feasts, festivals and other events have therefore become more and more frequent. The lakes offer breathtaking scenery, an entertainment in itself, and every year there are programmes of cultural events. In addition there are fine architectural and artistic works to be seen, lovely gardens to explore, and nature reserves to wander through.

The logo of the Caneva aquatic amusement park

SPORTS

If keeping in top physical shape is a priority, there are plenty of activities that serve the purpose at the lakes. Lake Garda is the domain of windsurfing; Torbole and Riva in particular being the most popular places for surfers both in summer and winter. Sailing fans will enjoy the Centomiglia, an annual regatta organized by the Circolo Vela Gargnano sailing club and held on the second weekend of September. For a more relaxing time, there are also opportunities to go fishing.

In the Garda hinterland, hiking has become very popular, and touring the area on a mountain bike is the most recent vogue. More adventurous souls can take lessons in paragliding.

Lake Maggiore offers not only many aquatic sports but is quite popular with golf enthusiasts. There are state-of-the-art golf courses in lovely natural settings that are enjoyed by Italian and foreign golfers alike.

The hills and valleys around the lake are ideal places for horse riding, hiking, mountaineering, free climbing, hang-gliding and paragliding and, in the winter, when snow covers the high ground, skiing and snowboarding.

The most popular sports at Lake Como are sailing and water skiing. Lessons are available from qualified instructors, whatever your age and experience.

Another enjoyable activity is canoeing. All the lakes have clubs where you can rent canoes and equipment.

A water skiing instructor and his pupil at Lake Como

For the more sedentary, there are many spas (terme) at the lakes or in the vicinity. These centres offer a variety of treatments.

OTHER ACTIVITIES

Visitors to Lake Garda, especially families with children, might want to visit the Gardaland amusement park (see pp152–3). It is recommended for children and adults alike, the ideal place to enjoy yourselves and even experience the occasional thrill. However, in peak season, be prepared for a very long wait at the most interesting attractions.

About 2 km (1 mile) from Gardaland is **Caneva**, the

A group of windsurfers in action at Lake Garda

Camels in the Natura Viva zoological park, at Bussolengo-Pastrengo near Lake Garda

The **Parco Giardino Sigurtà** lies 8 km (5 miles) from Peschiera. This 50-ha (123-acre) garden is a temple to ecology.

At Lake Maggiore the Villa Pallavicino park (see p137) has a lovely 20-ha (49-acre) botanic garden with 40 different species of animals.

largest water amusement park in Italy. Shows, water games and other displays, plus an area reserved for small children, make this a big aquatic attraction.

To take a closer look at some rare and endangered animal species, visit the **Parco Natura Viva**, a zoo located at Bussolengo-Pastrengo. A pleasant walk among ancient oak trees and plants takes visitors around the home of the 1,000 specimens in this lovely park. Cars are also allowed into the safari park, where a 6-km (4-mile) tour brings you into closer contact with some of the wild animals of the savannah.

Another popular place for lovers of interesting plants is the **Giardino Botanico della Fondazione André Heller** at Gardone Riviera: 1.5 ha (3.7 acres) of land with over 8,000 plants from every climatic zone in the world.

Logo of the Natura Viva zoological park

NIGHTLIFE

The best area for nightlife is Lake Garda, which boasts internationally known nightspots. Desenzano, in particular, has a number of pubs and other spots for evening entertainment, while in the outskirts are some of the largest discotheques in Italy. The undisputed king is **Dehor**, a gigantic and extremely popular place, especially in the summer. Another famous and very popular nightspot is **Fura**, a multimedia disco where theme evenings feature. On Friday there is funk, soul and "rare groove" music, while the other evening (and night) programmes are more unconventional.

At Lake Como, a popular spot for dinner and drinks with music is **Como Fashion Café**, which caters to a young and trendy crowd. For live music, go to **L'Ultimo Caffè**.

At Lake Maggiore, do not miss **La Rocchetta**, a disco situated in a splendid Art Nouveau villa with a view of the lake, and **Dancing Mirage**.

At Verbania, go to **Tam Tam**; **Byblos**, at Arizzano, is another lively spot.

(see p137)

DIRECTORY

ACTIVITIES

Caneva
Località Fossalta 58, Lazise.
Tel 045-69 69 900.
www.canevaworld.it

Giardino Botanico della Fondazione André Heller
Via Roma, Gardone Riviera.
Tel 033-64 10 877.
www.hellergarden.com

Parco Giardino Sigurtà
Via Cavour 1, Valeggio sul Mincio. **Tel** 045-637 10 33.
www.sigurta.it

Parco Natura Viva
Località Figara 40, Bussolengo-Pastrengo, Varenna.
Tel 045-717 01 13.
www.parconaturaviva.it

NIGHTLIFE

Byblos
Via Nuova Intra Premeno 6, Arizzano. **Tel** 0323-533 03.

Como Fashion Café
Via Sant'Abbondio 7, Como.
Tel 031-26 83 56.

Dancing Mirage
Viale Baracca 16, Arona.
Tel 0322-443 31.

Dehor
Via Fornace dei Gorghi 2, Lonato.
Tel 030-991 99 48.
www.dehor.it

Fura
Via Lavagnone 13, Lonato.
Tel 030-913 06 52.
www.fura.it

L'Ultimo Caffè
Via Giulini 32, Como.
Tel 031-27 30 98.

La Rocchetta
Via Verbano 1, Arona.
Tel 0322-83 26 89.

Tam Tam
Piazza Flaim 16, Verbania.
Tel 0323-40 32 10.

One of the bars at the Dehor discotheque at Lake Garda

SURVIVAL GUIDE

PRACTICAL INFORMATION

Milan is one of Italy's most efficient and business-like cities, with an excellent public transport network and good public services. In the capital of fashion, appearances do matter, and you are likely to receive better service and attention if you are smartly dressed. Milan has its share of petty crime, and it is advisable to take some basic precautions in order to enjoy your stay to the full. Keep bags and cameras close to you at all times, and take extra care travelling on public transport, where pickpockets

Logo of the City of Milan

may be operating. The public transport system is, however, the best way to get around the city. Walkers should stay alert in the chaotic traffic, and take particular care crossing streets. Tourist offices are the best places to go for practical information, including maps. At the lakes, brochures are available from IAT offices, with information on local festivals and other entertainment. Information can also be obtained ahead of your visit from the Italian tourist office (ENIT) in your home country.

Visitors on the roof of the Gothic Duomo

WHEN TO GO

Although Milan is great to visit year-round, the mild climate in June makes it one of the best months to go. The balmy spring months are also pleasant with cool breezes. Milan in August can be brutally hot and many shops and restaurants are closed. Most tourist attractions remain open, however. Winter in Milan can be very cold. The lakes are best visited from April to October, but they are packed in July and August.

VISAS AND PASSPORTS

Italy is part of the Schengen Agreement, whereby travellers moving from one Shengen country to another are not subject to border controls, although there are spot checks.

Other EU nationals and citizens of the US, Canada, Australia and New Zealand do not need visas for stays of up to three months.

All visitors to Italy must register with the police within eight working days of arrival. If you are staying in a hotel, this will be done for you. Otherwise, contact the local *questura* (police station). Anyone wishing to stay for more than three months (eight working days for citizens from countries other than those mentioned above) will have to obtain a *permesso di soggiorno* (permit to stay). EU citizens can apply for a permit at any main police station. Non-EU citizens must apply in advance in their home country.

If you lose your passport contact your embassy.

IAT logo

TOURIST INFORMATION

Information on hotels and local amenities is available from the Italian tourist board, **ENIT (Ente Nazionale Italiano per il Turismo)**, which has offices in many major cities, including London and New York. In Milan, **IAT (Informazione e Accoglienza Turistica)** offices have information on the city, including free lists of hotels and restaurants, and details of cultural events.

At the lakes, look for IAT offices in larger towns, and Pro Loco tourist offices in smaller towns and villages; these are usually located in the town hall *(comune)* and are sometimes open only during the tourist season.

OPENING HOURS AND ADMISSION PRICES

Most state-owned museums in Milan are open from Tuesday to Sunday, while privately owned museums operate their own timetables. Churches are open daily but often close for lunch.

EU residents aged under 18 and over 60 benefit from discounts in most state-run places, though proof is required. The Milano Card gives free public transport and reduced entry to several museums and galleries. A three-day card, available from www.milanocard.it, is €13 plus shipping costs.

TRAVELLERS WITH SPECIAL NEEDS

Milan is a challenging city for disabled travellers. Pavements can be uneven or blocked by parked cars, and tram lines can make crossing the road difficult. However, the majority of Milan's metro system is wheelchair-accessible, as are the green, low-level trams. An excellent source of information for disabled travellers is the **AIAS Milano Onlus** website.

International Student Identity Card

STUDENT TRAVELLERS

The **Centro Turistico Studentesco (CTS)** issues the **International Student Identity Card (ISIC)** and discount tickets to people under 26; these can be used for travel not only in Milan, but also in the rest of Italy and Europe.

There are two youth hostels in Milan: the **Ostello della Gioventù P Rotta**, where you need an annual membership card (which can be bought at the hostel), and **La Cordata (Casa Scout)**. For information on youth hostels around the lakes, contact the **Associazione Italiana Alberghi per la Gioventù** (Italian Youth Hostelling Association).

ITALIAN TIME

Milan is 1 hour ahead of Greenwich Mean Time. This means New York and Los Angeles are 6 and 9 hours behind Italian time, and Moscow is 2 hours ahead. Tokyo and Sydney are 8 and 9 hours ahead respectively.

RESPONSIBLE TRAVEL

Milan doesn't immediately impress the eco-conscious visitor. Things are greener beneath the surface, however, particularly when it comes to food. Piazza Gramsci, in the Sempione district, has a small organic market on the first Sunday of each month, while Via F Confalonieri, in the Garibaldi area, hosts a similar market on the second Sunday of each month. **Simply SMA** is the city's first eco supermarket, and **Natura Si** is a chain selling organic and natural products.

Recycling bins are everywhere, while in metro stations, the *salvagiornali* bins are a response to the nuisance of free newspapers. **Agriturismi Bio** lists farm or country holidays considered fully or partly organic.

Colourful produce at one of Milan's organic markets

DIRECTORY

CONSULATES

UK
Via San Paolo 7.
Tel 02-72 30 01.

US
Via Principe Amedeo 2/10.
Tel 02-29 03 51.

TOURIST INFORMATION

ENIT UK
1 Princes Street, London
W1B 2AY. www.
italiantouristboard.co.uk

ENIT US
630 Fifth Avenue,
Suite 1565, NY 10111.
www.italiantourism.com

IAT Offices

Milan
Piazza Castello.
Tel 02-77 40 43 43.
www.visitamilano.it

Lake Como
IAT di Bellagio
Piazza G Mazzini 12.
Tel 031-95 02 04. www.
bellagiolakecomo.com

IAT di Cernobbio
Via Regina 33.
Tel 031-51 01 98.

IAT di Como
Piazza Cavour 17.
Tel 031-26 97 12.
www.lakecomo.it

IAT di Lecco
Via Nazario Sauro 6. *Tel*
0341-29 57 20. www.
turismo.provincia.lecco.it

IAT di Tremezzo
Via Regina 3.
Tel 0344-404 93.
(Seasonal opening only).

Lake Garda
IAT di Desenzano
Via Porto Vecchio 34.
Tel 030-374 87 26.

IAT di Gardone
Corso Repubblica 8.
Tel 0365-203 47.

IAT di Sirmione
Viale Marconi 8. *Tel* 030-
91 61 14 or 030-91 62 45.

IAT di Toscolano Maderno
Via Sacerdoti 1.
Tel 0365-64 13 30.

Lake Iseo
IAT di Iseo
Lungolago Marconi 2.
Tel 030-98 02 09.

Lake Maggiore
IAT di Laveno
Piazza Italia 2.
Tel 0332-66 87 85.

IAT di Varese
Via Romagnosi 9.
Tel 0332-28 19 13.
www.vareseland
oftourism.it

TRAVELLERS WITH SPECIAL NEEDS

AIAS Milano Onlus
www.milanopertutti.it.
org

STUDENT TRAVELLERS

Associazione Italiana Alberghi per la Gioventù
www.aighostels.com

Centro Turistico Studentesco
Largo Gemelli 1,
c/o ISU Cattolica.
Tel 02-80 25 55 95.
www.cts.it

International Student Identity Card
www.isic.org

La Cordata
Via Burigozzo 11.
Tel 02-58 31 46 75.
www.lacordata.it

Ostello della Gioventù P Rotta
Via Martino Bassi 2.
Tel 02-39 26 70 95.
www.hostelmilan.org

RESPONSIBLE TRAVEL

Agriturismi Bio
www.agriturismibio.it

Natura Si
www.naturasi.it

Simply SMA
Via Novara 15.

Personal Security and Health

Italian pharmacy sign

In Milan, there is widespread petty crime, a problem common to all large cities. Stay wary, particularly in crowded areas, and keep a close eye on personal property such as bags and cameras, especially in the evening. The towns and villages around the lakes are very safe areas, however, and there should be no cause for concern. Should you fall ill during your stay, Italian pharmacists can advise on minor ailments.

A municipal policewoman directing traffic in Milan

POLICE AND EMERGENCIES

There are several police forces in Italy. The *polizia* (state police) deal with all kinds of criminal offences and issue *permessi di soggiorno* (residence permits) to foreigners and passports to Italian citizens.

The *vigili urbani* (municipal police) wear blue-and-white uniforms in winter and white ones in summer; they regulate traffic and parking offences.

The *carabinieri* (military police) deal with everything from speeding offences to drug-related crimes.

Police stations *(questura)* and hospitals *(ospedale)* with a casualty unit/emergency room *(pronto soccorso)* are shown on the Street Finder maps *(see pp224–37)*.

For urgent medical attention see *Hospitals and Pharmacies*. Emergency phone numbers are listed in the Directory.

WHAT TO BE AWARE OF

Pay attention when walking alone at night in poorly lit streets away from the city centre. Unaccompanied women should take particular care. Petty theft is a perennial problem, so keep a tight grip on your bag, especially in trams and on the metro. Pickpockets are common and well organized. Keep your handbag closed and do not carry backpacks or shoulder bags on your back. Keep valuables such as your wallet or purse, camera and mobile phone well out of sight. When walking along the street, keep handbags on the inside, away from the road.

Visitors with cars should take all the usual precautions appropriate in a big city. Do not leave personal belongings or car radios visible inside the car. Whenever possible, leave your car in an attended parking space *(parcheggio custodito)*.

LOST PROPERTY

If you lose documents or other personal property, report the loss immediately at the nearest police station. An official report will be needed for insurance claims. It may also be worth contacting the city's **Ufficio Oggetti Smarriti** (Lost Property Office, c/o Railway Police). If you lose something on a train or in a station, contact the lost property office on the ground floor of the **Stazione Centrale**.

Should an interpreter be needed, ask at your hotel or try the Yellow Pages *(Pagine Gialle;* www.paginegialle.it). where agencies will be listed. The **Associazione Italiana di Traduttori e Interpreti (AITI)** also has a list of qualified translators and interpreters. Your consulate should be able to provide interpreters too.

It is advisable to take photo-copies of all important documents, including passport pages, before travelling.

HOSPITALS AND PHARMACIES

Milan has state-of-the-art health facilities should you become ill during your stay. If the ailment is minor, go to a pharmacy *(farmacia)* first. Italian pharmacists are well trained to deal with routine problems. Pharmacies can be identified by a neon green cross over the door. A list of pharmacies open at night

Milanese police at a road block

Fire engine

Ambulance

Police car

the city is also particularly bad). Always remember to apply insect repellent cream or spray.

Tap water is safe to drink in Italy, but many people prefer to drink bottled water *(acqua minerale)*, which may be either fizzy *(frizzante* or *con gas)* or still *(naturale).*

Milan's pollution and its notorious smog, which is particularly prevalent in winter, can be problematic for people with breathing difficulties who should consider wearing anti-pollution masks.

(servizio notturno) and on public holidays will be on display. A useful chemist is the **Farmacia della Stazione Centrale**, at the main railway station, open 24 hours a day.

Pronto Farmacia is a free emergency service that will deliver urgent medicines. The 24-hour service also gives advice and information on pharmacies that are open at night and on Sundays.

If you need urgent medical assistance, call the **Emergenza Sanitaria/Ambulanze** (Health Emergencies/Ambulance) or go straight to the Pronto Soccorso (Casualty Department/Emergency Room) at the nearest hospital.

If you should need a doctor at your hotel, contact the **Guardia Medica** (Night Duty Physician). In the event of dental problems, go to the emergency dentist **Pronto Soccorso Odontoiatrico**.

MINOR HAZARDS

Mosquitoes *(zanzare)*, which appear at the first sign of warm weather, can be a real pest. Despite the various anti-mosquito devices such as burning coils and plug-ins, it is difficult to fend them off altogether, especially when sitting at outdoor cafés at the lakes (the Navigli quarter in

TRAVEL AND HEALTH INSURANCE

All EU citizens should travel with the European Health Insurance Card (EHIC), available from the UK Department of Health (www.dh.gov.uk) or a post office. The card entitles the holder to free emergency treatment and reciprocal health care in Italy. It is wise, however, for visitors to have additional health insurance.

Always take out adequate travel insurance before leaving for Italy, and remember to report any loss or theft at a local police station.

SAFETY OUTDOORS

Aside from the high levels of pollution and strong sun in summer, Milan poses little environmental danger. Visitors to the lakes are unlikely to experience anything more alarming than the odd mosquito. Those keen to practise watersports should follow certain guidelines. At Lakes Maggiore and Como, cold water and strong currents challenge even experienced swimmers. On Lake Garda, windsurfers may be taken by surprise by sudden gusts of wind, particularly in the areas around Torbole and Riva (the northern part of the lake).

DIRECTORY

POLICE AND EMERGENCIES

Emergenza Sanitaria/ Ambulanze (Health Emergencies/Ambulance)
Tel 118.

General Emergencies
Tel 113.

Fire
Tel 115.

Police
Tel 112 (Carabinieri).
Tel 02-77 27 01 00 (Vigili Urbani).

LOST PROPERTY

Associazione Italiana di Traduttori e Interpreti
www.aiti.org

Stazione Centrale
Piazza Duca d'Aosta
(Platform 21).
Map 4 F1. *Tel* 02-63 71 24 28.
🕐 24 hours.

Ufficio Oggetti Smarriti
Via Friuli 30. **Map** 8 F4.
Tel 02-88 45 39 00.
🕐 8:30am–4pm Mon–Fri.

HOSPITALS AND PHARMACIES

Farmacia della Stazione Centrale
Map 4 F1.
Tel 02-669 07 35.

Guardia Medica
Tel 02-345 67.

Pronto Farmacia
Tel 800-80 11 85 (free).

Pronto Soccorso Odontoiatrico
Via della Commenda 10.
Map 8 E2. *Tel* 02-55 03 25 14.

Canoeing, a popular outdoor activity in the lakes in Lombardy

Banking and Currency

Cashpoint (bancomat) logo

Milan has very good public services. There is a bank on almost every street corner, and most of them have automatic cash dispensers. In the smaller villages around the lakes, banks with cash dispensers are less easy to find, so plan ahead and take some cash with you. Credit cards are widely accepted by all but the smallest of businesses. Currency can be exchanged at post offices, banks, bureaux de change and, at a less competitive rate, some hotels. Always compare rates to find the most favourable one.

Main branch of the Credito Italiano bank, in Piazza Cordusio

BANKS

Milanese banks are open 8:30am–1:30pm and 3–4pm Monday to Friday; note that opening times may vary by about a quarter of an hour from bank to bank. Most banks have cashpoint machines (or ATMs), which take all major credit cards, including American Express and Visa.

CURRENCY EXCHANGE

It is a good idea to bring some euros with you to avoid poor exchange rates and/or high charges, but it is possible to change money at the airports. **Forexchange Linate** in the arrival lounge of Linate airport, is open 7am–midnight daily; the office in the departure lounge is open 6am–10pm. **Forexchange Malpensa**, in Malpensa airport departures, is open 7am–11pm daily.

Larger post offices and banks also offer exchange services at attractive rates; however, using an ATM to withdraw cash can often be a more economical option.

ATMS

ATMs *(bancomat)* are ubiquitous in Milan. Be aware, though, that some of the smaller villages around the lakes may not have either a bank or an ATM. The majority of ATMs have instructions in English and other European languages. Always use caution when withdrawing cash and avoid any machine you are unsure about.

CREDIT CARDS AND TRAVELLER'S CHEQUES

Both in Milan and at the lakes, most businesses accept **MasterCard** and **Visa**, while **American Express** and **Diners Club** are less frequently accepted. However, some restaurants, cafés and shops may require a minimum expenditure to accept credit card payment. Always make sure you have some cash in case your credit card is not accepted. Note that petrol stations do not take credit cards, only cash.

To avoid problems using your card while abroad, inform your credit card company before travelling. In the event of the loss or theft of your credit card, contact the numbers listed in the Directory immediately.

Traveller's cheques are not as popular as they used to be and tourists are finding it increasingly hard to cash or spend them. If you decide to use them, choose a well-known name such as American Express.

CURRENCY

Italy's currency is the euro. Euro banknotes have seven denominations. The €5 note (grey) is the smallest, followed by the €10 note (pink), €20 note (blue), €50 note (orange), €100 note (green), €200 note (yellow) and the €500 note (purple). The euro has eight coin denominations: the €1 and €2 coins are both silver and gold in colour; the 50-, 20- and 10-cent coins are gold; and the 5-, 2- and 1-cent coins are bronze.

Do not carry large amounts of cash on you, and never underestimate the need for coins and small notes in Italy. Taxis and smaller shops and museums can rarely change large notes.

DIRECTORY

BANKS

Banca Popolare di Milano
Piazza Filippo Meda 4.
Map 4 D5. *Tel* 02-770 01.

Banca Popolare di Lodi
Piazza dei Mercanti 5.
Map 7 C1. *Tel* 02-850 81.

CURRENCY EXCHANGE

Forexchange Linate
International arrivals.
Tel 800-30 53 57.

Forexchange Malpensa
International departures T2.
Tel 800-30 53 57.

LOST AND STOLEN CREDIT CARDS

American Express
*Tel 06-72 90 03 47 or
800-87 43 33 (toll free).*

Diners Club
Tel 800-39 39 39 (toll free).

MasterCard
Tel 800-87 08 66 (toll free).

Visa
Tel 800-87 72 32 (toll free).

Communications and Media

Logo of
Telecom Italia

Public phones are increasingly hard to find in Milan, as access to Internet services and the use of mobile phones have increased. Mobile phone users should consider purchasing a SIM card for use in Italy before they travel, or a prepaid phone on arrival. In addition to Internet cafés, Wi-Fi hotspots are ever more common in bars, restaurants and hotels. Newsstands carry a huge range of publications, and many sell English-language newspapers too. The postal service in Italy, once notoriously slow, is much improved.

INTERNATIONAL AND LOCAL TELEPHONE CALLS

The area code *(prefisso)* for Milan is 02. Be aware that it is necessary to dial telephone numbers in full, including the area code, even for local calls. For information in English concerning international calls, dial 4176. To make an international reverse charge (collect) call, the number to dial is 170. For Italian directory enquiries, dial 1254.

MOBILE PHONES

GSM mobile phones work in Italy, but North American phones may not work abroad if they are locked or will not accept other SIM cards. If you know that your handset will function and is unlocked, consider buying an Italian SIM. Most offer free incoming calls and low outgoing call rates.

If your phone is locked, you could buy a prepaid phone once in Italy, though some shops will ask for a tax code, which you won't be able to provide. You can find shops for Milan's mobile providers (**Vodafone**, **Negozio TIM** and **Negozio Wind**) all over the city.

PUBLIC TELEPHONES

Most telephone booths in Milan are scheduled to disappear by 2015; around the lakes they are still quite commonplace. Public phones usually operate with telephone cards *(schede telefoniche)*, sold at Internet shops, tobacconists and newsstands. An international card *(scheda telefonica internazionale)* is the cheapest way of calling home.

Internet café in Milan

INTERNET ACCESS

There are Internet cafés all over Milan, including **Hard Disk Café** and **Mondadori**, and in the main lake towns. Wi-Fi is common in bars, restaurants and hotels. It can also be accessed both inside and outside public buildings such as libraries, schools, museums and more.

POSTAL SERVICES

Post offices are usually open 8am–7pm on weekdays and 8:30am–12:30pm on Saturday. The **Ufficio Centrale** offers a poste restante *(Fermo Posta)* service and it is possible to change money there.

You can buy stamps *(francobolli)* from post offices and any tobacconist with the black-and-white T sign.

NEWSPAPERS AND MAGAZINES

Milan dailies, such as *Il Corriere della Sera*, have local news sections and entertainment listings. The free *Milano Mese* (available at IAT offices) has listings of cultural events.

Websites such as www.tuttomilano.it, www.aboutmilan.com and http://ciaomilano.it have information on cultural activities.

DIRECTORY

MOBILE PHONES

Negozio TIM
Tel 02-80 92 32.

Negozio Wind
Tel 02-67 48 18 56.

Vodafone
Tel 02-34 22 08.

INTERNET CAFES

Hard Disk Café
Corso Sempione 44.
Map 2 E2.
Tel 02-33 10 10 38.

Mondadori
Via Marghera 28.
Map 1 C5.
Tel 02-48 04 71.
Piazza del Duomo 1.
Map 7 C1.
Tel 02-454 41 10.

POSTAL SERVICES

Ufficio Centrale
Via Cordusio 4. **Map** 7 B1.
Tel 02-87 91 44 46.
www.poste.it
Other Post Offices
Via Sammartini 2, off Piazza Duca d'Aosta (Stazione Centrale, ground floor).

Newsagent selling national and international publications

TELEVISION

There are three state-owned television channels in Italy (RAI 1, RAI 2 and RAI 3) and many private channels, some of which are owned by Mediaset (Retequattro, Canale Cinque, and Italia Uno). There are also many local channels. Most hotels 3-stars and above have satellite TV with BBC and CNN news in English, as well as German and French channels.

TRAVEL INFORMATION

An Alitalia airplane

Three airports link Milan with the rest of the world. Linate airport is only a few kilometres from the city centre and connects the capital of Lombardy with the main Italian and European cities. Malpensa is an intercontinental airport about 50 km (30 miles) from Milan, while Orio al Serio, which handles many European budget flights, is located 45 km (27 miles) away, near Bergamo. There are car rental offices at all the airports, though it is usually cheaper to book a fly-drive deal ahead rather than arrange hire on arrival. There are excellent train links between Milan and other cities in Italy. The city is also well connected to the rest of Europe, with fast, easy routes to France and Switzerland, and to Austria and Germany via Verona. Visitors arriving by car will use the excellent road and motorway networks. Exits from the ring road around Milan are clearly marked. However, these roads are often congested with traffic, particularly at rush hour, so journey times can be slow.

Linate Airport, located within easy reach of the city centre

ARRIVING BY AIR

Visitors from outside Italy arriving in Milan by air are likely to fly into either Malpensa or Orio al Serio airports (the latter is often referred to as Bergamo airport). Linate airport handles more domestic than international flights. Frequent flights between London and Milan are operated by **Alitalia**, **British Airways** and **easyJet**. The majority of low-cost airlines, such as **Ryanair**, fly to Orio al Serio in Bergamo.

British Airways and **Lufthansa** offer a good choice of direct flights from the United States, linking Milan with Boston, New York, Chicago, Miami and Los Angeles. Alitalia also has good connections from Toronto, Vancouver and Sydney; however, many of its flights from the US go via Rome, necessitating a connection to Milan.

LINATE AIRPORT

Linate handles a small number of European flights with airlines such as Alitalia, **Air France**, British Airways, **BMI**, Lufthansa and **KLM**, and domestic flights with carriers such as **Meridiana**.

The airport has left luggage facilities, car rental offices including Avis and Hertz (see pp222–3), and plenty of car parking space.

Getting from Linate to the centre of Milan is easy. Taxis take around 20 minutes (longer in rush hour) and cost about €30. A taxi stand is situated right in front of the airport exit.

ATM bus No.73 runs from 6:05am to 0:55am, linking the airport with the city centre, going as far as Piazza San Babila. There are two services – a regular service and a non-stop one. Tickets (€2.50) are sold at the vending machine near the bus stop. They can also be bought on the non-stop bus. The **Starfly** bus runs every 30 minutes between 5:30am and 11:45pm, connecting Linate and Milan's central station. Tickets cost €5 and can be bought on board.

MALPENSA AIRPORT

Located 50 km (30 miles) from the city, Malpensa is the largest of the Milan airports, with two terminals.

The **Malpensa Express** rail service links the airport with Stazione Nord in Piazza Cadorna and Stazione Centrale (€7). The journey times vary from 29 to 52 minutes, with trains leaving the airport every 30 minutes between 5:26am and 0:29am. The last coach to Cadorna is at 1:30am. Trains from Milan depart from 4:28am to 0:28am. A one-way ticket costs €11; the only returns available are day returns.

A view of Malpensa airport

The ring road *(tangenziale)* around Milan, often congested with traffic

Two coach lines also offer a good airport service. The **Malpensa Shuttle** runs every 20 minutes, starting at 5am from the Stazione Centrale (there is an earlier coach at 4:15am), and 5:30am from Malpensa; the last coach from the airport leaves at 1:20am. The journey time is about 1 hour; tickets cost €7.50 for a single or €12 for a return.

The **Malpensa Bus Express**, operated by Autostradale, runs approximately every 20 minutes starting at 4am from the Stazione Centrale and 6am from Malpensa. A single journey costs €7.50.

An **Airpullman** bus links Malpensa and Linate every 90 minutes, starting from 9:30am; the last coach leaves Linate at 4:30pm and Malpensa at 6:20pm. The journey time is 70 minutes and tickets cost €13.

A taxi from Malpensa takes around an hour (more in rush hour) and costs €90 to Milan.

ORIO AL SERIO AIRPORT

Used by several European carriers (including many low-cost airlines), Orio al Serio has only one terminal, meaning that crowds and queues are commonplace.

Autostradale runs an efficient bus service between the airport and Milan's Stazione Centrale, leaving every 30 minutes during the day. The journey time is about 1 hour, and a ticket costs €10.

An urban bus route (No.1) links the airport to Bergamo train station every 25–35 minutes (6:05am–0:15am Mon–Sat; service is less frequent on Sundays); tickets cost €1.60.

A taxi to Milan takes 45–60 minutes and costs about €100.

ARRIVING BY CAR

Visitors arriving from the *autostrada* (motorway) will approach Milan via the ring roads, *tangenziale est* (east) and *tangenziale ovest* (west), which are often congested with traffic. Approaching the centre, look for an official car park *(see p219)*, then use public transport. The alternative is to use the ATM parking areas *(see chart below)* that are on the outskirts but well served by the metro. Fees vary from €1 for half a day to €2 for up to 8 hours. Some ATM parking is free after 8pm.

Car parks closer to the city centre are more expensive.

ARRIVING FROM	MOTORWAY EXITS	CAR PARK	NUMBER OF CARS	METRO AND BUS	DISTANCE FROM CITY CENTRE
Trieste **Venice** **Verona** **Brescia**	Cavenago/Cambiago	Gessate	500	M 2 (30/35 min.)	23 km (14 miles)
	Sesto San Giovanni/V.le Zara	Sesto Marelli	250	M 1 (20 min.)	8 km (5 miles)
	Tang. est/Cologno Monzese	Cologno Nord	500	M 2 (30 min.)	9 km (5.5 miles)
	Tang. est/Viale Palmanova	Cascina Gobba/ Crescenzago	800 600	M 2 (20 min.)	6 km (4 miles)
	Tang. est/ Viale Forlanini	Forlanini	650	🚋 12 🚌 73	6 km (4 miles)
Turin **Aosta** **Como** **Chiasso** **Varese** **Gravellona**	Viale Certosa	Lampugnano	2,000	M 1 (20 min.)	5 km (3 miles)
	Pero	Molino Dorino	1,600	M 1 (25 min.)	8.5 km (5 miles)
	Tang. ovest/Milano Baggio	Bisceglie	900	M 1 (20/25 min.)	6 km (4 miles)
Ventimiglia **Genoa**	Viale Liguria/Centro Città/ Filaforum	Romolo/ Famagosta	250 560	M 2 (20 min.)	4–5 km (2.5–3 miles)
Naples **Rome** **Florence** **Bologna**	Milano/Piazzale Corvetto	Rogoredo/ San Donato	350 2,400	M 3 (20 min.)	5–7 km (3–4 miles)

An ETR Eurostar train at the Stazione Centrale in Milan

ARRIVING BY RAIL

The main railway station in Milan is the **Stazione Centrale**, where all the major domestic and international trains arrive. Connections with your destination in town can be made by taxi, metro (underground) lines 2 and 3, and many trams and buses, all of which are just outside the entrance. **Porta Garibaldi**, in the Centro Direzionale area, and Milano Lambrate (near Città Studi) are much smaller railway stations. Both can be reached via metro line 2. Metro line 3 links **Rogoredo** station, near San Donato Milanese, with central Milan.

A regional train service run by the **Ferrovie Nord Milano** connects the city with Como, Varese and the Brianza region. Trains depart from Piazzale Cadorna, where metro lines 1 and 2 converge.

The Passante Ferroviario (*see p221*) is a suburban railway link network that connects various metro lines with the Porta Garibaldi station, run by the **Ferrovie dello Stato** (state railway), and with the Milano–Bovisa station, run by Ferrovie Nord.

A number of different types of train operate on Italy's railways. The fastest trains linking Milan and the main national and international cities are the ETR Eurostar trains (*le freccie*). The ticket price includes a supplement and obligatory seat reservation. International

Eurocity trains also offer fast links to major European cities such as Zurich, Paris and Barcelona. Intercity trains link Milan and the main cities within Italy, such as Florence and Rome. On both Eurocity and Intercity services, tickets should be booked ahead. A supplement is charged.

The other types of train are slower, but the fares are very reasonable and calculated by the kilometre. *Espresso* trains stop only at main stations, *Diretto* trains stop at most stations and the *Locale* ones stop at every single station along the route.

There are also trains with sleeping cars for people travelling at night. It is possible to reserve a *cuccetta* (bunk bed) in a compartment holding four to six beds. A more expensive but more private and comfortable alternative are the Wagons-Lits

carriages *(vagoni letto)*. These compartments have washing facilities, and breakfast is provided. A first-class ticket is obligatory to secure a one-bed cabin.

RAIL TICKETS

Train tickets can be purchased online on the Trenitalia website (www.trenitalia.com), at railway stations or in travel agencies. E-tickets and ticket-less purchases sent to your mobile phone are also available. Standard tickets must be validated before departure by date-stamping them at the small yellow stamping machine at the entrance to each platform *(binario)*.

Tickets are valid for two months from the time of purchase; however, once date-stamped, they must be used within 24 hours. If you are adversely affected by a railway strike, tickets for travel should be stamped by a ticket inspector or cashier in order to claim a refund.

Online re-imbursements are also possible for those with ticket-less purchases.

Should you need to amend a booking, Trenitalia offers a range of possibilities – and restrictions. Full details are available online.

FERROVIE DELLO STATO

The Ferrovie dello Stato logo

ARRIVING BY COACH

Coaches (in Italian, *pullman*) arriving in Milan end their journey at the coach terminus at Lampugnano, next to the metro stop of the same name (line 1). The most important

The concourse at Milan's Stazione Centrale

service connecting Milan with Rome, Venice and Florence.
Long-distance coaches are comfortable, with reclining seats, air conditioning, toilets and television. They make regular stops at motorway service stations.

COACH TICKETS AND FARES

Tickets for coach travel can be purchased directly at the bus terminal in Lampugnano or online at **Bus Italia**. There are also Autostradale offices in Piazza Castello and at Orio al Serio. Timetables and rates vary according to the length of the journey and the season. Reductions are often available for children aged 2–14 and people over 60.

Autostradale coaches parked at a terminus in Milan

coach carrier connecting Milan with the rest of Italy, including Sicily, is **Autostradale Viaggi**; the company also run airport buses that can be booked online. **SAFduemila** links Milan to Lake Maggiore, going to Arona, Stresa and Verbania. It also has a service that connects Malpensa airport to Stresa, Arona and Intra. Reserve tickets the day before travelling before 11am.

For destinations in the rest of Europe, the main firm is **Eurolines**, which also offers a

DIRECTORY

ARRIVING BY AIR

Air France
Tel 0871-663 37 77.
www.airfrance.co.uk

Alitalia
Tel 06-656 49.
www.alitalia.it

BMI
www.flybmi.com

British Airways
Tel 199-71 22 66.
www.ba.com

Easyjet
Tel 199 20 18 40.
www.easyjet.com

KLM
www.klm.com

Lufthansa
Tel 199-400 044.
www.lufthansa.it

Meridiana
Tel 89 29 88.
www.meridiana.it

Ryanair
Tel 899 01 88 80.
www.ryanair.com

LINATE AIRPORT

ATM
Tel 800-80 81 81
(toll free).
www.atm-mi.it

First Aid
Tel 02-74 85 22 23.

Information
Tel 02-23 23 23 (call centre). *www.sea-aeroportimilano.it*

Left Luggage
Tel 02-71 66 59.

Lost Property
www.sea-aeroporti milano.it/en/pdf/lost_property_form.pdf

Starfly
Tel 02-58 58 72 37.

MALPENSA AIRPORT

Airpullman Linate – Malpensa
📱 *02-58 58 10 64.*
www.airpullman.com

First Aid
Tel 02-74 85 44 44 (T2).

Information
Tel 02-23 23 23 (call centre). *www.sea-aeroportimilano.it*

Left Luggage
Tel 02-58 58 02 98 (T1).

Lost Property
www.sea-aeroporti milano.it/en/pdf/lost_property_form.pdf

Malpensa Bus Express
Tel 02-58 58 73 04.
www.autostradale.it

Malpensa Express
📱 *02-202 22.*
www.malpensaexpress.it

Malpensa Shuttle
📱 *02-58 58 31 85.*
www.airpullman.com

ORIO AL SERIO AIRPORT

Autostradale
Tel 02-63 79 01
or 035-31 84 72.
www.autostradale.com

Information
📱 *035-32 62 97.*
www.orioaeroporto.it

ARRIVING BY RAIL

Ferrovie dello Stato
Tel 89-20 21.
www.ferrodellastato.it

Ferrovie Nord Milano (Cadorna)
Piazzale Cadorna 14.
Map 3 A5.
Tel 02-202 22.
www.ferrovienord.it

Porta Garibaldi
Map 3 C1.
Tel 02-63 71 62 75
(information).

Rogoredo
Tel 02-63 711 or 89-20 21.

Stazione Centrale
Map 4 F1.
Tel 89-20 21
(state railway call centre).
Tel 02-77 40 43 18
(tourist information).
Tel 02-63 71 22 12
(left luggage).
Tel 02-63 71 24 28
(railway police).

ARRIVING BY COACH

Autostradale Viaggi
Lampugnano.
Tel 02-30 08 91.
www.autostradale.com

Eurolines
c/o Autostradale Viaggi, Lampugnano.
Tel 02-30 08 91, 055-35 71 10 (main office).
www.eurolines.com

SAFduemila
Tel 0323-55 21 72.
www.safduemila.com

COACH TICKETS AND FARES

Bus Italia
www.busitalia.it

Getting around Milan

Ticket for a car park in Milan

Although there are some traffic-free areas, such as Brera and the historic centre, Milan is not very pedestrian-friendly. Traffic is heavy and chaotic, and parking space is hard to find. Public transport *(see pp220–21)* is the best way of getting around. The tram, bus and metro network is efficient, and a flat fare operates in the city centre. One- and two-day passes offer good value. All tickets, including the passes, must be date-stamped before use. Fines are imposed on anyone caught having a "free ride".

GREEN TRAVEL

The biggest problems facing Milan are traffic and the lack of parking space. However, the public transport system is well used and represents good value, with tickets valid on all forms of transport.

The **Area C** *(see Driving Around Milan)*, is the city council's attempt to curb traffic entering the city. All cars pay a €5 fee to access the city centre. Tickets are available from tobacconists, newsagents and some Banca Intesa San Paolo ATMs. Profits from this scheme are reinvested in more sustainable transport.

Milan's public transport authority, ATM *(see p221)*, is replacing traditional buses with hydrogen-powered and hybrid vehicles. Since 2008, around 250 "clean" forms of transport have been introduced in the city.

ATM also operate a bike-sharing scheme for residents and visitors, **BikeMi**. This popular initiative allows you to pick up a bike and return it to a designated place elsewhere in the city.

WALKING IN MILAN

Some areas of Milan are very pleasant to walk around. Strolling around the fashion district window shopping, for example, is always an enjoyable aspect of the city. Pedestrianized areas in Milan can be found around Corso Vittorio Emanuele, Via dei Mercanti, Piazza San Babila, Via Dante, Via della Spiga and the Brera quarter.

Another good area for people on foot is the Navigli quarter, which is a pedestrian zone after 8pm in summer.

However, outside of oases like these, the pedestrians' lot is by no means an easy one. The main problem is the heavy traffic. Drivers tend to treat the streets as race tracks, and even where people crossing the streets are using the zebra crossings, the road markings may be ignored by motorists. An additional problem is that the chronic lack of parking space means that cars are usually parked on the pavements, leaving pedestrians very little room to manoeuvre. This is a particular problem for those trying to get around with prams or pushchairs and for those who are wheelchair-bound.

STREET CROSSINGS

Theoretically, pedestrians have right of way at crossings when the green *avanti* sign is lit up; however, you won't have long to get across, so be alert. The red *alt* sign means that you must wait. Underground crossings are indicated by a sign reading *sottopassaggio*.

DRIVING AROUND MILAN

Driving in Milan is not recommended. The heavy traffic and no-entry areas, known as ZTL *(zona a traffico limitato)* for taxis, buses and emergency vehicles only, make driving difficult. From 8am to 8pm on-street parking (indicated by blue lines) is allowed for up to 2 hours by using a Sosta Milano card, which is a pre-pay parking ticket sold at authorized ATM sales points (tobacconists, newsstands and bars). Areas marked with yellow lines are for residents only, while white lines indicate free parking. Disabled drivers displaying a badge can park for free in designated areas. Alternatively, use the Private Car parking in the centre of Milan *(see chart opposite)* or the ATM parking areas on the outskirts of the city, which are well served by the metro *(see p215)*.

Cars entering central Milan between 7:30am and 7:30pm Mon–Fri have to pay an eco tax in the Area C. The Area C zone is clearly signposted, and the amount payable is €5; there is no access for diesel vehicles. The charge is payable on the day of entry or until midnight the following day. A multiple Area C ticket (worth €30, €60 or €100) entitles you to enter central Milan on different days, without having to pay on a daily basis. Most hotels will assist visitors with fulfilling the Area C requirements. For rental cars, it is best to check with the car hire company.

Corso Buenos Aires, heading to the city centre

**Motorbikes and scooters
parked in Piazza Cordusio**

SCOOTERS, MOPEDS AND BICYCLES

Scooters and mopeds *(moto)* are good means of getting around Milan and avoiding traffic jams. Bicycles *(biciclette)* can also provide an alternative, provided you are confident and keep your wits about you. The tram tracks can be a nuisance for bicycle wheels.

Companies that offer moped or bicycle hire (rent) include **AWS** (bicycles) and **Bianco Blu** (scooters).

TAXIS

Official taxis are generally white, but you may see yellow ones or taxis with the livery of their sponsors. Taxi stands are located throughout the city; all taxis have telephones, and the numbers are listed in the telephone directory. At the beginning of the ride the meter should read €3.20 for daytime weekday rides, €5.20 on Sundays and holidays, and €6.20 at night, to which a supplement for luggage is added. To call a taxi, ring the **Radio Taxi** service. Taxis leaving from the airport charge a minimum of €12.50.

DIRECTORY

GREEN TRAVEL

Area C
Tel *02-02 02; 800-437 437.*
www.areac.it

BikeMi
Tel *800-80 81 81.*
www.bikemi.com

SCOOTERS, MOPEDS AND BICYCLES

AWS
Via Ponte Seveso 33.
Tel *02-67 07 21 45.*
www.awsbici.com

Bianco Blu
Via Gallarate 33. **Tel** *02-308 24 30.* **www**.biancoblu.com

TAXIS

Radio Taxi
Tel *02-85 85; 02-40 40; 02-69 69.*

CAR PARKS IN THE CITY CENTRE

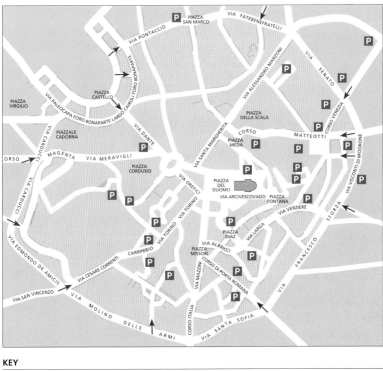

KEY

🅿 Parking

Resident parking

City centre

Pay on-street parking

➤ Area C zone

Travelling by Public Transport

**Logo of the Azienda
Trasporti Milanesi (ATM)**

To avoid stress and parking problems, the best and least expensive way to get around town is to use public transport. Milan has a very efficient city transport system, run by the Azienda Trasporti Milanesi (ATM), which comprises trams, buses, trolleybuses and the three lines of the underground railway *(metropolitana)*.

A tramcar going through the Navigli quarter

TRAMS AND BUSES

Trams, buses and trolleybuses in Milan are efficient and serve virtually the entire city. They are always crowded, especially at rush hour, and generally pass by every 7 minutes.

Bus and tram stops are easy to recognize. Each has a yellow sign displaying the route taken. Stops are often located on islands in the road, with seats for waiting passengers.

The yellow signs also have a timetable, but be careful to distinguish the summer *(estate)* from the winter *(inverno)* schedules, as they are posted side by side. Italian timetables always use the 24-hour clock.

On most buses and trams you can use any door to get on or get off. A few vehicles have signs indicating which door must be used to enter *(entrare)* and exit *(uscita)*.

Tickets must be bought before you get on from a nearby newsstand or bar, and date-stamped on the bus or tram. There is a small machine to validate *(convalidare)* your ticket; it is usually at the front, behind the driver, but on longer vehicles there are at least two, one in the front and one at the back.

When you want to get off, press the red button. A sign saying *"fermata prenotata"* will flash until the next stop is reached. The driver will usually open the doors when the tram or bus reaches the stop; if not press the button next to the doors.

The **ATM** runs a night bus called **Radiobus**. Call ahead to book a pick-up at your nearest stop. It costs €4 a ride.

Always keep a close eye on your personal belongings, including luggage, particularly on a crowded bus or tram. Pickpockets – including children – are on the look-out for handbags, mobile phones and wallets, and you must be wary.

Families travelling with prams and people in wheelchairs will find the newer, green trams easier to board.

USEFUL BUS AND TRAM ROUTES

This map shows the best bus and tram routes for sightseeing in Milan. The locations of major sights are marked, as well as the nearest useful stop. Sights should then only be a short walk away.

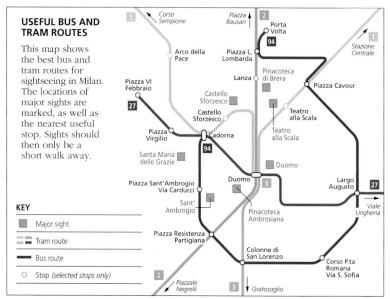

KEY

- ■ Major sight
- ▦ Tram route
- ■ Bus route
- ○ Stop (selected stops only)

THE METRO

There are three metro lines: number 1 (red), 2 (green) and 3 (yellow). Two further lines are being planned or constructed, with the proposed Line 4 connecting Linate airport to the city. Stations all have escalators and many have lifts for disabled passengers (see Back Endpaper), and they are usually located close to tram and bus stops. The trains run approximately every 2 minutes during rush hour and are often crowded. They run every 5 minutes at other times of the day. Once stamped, tickets can also be used for other means of public transport within 90 minutes.

PASSANTE FERROVIARIO

This commuter train service links the northwest of Milan with the metro. The line goes from Porta Vittoria to Bovisa, with intermediate stops at Porta Venezia, Piazza della Repubblica, Stazione Garibaldi and Via Lancetti.

TICKETS AND TIMETABLES

All tickets and travelcards can be used for above-ground transport, the metro and the Passante Ferroviario. Tickets are valid for 90 minutes on all lines. However, they cannot be used twice on the metro.

Tickets and electronic travelcards must be bought in advance as you cannot buy them on board. They can be purchased from newsstands, tobacconists and automatic

vending machines in metro stations, which operate with both coins and banknotes.

Tourist tickets are good value. They cost from €4.50/8.25 and are valid for 24/48 hours. Weekly and monthly passes (abbonamenti) are also available. The Milano Card, also available for tourists, gives free public transport for three days (see p208).

Milanese public transport usually operates from 6am to 12:30am, but some buses and trams run until 2am.

Ticket for the metro

GUIDED TOURS

A unique way of touring Milan is on an antique tram made into an Orient Express-style restaurant. Called **ATMosfera**, the tram, which offers dinner (and lunch, if you book the entire tram), leaves from Piazza Castello, on the corner of Via Beltrami, Tuesday to Sunday; the tour lasts around 2 hours. Reservations must be made by 7pm the day before and tickets cost €65.

Zani Grand Tour leaves twice daily from Foro Bonaparte at 9:30am and 2:30pm. From Tuesday to Sunday, this 3½-hour bus tour includes visits to Teatro alla Scala and its Museum, the Duomo and the Last Supper. Tickets cost €60 for adults and €30 for children aged 5–15. Zani also

DIRECTORY

TRAMS AND BUSES

ATM
Tel 800-80 81 81 (toll free).
www.atm-mi.it
For season tickets and travel passes:
Duomo, Cadorna, Centrale FS, Garibaldi FS, Loreto and Romolo stations.
⏱ 7:45am–7:15pm Mon–Sat.

Radiobus
Tel 02-48 03 48 03 (1pm–2am) to book time and route (service runs 8pm–2am).

GUIDED TOURS

ALGAT
Via Giovanni Aurispa 2.
Tel 02-55 21 04 77.
www.guideturistichemilano.it

ATMosfera Restaurant Tram
Tel 800-80 81 81.
www.atm-mi.it

Autostradale
Passaggio Duomo 2.
Tel 02-80 58 13 54.
www.autostradale.it

Zani Viaggi
Foro Bonaparte 76.
Tel 02-48 03 69 99/86 71 31.
www.zaniviaggi.it

runs two daily hop-on, hop-off open-topped buses, City Sightseeing, from Piazza Castello. Tickets cost €20 for adults and €10 for children, and are available online, at their office and on board (sightseeing tours only).

Autostradale offers two daily tours leaving from Passaggio Duomo at 9:30am and 11am, both with a visit to the Last Supper. The 3-hour tour costs €55 and the 1½-hour tour costs €35. Buy tickets online or at the office. They also organize walking tours from April to July and September to October. These start at €20.

ALGAT (Association of Lombard Guides) organizes private walking tours and museum visits.

Milan's antique ATMosfera tourist tram

Getting to and around the Lakes

The funicular
at Como in 1894

The lakes are easily accessible from Milan, both by car and by train. Visitors arriving by car will take the Autostrada dei Laghi motorway or the Valassina *superstrada*. There are good train links with all the lakes using either the Ferrovie dello Stato (FS) or the Ferrovie Nord Milano (FNM) railways. Both offer frequent services. Bus services link the various towns and villages around the lakes, or you may well prefer to use the hydrofoils or ferries in order to avoid traffic jams on the crowded roads, especially at weekends. Be advised that all lake ferry companies run a much reduced service in the winter months, generally between November and March.

A Ferrovie dello Stato regional train

CAR HIRE

At Malpensa, most car hire companies are located on the first floor of Terminal 1. Rental companies at the airport include **Hertz**, **Avis**, **Maggiore**, **Europcar**, **Budget** and **Sixt**. Desks are usually open from 7am to 11pm/midnight daily. At Linate, car hire firms are on the ground floor (arrivals). Opening times vary, with some desks – Europcar, for example – closed at weekends. Many car rental firms also operate from Orio al Serio. Arrange car hire before you travel for a better deal.

LAKE MAGGIORE

To get to Lake Maggiore from Milan by car, take the A8 *autostrada* and exit at Sesto Calende. From here, take the road to Angera to go to the Lombardy side of the lake, or the road to Arona to go to the Piedmontese side.

To get to the upper part of the lake, proceed northwards, turn off at Gravellona Toce and then follow the signs for Fondotoce and Verbania.

If you go to Lake Orta, take the Borgomanero turnoff and follow the signs for Gozzano–Orta San Giulio. The A8 *autostrada* is also the easiest way to get to Lake Varese from Milan: take the Varese exit and continue to Gavirate.

Lake Maggiore is also accessible by train. Trenitalia run a regular service from Stazione Centrale to Arona and Stresa (*see p217*); local trains go as far as Luino, via Gallarate. The Ferrovie Nord railway (*see p217*) has frequent daily train services to Laveno.

The most enjoyable way of travelling from one town to another on Lake Maggiore is to use the hydrofoils and ferries. The main towns are connected by the **Navigazione Lago Maggiore** service, which has a fleet of steamboats,

motor boats and ferries. The time-tables are posted at local hotels, restaurants and all the ports, and are subject to seasonal changes.

If you are travelling from outside Italy, Malpensa airport (about 50 km/30 miles from Milan; *see pp214–15*) is the closest to Lake Maggiore.

LAKE COMO

The shortest route from Milan to Lake Como by car is to take the A9 *autostrada*, better known as Milano–Laghi, and exit at the Como Nord signs. To get to the western side of the lake, from Como take the Statale 340 road, the ancient Via Regina, which goes as far as Sorico. If, however, you are headed for the other side, go up the state road 583, which passes through Bellagio and goes as far as Lecco.

Traffic can be very heavy during the weekend, and as there is not much parking space around, the best solution may be to use a combination of car followed by one of the frequent hydrofoil or car ferry services. The hydrofoils are particularly frequent on the Como–Colico line, with intermediate stops, while the ferries stop only at Cadenabbia, Bellagio, Menaggio and Varenna. For detailed information, contact **Navigazione Lago di Como**.

The town of Como is also served by the Ferrovie dello Stato (FS) and Ferrovie Nord railways. The FS trains depart from Stazione Centrale and go

A ferry connecting the main towns around Lake Como

to Como on the Milan–Chiasso line. The Nord trains leave from Piazzale Cadorna in Milan and arrive at Piazza Cavour.

If you travel by air, Malpensa (*see pp214–15*) is the closest airport to Lake Como.

LAKE GARDA

Verona is the nearest main town to the lake. It is on routes linking Milan with Venice, both road and rail.

To reach Salò from the Milan–Venice A4 motorway, exit at Brescia Centro and go eastwards on the *tangenziale* (ring road) until you see signs for the Salò *superstrada* (highway). Alternatively, exit at Desenzano del Garda (118 km/73 miles from Milan), cross the town and go up the Statale 572 road for 20 km (12 miles).

Navigarda tickets

A few kilometres past Salò is Gardone. Sirmione can be reached from Desenzano del Garda by following the southern side of Lake Garda for 9 km (6 miles) or leaving the *autostrada* at the Sirmione–San Martino della Battaglia exit.

To get to the Veneto side of the lake, take the A22 *autostrada* to Brennero and then exit at Affi.

To get to Lake Idro from Milan, take the A4 *autostrada* to Brescia Ovest and then proceed to Lumezzane.

Those coming from the east should take the state road that goes from Salò to Barghe, and then follow the signs for Madonna di Campiglio.

Lake Garda is also well served by trains. Desenzano del Garda and Peschiera del Garda are stops on the Milan–Venice line, and coaches will take you onwards from these stations to Sirmione, Salò, Gardone and Limone. For more information, contact the **Azienda Trasporti Verona**.

There is a good boat service on Lake Garda, except in the winter season. The hydrofoils are the fastest means of crossing the lake, while car ferries run between Maderno and Torri del Benaco and Limone and Malcesine. Boat services are run by **Navigazione Lago di**

Garda (Navigarda); see the website for timetables.

The nearest airport to Lake Garda is Verona-Villafranca (also known as Valerio Catullo airport). Other possibilities are Orio al Serio (*see p215*), Linate (*see p214*) and Marco Polo in Venice.

LAKE ISEO

The easiest way to get to Lake Iseo by car is to take the A4 Milan–Venice motorway. Come off at the Ponte Oglio and Palazzolo exits to get to Sarnico, and at the Rovato, Ospitaletto and Brescia Ovest exits to get to Iseo.

If you go by train, the state railway from Stazione Centrale takes you to Brescia; from there you can go on the Ferrovie Nord Brescia–Iseo–Edolo line; bicycles are allowed on board.

The best way to get to Sarnico and Lovere is by boat from Iseo. **Navigazione Lago Iseo** will provide timetables.

In spring and autumn (suspended in July and August), a steam train service, the **Treno Blu**, travels to Sarnico on the Palazzolo–Paratico–Sarnico line. It is run by the Ferrovia del Basso Sebino, which operates in the Oglio River Regional Park in cooperation with the WWF and other environmental associations. **Pro Loco Sarnico** has information.

The Ferrovie Nord railway station, in Piazzale Cadorna, Milan

DIRECTORY

CAR HIRE

Linate
Avis *Tel* 02-71 51 23.
Budget *Tel* 199 44 59 19.
Europcar *Tel* 02-76 11 02 58.
Hertz *Tel* 02-70 20 02 56.
Maggiore *Tel* 02-71 72 10.
Sixt *Tel* 02-70 20 02 68.

Malpensa Terminal 1
Avis *Tel* 02-585 84 81.
Budget *Tel* 02-74 86 73 47.
Europcar *Tel* 02-585 86 21.
Hertz *Tel* 02-58 58 10 81.
Maggiore *Tel* 02-58 58 11 33.
Sixt *Tel* 02-58 58 02 71.

Orio al Serio
Avis *Tel* 035-31 60 41.
Budget *Tel* 035-33 06 99.
Europcar *Tel* 035-31 79 92.
Hertz *Tel* 035-31 12 58.

LAKE MAGGIORE

**Navigazione
Lago Maggiore**
Tel 800-55 18 01.
www.navlaghi.it

LAKE COMO

**Navigazione
Lago di Como**
Tel 800-55 18 01.
www.navlaghi.it

LAKE GARDA

**Azienda Provinciale
Trasporti**
Tel 045-805 78 11.
www.atv.vr.it

**Navigazione Lago di
Garda (Navigarda)**
Tel 800-55 18 01.
www.navlaghi.it

LAKE ISEO

Navigazione Lago Iseo
Via Nazionale 16, Costa Volpino.
Tel 035-97 14 83.
www.navigazionelagoiseo.it

Pro Loco Sarnico
Via dei Lantieri, Sarnico.
Tel 035-426 13 34.
www.prolocosarnico.it

Treno Blu
Tel 030-740 28 51.

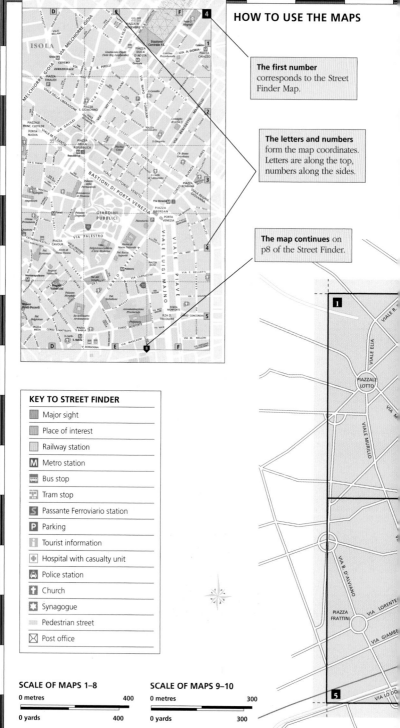

HOW TO USE THE MAPS

The first number corresponds to the Street Finder Map.

The letters and numbers form the map coordinates. Letters are along the top, numbers along the sides.

The map continues on p8 of the Street Finder.

KEY TO STREET FINDER

▨	Major sight
▨	Place of interest
▨	Railway station
M	Metro station
▦	Bus stop
▦	Tram stop
S	Passante Ferroviario station
P	Parking
i	Tourist information
✚	Hospital with casualty unit
▣	Police station
✝	Church
✡	Synagogue
▥	Pedestrian street
⊠	Post office

SCALE OF MAPS 1–8

0 metres	400
0 yards	400

SCALE OF MAPS 9–10

0 metres	300
0 yards	300

MILAN STREET FINDER

All the map references in this guide, both in the *Milan Area by Area* and in the *Travellers' Needs* sections, refer to the maps in this *Street Finder* only. The page grid superimposed on the *Area by Area* map below shows which parts of Milan are covered by maps in this section. Besides street names, the maps provide practical information, such as metro stations, tram and bus stops, post offices, hospitals and police stations. The key on the opposite page shows the scale of the map and explains the symbols used. The main sights are shown in pink. On page 219 there is a map of the Milan metro system, including the Passante Ferroviario.

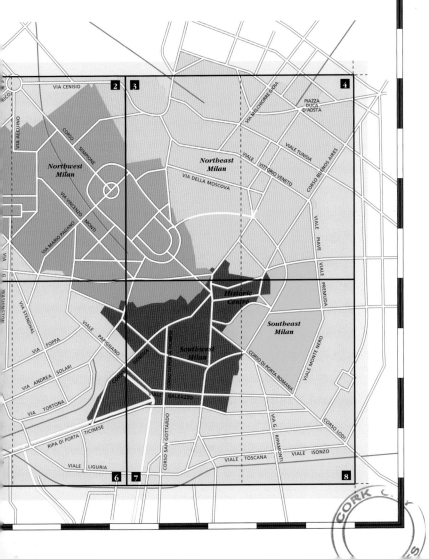

Street Finder Index

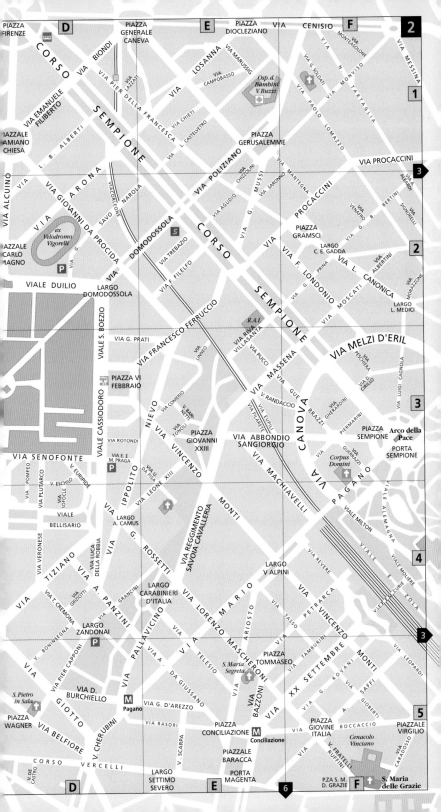

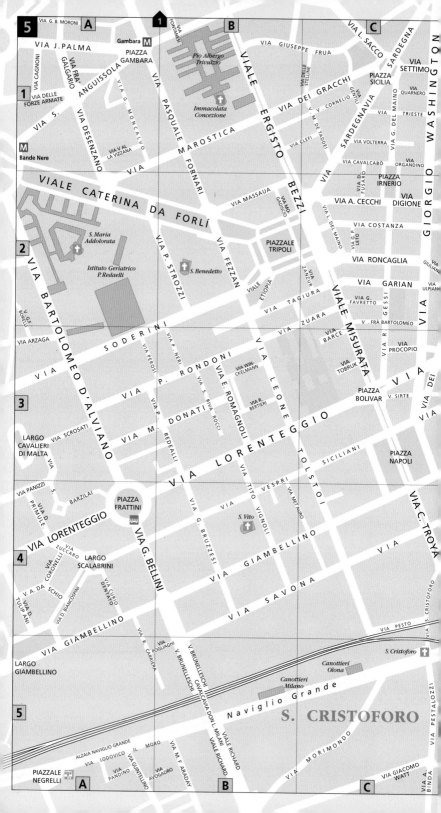

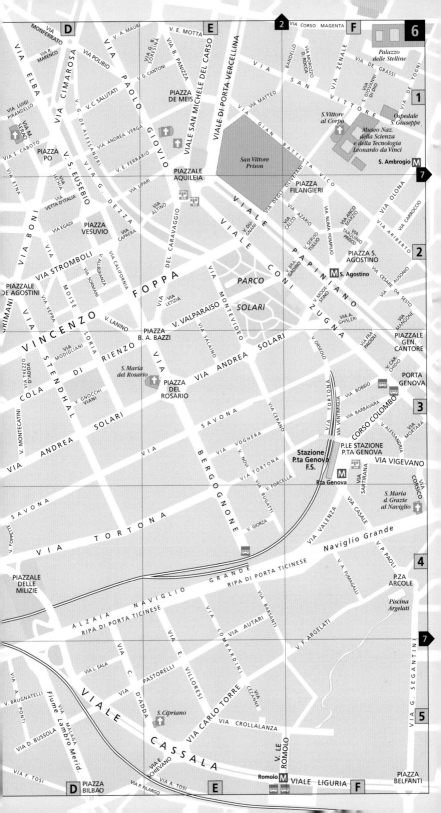

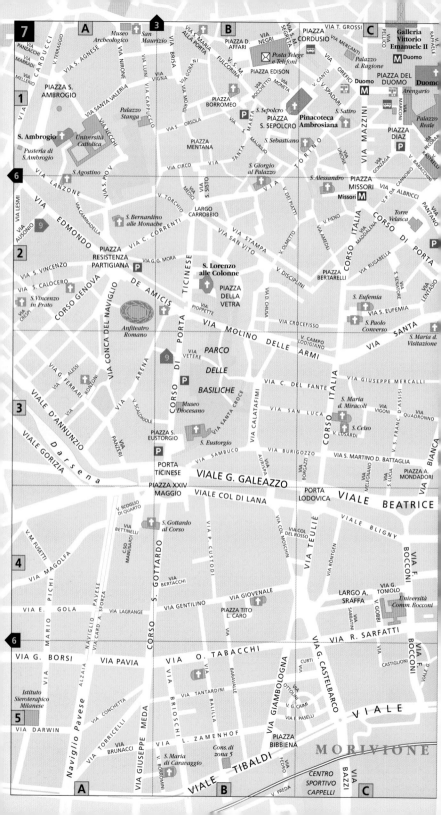

General Index

The numbers in **bold type**
refer to main entries.

Acknowledgments

Dorling Kindersley would like to thank all the people, organizations and associations whose contributions and assistance have made the preparation of this book possible. Special thanks are due to the following organizations and individuals: APT di Como (Sig. Pisilli), Silvia Dell'Orso, Direzione Civiche Raccolte d'Arte del Castello Sforzesco (Walter Palmieri), Giorgio Facchetti, Diana Georgiacodis, Alberto Malesani (Gardaland), Enrico Pellegrini, chef of the *Locanda degli Angeli* (Gardone), Augusto Rizza, Silvia Scamperle, Carla Solari, Crisca Sommerhoff, Valentina Tralli.

Revisions Team
Gillian Allan, Douglas Amrine, Marta Bescos Sanchez, Sonal Bhatt, Michelle Clark, Michelle Crane, Vivien Crump, Imogen Corke, Cristina Dainotto, DG Consulting s.a.s. di Julia Dunn & C, Conrad van Dyk, Louise Bostock Lang, Annette Jacobs, Priya Kukadia, Maite Lantaron, Delphine Lawrance, Jude Ledger, Hayley Maher, Cristina Minoni, Catherine Palmi, Rada Radojicic, Sands Publishing Solutions, Ellie Smith, Mary Sutherland.

Additional Assistance
Reid Bramblett, Sally Bloomfield, Susi Cheshire.

Picture Credits
Key: a-above; b-below/bottom; c-centre; f-far; l-left; r-right; t-top..

Every effort has been made to trace the copyright holders. The publisher apologizes for any unintentional omissions and would be pleased, in such cases, to add an acknowledgment in future editions.

All the photographs reproduced in this book are from the Image Bank, Milan, except for the following:

ALAMY IMAGES: Tibor Bognar 10cra; Chuck Pefley 209cr; Tom Thulen 213crb; CuboImages srl/Bluered 170cl; CuboImages srl/Eddy Buttarelli 35bl; CuboImages srl/Dario Mainetti; 171cb Adam Eastland 124clb; John Warburton-Lee Photography/Ian Aitken 11tr; Jon Arnold Images 42; David Sanger photography/Sam Bloomberg-Rissman 171tl.ARCHIVIO FOTOGRAFICO DEL TEATRO ALLA SCALA: 52bl, 53tl, 53br, 53bl; Andrea Tamoni 52cl.

ARCHIVIO FOTOGRAFICO ELECTA: 56-57 (all the photographs), 58tr, 58tl, 58c, 58bl, 59tr, 59c, 64cr(d), 146tl, 146tr, 148cr, 149tl, 149cr.ARCHIVIO FOTOGRAFICO STORICO ACHILLE BERTARELLI: 41tc, 157tc, 207tc.ATM S.P.A - ARCHIVIO FOTOGRAFICO: 220tl, 221bl, 221ca.

SIMONETTA BENZI: 36tl, 51tr, 51cl, 51cr, 68cr, 69cr, 74br, 75tr, 75cl, 78tr, 80br, 82tc, 85br, 87br, 88cr, 88br, 90c, 90bl, 97tl, 97cr, 97cb, 98cl, 100tl, 100br, 101br, 112tl, 113br, 122tr, 122cs, 122br, 123tr, 123cl, 123br. BOEUCC ANTICO RISTORANTE: 168bl.

CORBIS: Atlantide Phototravel/Mario Cipriani 208cl; Atlantide Phototravel/Massimo Borchi 40-1; The Gallery Collection 5t, 72tr, 72-73c; Massimo Listri 143t. CORPO NAZIONALEDEI VIGILI DEL FUOCO: 211tl.

DISCOTECA DEHOR: 205cb. DORLING KINDERSLEY PHOTO LIBRARY: Julia Dunn 218tl; Paul Harris and Anne Heslope 6clb, 42, 128-9, 132cl, 132-133t, 133bl, 140tr, 168cra, 213ca, 214cl; Neil Lukas 210tl; Ian O'Leary 170tr/cb/bl/br, 171bl/bc/br; 197bl.

EMPICS: 196t. THE EURAIL GROUP: 216br, 216tl.

FABIO DE ANGELIS: 29tl, 29cl, 32br, 33tl, 33tr, 33bl, 44tl, 45br, 49tl, 49c, 80tr, 83tr, 83cr, 83bl, 84tl, 85tc, 85bl, 88tm, 90tc, 96c, 96br, 98br, 99tr, 100c, 102tr, 111br, 112cr, 112br, 119bl, 119cr, 121tl, 149bl, 185br, 188bl, 196cr. FOTOLIA: Claudio Baldini 76

GARDALAND: 152r, 152-3. GETTY IMAGES: 211cl; Vincent Lombardo 68b. GIOVANNI FRANCESIO: 32bl. GRAND HOTEL VILLA SERBELLONI (BELLAGIO): 145tr, 159tl. GRANDI STAZIONI S.P.A: 216cr; GRAZIA NERI: Archivio Marcello Mencarini/La Scala Theatre Museum, Milan, Angelo Inganni (1852) The Theater in a painting 124tl; Archivio Marcello Mencarini/La Scala Theatre Museum, Milan Ulisse Surtini Portrait of Maria Callas 125tr; Barbara Seghezzi 124br, 126clb, 126tr, 127tc.

HOTEL DU LAC (VARENNA): 141cr. HOTEL FOUR SEASONS (MILAN): 158cr, 185br. HOTEL REGENCY (MILAN): 158bl. HOTEL VILLA CRESPI (ORTA SAN GIULIO): 159br.

IAT DI COMO: 144tr, 144bl. IL DAGHERROTIPO: 49br. INDEX, FIRENZE: Alberti 127crb; Pizzi 126c. KRIZIA: 36c.

MARKA, MILAN: 196bl, 223b; Roberto Benzi 125bl; Danilo Donadoni 10bl; Nevio Doz 11bl; Giovanni Rivolta 10tc; Alessandro Villa 217tl. MUSEO DIOCESANO: 90tl. MUSEO DEL RISORGIMENTO: 8–9c..

OMEGA FOTOCRONACHE: 27cl, 30tr, 30cl, 30bl.

PASTICCERIA COVA (MILAN): 185tr.

LAURA RECORDATI: 32cl, 54tl, 55br, 78br, 91br, 96tl, 98tl, 101c. RISTORANTE IL SOLE (RANCO): 169bl. RISTORANTE L'ALBERETA (ERBUSCO): 169tl. RISTORANTE VILLA FLORI (COMO): 169tl. SAPORETTI IMAGINI D'ARTE SNC: Comune di Milano, Galleria d'Arte Moderna, Milano 121bl. 121crb; MARCO SCAPAGNINI: 146cl, 158tc, 159cr, 168tc, 188tc. SOS MILANO: 211cla; STA TRAVEL GROUP: 209cla. MUSEO TEATRALE ALLA SCALA: 35crb

VERSACE: 106tl.

FRONT ENDPAPERS
ALAMY IMAGES: Jon Arnold Images cr.

SHEET MAP COVER
PHOTOLIBRARY: Superstock/Federico Cabello

JACKET
Front - PHOTOLIBRARY: Superstock/Federico Cabello. Back - AWL IMAGES: Ian Aitken bl; DORLING KINDERSLEY: Paul Harris and Anne Heslope cla, clb, tl.; Spine PHOTOLIBRARY: Superstock/Federico Cabello t

---

SPECIAL EDITIONS OF DK TRAVEL GUIDES

DK Travel Guides can be purchased in bulk quantities at discounted prices for use in promotions or as premiums. We are also able to offer special editions and personalized jackets, corporate imprints, and excerpts from all of our books, tailored specifically to meet your own needs.

To find out more, please contact:

(in the United States) **SpecialSales@dk.com**

(in the UK) **TravelSpecialSales@uk.dk.com**

(in Canada) DK Special Sales at **general@tourmaline.ca**

(in Australia) **business.development@pearson.com.au**

Phrase Book

In Emergency

Help!	Aiuto!	*eye-yoo-toh*
Stop!	Fermate!	*fair-mah-teh*
Call a doctor.	Chiama un medico	*kee-ah-mah oon meh-dee-koh*
Call an ambulance.	Chiama un' ambulanza	*kee-ah-mah oon am-boo-lan-tsa*
Call the police.	Chiama la polizia	*kee-ah-mah lah pol-ee-tsee-ah*
Call the fire brigade.	Chiama i pompieri	*kee-ah-mah ee pom-pee-air-ee*
Where is the telephone?	Dov'è il telefono?	*dov-eh eel teh-leh-foh-noh?*
The nearest hospital?	L'ospedale più vicino?	*loss-peh-dah-leh pee-oo vee-chee-noh?*

Communication Essentials

Yes/No	Sì/No	*see/noh*
Please	Per favore	*pair fah-vor-eh*
Thank you	Grazie	*grah-tsee-eh*
Excuse me	Mi scusi	*mee skoo-zee*
Hello	Buon giorno	*bwon jor-noh*
Goodbye	Arrivederci	*ah-ree-veh-dair-chee*
Good evening	Buona sera	*bwon-ah sair-ah*
morning	la mattina	*lah mah-tee-nah*
afternoon	il pomeriggio	*eel poh-meh-ree-joh*
evening	la sera	*lah sair-ah*
yesterday	ieri	*ee-air-ee*
today	oggi	*oh-jee*
tomorrow	domani	*doh-mah-nee*
here	qui	*kwee*
there	là	*lah*
What?	Quale?	*kwah-leh?*
When?	Quando?	*kwan-doh?*
Why?	Perchè?	*pair-keh?*
Where?	Dove?	*doh-veh?*

Useful Phrases

How are you?	Come sta?	*koh-meh stah?*
Very well, thank you.	Molto bene, grazie.	*moll-toh beh-neh grah-tsee-eh*
Pleased to meet you.	Piacere di conoscerla.	*pee-ah-chair-eh dee coh-noh-shair-lah*
See you later.	A più tardi.	*ah pee-oo tar-dee*
That's fine.	Va bene.	*va beh-neh*
Where is/are...?	Dov'è/Dove sono...?	*dov-eh/doveh soh-noh?*
How long does it take to get to...?	Quanto tempo ci vuole per andare a...?	*kwan-toh tem-poh chee voo-oh-leh pair an-dar-eh ah...?*
How do I get to...?	Come faccio per arrivare a...?	*koh-meh fah-choh pair arri-var-eh ah...?*
Do you speak English?	Parla inglese?	*par-lah een-gleh-zeh?*
I don't understand.	Non capisco.	*non ka-pee-skoh*
Could you speak more slowly, please?	Può parlare più lentamente, per favore?	*pwoh par-lah-reh pee-oo len-ta-men-teh pair fah-vor-eh?*
I'm sorry.	Mi dispiace.	*mee dee-spee-ah-cheh*

Useful Words

big	grande	*gran-deh*
small	piccolo	*pee-koh-loh*
hot	caldo	*kal-doh*
cold	freddo	*fred-doh*
good	buono	*bwoh-noh*
bad	cattivo	*kat-tee-voh*
enough	basta	*bas-tah*
well	bene	*beh-neh*
open	aperto	*ah-pair-toh*
closed	chiuso	*kee-oo-zoh*
left	a sinistra	*ah see-nee-strah*
right	a destra	*ah dess-trah*
straight on	sempre dritto	*sem-preh dree-toh*
near	vicino	*vee-chee-noh*
far	lontano	*lon-tah-noh*
up	su	*soo*
down	giù	*joo*
early	presto	*press-toh*
late	tardi	*tar-dee*
entrance	entrata	*en-trah-tah*
exit	uscita	*oo-shee-ta*
toilet	il gabinetto	*eel gab-bee-net-toh*
free, unoccupied	libero	*lee-bair-oh*
free, no charge	gratuito	*grah-too-ee-toh*

Making a Telephone Call

I'd like to place a long-distance call.	Vorrei fare una interurbana.	*vor-ray far-eh oona in-tair-oor-bah-nah*
I'd like to make a reverse-charge call.	Vorrei fare una telefonata a carico del destinatario.	*vor-ray far-eh oona teh-leh-fon-ah-tah ah kar-ee-koh dell dess-tee-nah-tar-ree-oh*
I'll try again later.	Ritelefono più tardi.	*ree-teh-leh-foh-noh pee-oo tar-dee*
Can I leave a message?	Posso lasciare un messaggio?	*poss-oh lash-ah-reh oon mess-sah-joh?*
Hold on.	Un attimo, per favore	*oon ah-tee-moh, pair fah-vor-eh*
Could you speak up a little please?	Può parlare più forte, per favore?	*pwoh par-lah-reh pee-oo for-teh, pair fah-vor-eh?*
local call	telefonata locale	*te-leh-fon-ah-tah loh-cah-leh*

Shopping

How much does this cost?	Quant'è, per favore?	*kwan-teh pair fah-vor-eh?*
I would like...	Vorrei...	*vor-ray*
Do you have...?	Avete...?	*ah-veh-teh... ?*
I'm just looking.	Sto soltanto guardando.	*stoh sol-tan-toh gwar-dan-doh*
Do you take credit cards?	Accettate carte di credito?	*ah-chet-tah-teh kar-teh dee creb-dee-toh?*
What time do you open/close?	A che ora apre/ chiude?	*ah keh or-ah ah-preh/kee-oo-deh?*
this one	questo	*kweh-stoh*
that one	quello	*kwell-oh*
expensive	caro	*kar-oh*
cheap	a buon prezzo	*ah bwon pret-soh*
size, clothes	la taglia	*lah tah-lee-ah*
size, shoes	il numero	*eel noo-mair-oh*
white	bianco	*bee-ang-koh*
black	nero	*neh-roh*
red	rosso	*ross-oh*
yellow	giallo	*jal-loh*
green	verde	*vair-deh*
blue	blu	*bloo*

Types of Shop

antique dealer	l'antiquario	*lan-tee-kwah-ree-oh*
bakery	il forno/ il panificio	*eel forn-oh /eel pan-ee-fee-choh*
bank	la banca	*lah bang-kah*
bookshop	la libreria	*lah lee-breh-ree-ah*
butcher	la macelleria	*lah mah-chell-eh-ree-ah*
cake shop	la pasticceria	*lah pas-tee-chair-ee-ah*
chemist	la farmacia	*lah far-mah-chee-ah*
delicatessen	la salumeria	*lah sah-loo-meh-ree-ah*
department store	il grande magazzino	*eel gran-deh mag-gad-zee-noh*
fishmonger	il pescivendolo	*eel pesh-ee-ven-doh-loh*
florist	il fioraio	*eel fee-or-eye-oh*
greengrocer	il fruttivendolo	*eel froo-tee-ven-doh-loh*
grocery	alimentari	*ah-lee-men-tah-ree*
hairdresser	il parrucchiere	*eel par-oo-kee-air-eh*
ice cream parlour	la gelateria	*lah jel-lah-tair-ree-ah*
market	il mercato	*eel mair-kah-toh*
newsstand	l'edicola	*leh-dee-koh-lah*
post office	l'ufficio postale	*loo-fee-choh pos-tah-leh*
shoe shop	il negozio di scarpe	*eel neh-goh-tsioh dee skar-peh*
supermarket	il supermercato	*eel su-pair-mair-kah-toh*
tobacconist	il tabaccaio	*eel tah-bak-eye-oh*
travel agency	l'agenzia di viaggi	*lah-jen-tsee-ah dee vee-ad-jee*

Sightseeing

art gallery	la pinacoteca	*lah peena-koh-teb-kah*
bus stop	la fermata dell'autobus	*lah fair-mah-tah dell ow-toh-booss*
church	la chiesa	*lah kee-eb-zah*
	la basilica	*lah bah-seel-i-kah*
closed for holidays	chiuso per le ferie	*kee-oo-zoh pair leh fair-ee-eh*
garden	il giardino	*eel jar-dee-no*
library	la biblioteca	*lah beeb-lee-oh-teb-kah*
museum	il museo	*eel moo-zeb-oh*
railway station	la stazione	*lah stat-tsee-oh-neb*
tourist information	l'ufficio del turismo	*loo-fee-choh del too-ree-smoh*

Staying in a Hotel

Do you have any vacant rooms?	Avete camere libere?	ab-veb-teb kab-mair-eb lee-bair-eb?
double room	una camera doppia	oona kab-mair-ab dob-pee-ab
with double bed	con letto matrimoniale	kon let-tob mah-tree-mob-nee-ab-leb
twin room	una camera con due letti	oona kab-mair-ab kon doo-eb let-tee
single room	una camera singola	oona kab-mair-ab sing-gob-lab
room with a bath, shower	una camera con bagno, con doccia	oona kab-mair-ab kon ban-yob, kon dot-chab
porter	il facchino	eel fab-kee-nob
key	la chiave	lab kee-ab-veb
I have a reservation.	Ho fatto una prenotazione.	ob fat-tob oona preb-nob-tab-tsee-ob-neb

Eating Out

Have you got a table for...?	Avete un tavolo per...?	ab-veb-teb oon tab-vob-lob pair...?
I'd like to reserve a table.	Vorrei riservare un tavolo.	vor-ray ree-sair-vab-reb oon tab-vob-lob
breakfast	colazione	kob-lab-tsee-ob-neb
lunch	pranzo	pran-tsob
dinner	cena	cheb-nab
The bill, please.	Il conto, per favore.	eel kon-tob pair fab-vor-eb
I am a vegetarian.	Sono vegetariano/a.	sob-nob veb-jeb-tar-ee-ab-nob/nab
waitress	cameriera	kab-mair-ee-air-ab
waiter	cameriere	kab-mair-ee-air-eb
fixed price menu	il menù a prezzo fisso	eel meb-noo ah pret-sob fee-sob
dish of the day	piatto del giorno	pee-ab-tob dell jor-no
starter	antipasto	an-tee-pass-tob
first course	il primo	eel pree-mob
main course	il secondo	eel seb-kon-dob
vegetables	il contorno	eel kon-tor-nob
dessert	il dolce	eel doll-cheb
cover charge	il coperto	eel kob-pair-tob
wine list	la lista dei vini	lab lee-stab day vee-nee
rare	al sangue	al sang-gweb
medium	al puntino	al poon-tee-nob
well done	ben cotto	ben kot-tob
glass	il bicchiere	eel bee-kee-air-eb
bottle	la bottiglia	lab bot-teel-yab
knife	il coltello	eel kol-tell-ob
fork	la forchetta	lab for-ket-tab
spoon	il cucchiaio	eel koo-kee-eye-ob

Menu Decoder

l'acqua minerale gassata/naturale	lab-kwab mee-nair-ab-leb gab-zab-tab/nab-too-rab-leb	mineral water fizzy/still
l'agnello	lab-niell-ob	lamb
l'aceto	lab-cheb-tob	vinegar
l'aglio	lal-ee-ob	garlic
al forno	al for-nob	baked
alla griglia	ah-lab greel-yab	grilled
l'aragosta	lab-rab-goss-tab	lobster
l'arrosto	lar-ross-tob	roast
la birra	lab beer-rab	beer
la bistecca	lab bee-stek-kab	steak
il brodo	eel brob-dob	broth
il burro	eel boor-ob	butter
il caffè	eel kab-feb	coffee
i calamari	ee kab-lab-mab-ree	squid
i carciofi	ee kar-choff-ee	artichokes
la carne	la kar-neb	meat
carne di maiale	kar-neb dee mab-yab-leb	pork
la cipolla	la chip-ob-lab	onion
i contorni	ee kon-tor-nee	vegetables
i fagioli	ee fab-job-lee	beans
il fegato	eel fay-gab-tob	liver
il finocchio	eel fee-nok-ee-ob	fennel
il formaggio	eel for-mad-job	cheese
le fragole	leb frab-gob-leb	strawberries
il fritto misto	eel free-tob mees-tob	mixed fried dish
la frutta	la froot-tab	fruit
frutti di mare	froo-tee dee mab-reb	seafood
i funghi	ee foon-ghee	mushrooms
i gamberi	ee gam-bair-ee	prawns
il gelato	eel jel-lab-tob	ice cream
l'insalata	leen-sab-lab-tab	salad

il latte	eel labt-teb	milk
il lesso	eel less-ob	boiled
il manzo	eel man-tsob	beef
la melanzana	lab meh-lan-tsab-nab	aubergine
la minestra	lab mee-ness-trab	soup
l'olio	lob-lee-ob	oil
il pane	eel pab-neb	bread
le patate	leb pab-tab-teb	potatoes
le patatine fritte	leb pab-tab-teen-eb free-teb	chips
il pepe	eel peb-peb	pepper
la pesca	lab pess-kab	peach
il pesce	eel pesb-eb	fish
il pollo	eel poll-ob	chicken
il pomodoro	eel pob-mob-dor-ob	tomato
il prosciutto cotto/crudo	eel pro-shoo-tob kot-tob/kroo-dob	ham cooked/cured
il riso	eel ree-zob	rice
il sale	eel sab-leb	salt
la salsiccia	lab sal-see-chab	sausage
le seppie	leb sep-pee-eb	cuttlefish
secco	sek-kob	dry
la sogliola	lab soll-yob-lab	sole
gli spinaci	lyee spee-nab-chee	spinach
succo d'arancia/di limone	soo-kob dab-ran-chab/dee lee-mob-neb	orange/lemon juice
il tè	eel teb	tea
la tisana	lab tee-zab-nab	herbal tea
il tonno	eel ton-nob	tuna
la torta	lab tor-tab	cake/tart
l'uovo	loo-ob-vob	egg
vino bianco	vee-nob bee-ang-kob	white wine
vino rosso	vee-nob ross-ob	red wine
il vitello	eel vee-tell-ob	veal
le vongole	leb von-gob-leb	clams
lo zucchero	lob zoo-kair-ob	sugar
gli zucchini	lyee dzu-kee-nee	courgettes
la zuppa	lab tsoo-pab	soup

Numbers

1	uno	oo-nob
2	due	doo-eb
3	tre	treb
4	quattro	kwat-rob
5	cinque	ching-kob
6	sei	say-ee
7	sette	set-teb
8	otto	ot-tob
9	nove	nob-veb
10	dieci	dee-eb-chee
11	undici	oon-dee-chee
12	dodici	dob-dee-chee
13	tredici	tray-dee-chee
14	quattordici	kwat-tor-dee-chee
15	quindici	kwin-dee-chee
16	sedici	say-dee-chee
17	diciassette	dee-chab-set-teb
18	diciotto	dee-chot-tob
19	diciannove	dee-chab-nob-veb
20	venti	ven-tee
30	trenta	tren-tab
40	quaranta	kwab-ran-tab
50	cinquanta	ching-kwan-tab
60	sessanta	sess-an-tab
70	settanta	set-tan-tab
80	ottanta	ot-tan-tab
90	novanta	nob-van-tab
100	cento	chen-tob
1,000	mille	mee-leb
2,000	duemila	doo-eb mee-lah
5,000	cinquemila	ching-kweb mee-lah
1,000,000	un milione	oon meel-yob-neb

Time

one minute	un minuto	oon mee-noo-tob
one hour	un'ora	oon or-ab
half an hour	mezz'ora	medz-or-ab
a day	un giorno	oon jor-nob
a week	una settimana	oona set-tee-mab-nab
Monday	lunedì	loo-neb-dee
Tuesday	martedì	mar-teb-dee
Wednesday	mercoledì	mair-kob-leb-dee
Thursday	giovedì	job-veb-dee
Friday	venerdì	ven-air-dee
Saturday	sabato	sab-bab-tob
Sunday	domenica	dob-meb-nee-kab